BLOOD

AND

HONOR

BLOOD
AND
HONOR

INSIDE
THE SCARFO MOB—
THE MAFIA'S
MOST VIOLENT
FAMILY

George Anastasia

WILLIAM MORROW AND COMPANY, INC.
New York

It is the policy of William Morrow and Company, Inc., and its imprints and affiliates, recognizing the importance of preserving what has been written, to print the books we publish on acid-free paper, and we exert our best efforts to that end.

Library of Congress Cataloging-in-Publication Data

Anastasia, George.
    Blood and honor : inside the Scarfo mob—the Mafia's most violent family / George Anastasia.
      p. cm.
    ISBN 0-688-09260-8
    1. Mafia—Pennsylvania—Philadelphia Metropolitan Area—Case studies. 2. Scarfo, Nicodemo Domenic, 1929–   . I. Title.
    HV6452.P4M3425   1991
    364.1′06′0974811—dc20   91-10745
                                                                     CIP

Printed in the United States of America

First Edition

1 2 3 4 5 6 7 8 9 10

For my father,
and his father before him

ACKNOWLEDGMENTS

This book could not have been written without the advice, encouragement, and support of many editors, reporters, and friends whom I have worked with over the years.

I would especially like to thank Bill Marimow, who thought of me when this project was first being discussed and who is most responsible for my involvement in it. Also Bob Samsot, an editor and friend who will recognize sections of what follows.

There are also dozens of reporters, law enforcement officials, and attorneys who worked on various aspects of the Scarfo story or investigation—as the case may be—and whose excellent work and willingness to cooperate made my job easier. These include the criminal and court reporters at the *Philadelphia Inquirer* and *Daily News*, detectives with the New Jersey state police and Philadelphia police department, members of the FBI and U.S. Attorney's Offices in Philadelphia, Atlantic City, and Newark, and officials with the New Jersey State Commission of Investigation and the Pennsylvania Crime Commission.

In Atlantic City, I would like especially to thank Michael Schurman, a friend and former reporter who was one of the best in the business.

Special thanks also to Susan Leon, whose hard work and determination helped shape this manuscript, and to Jerry Perles, for his wisdom and counsel.

Finally, I'd like to say thank you to my wife, Angela, and daughters, Michelle and Nina, for their support and encouragement and for their love.

THE PLAYERS

Leland Beloff   Former Philadelphia city councilman. Sentenced to ten years in prison after being convicted of conspiring with the mob in a $1 million shakedown of a major waterfront developer.

Chelsais "Stevie" Bouras   Head of Philadelphia's Greek mob. Killed in a South Philadelphia restaurant on May 27, 1981, in a dispute over methamphetamine dealing.

Angelo Bruno   Mafia boss of Philadelphia and southern New Jersey from about 1959 until his assassination on March 21, 1980. His death set in motion five years of internecine warfare that left more than twenty mob members and associates dead and Nicodemo Scarfo as the boss of a new and more violent Mafia family.

John Calabrese   Mob associate involved in drug dealing and loan-sharking operations with Antonio Caponigro. Murdered on October 6, 1981, after failing to fall in line under Scarfo.

Antonio "Tony Bananas" Caponigro   Bruno's consigliere and head of the Newark branch of the family. Suspected of plotting Bruno's murder. Found dead in the Bronx on April 18, 1980.

Nicholas "Nicky Crow" Caramandi   Scarfo soldier and top money earner. Became a government witness after being marked for death. Testified at eleven trials resulting in fifty-two convictions. Pleaded guilty to racketeering and conspiracy charges. Sentenced to eight years. Released in October 1990. Now in Federal Witness Protection Program.

Peter Casella   Bruno capo elevated to underboss by Philip

9

Testa. Fled to Florida after planning Testa's murder in 1981. Died of natural causes two years later.

Joseph "Chickie" Ciancaglini Scarfo capo sentenced to forty-five years in prison following conviction on federal RICO charges in 1988.

Michael "Mickey Coco" Cifelli Suspected drug dealer murdered for selling drugs to the son of a mob figure. Gunned down in a South Philadelphia bar on January 4, 1979.

Ralph "Big Ralph" Costobile Caramandi associate and South Philadelphia bar and construction company owner. Pleaded guilty to labor racketeering charges. Sentenced to three years in prison.

Albert Daidone Atlantic City Bartenders Union official. Convicted with Raymond Martorano of plotting the murder of John McCullough.

Frank "Frankie Flowers" D'Alfonso Top Bruno associate and big-time money earner for the organization. Brutally beaten on Scarfo's orders on October 29, 1981. Murdered on July 23, 1985.

Thomas "Tommy Del" DelGiorno Former Scarfo capo. Became a government witness after being demoted to the rank of soldier. Believed he was marked for death. Testified at a dozen trials. Pleaded guilty to a federal racketeering charge. Sentenced to five years in prison. Released in May 1990. Now in the Federal Witness Protection Program.

Dominick "Mickey Diamond" DeVito Nick Caramandi's original mob mentor. Found murdered on February 25, 1982. Victim of a twenty-year-old Scarfo grudge.

Ronald "Cuddles" DiCaprio Mob associate. Driver for Pat Spirito murder. Convicted of racketeering charges. Currently serving twenty-year prison sentence.

Anthony "Spike" DiGregorio Associate of Nicodemo Scarfo and Nick Caramandi. Served as caretaker at Scarfo's Fort Lauderdale home.

Angelo "Chick" DiTullio South Philadelphia drug dealer. Victim of Mafia P-2-P importation scam. Convicted of federal drug charges. Serving eighteen-year prison term.

Vincent Falcone Atlantic City cement contractor killed for insulting Scarfo and his nephew Philip Leonetti. His body was found in the trunk of his car in Margate, New Jersey, shortly after the December 16, 1979, slaying.

George Fresolone   Scarfo soldier who secretly recorded his own Mafia initiation ceremony while working undercover for the New Jersey state police. Now a cooperating witness for the New Jersey Attorney General's Office.

Joseph Grande   Scarfo soldier. Convicted of RICO charges. Currently serving a forty-year prison sentence.

Salvatore "Wayne" Grande   Brother of Joe Grande. Hit man in Salvatore Testa murder. Convicted of federal RICO charges. Currently serving a thirty-eight-year prison sentence.

Edwin Helfant   Atlantic City lawyer and part-time municipal court judge. Killed in a cocktail lounge on February 15, 1978, after failing to follow through on a promise to rig a judicial proceeding.

Robert Hornickel   Suspected drug dealer. Found murdered in South Philadelphia on January 27, 1983.

Francis "Faffy" Iannarella, Jr.   Scarfo family capo. Convicted of RICO charges and of Frank D'Alfonso murder. Sentenced to consecutive forty-five-year and life sentences.

Charles "Charlie White" Iannece   Caramandi's Mafia partner in crime. Triggerman in Pat Spirito murder. Convicted of RICO charges. Sentenced to forty years in prison.

Joseph Ida   Philadelphia Mafia boss who fled to Italy after the 1957 mob conclave in Apalachin, New York.

Saul Kane   Former Atlantic City bail bondsman and longtime Scarfo associate. Convicted in separate cases of federal drug charges and extortion. Serving twenty-five-year prison sentence.

Philip "Crazy Phil" Leonetti   Scarfo's nephew and underboss. Convicted of RICO charges. Sentenced to forty-five years in federal prison. Became a cooperating government witness in June 1989.

Joseph Ligambi   Scarfo soldier. Hit man in Frank D'Alfonso murder. Convicted of murder and gambling charges. Serving a life prison term.

John McCullough   Boss of Philadelphia Roofers Union Local 30. Tried to set up union operations in Atlantic City. Killed in the kitchen of his Philadelphia home on December 16, 1980.

Alphonse "Funzi" Marconi Scarfo soldier suspected in the Dominick "Mickey Diamond" DeVito murder.

Guerino "Mark" Marconi Scarfo soldier, brother of Alphonse. Also a suspect in the DeVito murder.

Rocco Marinucci Mob associate linked to Peter Casella. Suspected of detonating the bomb that killed Philip Testa. Found brutally murdered on March 15, 1982, the first anniversary of the Testa bombing.

Frank Martines Riccobene associate. Wounded outside his home on October 14, 1983. Caramandi planned and supervised the hit.

George "Cowboy" Martorano Son of Raymond Martorano. Major Philadelphia drug dealer and suspected hit man. Currently serving a life prison term after pleading guilty to federal drug charges.

Raymond "Long John" Martorano Longtime Bruno associate. Became a "made" member under Scarfo. Convicted of murder in the death of John McCullough and of drug dealing in a separate federal case.

Michael J. Matthews Former mayor of Atlantic City. Accused of selling his office to the Scarfo mob. Sentenced to a fifteen-year federal prison term after pleading guilty to a bribery charge. Released in May 1990.

Lawrence "Yogi" Merlino Former Scarfo family capo. Convicted of RICO and first degree murder charges. Became a government witness prior to sentencing in RICO case in May 1989.

Salvatore "Chuckie" Merlino Scarfo's underboss and oldest friend in the mob. Brother of Lawrence Merlino. Demoted to soldier by Scarfo in 1985. Convicted of first degree murder in Frank D'Alfonso murder case. Convicted of RICO charges. Currently serving life plus forty-five years.

Eugene "Gino" Milano Mob soldier convicted in RICO trial. Later became a government witness in Frank D'Alfonso murder trial. Testified against Scarfo and seven others, including his own brother, "Nicky Whip" Milano.

Nicholas "Nicky Whip" Milano Hit man in Sammy Tamburrino murder. Convicted of the Frank D'Alfonso murder. Sentenced to life in prison.

Frank Monte Scarfo's consigliere. Killed on May 13, 1982. The first victim of the Scarfo-Riccobene war.

Willard "Junior" Moran Confessed hit man in McCullough killing. Became a government witness and testified against Raymond Martorano and Albert Daidone.

Frank "Chickie" Narducci, Sr. Mafia capo who planned the Philip Testa murder. Gunned down by Testa's son, Salvatore, on January 7, 1982.

Frank Narducci, Jr. Adopted son of Chickie Narducci. Became a hit man for the Scarfo family. Convicted of the murder of Frank D'Alfonso and of federal RICO charges. Serving a life sentence plus thirty-five years.

Philip Narducci Son of Chickie Narducci. Convicted of the murder of Frank D'Alfonso and of federal RICO charges. Serving a life sentence plus thirty-eight years.

John Pastorella Caramandi's construction company partner. Secretly worked for the FBI and taped hundreds of conversations used in the Rouse extortion case.

Albert "Reds" Pontani Scarfo soldier in charge of Trenton operations. Convicted of federal drug charges. Sentenced to thirty years in prison.

Anthony "Anthony Pung" Pungitore, Jr. Scarfo soldier. Convicted in RICO trial. Serving a thirty-year prison term.

Joseph "Joey Pung" Pungitore Scarfo soldier. Brother of Anthony Pungitore. Set up Salvatore Testa. Convicted of RICO charges. Serving a forty-year prison term.

Robert "Bobby" Rego Riccobene associate who later became the legislative aide of Leland Beloff. Convicted of Rouse extortion and of drug dealing. Currently serving an eight-year prison sentence.

Enrico Riccobene Son of Mario Riccobene. Committed suicide on December 14, 1983, because he thought Scarfo gunmen were stalking him.

Harry "the Hump" Riccobene Target of Scarfo hit teams. Escaped several assassination attempts. Convicted of the Frank Monte murder. Currently serving a life prison sentence.

Mario "Sonny" Riccobene Half brother of Harry Riccobene. Target of Scarfo hit teams. Jailed on racketeering and murder charges. Testified for the government in the Frank Monte murder case.

Robert Riccobene Brother of Mario Riccobene, half brother of

Harry Riccobene. Gunned down in his mother's back yard on December 6, 1983. Last murder in the Scarfo-Riccobene war.

Willard Rouse III Philadelphia developer chosen to do the Penns Landing project. Target of $1 million shakedown by Scarfo mob and city councilman Leland Beloff.

Joseph "Mr. Joe" Rugnetta Bruno's family consigliere and head of the Calabrian faction of the organization (Bruno was of Sicilian descent). Died of natural causes in 1977.

Alfred Salerno Caponigro's brother-in-law and driver. Possible triggerman in the Bruno murder. Found dead in the Bronx on April 18, 1980.

Joseph Salerno, Jr. Atlantic City plumbing contractor and witness to the Falcone murder; no relation to Alfred. Testified against Scarfo. Now in the Federal Witness Protection Program.

Salvatore "Tory" Scafidi Scarfo soldier. Convicted of RICO charges. Serving forty-year prison sentence.

Nicodemo "Little Nicky" Scarfo Became mob boss after the death of Philip Testa in 1981 and launched a bloody reign of terror that ultimately led to the demise of the organization. Currently serving consecutive terms of fourteen years, fifty-five years, and life following convictions on conspiracy to commit extortion, RICO, and murder charges.

John "Johnny Keyes" Simone Mafia family capo linked with Caponigro in the plot to kill Bruno. Found murdered near a landfill in Staten Island on September 19, 1980.

Frank Sindone Mafia loan shark extraordinaire. Linked to the plot to kill Bruno. Found shot to death behind a South Philadelphia variety store on October 29, 1980.

Pasquale "Pat the Cat" Spirito Scarfo soldier and reluctant hit man. Ordered murdered after botching several contracts during the Scarfo-Riccobene war. Caramandi's mentor and first murder victim. Killed April 29, 1983.

Ralph "Junior" Staino Scarfo soldier. Convicted of RICO and federal drug charges. Serving concurrent thirty-three-year and twelve-year prison terms.

John Stanfa Philadelphia construction company owner and mob associate who drove Bruno home on the night he was killed. Sentenced to eight years in prison after being convicted of lying to the grand jury investigating Bruno's murder. Released in 1987.

Salvatore "Sammy" Tamburrino   Riccobene associate. Shot to death in a Southwest Philadelphia candy store he operated on November 3, 1983.

Philip "Chicken Man" Testa   Bruno's underboss and successor. Killed in a bomb blast as he stepped on the porch of his South Philadelphia home early in the morning of March 15, 1981.

Salvatore Testa   Son of Philip Testa. Youngest Mafia capo in America. Betrayed and murdered on Scarfo's orders on September 14, 1984.

Frank "Funzi" Tieri   Genovese family crime boss. Set up double cross in which Antonio Caponigro thought he had Mafia Commission approval to kill Angelo Bruno.

Stephen Traitz, Jr.   John McCullough's successor as head of Roofers Union Local 30. Became Scarfo's liaison to organized labor. Convicted of racketeering. Currently serving a fifteen-year prison term.

Steven Vento, Sr.   Convicted South Philadelphia drug dealer whose methamphetamine operation became the target of a Scarfo shakedown. Testified against Scarfo organization in subsequent drug trial.

Steven Vento, Jr.   Son of Steven Sr. Wounded on May 27, 1986, by Scarfo gunmen during drug dispute over methamphetamine shipment.

Nicholas "Nick the Blade" Virgilio   Scarfo soldier. Hit man in Helfant murder. Convicted of federal RICO charges. Currently serving a forty-year prison sentence.

THE HITS

1978
February 15   Edwin Helfant

1979
January 4   Michael "Mickey Coco" Cifelli
December 16   Vincent Falcone

1980
March 21   Angelo Bruno
April 18   Antonio "Tony Bananas" Caponigro
April 18   Alfred Salerno
September 19   John "Johnnie Keyes" Simone
October 29   Frank Sindone
December 16   John McCullough

1981
March 15   Philip "Chicken Man" Testa
April 27   Chelsais "Stevie" Bouras
October 6   John Calabrese

1982
January 7   Frank "Chickie" Narducci
February 25   Dominick "Mickey Diamond" DeVito
March 15   Rocco Marinucci
May 13   Frank Monte

17

1983

January 27	Robert Hornickel
April 29	Pasquale "Pat the Cat" Spirito
November 3	Salvatore "Sammy" Tamburrino
December 6	Robert Riccobene
December 14	Enrico Riccobene (self-inflicted)

1984

| September 14 | Salvatore Testa |

1985

| February 8 | Frank J. Forlini, Jr. |
| July 23 | Frank "Frankie Flowers" D'Alfonso |

THE CONVICTIONS

May 6, 1987—Mob boss **Nicodemo Scarfo** convicted of conspiracy to commit extortion in the $1 million shakedown of waterfront developer Willard Rouse III.

May 6, 1987—Mob associate **Ronald DiCaprio** convicted of federal racketeering charges, including the murder of Robert Hornickel.

July 5, 1987—Former Philadelphia city councilman **Leland Beloff** and his aide, **Robert Rego**, convicted of federal conspiracy charges in the Rouse extortion and the shakedown of two other developers. An earlier trial had ended in a hung jury and acquittal on several minor charges.

November 23, 1987—**Stephen Traitz, Jr.**, and twelve other members of Philadelphia Roofers Union Local 30 convicted of federal racketeering charges.

March 7, 1988—**John Renzulli** and eleven others convicted of federal drug charges in a major P-2-P importation and methamphetamine distribution ring.

April 21, 1988—**Angelo "Chick" DiTullio** and three others convicted of federal drug charges in the P-2-P/meth case.

July 15, 1988—**Ralph "Junior" Staino** convicted of federal drug charges in the P-2-P/meth case.

November 19, 1988—Mob boss **Nicodemo Scarfo** and sixteen others convicted under the Racketeering Influenced and Corrupt

Organizations (RICO) Act. RICO charges included drug dealing, loan-sharking, extortion, and murder. Murders included the deaths of Edwin Helfant, Michael Cifelli, Vincent Falcone, Frank Narducci, Sr., John Calabrese, Pasquale Spirito, Salvatore Tamburrino, Robert Riccobene, and Salvatore Testa. Charges also included the attempted murders of Harry Riccobene, Frank Martines, Joseph Salerno, Sr., and Steven Vento, Jr. Convicted with Scarfo were **Salvatore Merlino, Lawrence Merlino, Philip Leonetti, Frank Iannarella, Jr., Joseph Ciancaglini, Charles Iannece, Nicholas Virgilio, Salvatore Grande, Joseph Grande, Salvatore Scafidi, Joseph Pungitore, Anthony Pungitore, Jr., Frank Narducci, Jr., Philip Narducci, Ralph Staino**, and **Eugene "Gino" Milano**.

April 5, 1989—Mob boss **Nicodemo Scarfo** and seven others convicted of first degree murder in the 1985 slaying of mob associate Frank "Frankie Flowers" D'Alfonso. Convicted with Scarfo were **Salvatore Merlino, Lawrence Merlino, Frank Narducci, Jr., Philip Narducci, Nicholas Milano, Joseph Ligambi**, and **Frank Iannarella, Jr.**

PART
ONE

PROLOGUE

O cean City, Maryland, is a bustling seashore town three hours south of Philadelphia. It is a summer getaway for the middle class, a city that bulges from May to September with tourists who flock to the condominiums and high-rise hotels that line the Atlantic Ocean.

A pristine beach. Clean, wide streets lined with shopping centers, restaurants, movie theaters, and bars. A boardwalk jammed with rides and amusements for the kids. Ocean City has it all.

It is bigger, brighter, and cleaner than Wildwood, New Jersey, more family-oriented than Atlantic City, and more sophisticated—in its own tacky way—than anything on Long Beach Island, another Jersey shore area.

In the summer of 1988, Ocean City, Maryland, was also the home of Nicholas Caramandi, mobster turned informant, hit man turned government operative, and witness extraordinaire. Caramandi, fifty-four, was preparing for the most important court appearance of his life, a federal case in which Philadelphia organized crime boss Nicodemo Scarfo and seventeen of his top associates were charged under the Racketeering Influenced and Corrupt Organizations Act with assorted counts of murder and mayhem. It was the biggest RICO case in Philadelphia history, a trial that federal authorities were predicting would bring down the notorious Scarfo organization.

Caramandi was the federal point man, the witness whose testimony would make or break the case. He was in hiding, living with teams of federal agents who worked week-long shifts serving as his bodyguards. They had checked into a condominium in Ocean City early in the year, long before the tourist season began. Ocean City seemed ideal. It was close to Philadelphia, yet removed from the Philadelphia axis. Few Philadelphians vacationed there. When they went to the shore, it was usually in New Jersey. Ocean City attracted visitors from Delaware, Maryland, and the District of Columbia; people who read the papers and watched the television news out of Washington and Baltimore; people who knew little and cared less about Nicodemo "Little Nicky" Scarfo and the Philadelphia mob.

On a Monday morning late in August, I pulled my car into the parking lot of the Sheraton Hotel on the main drag in Ocean City. It was shortly before 10:00 A.M., and the town was alive with tanned and sunburned tourists. Mothers walked with children toward the ocean, buckets and shovels, suntan lotion, and magazines stuffed into beach bags, towels and blankets and umbrellas clutched under their arms. A steady stream of cars pulled up to the doors of the hotels. Luggage was unloaded. Sunglasses perched on their heads, men and women emerged stiff-legged from the vehicles as their kids, some already wearing bathing suits, burst from the backseats and scampered into the hotel lobbies.

It hardly seemed the spot for a rendezvous with a mobster, but ten minutes later there he was, blending in with the crowd. He wore tan jogging pants, white Reebok sneakers, a "Hard Rock Café" T-shirt, and a white baseball cap with the word "Cacún" scrawled in black across its crown. Dark designer sunglasses shielded his eyes.

I recognized the walk before I recognized the face. Slightly stooped of shoulder, short and stocky, Nick Caramandi moves like a banty rooster, quick and light on his feet.

"Heh, buddy, how ya doing?" he said.

I had met Caramandi two or three times previously and had had several brief discussions with him. But this trip to Maryland was to be the first of several long sessions in which he would explain how the mob worked and how he became a part of it.

Caramandi, it turned out, was hiding in plain sight. He was on a very long federal leash, a fact that would surprise and shock certain people back in Philadelphia who assumed that he was unreachable. That was hardly the case. He jogged three miles every day on the beach . . . alone. He had a membership at a local health club, where he would show up a couple times a week for workouts and steam baths. He was a regular at certain restaurants and bars. He was a tourist named Joe who was down for the summer, and while he never got particularly close to anyone, he became friendly with several bartenders and waitresses who liked his easy, outgoing manner. He moved around town by bus or on foot. Dressed casually. Always wore sunglasses and seldom was without a cigarette.

During two days of interviews in August, he called to check in with his federal watchdogs on a regular basis, but other than the phone calls, his time was his own. I had to wonder what his fellow tourists would have thought about rubbing shoulders with a Mafia hit man. And how they would have reacted had they known that the man who was sitting at the bar or at the table near them in the restaurant or with whom they shared the elevator or a stretch of beach was an individual marked for death by a despotic mob kingpin who that very moment was rotting in a prison cell in Philadelphia. Nicky Scarfo's world was coming to an end, and it was all because of this suntanned tourist in the Hard Rock Café T-shirt.

One of the movies featured on the hotel's pay-TV channel that week was *Wall Street*, starring Michael Douglas. The movie is about greed and ambition and how it powers the American economy.

"Greed, for want of a better word, is good," says Douglas at one of the key points in the film. "Greed works."

In a series of interviews that began in Ocean City, Caramandi would say much the same thing. Greed and ambition are the tools that the mob uses to advance its interests and to subvert and co-opt society. Money and power are what make the Mafia America's second government, a violent, corrupt, and unaccountable national force whose influence stretches from the boardrooms of corporate America to the Boardwalk in Atlantic City and from the corridors of City Hall to the drug-infested alleys of the ghetto.

Forget any fancy or idealistic notions about the "men of honor" who make up the mob. If they existed at all, they died a generation ago. La Cosa Nostra today is an amoral organization, put together to make money—no matter the manner—for its bosses. Murder, money, and corruption were the things

Caramandi talked about over and over again for the next twelve months.

A gifted raconteur, he was often charming and entertaining as he described the scams and swindles that propelled his early life. Some brought him hundreds of thousands of dollars, others left him empty-handed and frustrated. But each seemed to bring him closer to the mob.

By 1980, after twenty-five years as a thief, con man, and flimflam artist, he was a recognized mob associate. Two years later he was a "proposed" member. And after taking part in a series of murders, he was, in 1984, formally initiated into the bloodiest and most violent Mafia family in America.

Two years after that rite of passage, however, Nick Caramandi found himself a target of Scarfo's paranoia. And so he began the process of taking the family down. In appearances before more than a dozen grand juries and in testimony at eleven different trials, Caramandi destroyed the Philadelphia organization he had sworn to defend with his life. Not since Joe Valachi shattered the Mafia's time-honored code of silence in 1963 had a mob figure provided such a detailed and up-to-date account of the way the organization operates.

While the Philadelphia family was relatively small—there were sixty made members and nearly two hundred associates—it was strategically positioned within La Cosa Nostra. Its boss sat on the seven-member Mafia Commission, dubbed "the mortgage company" by local mobsters, and dealt frequently with the leaders of New York's powerful Genovese and Gambino organizations. Philadelphia's status within the Mafia underworld was also enhanced by the fact that its orbit of influence extended all the way to Atlantic City.

While other families were permitted to operate in the East Coast gambling capital—the mob had declared Atlantic City, like Las Vegas, an "open" city—the Philadelphia family dominated the local rackets there and had a piece of almost everyone's action.

One way to measure the impact of Caramandi's defection is through the prosecutions and convictions that have dismantled the Philadelphia mob. In no other city in America has law enforcement scored as many repeated "hits" on La Cosa Nostra. But Caramandi's usefulness to the authorities has not stopped there. He has been the catalyst for a series of broader investigations that now have the FBI focusing on those who sit atop the Mafia underworld in Manhattan.

Caramandi's story is a tale of greed and murder within the most ruthlessly corrupt crime family in America. It is a first-hand account of La Cosa Nostra in the 1980s and a warning for the 1990s.

"People don't understand about this thing," he said over a dinner of steak and lobster tail during our first night in Ocean City. "There's not an industry you could name—entertainment, casinos, construction, the unions—where we don't have something. Wherever there's money, that's where we are. Wherever there's power. You understand?

"It's a second government. We reach all over, in every major city in the United States. It's nationwide. It's one organization."

Caramandi was the man who bought the politicians, judges, and union leaders who provided the Scarfo family with its clout. He was on the inside when plans were hatched to take over the mayor's office in Atlantic City. He was the mob's go-between in a $1 million extortion scheme with a Philadelphia city councilman.

He traveled from the union halls and political back rooms of Philadelphia to the casino floors of Atlantic City, wheeling and dealing for La Cosa Nostra. Drug dealers, loan sharks, and bookmakers had to pay him a "street tax" to do business. Union leaders and construction company owners had to pay kickbacks.

Mayors, judges, and councilmen had to pay homage.

Those who refused had to pay with their lives.

CHAPTER ONE

Defense attorney:	When you were growing up, did you learn the Ten Commandments?
Caramandi:	Yes.
Attorney:	Did you learn "Thou shalt not steal"?
Caramandi:	Yes.
Attorney:	"Thou shalt not kill"?
Caramandi:	"Yes."
Attorney:	"Thou shalt not lie"?
Caramandi:	"Yes."
Attorney:	The three commandments I just mentioned, how many of them did you break?
Caramandi:	I broke them all.

hortly before 10:00 P.M. on the night of March 21, 1980, a maroon Chevrolet Caprice Classic eased up to the curb in front of a two-story brownstone at the end of the 900 block of Snyder Avenue in South Philadelphia.

John Stanfa, a Sicilian immigrant and owner of a small construction company, sat behind the wheel of the car. In the passenger seat beside him was Angelo Bruno, the longtime boss of the Philadelphia mob.

Bruno was sixty-nine at the time, in relatively good health and enjoying the fruits of more than twenty years at the helm of a prosperous, low-key, smoothly run organization. The slightly balding, soft-spoken mob boss was noted in both law enforcement and underworld circles for his conciliatory style.

He was a master of compromise, a Mafia diplomat, a true man of honor.

Earlier that evening, Bruno had had dinner with his lawyer at Cous' Little Italy, a popular neighborhood restaurant whose hidden owners included two members of his organization. Bruno had pasta and chicken, a dish he savored and ordered frequently.

Stanfa showed up at the restaurant just as Bruno was finishing his meal and was asked to give the mob boss a ride home. The trip takes less than fifteen minutes. They drove down South Broad Street and stopped at a newsstand on the corner of Broad and Snyder, where Bruno bought a copy of the next morning's *Philadelphia Inquirer*.

Bruno wore a dark blue topcoat over a business suit, white shirt, and tie. On the seat next to him was his trademark white woolen cap.

As Stanfa pulled his car up to the curb in front of Bruno's home at 934 Snyder Avenue, a man who had been waiting in the shadows began moving toward it. Stanfa pushed a button and the window next to Bruno began to lower. It was 9:45 P.M.

The man in the shadows moved swiftly and directly toward the now opened window. He pulled a 12-gauge shotgun out from under his coat and pressed the gun to the back of Angelo Bruno's head.

The blast punctured the quiet South Philadelphia night. Bruno's body lurched forward, his face frozen in a soundless, gape-mouthed scream. Blood from a massive wound behind his right ear flowed down his back. By the time police arrived minutes later, the white woolen cap on the seat beside him was crimson and the newspaper was soaked in blood.

Stanfa was sprayed with pellets in the right arm and hand, but escaped serious injury. The man with the shotgun ran to a waiting car and sped off.

The assassination of Angelo Bruno set in motion one of the most violent mob wars in history. Over the next five years, twenty-eight members or associates of the sixty-member Philadelphia branch of La Cosa Nostra would die. Nail bombs, bullets, knives, and garrotes left a bloody trail that stretched from New York to Atlantic City as the mob that Bruno had run so quietly and efficiently turned on itself and longtime friends, and family members hacked away at each other in a grab for power, wealth, and revenge.

In the midst of that carnage, Nicodemo "Little Nicky" Scarfo rose to the top of the heap, head of a revamped organization with a philosophy that was decidedly different from Bruno's.

Scarfo was a mob boss for the 1980s, a greedy, ruthless despot whose family coat of arms could have been a pair of crossed .357 magnums mounted on a blood-red shield embossed with the words "Kill or be killed." Not since the late Albert Anastasia, the Mad Hatter of New York's Murder Inc., had a major American Mafia family been ruled by a man who gloried in such wanton, ruthless, and senseless violence.

There are three dominant institutions in the Italian-American neighborhoods of South Philadelphia: the Catholic Church, the Democratic Party, and the mob. Not everyone believes. Not everyone belongs. But by and large, almost everyone accepts or tolerates the presence of those institutions.

South Philadelphians go to Mass on Sunday and see the priest to arrange such things as baptisms, First Communions, marriages, and funerals. They look to their ward leader or Democratic Party committeeman to fix parking tickets, arrange zoning variances, and navigate the bureaucracy that is city government.

And the mob, by and large, they ignore.

The attitude of the community is captured in a piece of Sicilian wisdom handed down through the ages: "He who is deaf, blind, and silent lives a thousand years."

"I don't bother them, they don't bother me" is one common refrain when a South Philadelphian is asked about the organization.

"I don't know nuthin'" is another.

Nick Caramandi grew up on the streets of South Philadelphia, living in one of the thousands of two-story brick homes that are packed one next to another along a gridwork of narrow, congested streets that stretch across several square miles in the city's southeast quadrant. Corner grocery stores and parish churches define the community. Commerce is conducted along East Passyunk Avenue, where the quality and diversity of the shops, stores, and restaurants far outshine those of any suburban mall. And what isn't there can be found along the Ninth Street Italian Market, where dozens of stores and open-air stalls attract thousands of customers each day.

So densely populated is South Philadelphia that for years residents have routinely parked their cars between the yellow median lines that separate north- and southbound traffic along Broad Street, the four-lane thoroughfare that runs from the stadium complex to City Hall.

Periodic attempts by the police and parking authority to ticket those illegally parked cars set off street demonstrations, phone calls to ward leaders, and howls of protest. There are, a parking authority survey once showed, several thousand more cars than there are legal parking spaces in South Philadelphia. And so, with a wink and a nod, the police ignore the cars and the populace parks wherever it damn well pleases, including the middle of the city's main thoroughfare.

It is a minor but telling point, a victory for reality over authority.

Nick Caramandi always accepted the reality of the streets, of his life, and of his prospects for success.

"I'm a thief," he would say without shame or apology. He could also be described as a murderer, extortionist, and drug dealer, but in his own mind what he was, first and foremost, was someone who stole for a living. Guys in the neighborhood gave him the nickname Crow, he said, because "a crow is a shrewd bird." He took pleasure in that. And also in the fact that over the course of his lifetime, he rose to the top of his field.

He came of age surrounded by people like himself, first- and second-generation Italian-Americans, people who traced their family roots to dirt-poor sections of Sicily and Calabria. They were men and women of modest ambition who believed in hard work and in minding their own business. They lived in row houses around the corner or down the block from their sisters, brothers, cousins, and uncles, insulated in large degree not only from the rest of the country but also from the rest of the city.

Nurtured by family ties and Old World values, residents of South Philadelphia have given the city a long list of prominent doctors, lawyers, judges, athletes, artists, and teachers who have had a positive impact on the community. Their contributions far outweigh the impact of crime and corruption generated by the neighborhood's one nefarious institution. But there is no denying that South Philadelphia has stocked the mob for three generations, supplying a core group of thieves, loan sharks, extortionists, and murderers who have corrupted and bastardized those same family ties and values.

Nick Caramandi had no chance to be a doctor, lawyer, or teacher. That, he says, is not an excuse, simply a fact. He was, by his own admission, a born hustler and a natural con man. And the mob was the only institution that put any stock in those talents. It was a distortion of the value system of his community. The dark side of the Italian-American work ethic. A marriage of convenience.

The courtship began on the corner at Seventh and Morris where Caramandi, a fifteen-year-old high school dropout, hung out with a group of older teenagers. Their talk was of drugs and money and girls. Their heroes were the guys from the neighborhood with connections and juice—the bookmakers, gamblers, and loan sharks who worked with or for the Angelo Bruno organization.

Caramandi listened and learned.

His parents had split when he was ten years old. He and his younger brother lived with their mother. After he dropped out of school, Caramandi went to work in a tailor shop and began hanging on a corner every night after work and on weekends. By the time he was eighteen he was a streetwise punk with a pregnant girlfriend and a job driving a cab. Marriage and two young children quickly followed. So did a gambling habit that would dog him the rest of his life.

"I used to like to bet horses. I used to bet two dollars on horses with the local bookmakers. Small bets. Things were tough. We lived in a one-bedroom apartment. I started with Yellow Cab in 1954, and it was really an education. I met all types of people. I wasn't too bright about the world, but I started to get street-smart.

"I started to steal the paychecks from the cab company. They used to pay on a Friday, and the dispatcher used to have the checks in the office. I used to wait until he left and I would steal four or five checks. I did that for a good while. They couldn't figure out who was doing it. But I was desperate for money. I was dead broke. No money. No food. I used to gamble all the money away playing poker.

"There was this check-cashing place where I used to take the Yellow Cab checks. I figured on sticking this place up. So I got a toy gun, my kid's toy gun, and I got an overcoat. I remember it was a Friday morning. This guy used to have the money in a cigar box behind the counter. I remember being concerned about the people getting off the trolley cars, that they might come in and see me. So I go in there and, I'll never forget, I said, 'This is a stickup.' He was just a little guy. He put his hands up and I said, 'Back away.' And he opened the register. I go for the register. I put the change in my pocket. I don't even think about the cigar box with all the money in it, and I run to my cab, I had my cab parked around the corner, up another little street, and I took off. I drove home. I counted the money when I got home. It was thirty-five dollars. Then I realized... I forgot all about the cigar box."

Real or fake, it was one of the few times until his days with the mob twenty-five years later that Caramandi would ever use a gun to commit a crime. Over the next two decades he would earn millions, and his only weapon would be guile. That and an abiding belief in the power of greed.

"You show me a fucking guy that's greedy, and I'll rob him," he boasted during one interview. "No matter how, I'll find a way to rob him. Because if he's got greed in him, there's always a way. Just find the thing that he likes the most. When a guy's greedy, you could make him believe blue is white. You could make him believe orange is black. I mean, this is what kind of fuckin' suckers there are. Show a guy something. I take guys to trucks. 'You see that truck, it's loaded with televisions.' They believe it. 'It's loaded with tuna fish.' They believe it. Give me the money. 'See that truck, it's loaded with pizza sauce. California All Red, the best pizza sauce.' Whatever."

It was a philosophy Caramandi developed over the years as he honed his skill as a con man and hustler. Always steal from a crook, he said. Never from an honest man.

A few years after the aborted stickup, Caramandi and his wife split up. She moved out of the city, taking their two young sons with her. And the Crow moved farther across the line, abandoning all pretense of legitimacy, as he lied, robbed, and cheated his way up the underworld ladder. It was not a question of being immoral. Caramandi was completely amoral.

His days were spent conning and flimflamming and his nights and weekends chasing broads, booze, and Lady Luck. He would marry and divorce once more, but marriage was just another institution to be flouted. There was always a girlfriend, whether or not he had a wife. And in addition to the girlfriend, he was open to almost any other female proposition that might happen his way.

When he had money in his pocket he dressed the part of a

South Philadelphia wiseguy in a tailored suit and silk tie, or a cashmere sports jacket and Italian leather loafers. Short and stocky with thick black hair and an engaging, roguish style, Caramandi was playing the role of a mobster long before he became one. And the women, at least those he came in contact with, seemed to love it.

More often than not, however, they were third on his list. Money was always first. And for a long time booze was a solid second.

As his gambling habit increased, he became a regular at mob-run card and dice games. During the week he'd hustle his way to a score that would net him several hundred to several thousand dollars. And during a weekend he'd blow that and more. This would lead him to a loan shark and a debt that had to be repaid. And so he would rob some more to pay his gambling debts and then gamble some more and get ever deeper in debt.

He worked part-time as a cab driver, bartender, and parking lot attendant, but he rarely had a current driver's license and never filed an income tax return. His was a cash-and-carry operation, a philosophy of personal finance that said whatever he could grab, he could keep. And so he was always on the lookout, trolling for suckers.

"My first big score came while I was working at this parking lot during the day. I met this fella named Lester who worked at a bank at Seventh and Walnut. I got friendly with the guy. He used to park his car there every morning. We get to talking and I find out he wants to get into the still business, bootleg whiskey.

"This was my first con job. I get an older guy from the neighborhood named Charlie and we make a meet, the three of us, and this Charlie tells him we'll set up this still but it will be in Jersey and he can't go near the still because he's a banker and there might be heat and we didn't want to put any heat on him. So we ask him for eight thousand dollars in the front to buy the sugar, and we hadda get a plumber for the piping. Charlie gave him a really, really good con.

"Lester said he'd have the money for us in a couple days. He was supposed to meet us at Eighth and Morris streets. So here's this Charlie and me sitting in the bar. We got a dollar between us. He's supposed to meet us at nine o'clock. Nine o'clock comes and we go outside. Lester is in his car, he's got the eight thousand. Man, you never seen two happier guys. We cut up four thousand apiece and then it was every week we were taking money from him.

"We'd tell him we needed money for this, for that. We needed money for the cooker, for the mash, all kinds of stories. We musta took, in a period of six months, a hundred thousand dollars off the guy. We both were living high. I was going to the racetrack. I quit my job.

"See, Lester had access to these books. People would leave their savings books in the bank. So we devised a plan. He'd get me the books of people that had money in the bank, thirty thousand, forty thousand, fifty thousand. In those days, if you wanted to draw over three thousand dollars out, you had to wait three days. If it was under three thousand you could get the money on the spot. I used to forge the names and get the money. We did this over and over. Then one time we tried to pull some money out of an account at a branch office. I'll never forget the guy's name. He lived in Jersey and had about thirty thousand dollars in the bank.

"Now the thing was, they would have an identification signature at the branch bank. The amount that I was going to ask to withdraw would be twenty-nine hundred. The girl would go to the box and look for the signature. If the signature matched, she'd give me the money. So I go into the bank and I hand the cashier the withdrawal slip. She looks at it and says, 'Just a minute.' She comes back and she says, 'Would you mind signing this over again?' Well, this took me by surprise. But I stood there and I signed it over again. I had practiced the guy's signature for three or four days. You do it often enough, it comes natural. I could do it in my sleep. The signature was perfect. She made out the withdrawal and I signed the signature. But little did I know they were having a problem with the signature card. They couldn't find it. Lester had called to make sure the signature card was there and somehow afterward the card got lost.

"So I'm standing there waiting and the manager comes over, a little bald-headed guy. He calls me to the back of the bank, on the second floor, and the first question he asks me is what's your name. I give him the name that's on the signature card. So he says, 'We seem to be having some problem with the identification,' and asks if I have any ID on me. I knew I had a problem. There was a lot of security guys in there. So I said,

'Listen, I got my ID in the car. Just let me go get it and I'll clear this thing right up.'

"So I turn around and start walking. I don't know if I'm gonna get arrested or what. That walk out of that bank seemed like a hundred miles. I hit the escalator stairs, jump down the steps, and, boom, I was out.

"With this, the con blew up. It was a mess. We told Lester the cops were checking the still. Then we told him the still got busted, but he didn't read anything about it in the papers, so he knew we'd robbed him. But the kid took it on the chin, him and another guy he was involved with in the bank. They got five years."

Caramandi walked away clean. More important, he learned that a good con was better than a gun.

As he became more and more involved—and respected—in the underworld, he developed the second major asset of any thief, burglar, or con man: information. Knowledge is the key to any scam. If it's a flimflam and you're trying to sell a product, you've got to know the intricacies of its marketing. Is it sold by the pound, the gallon, the ounce, or the gross? Does it come in cases, cartons, bottles, or crates? What's the retail price? What's the wholesale price? Who's in the market?

Information. Caramandi dealt in information. He wanted to know who had money and where they stashed it. If the booty was big enough, he'd go for it.

The early results were mixed.

"There was a guy by the name of Heschie Price whose brother-in-law has a brother-in-law that's a rabbi. He says this rabbi's made a fortune over the years with circumcisions, marriages, and so on. But according to his brother-in-law, the rabbi doesn't bank and, what's more, he never goes out. Never spends any money. He stays home, just him and his wife. The only time he goes out is on a Saturday morning for services.

"So Heschie gives me all the information and we go up there and we watch the rabbi and his wife leave the house. Bingo. I go right to the door. Boom. I pick the lock. I'm in the house in a half a minute. Me and this kid Ricky. Now we go upstairs. We're looking all around. The guy said there was a safe in the house. We're looking, but we can't find it. We go into the bedroom. We're looking all around, in the other bedrooms. All over.

"Finally, we go in the bathroom. The bathroom has a closet door. Sure enough, there's a big fucking safe. The safe musta weighed six hundred fucking pounds . . . and it's on the second floor. It musta taken us a half hour to get the safe down. Anyway, we wave to this guy Boozie who's waiting down the street to bring the car around. He waves us to come over—it's maybe seven-thirty in the morning now. He can't get the car started.

"I says, 'Why can't you get the car started?'

"He says, 'I shut it off. I don't know.' I started screaming at him. I said, 'Let's push the fucking car.'

"Anyway, a newspaper delivery truck comes down the street. I said, 'Hey, buddy, gimme a push?' And he does. We get the car started and we pull it in front of the house. I gave the truck driver twenty dollars for helping us get started.

"So, finally, we get the safe into the trunk of the car. But we had no blanket to hide it. We just were anxious to get away. We had the trunk up and we drove all the way downtown with that safe, you could see it. If a cop had passed, we would have been history.

"As we're driving we're saying to ourselves God knows how much money's in there after twenty-five, thirty fucking years of saving. And the way the safe was concealed in the house.

"We go to this guy's garage. We pull out a sledgehammer, crowbar, and chisel. I knew a little bit about safes. This was one of them old-fashioned types with hinges on the side and the combination on the front. After about half an hour, boom, we busted the safe open. We knocked the hinges. We hit the combination and boom, the door goes. So what do you think is in there?

"About fifteen to twenty fucking bankbooks, a bottle of fuckin' Crown Royal, and some Israel bonds. Ah, we coulda died. Our hopes were so high, and, bango, a blank.

"All that work and effort.

"I mean, yeah, there was three or four or five hundred thousand in money, but it was in bankbooks. And they were worthless to us.

"Another time, a buddy and I made a better connection with a kid named Jerry who worked in a parking garage. He and another guy would tip us off when people would come in driving expensive cars and all dressed up. Rich people. Usually they would leave their owner's card in the car, some kind of identification and an address. And usually the key to their house was on the keychain. We would go get a copy made and bring the original keys back to Jerry. He would put them back in the car. And we would go to the house. They were on the Main Line, mostly, suburbs like Wynnewood and Radnor. We started doing that every night, going in and robbing.''

Cash, furs, and jewelry were the big-ticket items they looked for. They would find a fence for the jewelry and the furs, then whack up the take. Caramandi could make from several hundred to several thousand dollars in a good week. And all the while he was expanding his circle of contacts, moving closer to the men with the juice and the connections.

He also was learning that the rich were not very different from him and his friends. Everyone, it seemed, was looking for an edge, for a way to get over on somebody else.

"There was this big Philadelphia realtor who lived in Radnor. I robbed his house. What a house. One of these beautiful homes you see in magazines. The next day in the paper the headline says, 'Fifty Thousand Dollars in Gems Stolen from Realtor.' And I had a big beef with the guys at the garage because they thought I got fifty thousand dollars in gems. I couldn't get two hundred for the fucking stuff. It was paste.''

Caramandi is certain, however, that some insurance company came across with the $50,000, or something close to it, and that he and his partners inadvertently helped the rich get a little richer.

"Things like this happened over the years. Then we didn't know anything about silverware or antiques. We just used to go for the money and furs, diamonds. We were green with that shit.

"But one time we busted into a house and the payoff was unbelievable. This was up in Northeast Philly. The guy was a bookmaker. We found money, cash, everywhere. In every pocket, pants pocket, jacket pocket. There was so much money I went down to the cellar and found a suitcase, a big suitcase, which we loaded. I mean, we just kept finding money. As soon as we got upstairs we found money on top of the dresser, in just about every drawer, in the closet. The money was folded in wads and wrapped with rubber bands. We filled a whole suitcase and loaded as much else as we could in our pockets.

"We knew there was plenty there, 'cause you could see fifties and hundreds, and when we got back downtown and counted it, it was over a hundred thousand dollars. Now that was a big score. I winded up with maybe thirty thousand, thirty-five thousand plus maybe another twenty thousand from what was stashed in my pocket."

Caramandi and one of his partners took part of their "earnings" and invested in a South Philadelphia bar and after-hours club. They began booking numbers out of the joint and, with the mob's approval, opened up a crap game in a room upstairs. For more than a year they were legitimate entrepreneurs by day, gambling-house impresarios by night. They paid off the cops and magistrates to stay in business, and they attracted a well-heeled clientele that included some of the top gamblers, loan sharks, and bookmakers in the South Philadelphia underworld, including Dominick "Mickey Diamond" DeVito, who would become Caramandi's first mob mentor.

"We were making all kinds of money," Caramandi said. "Cabareting every night. Living high off the hog."

The club, however, was an economic meteor for Caramandi and his partner. For several months it was a flash point in the South Philadelphia nightlife. Then it fizzled and abruptly disappeared. By 1969, Caramandi was out of the bar business and basically out of money. But the contacts he had made put him on the verge of some of his biggest scores. Through Mickey Diamond he was meeting other wiseguys, including Joseph Rugnetta, a wily old-time mobster known throughout the neighborhood as Mr. Joe. Rugnetta was the consigliere of the Angelo Bruno organization and, like Bruno, a man schooled in the traditional ways of the mob. Rugnetta was also the titular head of the Calabrian faction of the Philadelphia mob. Bruno, a Sicilian, made a point of selecting a Calabrese as his counselor. It made for less petty friction within the organization and helped Bruno consolidate his power.

For years Bruno, with Rugnetta at his side, ran an organization that made money without making waves. Both men understood the limits of their power, knew when to push and when to pull back.

Nicky Scarfo, who dominated the Philadelphia mob after Bruno's death, sorely lacked that understanding. Caramandi and nearly everyone else associated with the Scarfo organization would suffer the consequences.

CHAPTER TWO

Angelo Bruno's rise to the top of the Philadelphia mob began with one of the cataclysmic events in organized crime history, the notorious 1957 mob conclave in Apalachin, New York. Some sixty mob leaders from across the country had gathered in the tiny upstate New York hamlet on November 14, 1957, for what they would later say was a barbecue at the home of one Joseph Barbara, a mob boss whose territory stretched from Pittston, Pennsylvania, to Binghamton, New York. In fact, the national conference had been called to smooth out some ruffled feathers and allay any fear stemming from the murder three weeks earlier of Albert Anastasia, the hair-triggered leader of Murder Inc.

Anastasia met his end as he sat in a barber chair in New York City's Park Sheraton Hotel, his face wrapped in hot towels in preparation for a shave. The Mafia's Mad Hatter had become a problem to the organization. His penchant for violence and ruthless killings, an asset in earlier years, had turned into a liability as the mob, in the late 1950s, tried to move into a more sophisticated era. Carlo Gambino, an Anastasia lieutenant who would later become "boss of bosses," is believed to have plotted the Park Sheraton hit, apparently with the tacit approval of Vito Genovese, then the most powerful mob boss in New York. As Anastasia waited for his shave that morning, his two bodyguards quietly took their leave. Then two gunmen walked into the shop off the hotel lobby, pulled out revolvers, and pumped his body full of lead.

There were few organization members who mourned the death of the violent mobster. But the murder had a destabilizing effect on the organization. Was this an isolated killing, or the start of a new round of warfare? Thus the call by Genovese for a national meeting. Originally, the session had been planned for Chicago, but Stefano Magaddino, who controlled the Buffalo, New York, area, argued that a meeting would attract less attention if it were held away from the major metropolitan centers, where the feds were likely to observe the comings and goings of top organization members.

Only by happenstance did police stumble upon the Apalachin conclave. An alert New York state trooper noticed a number of big cars in town and began running license checks. The raid that followed sent some of the most prominent Mafia leaders in America scurrying for cover. One of those was Joseph Ida, then head of the Philadelphia family. Ida was one of dozens of mob bosses arrested and questioned by police. While no one was charged with any serious offense, the discovery of the meeting was an eye-opener for law enforcement officials, who for the first time had definitive evidence of a national crime syndicate. Shaken by the encounter, Ida decided not to stick around for the long-term repercussions. A short time after the Apalachin meeting, he fled to Italy, leaving his Philadelphia organization in the hands of his underboss, Antonio Dominick Pollina.

At the time, Angelo Bruno was a capo in the Ida organization and a dominant member of the Philadelphia rackets. Born Angelo Bruno Annaloro in Villalba, Sicily, he had come to America with his family in 1911. His father, Michele, ran a grocery store in South Philadelphia.

While still a young man, Angelo dropped the name Annaloro and began using Bruno, the maiden name of his paternal grandmother. Angelo Bruno is the name that appears on police records from the 1930s detailing his arrests on bootlegging and gambling charges. Through the 1940s and early 1950s, Bruno continued a steady rise in the organization. Initiated into La Cosa Nostra by Michele Maggio, a prominent Philadelphia mob figure, Bruno moved from small-time bookmaker and gambler to major numbers writer and loan shark. By 1951, Bruno, operating with then mob underboss Marco Reginelli and fellow capo Peter Casella, was part of what local authorities derisively called the Greaser Gang. Their bookmaking, gambling, and loan-sharking operations were said to generate $50 million annually, and they became the targets of a major law enforcement crackdown.

One of Bruno's several brushes with the law at that time came in 1953 after a police raid uncovered about seventeen thousand numbers slips at his gambling headquarters. Bruno was prosecuted by a young assistant district attorney named Samuel Dash, who two decades later would play a prominent role as counsel to the U.S. Senate committee that investigated President Richard M. Nixon. Dash won a conviction and sought a jail sentence for Bruno. But a judge, much to the young prosecutor's consternation, levied a fine and placed Bruno on two years' probation.

Bruno managed to dodge several other prosecutions and continued to prosper as a major bookmaker and loan shark. He was a respected and highly regarded member of the Philadelphia family with his own loyal following when Pollina assumed the reins of the organization. But to Pollina, unsure of his hold on the family and anxious to consolidate his power, Bruno was a rival who had to be eliminated.

Pollina selected Ignazio Denaro to carry out the contract. Instead, Denaro went to Bruno and informed him of the plot. Bruno, demonstrating the intelligence and savvy that were to become his trademarks, sought a hearing before the Mafia Commission in New York. Ever the Mafia diplomat, Bruno showed both his loyalty to the organization and a certain fearlessness that would earn him even more respect from his peers. In effect, Bruno was putting his life in the hands of the mob bosses who ran La Cosa Nostra. There was no guarantee that he would win a dispute with his own boss. Yet he was willing to submit the issue to arbitration. A ruling in Pollina's favor would have meant a death sentence for Bruno.

To this day, no one outside the organization knows what was said at the Mafia Commission hearing. But informants later told members of the Pennsylvania Crime Commission the outcome: The New York bosses ruled in Bruno's favor and deposed Pollina. Bruno was named the new boss of the Philadelphia organization and was given permission to eliminate Pollina in much the same way Pollina intended to eliminate him.

But Bruno, setting the tone for his twenty-one-year reign, opted not to exercise that ultimate authority. Instead, he ordered Pollina into retirement. Pollina was never again a factor in the mob. Bruno, meanwhile, prospered as the local boss and was eventually named to the seven-member Commission that by the mid-1960s was headed by his good friend and Mafia mentor Carlo Gambino.

The Gambino alliance enhanced the power and authority of Bruno, and his control of the rackets in the Philadelphia–South Jersey area went unchallenged for nearly two decades. It was during this period of stability within the local organization—a period of Pax Mafia Philadelphia—that Nicholas Caramandi moved from local hustler to mob associate.

"I was with Mickey Diamond [Dominick DeVito] and Joe Rugnetta from about 1969. I musta been about thirty-one years old then. Mickey was a soldier and Joe Rugnetta was the consigliere with the Angelo Bruno family. In those days I really didn't know what the Mafia was about. But word on the street was that I was a good hustler. An older guy I used to work with introduced me to Joe Rugnetta and Mickey Diamond. We made a deal with them that anything that we did we would give them a third of the profit in exchange for their protection. And that's how I really got involved with the Mafia stuff, with Mickey Diamond and Mr. Joe."

Caramandi had already established a reputation that carried weight within La Cosa Nostra. He was known as a guy who would do anything for money. And he had shown himself to be a man who recognized that sometimes, along the way, people die; that sometimes death is a part of doing business.

Two incidents prior to his formal association with Mickey Diamond and Joe Rugnetta point this out. One involved a hapless pharmacist hooked in one of Caramandi's patented flimflams. The other involved a bloody bank robbery.

"It was 1966 and I was living with a girl on Fourth and Snyder. I'm dead broke. Across the street, this young guy just took over a drugstore.

"Iggie, I think his name was. So one day I go across the street to buy a pack of cigarettes. Iggie says, 'Oh, you live across the street?'

"I said, 'Yeah.' I get in a conversation with him. A real fucking donkey, this guy. He's telling me he would like to put a line of toys in the drugstore. I said, 'I can get ya some toys. What kind of toys ya want?'

"So he tells me what he wants. I tell him I can get them, but I say to him, 'You can't bring the stuff here all at once.' So I says, 'What are you lookin' to spend?' And he says, 'See what kind of deal you could get me.'

"So I go and try to find out about these fucking toys. I come back with a list. 'I can get ya this, I can get ya that, I can get ya this.' This is the following day. I had everything set up. It comes to about three or four thousand dollars' worth of stuff. I said, 'Look, I gotta pay the guy. You gotta give me all the money. We got a garage, a warehouse. As you use it, I'll bring ya more of the stuff.'

"This guy's a real fucking lamb chop. He gives me thirty-five hundred bucks. And man, that was big, because I was dead out. Now I start to angle. I go to the guy and I say, 'Look, we got a load of spray net, Aquanet. How much do you pay a case?' Let's say he was paying sixteen dollars. I said, 'I could get it for you for eight. You could use it as a [loss] leader. You could advertise it. You could sell it for fifty cents a fucking can. Who's gonna know any different? Because you're using it as a leader, you're losing money.' Everybody else was selling it for, maybe, a dollar twenty-nine. Oh, he was foaming from the mouth. I told him we had five hundred cases in the warehouse.

"Now, it would take this guy a fucking month to sell three cases. So I went out and bought three or four cases. It cost me twenty-two or twenty-four dollars a case at the time. I bring him these, and just like with the toys, I tell him the rest are in the warehouse. He gives me four thousand dollars just like that. Now, every fucking day I go to him. And I come up with different items. Maalox. I say we got a load of Maalox. And I get the price for Maalox, the liquid and the tablets. Same story, we got five hundred cases of that. This guy couldn't sell anything close to that—I mean, if he sold fifty bottles a week, that was a lot. It would take him years to sell five hundred cases of Maalox. He was so greedy that he didn't see beyond his greed. All he could see was all the money he was gonna make. But he didn't realize how long it's gonna take him to sell this stuff.

"Now I tell him I can get drugs, prescription medicine. And I give him a list of prescription medicine. I sold him so much of the sundries, I hadda come up with something else. I stocked the fucking store up. All the stock that was in there was mine, that I was buying and telling him that we had, you know, five hundred cases of this, three hundred cases of that.

So I had to come up with something else, gettin' him drugs.

"The deal comes to six thousand or eight thousand, something in that area. I say, 'Listen, I'm gonna bring you the stuff. You be outside. I want you to put the stuff in the car. You take it home. You don't touch it. You bring it in a little bit at a time.'

"So I gave him a list of all these different drugs, and, oh, he was foaming from the mouth again. He had a hell of a prescription business. It was a neighborhood prescription business, but he was doing three thousand to four thousand a week. He worked like a fucking dog in there. All day. He was in there from seven in the morning till nine at night.

"Well, of course, I didn't have the drugs to deliver to him. But I didn't need any, 'cause I had this plan. I got this big box and I filled it with bricks and phone books. Then I taped it shut real tight and then wrapped it up with string. I gave him the box and took his money. And I tell him again, 'Put that box in your car and take it home. Don't put all these drugs in your store. Just bring 'em in from home as you need them. Ya understand?'

"So he puts the drugs in the trunk of his car and parks it up the street. I had borrowed his car about a week before and had a copy of the keys made. So later that day, I had a guy take the car and drive it to a neighborhood where I knew it would be stripped.

"About eight o'clock that night he calls me up and he says, 'You won't believe it—my car's missing.'

"'Your car's missing? How the fuck's that?' Even though I was the one who used to borrow his car, this guy couldn't put nuttin' together. I said, 'You can't report it to the cops. You got that stuff in there. Did anybody know? Did you tell anybody?'

"'No,' he said. 'I didn't tell nobody.' Well, I said, 'You can't call the fucking cops. You just gotta wait and see if it turns up. Maybe some kids took it.'

"'Yeah, I locked the doors.'

"He was so fucking scared. I had him scared to death of me. Anyway, we found the car like weeks later. It was all stripped.

"After this, I got a friend to go over there and say that I had been locked up and that the warehouse was found and they took all the stuff out and the FBI was looking for who owned this stuff. And he gives my friend twelve hundred dollars to bail me out of jail. This is how fucking dumb he was.

"But then he caught on, and he called the cops on me. Tried to have me locked up. When we go to the police station I tell the captain at the police station, 'This guy's jealous 'cause I sell spray net cheaper than him.'

"The captain can't believe the story he's tellin'. He says to him, 'You're tellin' me a story that... it's a Damon Runyon story. How could I believe a story like this? And you wanna lock this guy up? It's incredible the story you're tellin' me, what this guy did to you. How could you prove it? You got any proof of this? Now get outta here before I lock you up.'

"I broke the guy. I musta took, in a six-month period, maybe a hundred thousand off him. Soon he went broke, and whaddya think this guy did? He killed himself. Went into his garage and turned on the motor. It's un-fucking-believable the way some people are suckers. But it's only the fucking greed. You know, when a guy's greedy... people believe anything through greed."

Caramandi's other brush with death came later that same year and involved a guy named Tony Esposito whom he knew from the streets. They had pulled some burglaries together and other assorted scams. Esposito's brother, Lulu, was a member of the Bruno family and had helped Caramandi by supplying merchandise that he used in several low-level flimflams.

"One day Tony comes to me and he says, 'Listen, I'm gonna put you in with a bank robbery. We got three fuckin' banks to look at. We're gonna go case 'em. I want you to go in and get quarters and just see what you could see. Get in line. Get, like, fifty dollars' worth of quarters.'

"I says all right and he says, 'You're in. You got a piece. Whatever we do, you're a full partner.' There was William Bakey, who had just come out of jail, Tony's friend Anthony Perpiglia, and him. So I woulda been the fourth man. Now these guys don't go for the fuckin' drawers, they go for the fuckin' safe. They want the safe in the bank.

"So, he's got three banks to look at. One bank is on Twenty-fourth and South. I go look. Now this is all brand-new to me, and what do I know? Tony asked me how many tellers there were and what did I think. I said, 'I don't know, Tony. You gotta come and look. There's a couple tellers.'

"He's got another bank for me to check out. But it was one of those temporary trailer banks, it was a trailer sitting on an empty lot. I looked in there and I figured this would be easy; they only had two or three people working there. But how much money could there be?

"Now, the last bank I had to look at was on Third and Packer Avenue, right near the Food Distribution Center. A lot of people used that bank. I go there and get the quarters. From what I could see, there were three or four tellers and this big fuckin' safe.

"I thought this bank looked pretty good. So I had Tony come back with me. He looks at it and he likes it. There was two broads behind the counter, but not too many people, as far as I could see. But there was a room that faced west, toward Broad Street. When you pulled into the parking lot you could see a couple of windows facing Broad Street.

"When we come out of the bank I said, 'Tony, they got a room there and we don't know who's in there.' He said, 'Whaddaya, paranoid?'

"I said, 'No, I'm just saying we should find out who's in that fuckin' room.'

"'Ah, don't worry about it.'

"So now he and the other two guys decide they're gonna take this bank on Third and Packer Avenue. At first they told me my job would be to drive the getaway car. Well, I didn't have the balls for that in those days. I was just a fuckin' kid. So instead it was decided that they'd have their own car, some junker they stole, and that after they robbed the bank, they were gonna take the masks they'd be wearing and the guns and the money and put everything into this big suitcase.

"I was able to get hot cars back then, stolen cars, and I had a brand-new Thunderbird. We picked a spot near the bank where I parked this Thunderbird. They were gonna drive from the bank, stop and put the suitcase in the trunk of the Thunderbird, then get back in their car. Then they'd drop one guy off at Oregon Avenue and another guy at Shunk Street, and the driver would go a few more blocks and dump the car. They'd meet at Tony's mother's house. Then they would call me and I'd go get the Thunderbird, drive it over, and bring them the suitcase. This was the plan.

"But I musta said to Tony four or five times, 'You sure this is gonna be okay? You know, we don't know who's in that fuckin' back room.' He says, 'Stop being paranoid. I like it. I like it. We'll get this bank on a Monday morning, because all these wholesalers deposit the money from the supermarkets over the weekend. It'll be all fuckin' cash. There's no telling what'll be in there. There might be a half a million in there.'

"So I said all right. You know, I was a lot younger and less experienced than these guys. So it's all set. All I hadda do is wait at my apartment. The cars are parked. They go there this Monday morning. What happens? The fucking bank's closed. Some kind of holiday."

"Two days later, on a Wednesday morning, it's on again. I'm waitin' in my apartment. It's ten o'clock, ten-thirty, eleven o'clock. So I turn on the fuckin' news hoping to hear something. All of a sudden, around eleven-thirty, I hear the report. Daring bank robbery. Two men dead. One critically wounded. Holy Christ almighty. What the fuck happened?

"Well, these guys pulled up with their masks. Pulled up into the parking lot. They get out of the car. The three of them go into the bank. This Tony Perpiglia is in the center of the bank, and he makes the announcement, 'This is a stickup.' Now, can you believe they had a fuckin' stakeout team in this bank? So when these guys got out of the car, they'd seen 'em through the window that I had told Tony about, that faces west, in that room I was worried about.

"As soon as Tony Perpiglia makes the announcement, these guys were ready for them. Ba-boom, ba-boom. They had, like, fuckin' shotguns. They blast 'em both, him and Bakey. Tony [Esposito] got a couple of shots off and got critically wounded.

"Holy Christ almighty. This is what's on the radio. Now you gotta understand, this Tony's brother is a made guy. Now Tony's in the hospital. He's dying. He's on the critical list. His brother, Lulu, goes and sees him and he wants to know if anybody gave him up.

"Now, I'm the only fuckin' guy that knew about it. I'm the fourth guy. Lulu sends for me and he asks me what happened. Now, you gotta understand, I wasn't around Mickey Diamond then. I had nothing goin' for me, if you understand what I'm trying to say.

"I said, 'Hey, I had a piece. My fuckin' car was there. I had a piece of the action. But I didn't say nothin' to nobody.' And he believed me,'cause of something else that happened that day.

"It turns out that one of the stakeout guys, the cop who shot Tony, had grown up in his neighborhood and knew Tony Esposito and his family. And it was just a fluke thing that he and his stakeout team were working there that day. So the story got around and I got off the hook. But I was scared to death, because it looked like it was a fuckin' trap for these guys. But it was just one of those things. They had just come out with these stakeout teams for these banks.

"When the guy pulled Tony's mask off and seen Tony, he started to cry. It was something. So Lulu knew I was sincere and nothing happened. In fact, Joe Rugnetta brought it up over the years, after I got to know him real good, about Tony and what happened. And I said, 'It was just one of those things. What could I do? I told and told the guy about that back room.'

"But Tony had a hard head and didn't want to listen. There was nothing I could do. Lulu understood, and even though Tony died in the hospital, Lulu was satisfied or else I woulda been gone. I woulda been history."

CHAPTER THREE

Prosecutor: Now would you tell the jury what types of flimflams . . . you were involved in.

Caramandi: It is known as theft by deception. I used to sell things I didn't have, cigarettes, anything, any commodity that the buyer would want, I would tell them I would have it.

Prosecutor: And how were you able to get these individuals to become victims of these flimflams?

Caramandi: Because they were crooks. They thought they were getting a bargain, and I guess greed got them. . . .

y the time Caramandi hooked up with Dominick "Mickey Diamond" DeVito and Joe Rugnetta in the late 1960s, he was an accomplished flimflam man and street hustler with contacts throughout the underworld.

He was earning several hundred to several thousand dollars a week and, as always, spending an equal amount—or more— at the track, with his bookmaker, and in the bars and restaurants he frequented.

"I was into everything back then," he said. "It didn't matter. I'd wake up on a Monday morning tapped out from the weekend and I'd go out to do a scam. It didn't matter what. We used to figure if you had ten deals working and you just hit on one, you'd make enough for the week."

Caramandi stole cars on a regular basis from the Garden State Racetrack in Cherry Hill, New Jersey.

"Valet parking," he said. "I'd just go over there and pick out the big cars in the valet parking lot. The keys were right in them. I had a contact in motor vehicles. I used to be able to get sets of licenses, registrations, whatever. So these cars were good. I'd get the phony registrations made up and I'd sell them. In fact, these registrations were so good, you used to be able to use them to get bank loans on the cars, that's how good they were."

He also dealt in counterfeit checks, stolen securities, and counterfeit $20 and $50 bills. But his staple was the flimflam, the classic con in which you sell what you don't have.

"We used to figure we had the whole week to grab a sucker. Here's how we would do it. Let's say, for instance, there were four stores on a corner. A gas station on one corner, a drugstore on another, a tailor shop, and a barber shop. And let's say we wanted to rob the druggist. To make the connection to get introduced to him we would go into the barber shop across the street. Say the guy's name is on the outside of the shop, Sal's Barber Shop.

"So we go, 'Sal, listen, you come highly recommended. Do you know that druggist across the street?' 'Oh, yeah, I know him good.' So I'd say, 'Listen, we got something for this guy and we've been told that this guy's a buyer, but we don't know him. What kind of guy is he?'

"And he would run the guy down to us. 'Oh, he's a good guy. Man, I could talk to him. Yeah, he's an okay guy.' So, I would say, 'Tell the guy I'm your brother-in-law. This way he's gonna trust me. Because, you know, some of these guys, they don't trust ya.' 'Oh, yeah. Sure,' he says. And I tell him he's got a good note out of this. 'Just introduce me to the guy and tell him I have something for him. I'm your brother-in-law. I'm a good man. And tell him if he makes any money, don't forget you. And I'll take care of ya. That way you'll make money on both ends.'

"And these guys would take me into guys and introduce me. Now I got the guy in a relaxed feeling when I start to talk and run through my spiel to the guy."

The spiel was almost always the same. Only the product changed. There was a truckload of goods. Spark plugs. Hams. Pizza sauce. Tuna fish. Tires. Golf balls. It all depended on the sucker. Later, as Caramandi got more sophisticated, it would be Krugerrands, bars of gold, or $1,000 bills. The stuff was hot. That was understood, but never spoken. Caramandi was looking to unload at a good price. That was the lure, the hook.

"Spark plugs," he said. "If they sold for eight cents apiece by the gross, I would offer them for four cents."

It was all access and marketing. Know your product. Know your customer. And never, ever, underestimate the power of greed.

"We made some big scores this way," Caramandi said with some pride. "These are the kinds of things the flimflam business is all about. One day we would sell spark plugs. The next day pizza sauce. The following day coffee. We used to go all over the state and out of state, all fucking South Jersey and North Jersey. We even went into New York, but in New York you're always running into wiseguys."

Early on he made several scores selling "colored television" sets off the back of a station wagon. He would pull into a gas station and offer the owner a deal on the sets. Nineteen-inch color sets sold for about $400 apiece. Caramandi would ask for $250.

"Could ya use them?" he would ask the gas station owner conspiratorially. The TVs would still be in their boxes in the back of the station wagon. Scattered around them would be brochures that screamed, "Color, color, color."

Caramandi would act nervous, anxious. "Look, I don't have all day for this," he would say. "Could you use them or not?" The deal would be struck. He'd settle for $200 a set.

He'd drive out of the gas station with $800 in cash in his pocket. The gas station owner would have four televisions that he no doubt intended to sell for a nice profit. Then he'd plug one in and spend twenty minutes trying to adjust the color before he realized that what he had bought for $200 apiece were four $99 black-and-white sets.

"The beaujours," Caramandi would say in his fractured vocabulary, "that's what sold 'em." And he'd tell the story two or three times before it became clear that he meant "brochures."

"They saw all the beaujours," he said. "And their greed blinded them. By the time the guy plugged them in, before he knew what was happening, we were home. This went on, and we were making three hundred or four hundred a day with no problem. We'd go out, and sometimes to the first guy we talked to, we'd sell the televisions. Sometimes we'd just sell two. Some days we'd sell none. Some days we'd sell the whole four. But we were grabbing seven hundred, eight hundred, maybe a thousand a week, and this was keepin' the wolves away."

At least the television scam involved a product. Most of Caramandi's deals were complete fiction. He had no spark plugs, no hams, no pizza sauce. But that didn't matter. All he needed was a spiel, a partner, and a double door.

"To double-door a guy I'd meet with the sucker after we set up the deal and get in his car. He drives me to a spot. The spot we pick out would have two doors. We had places all over the city. The best one we used to use was this bar, Dave's Bar, on Third and Fairmount. There were always guys hung in there who we would get to pretend like they were the driver of this truck with the stuff in it.

"I'd pull up. I got the sucker in the car. He's got the money. I'm taking him to the stuff. Now my partner is standing on the step in front of the bar. I'd be facing north. Our car was on the next street facing south. Now I'd have the sucker pull up so that he couldn't see the back door and park him there. I'd sit in the car and I'd ask him for the money. So now we had signals. If the guy was going to stay in the car after he gave me the money, my partner would put his hand on his shoulder. I would walk up to him. He would put his hands out and pretend like we were talking, but he's telling me, 'Okay, the guy's still in the car.' Then we'd go in the bar and run out the back door.

"By the time the sucker got out to see what happened, we'd be gone. In our car and down Delaware Avenue to South Philly, bing, in five minutes. That's how easy it was.

"We had places all over the city. Double-door spots. We'd show 'em the front door, but they would never see the back door. They didn't know about double doors. Most of these guys were greedy. We robbed guys with cigarettes. Five thousand. Three thousand. We'd sell guys meat, hams, quarter hinds. I mean, there were so many things we sold. Every item you could think of....

"This was the con. Everything was to the double door. And we got pretty good at it. One time we robbed two guys in one day. We grabbed twelve thousand dollars. Me and this fella Rickey. He had one guy and I had another guy. They just clicked up. It was easy money."

*   *   *

Not every deal went off without a hitch. Sometimes the sucker wouldn't turn over the money without seeing the product, in which case Caramandi would throw a fit and walk off in disgust, offended at this affront to his honesty and integrity. Other times, the guy would get out of the car and try to follow Caramandi and his money into the bar. On a signal from his partner, Caramandi would wheel around and confront the sucker.

"What are you doing?" he would scream. "Didn't I tell you to wait in the car? You want to blow this whole deal? The people I do business with don't want to see you. What's the matter with you?"

Cowered, the sucker would return to the car, and Caramandi and his partner would quickly make their way to the back door.

Caramandi earned hundreds of thousands of dollars as a flimflam artist over the years and was caught only once. Back in 1971, he and Johnnie Boozie tried to sell a load of golf balls to the manager of a New Jersey country club.

"It was Labor Day or Memorial Day. I can't remember which. It was a holiday, a Monday. We went to Jersey. My partner, Johnnie Boozie, he had robbed a guy in Delaware with this golf-ball deal but we didn't know the guy had reported it.

"So we go to Jersey. We're in Voorhees Township. Boozie goes into the clubhouse to try to talk to the owner to sell him golf balls. I'm outside. He comes out and says, 'The owner ain't here. He'll be back in five minutes.'

"So we waited. He goes back in. We had two plastic bags of golf balls. He goes inside, talks to the owner, and comes back out and says it looks good. The guy's gotta see how much money he's got. So we're just standing there waiting when all of a sudden I see a state police car and then another one. I say, 'Yo, Boozie, we got a problem here.'

"I says, 'Listen, let's take off. Leave the wagon here. You go this way. I'll go that way.' Across the golf course we start running. But now he can't run. He's got a bad ticker, even though he was only fifty-two or fifty-four at the time. So he calls to me, 'Wait, wait, I can't run.' Now, I know I woulda got away,'cause I was really flying, but I stop, and before you know it, ten or fifteen cops are there. They fire a gun in the air. 'Stop, halt or we'll shoot.'"

Boozie and Caramandi spent the night in the Camden County jail, guests of Jersey Joe Walcott, the former heavyweight champion, who was the county sheriff at that time.

"What a dungeon this joint was," Caramandi said. "We go upstairs. There's like four cells and there's only room for twenty guys. But they got forty, fifty guys in there. We bought a bunk for five bucks. If not, we would have had to sleep on the floor."

The next morning, detainers started to drop on Boozie and Caramandi. They were wanted in three states for assorted cons and flimflams. For twelve days they sat in the Camden County jail, waiting for a hearing and hoping to make bail.

"Our lawyer comes to the prison there, on the sixth floor, and we go to this room where we're gonna talk, and a riot breaks out. They start burning the joint. Oh, it was horrible. We're locked in this room, me, Boozie, a couple of other inmates, young kids, and the lawyer. We got on the floor. We wet some towels and covered our faces and tried to breathe the air in. We thought we were going to burn to death in there. Our lawyer was scared shitless."

The riot was quickly contained, and a few days later Boozie and Caramandi made bail. A few months later they were in Mays Landing, New Jersey, for a hearing on several of the outstanding charges. Ultimately, Boozie was sentenced to two years in prison. Caramandi got just ninety days.

"It turned out there was only one beef on me," Caramandi said. "The rest were on Boozie. They couldn't ID me, because I didn't work with him that much. You see, he used to rob honest guys. I used to rob crooks. Guys that I figured wouldn't go to the cops."

Caramandi ended up doing sixty days. It was a horrible experience, he says, but even there his connections to Mickey Diamond and Joe Rugnetta were valuable.

"Even while I was in that jail, I had the protection of Mr. Joe. Remember, by this time, I was sharing what I earned with Mickey Diamond and Mr. Joe. There was a guard there who used to do the plumbing work. So we made a connection and I got a job as his helper. It wasn't bad. The work was easy. And it helped pass the time."

When he got out of the county jail, Caramandi went right back to flimflamming. Only this time he went upscale. He had played out the market on spark plugs, cigarettes, television sets, and hams. So he traded in his blue-collar hustle for a suit-and-tie deal. Soft-spoken, sophisticated, hair neatly trimmed, nails manicured, Nick Caramandi was moving up the ladder in the underworld. Instead of pocketing $300 or $400 per scam, he was now making $3,000 or $4,000. He was still "with" Mickey Diamond, but he was also making other mob connections, including one with a skinny former amateur boxer who controlled the rackets in Atlantic City for Angelo Bruno.

It was 1971. Atlantic City was on the skids. The once proud resort had bottomed out. Hotels were closing. The convention trade was dying. Vacationers with money were hopping on a plane for Florida, Bermuda, the Bahamas, or Vegas. Middle-class families were opting for two weeks each summer in Wild-wood or Sea Isle City.

The Queen of Resorts was now a city of the old and the poor. And Little Nicky Scarfo was struggling to make a buck with a second-class rackets operation in a second-class city. In ten years all of that would change, but in 1971, when Caramandi pulled his first scam for Scarfo, the future mob boss was, like the city in which he lived, on the ropes.

"I got hooked up with this guy Spike [Anthony DiGregorio]. He was with Chickie Narducci [Philadelphia mob figure Frank Narducci, Sr.], but Nicky Scarfo had borrowed him from Narducci. This is when I first got hooked up with Nicky.

"We went down to Atlantic City, around Margate. Me and this guy Spike flimflammed a few people. Spike was a good hunting dog. He knew how to dig up guys. He would go in and meet people and tell them he's got this or that and I would go in and do the selling.

"Spike came up with this guy from Atlantic City, and we made this pretty good score. I'll never forget it, because the day we made it, Nicky's father was being laid out. His father had died.

"We met these guys and I sold them the thousand-dollar-bill deal."

The $1,000-bill deal was one of Caramandi's best cons, one that he would resort to again and again whenever he needed to make a score. Like most of his other deals, it was a matter of selling what he didn't have, of creating a product and a market and playing off the greed of the hapless consumer. This is how it worked:

"I used to get a thousand-dollar bill and two five-hundred-dollar bills. These were my samples to show the suckers. Now I had a spiel that I used that sounded so convincing that people just drooled over it. I seldom missed with this scam, because it sounded so authentic.

"Now if I got a sucker, usually he had to have money or be around money and have connections with money. I used to make sure the guy wasn't a peddler. When I'd get the sucker, I'd sit him down, usually at a nice restaurant. I'd get one of them phony Rolexes. My fingernails were manicured. I'd really look the part, suit and tie.

"I'd start out, and right away I try to read the guy. As soon as the guy talks, after a couple words, I could make him right away. That's my extra sixth sense. This is what made me so good in the con business. I could read people pretty good.

"So, I sit the sucker down and I say, 'See these bills? Let me explain where these bills come from. Remember when Batista was in Cuba. The wiseguys controlled Cuba then. They had the casinos, and in them days, in the forties and fifties and early sixties, they used to use thousand-dollar bills.

"'Now, what happened, when Castro overthrew Batista, was that all these wiseguys got out of Cuba and took their money with them. A lot of them winded up with large amounts of thousand- and five-hundred-dollar bills. In 1970 the government stopped making thousand-dollar bills, because, you know, it's tough enough to cash a fifty-dollar bill, let alone a thousand-dollar bill.

"'The point is, there's no crime in having a thousand-dollar bill. The crime is, how do you show it on your income taxes. If I'm carrying a hundred thousand dollars' worth of thousand-dollar bills, the government can't lock me up, because these bills are not stolen. It's not ransom money. It's not counterfeit money. There's no problem. They can't charge me with any kind of crime.

"'But suppose the IRS comes in for income tax purposes. Now say you're a legitimate businessman making fifty thousand, sixty thousand a year and you claim so much in taxes. Now they want to know how'd you get this hundred thousand in thousand-dollar bills, and they're gonna want to know if you paid taxes on it. So you got a problem. An IRS headache. You lied on your income tax returns. So this is what makes it so difficult.

"'More difficult is when you go into a bank and try to cash one. You cash one bill, they make a W-2 form up. And you gotta show ID. That's another headache. All right, you might be able to get away with one, but that's it, because three days later the IRS is gonna come a-knocking on your door.'

"So this is the spiel I'd give the sucker, and it sounds pretty sensible. And I tell him, 'Listen, I been all over the country, to Chicaco, L.A. I been in banks where bank presidents have said they were gonna switch the money and they couldn't do it.'

"This way I make him think I'm sincere about the deal. I'd say, 'I had all kinds of deals offered to me, and it never worked out. I've sold them. I've sold a few million dollars' worth, but my point is this: You wanna take twenty-five and go peddle them, you could go one bank here, one bank there. But you're gonna burn out the area. You've got to have a good connection. A guy that could show that somehow he could get rid of these bills. I'm not looking to sell twenty-five. I'm looking to sell a couple million dollars' worth. But you gotta buy no less than a hundred thousand dollars' worth. My thing is, you could have these bills for seventy points. In other words, seven hundred on a thousand.'

"Now, I knew usually they'd try to cut me down, like sixty-five percent or sixty percent. I'd go even for fifty percent. But they had to buy a large amount.

"They go, 'Yeah, yeah, yeah.' I show 'em the bill, but I would never give it to them. If they wanted to take the serial number, okay. Usually I was dealing with high-level guys, white-collar guys. And these guys are the biggest fucking suckers in the world, because they don't have any street smarts. They know dollars and cents. And this is how I grabbed these guys.

"I musta did something like fifteen guys. The highest I ever took was maybe fifty thousand.

"See, the bottom line is that once I gave the guy the pitch, I wasn't really selling the thousand-dollar bills, I'm selling myself. The guy believes in me. And then I would tell the guy, 'Listen, I do business in a bank. Now I'm not gonna make couriers come in—these bills are not here, they're not in Philadelphia. I'm not gonna make a guy travel with a million dollars' worth of bills and risk his getting caught with a million dollars' worth of bills. I'll make a guy take in a hundred thousand the first shot, and after we do business, then we'll go from there.

"'But you gotta be the right guy,' I'd tell 'im. 'I just wanna do business with you. I do business in a bank. We have banks that we use, and this is the way it goes. I don't do business in alleys and hotel rooms. We do business in a bank.'

"Now, all I want is the sucker to meet me with the cash and to come to the fucking bank. I used to use a bank on Broad and Walnut streets. Sometimes I'd meet them at the Bellevue Stratford Hotel, which was right near the bank. Now if I couldn't grab their money in the Bellevue, then I would walk 'em to the bank. I had two plans, Plan A and Plan B. Sometimes I grab them right in the Bellevue. I'd say, 'Wait here. You can't meet the vice president of the bank.' See, I'd always say I had somebody on the inside. I'd save that story till the guy came with the money.

"If they insisted on coming with me, I'd make them sit down in the bank. My partner would be there already talking to some loan officer. He'd go in there first and go up to one of the desks, so to the sucker it looks like we know a guy at the bank. Then my partner would come over and I'd say, 'Give 'im the money. He's gonna get the bills for ya.' Then my partner would walk back toward the bank officer and turn around and signal for me to come over. I tell the sucker, 'Let me go see what he wants.' Then it was just like the double door. If the sucker stays there, my partner gives me the signal to keep coming. If he gets up, I get another signal and turn around and holler at the guy.

"These guys didn't know any better. I used to scare them once we got in a bank. 'Hey, I ain't got no license to do this stuff.' My personality would change on them, you know. I had to get a little tough on them. But we're in a bank, so it all looks legitimate. If the sucker stays put we keep walking out a side door of the bank. We'd have a car waiting up the street, and before he knew it, we'd be gone."

One of the first scores he ever shared with Scarfo was the $1,000-bill scam set up by Spike back in 1971. Caramandi took $15,000 from two suckers. The sting, carried out in a Philadelphia bank, went like clockwork. Before the day was over, Scarfo had his piece of the action.

"Me, Spike, my partner Ricky, Mickey Diamond, and Scarfo all got a piece. Out of the fifteen thousand we each ended up with three thousand. Spike brought the three thousand right down to Atlantic City. In fact, Nicky was at the funeral parlor because of his father, and you know how you stand by the coffin? Spike gave him the three thousand dollars right there. Nicky says, 'How much is here? How much is here?' It was a big score, 'cause at this time Nicky was making it just on the hustle."

*   *   *

Off and on over the next two or three years, Caramandi would
work other scams and hustles for Scarfo. In addition, he used
his contacts and influence to help the future mob boss in legitimate deals. He once arranged for Scarfo to buy a set of
living-room furniture for his apartment in Atlantic City at a
reduced rate from a furniture salesman in Northeast Philadelphia who owed Caramandi a favor.

Ironically, the salesman would later spend four years in jail
after being mistakenly identified as the hit man in a mob murder carried out by the Scarfo organization. The man was eventually cleared and released from prison, but the murder of
Greek mob boss Stevie Bouras remains unsolved. The police
now believe it was carried out by a Scarfo family associate in
a dispute over control of the methamphetamine trade in the
city.

"Over the years I had a lot of dealings with this guy Spike,
and that's how I got to know Scarfo. Now here's a made guy,
Scarfo, who can't make no fuckin' money. Understand what
I'm trying to tell you. In other words, what did he have? He
had a little bookmaking, a little numbers business going. I
think one time he had a piece of a dirty bookstore in Atlantic
City. But it was nothing. He was always looking to make
money. He never had anything. And this is why, later on, when
he got the power, he wanted more and more. He could never
have enough money, Scarfo. He was a very greedy guy."

CHAPTER FOUR

O n November 2, 1976, voters in New Jersey over-whelmingly approved a proposal to legalize casino gambling for Atlantic City. The decision would spark an economic rebirth in that struggling South Jersey resort. It would also be the under-lying cause of the bloody turmoil that would change the face of the Philadelphia mob.

More than $1 billion would be spent building the Boardwalk gambling palaces that later made the city the most visited tourist destination in America. More than thirty million people, from high rollers in Lear jets and limousines to gray-haired grandmothers on one-day excursion buses, now flock to the gaming tables and slot machines each year. Forty thousand new jobs have been created in the casino-hotels. Thousands more have spun out of the legitimate and illegitimate casino service industries: food and liquor distribution, restaurant supplies, laundry service, entertainment, trash hauling, junket operations, loan sharking, bookmaking, prostitution, and drug dealing.

Governor Brendan Byrne, New Jersey's top executive at the time gaming was legalized, stood on the Boardwalk a short time after the referendum and issued a warning to the mob: "Keep your filthy hands out of Atlantic City," he said. Sea gulls squawked and the surf roared in the background. The governor's proclamation was noted by the media that swarmed around him. And then everybody went back to the business of preparing the city for the big gambling boom that was to follow.

Construction companies bid on contracts and hired mob-

connected firms to do millions of dollars' worth of the subcontracting work. Unions linked to the mob organized thousands of casino-hotel workers. Mobsters bought land and
joined in the real estate speculation frenzy that turned the
city into a Monopoly board. Here was the late Paul Volpe, then
boss of one of the big Canadian families, buying up parcels of
land all over the city. Here was Manny Gambino, a cousin of
the New York Gambinos, posing as Matty DiNardo as he bid
on one of the Boardwalk hotels. Even Meyer Lansky, then
living in semiretirement in Florida, sent an emissary to check
out the prospects.

Nick Caramandi sat out the early mob maneuverings in Atlantic City as a guest of the federal government in a penitentiary in Lewisburg, Pennsylvania.

His imprisonment capped a hectic five-year period in which
he bounced between Philadelphia and the Fort Lauderdale,
Florida, area. He first went south in 1971 and worked his
various scams and hustles before returning to Philadelphia
in late 1973. At that point, he got involved with a counterfeit
ring and became a major distributor of fake $20 and $50 bills.
It was a highly lucrative operation, but it would lead to his
first major bust.

"I came back to Philly and got involved with an old-timer
named Genie Taylor. He was with the old mustache mob. He
wasn't a made guy or anything, but he was around wiseguys.
He hooked me up with a printer that could print this counterfeit money.

"I told Mickey Diamond about it, and he said go ahead. So
I got involved with this printer and he started making these
bills, which I would then sell wholesale [at 10 to 20 percent
of their face value]. I musta made a couple hundred thousand
right away. This went on for eight or nine months. The feds
was going crazy. In fact, there was a big article in the paper
about how they didn't know how these bills were being made
and that the Secret Service was going crazy.

"After a while, the printer made up a new batch of ten-
dollar bills for me, two hundred thousand worth. So I met
with him and he gave me the package, a big box, out of which
I made five-thousand-dollar packages. The bills were good,
good quality. We switched to ten-dollar bills 'cause we had
burned the town up with twenties. I mean, these bills went
all over the country. In fact, when I got convicted they claimed

that millions of dollars of them had been passed and cir-
culated.

"Anyway, I had this guy Shorty with me, to help count
and separate the money and put it in bundles. I was driving
a '68 Buick at the time. I went to a friend of mine who had
an auto body shop and had him cut out a door under where
the spare tire sits in the trunk and put in a cable leading
from the side of my seat to inside the trunk that would hold
the door closed. If I pulled on the cable, the door would open
and anything sitting in there would drop to the ground. I
used to make the deliveries with this car and also keep the
money in the tire well. I figured if I was being followed or
something was happening, I could pull the pin and I wouldn't
have the stuff.

"So one day, a Saturday, it was July 1974, I got the packages
separated and had maybe five sales to make. But a couple of
days before, this Shorty stole some of the bills when he was
helping me count. Maybe a thousand dollars' worth. He gives
them to a young girl, like nineteen years old, and the girl got
caught with them. So she takes a Secret Service agent over
to his house and she says, 'Listen. This is my boyfriend. He
wants to buy some of them bills.'

"This was on a Friday. And Shorty tells the Secret Service
agent, 'I don't have any bills today. But tomorrow I'll have all
you want.' This fuckin' goof does this, right.

"Now the Secret Service sets up a surveillance. There were
about forty of them, on bikes, motorcycles, trucks. The next
day I call Shorty and tell him to come over. I'm gonna make
a move today. He comes over about ten o'clock in the morning. I had these five guys lined up I was gonna sell to.

"I come outside and I see a guy and girl walking with a dog.
It was kind of suspicious. Later, it turns out they were Secret
Service. They had been watching Shorty.

"I get into the Buick and drive to another car where the
bills are, wrapped in packages of five-thousand-dollar bundles.
I had like seventy, eighty thousand sold that day. So I get the
money and I put it in the well of my car and I start dropping
the money off here and there. The Secret Service, though, they
can't set up their surveillances fast enough.

"Now I come to the house of the last guy, the last customer.
I got, maybe, a ten-thousand-dollar bundle. This was his first
batch of these ten-dollar bills and he just wanted to try them
out, to see what he could do with them. But the fucking guy

ain't home. His wife says he went to his sister's house. So I say, 'Well, call him up.' She calls and he says he'll be right there.

"So I'm waitin' for the guy. All of a sudden I see a guy turn the corner and this guy's got a jacket on. Hey, it's a hot summer day. It musta been a hundred degrees that day. No way, I thought. So I said, 'Shorty, there's something wrong. Get that bag and put it under that car.' I walk to the corner and I see a bunch of guys coming up one way. I look down the street and I see like the whole area is surrounded. They're zeroing in on me. All of a sudden, here comes a fuckin' helicopter. They got a fuckin' helicopter.

"Now, all the people start to gather. And there's a woman in the helicopter, she's got a bullhorn. And she says, 'The man in the brown shirt, disperse from the crowd.' And I see these Secret Service agents running, and bing, they grab me.

"They threw me on the ground. One guy put a .357 magnum in my mouth. Another guy put a shotgun to my head. 'Move and we'll blow your head off.' They grabbed Shorty and they took us to Sixth and Market [the Federal Building]. They had him in one room and me in another. And they're telling me, 'You know, in Africa, they cut your head off for counterfeiting. You're gonna get a lot of time.' "

Caramandi was, in fact, charged, arraigned, and eventually released on $25,000 bail. In a move that demonstrated the arrogance and bravado that won him standing on the street corner, he went right back into the counterfeiting business, trying, he said, to raise enough money to pay for his defense. But by that point, the Secret Service had gotten a line on the printer and several of his associates. Feeling the heat, Caramandi decided he'd be better off in a warmer climate. So he jumped on a plane and headed back to Fort Lauderdale to await his April 1975 trial date. There he hooked up with Ralph "Junior" Staino, a longtime friend and fellow South Philadelphia mob associate.

For eight months prior to his trial and for about a year while he was appealing his conviction, Caramandi worked his hustle in the Florida sun. There was never any thought of skipping out on the charge or bolting after his conviction. Where would he go? What would he do? He had been caught and he had been convicted. Now he'd have to do time. It was part of the price he paid for the business he was in.

But first there were more suckers to be fleeced. He worked the $1,000-bill scam and some credit card fraud and then he and Staino sank their hooks into a small hotel called the Galt Ocean Manor.

"Me and Junior nearly took this place. It was in receivership, Chapter 11. These two guys, some crooked lawyer and his partner, were milking the joint dry. They were selling guys condos and parts of the hotel. They were robbing everybody. We muscled in on them, me and Junior. We took over all the food and beverage stuff.

"I charged everybody three thousand dollars for their little beach places, you know, the cabanas outside the pool. I would charge them three thousand or thirty-five hundred to sign new contracts. These were the people that lived in the hotel.

"We were also passing [stolen] credit cards, putting like three thousand or four thousand a day on these cards. In fact, one of the investigators from American Express came around, a retired cop from New York. He came in to the hotel and said, 'Look, I know what youse are doing. You gotta stop. I mean, you guys are too much.' But they couldn't prove it.

"We used to get a piece of glass and a light bulb and copy the customer's signature over it. It would come out perfect. A guy would come in to the hotel from out of town and we'd use his card for the whole fucking month. We had a system with these credit card people. It was easy to rob them.

"When a guest would give the waitress his card, the girl would bring it to me. I'd call the American Express and get an authorization number. But I would punch out four or five blank receipts with the guy's card. By the time he got the bill, he'd have three thousand, four thousand, five thousand in charges. And he'd call up screaming, but there was nothin' he could do about it. We'd say, 'I don't know. Somebody musta used your card.' We did this for months. We robbed that fucking place blind."

Caramandi and Staino were eventually arrested for credit card fraud. But by that point, their Florida escapade had run its course. One of the Florida papers did a piece announcing that the "Bruno mob" had invaded Fort Lauderdale. The police stopped by and recommended that the Crow and Junior leave town.

"They threw us out of town," Caramandi recalled with some

pride. "They actually escorted us, the cops, and threw us out of town. It could have gone on, someplace else. But I had to come back to Philly. I knew I had to go to jail.

"In January, January 8th, my appeal was denied, and in July of 1976, I went to jail."

CHAPTER FIVE

"**A**t Lewisburg, I met a few fellas from Philadelphia who were there for drug charges. Louie Fresta, who I knew from the neighborhood. Joe Mouse and Stevie Vento—these were guys I knew throughout my life.

"I was there about seven, eight months. It took a little time to get accustomed to prison life. Then Mickey Diamond sent word to another member of the Philadelphia mob at Lewisburg, Tommy DiNorsio, who approached me one day and said, 'I heard some nice things about ya. If you ever need anything in here, just let me know.'

"After that I got friendly with him and we winded up celling together. He made arrangements that I be moved to his block, J Block, which was the prison honor block. Tommy introduced me to another member of the Philadelphia mob, Tony Caponigro, also known as Tony Bananas. When Tommy got paroled, Tony moved in with me."

Caponigro was a made member of the Newark branch of the Bruno organization. Bruno, in an accommodation with the New York families, had been permitted in the late 1950s, shortly after Apalachin, to initiate several members from the Newark area. At that time the New York families, fearing government infiltration, had closed their books to new members.

Caponigro was a major bookmaker and loan shark in Newark, operating out of a bar, the 311 Club, he owned in the city's Ironbound section. He was also suspected of dealing in narcotics despite a Mafia ban on such activity. Like Caramandi, he was a major money-maker, both before and after his formal initiation into the mob. He was also, according to Caramandi,

69

one of the triggermen in the 1951 murder of Willie Moretti, a Newark mobster. Moretti was killed because he had become senile and had begun to talk openly about family business. It was common knowledge among mob members, Caramandi said, that Caponigro carried out the Moretti contract, although by the time Caramandi heard the story, some twenty-five years later, the details were somewhat distorted.

"He went up to him right on a street corner and banged him," Caramandi said. "Blew his head right off. Right on the street corner."

Moretti was killed on October 4, 1951, in a Cliffside Park, New Jersey, restaurant. According to an FBI report, Moretti was sitting in a booth in the restaurant with four other men. Their waitress walked into the kitchen. When she returned, Moretti was slumped dead in his seat. His four companions were gone.

Despite being the focus of several federal and state investigations, Caponigro had managed to avoid prison for most of his adult life. Even the New Jersey State Commission of Investigation, which in the early 1970s put dozens of mobsters behind bars with contempt citations, was unable to get its hands on Tony Bananas. By this point Caponigro was a caporegime, heading a crew of eight to ten members and twenty to thirty associates for the Bruno organization in New Jersey's Essex and Hudson counties, just south of New York City. His activities had long attracted the attention of federal and state investigators, and by 1974 the SCI had a subpoena out for Caponigro. The subpoena required his appearance and testimony at an SCI hearing. In more than a dozen similar cases, mobsters, including Bruno and Scarfo, had been served, had appeared, and had declined to testify. The result was a jail term, usually for a year or more, in a state institution.

Caponigro had managed to avoid all that by the simplest of all methods. He moved to Manhattan, where an SCI subpoena was unenforceable. Occasionally and clandestinely, he would return to New Jersey to visit his club or spend some time at a lavish home he maintained outside of Newark. On New Year's Eve 1974, Tony Bananas made such a visit to his home. He figured state process servers would have better things to do that day than bother with his subpoena. But as he walked out of his house, he spotted a car blocking his driveway. He panicked, jumped into his own car, and rammed the vehicle blocking his escape.

Tony Bananas was right. There was no subpoena server working on New Year's Eve. The car blocking his driveway belonged to an FBI agent who had tailed him to his home. Caponigro wasn't served with a subpoena. Instead, he was charged with assaulting a federal officer and ultimately was sentenced to thirty months in prison.

That's what led him to Lewisburg and, eventually, to a cell with Caramandi. It turned out to be beneficial for both men. Caramandi had someone who was able to look out for his interests, both inside the prison walls and later on the streets of South Philadelphia. And Caponigro, whose ambition stretched far beyond his Newark operation, was able to cultivate another ally in Angelo Bruno's back yard.

"You learn a lot of shit in prison. It seems like everybody's got a personality clash. The guys from New York, Harlem, don't like the guys from Brooklyn. The guys from Brooklyn don't like the guys from Manhattan. The guys from Manhattan don't like the guys from Harlem. It's one vicious circle with these New York guys. But basically most of them were pretty decent to me. I was around Tony a lot and I used to stay with the wiseguys. Tony took me under his wing.

"It wasn't easy. When I first went in there you had all them Washington blacks. They would rob ya. You had to watch when you walked down a corridor. When you went up steps. They would lay for you in gangs, three, four at a time. There was one guy who'd robbed a bank and had been sentenced to ten years. We used to call him Beep-Beep. He ain't in jail a year when he goes and buys a radio. A couple of these guys are waiting for him. They throw him down the steps, cripple him for life. They had him in a wheelchair.

"I met guys there from all over the country. One fella, from Detroit, had embezzled a bank for twenty-five million. This guy had more moves. There's, like, a hundred and thirty credit cards. He got them all. He took tons of money out of banks. He set up deals. I wrote a lot of his stuff down, but I never put it into play.

"And you hear everybody's story. Everybody's innocent. Everybody got ratted out. Every day you heard a different fuckin' story. Guys stole all their lives and they get caught for one beef and they're crying."

Caramandi listened and learned. From the con men and embezzlers he picked up new moves. And from the wiseguys, especially Caponigro, he came to understand more about the mob. Caramandi was a recognized Mafia associate when he went into jail. When he came out he was one step closer to being a made member.

"We used to get the newspaper every day at four o'clock in the afternoon. One day in the paper was a picture of Mickey Diamond standing over a gravesite. Mr. Joe Rugnetta had died. He was the consigliere of the Philadelphia family. I says to Tony, 'Look who died,' and I showed him the newspaper.

"He was very upset about it. He said he had a very close relationship with Mr. Joe. The fella that I was with, Mickey Diamond, was very close to Mr. Joe, too. Anyway, Tony said to me, 'We lost a good man.' I guess at the time he didn't know what was gonna happen either. Who the new consigliere was gonna be.

"But Mr. Joe, before he died, musta got all the Calabreses together, about forty members at the time, and he picked this Tony Bananas to succeed him. Little did Tony know.

"Now, a few months later I was transferred to the prison farm, and Tony was still inside the wall. But when his time was up, he would correspond with me. He wrote me eight or ten letters. I wasn't really familiar with his new position. All I knew was that he was a soldier in the Philadelphia mob from Newark. I wish I still had those letters."

Late in 1979, after serving nearly three years of his seven-year prison term, Caramandi was released. At his direction, a public defender appointed by the court filed a brief for Caramandi seeking a new trial on the grounds that the lawyer who represented him at the counterfeiting trial also represented a codefendant in the case. The appellate court ruled in Caramandi's favor and ordered a new trial. Always ready to deal, Caramandi seized the opportunity and turned it to his further advantage. Instead of a new trial, he agreed to a guilty plea in exchange for time served. He was released from the prison farm and headed back to South Philadelphia, where Mickey Diamond and Tony Bananas were waiting.

"A couple days after I'm out, Mickey Diamond makes a meet for me to have dinner with Tony at the Warwick Hotel. Who's there but Frank Sindone, Mickey Diamond, myself, and Tony. We hugged and he took me aside, into the bathroom, to have a little conversation.

"He said, 'Look. I got plans for ya. Don't fool with no drugs. Try to stay low-key. Do what you're doing.' You know, my flimflams, because, he said, 'Things are gonna be different soon. Just be patient.' He asked if I needed anything, and I said I was okay.

"Me and Mickey Diamond had opened up a bar and restaurant called the Annin Street Café at Ninth and Annin in South Philly. We had it for two or three years, then we lost it, gave it up.

"Now, I find out that Tony is consigliere. Jesus Christ, I thought, that's a big job. That's a powerful, strong thing.

"He used to come to the restaurant to meet people. On the second floor we had a private room. And when he used to come we'd have sort of a banquet, with all different foods for him. He used to stay for a few hours. Different people would come up and see him with different problems.

"There was a beef one time with this fella Victor DeLuca. It seems him and a guy named Pete Rinaldi were shaking down a drug dealer by the name of Ronnie Raiton. But this Johnny Calabrese, who was with Tony Bananas, and another member of the Philadelphia mob, Felix Bocchino, also wanted to shake Raiton down. So there was a beef and Tony and Johnny Calabrese wanted to have DeLuca and Rinaldi killed.

"But Victor and Peter went to this friend from Florida, a guy named Mr. Amato, who was a member but from a different family, for protection. So there was a meeting to resolve this dispute. Angelo Bruno was there. Tony Bananas was there. And this Mr. Amato.

"In the meeting it was decided they would let these two guys go. They wasn't gonna kill 'em. They voted not to. Tony complained about this later—he said Angelo was too easy. Tony was mad because he wanted DeLuca and Rinaldi killed. But even though they let 'em go, these other fellas, Calabrese and Bocchino, were told they could shake down Raiton. DeLuca and Rinaldi couldn't anymore. It was a compromise. Raiton was a big drug dealer. They were gettin' three thousand or four thousand a week off this guy."

Ronnie Raiton was, in fact, a major supplier of phenyl-2-propanone (P-2-P), a chemical needed in the manufacturing of methamphetamine, the drug commonly known as speed. Given the proper ingredients, anyone with a knowledge of high school chemistry is capable of setting up a meth lab. And for years, the Philadelphia area has been the speed capital of the

United States. The manufacture, distribution, and sale of the drug fuels a multimillion-dollar underground economy that has created a series of lucrative but ever shifting alliances in the Philadelphia underworld. Semilegitimate businessmen like Raiton, mobsters like Calabrese and Raymond "Long John" Martorano, and outlaw biker clubs like the Pagans all became part of the network.

"Cookers" who had the chemical know-how would set up a lab in the basement or kitchen of a suburban home, in a shack out in the woods, or in an industrial warehouse in the city. A fifty-gallon drum of P-2-P, smuggled into the country from Europe or Central America, could be converted, in a week or two, into two hundred to three hundred pounds of speed. Sold wholesale by the pound and at street level by the quarter ounce, the meth created from fifty gallons of P-2-P could be worth anywhere from $6 million to $10 million, depending on the skill of the cooker and the quality of the product.

Raiton, also known as the Silver Fox, eventually became one of the biggest federal drug informants in Philadelphia history and helped build narcotics cases against several major members and associates of the Philadelphia mob, including Martorano. He is now in the Federal Witness Protection Program. His cooperation, however, had a minimal effect on the flow of the drug into the city. By 1986, the Scarfo organization was generating hundreds of thousands of dollars in income simply by assessing a $2,000-a-gallon "street tax" on all P-2-P brought in by meth dealers. Caramandi himself collected more than $500,000 for the Scarfo family from local drug dealers. He also helped grab $1 million in a smuggling scam set up by the organization and was setting up another $2 million score when he became a government informant.

It was all part of the strange and illogical code of the Mafia. Here was an organization that, in theory at least, prohibited members from kidnapping and counterfeiting and, more important, from dealing in drugs. But both the financing of drug deals and the shakedown of drug dealers was permitted. As he learned more about the ways of the Philadelphia mob, Caramandi readily accepted those distinctions, and to this day he insists that he was not a drug dealer. But in 1979, drugs were not an issue. Caramandi was getting reestablished as a con man and flimflam artist. He had come out of prison not only with a new ally in Tony Bananas, but also with a new scam.

Gold.

* * *

"When I got out of jail I really went into high-class flimflamming. This time it was gold. I used to buy maybe fifteen pounds of brass wire, which I'd have dipped in gold. It used to cost me a hundred and fifty dollars. Then for another two hundred I used to buy two pieces of gold, maybe twelve inches. I'd fuse this gold, seventeen-karat, on both ends of the brass wire. And then I'd go look for suckers.

"'You wanna buy gold?' And I'd show 'em the brass wire that was dipped in gold. They'd cut a piece off and see it was seventeen-karat. And I'd get twelve thousand, fifteen thousand dollars for a roll, depending upon the sucker. For instance, if gold was selling for three hundred an ounce, I'd charge 'em like a buck and a half—a hundred and fifty. Greed. The greed used to get them. The first six months I was out of prison I must have made seventy-five thousand dollars. And gold was starting to go up.

"Now remember, I was around Mickey Diamond. I sorta looked to him for protection, and he was always interested in what I was doin'. I was a big fuckin' money-maker for this guy, me and the partner I was working with. We were making money hand over fist, and Mickey was gettin' a piece of everything we did. He was like a silent partner. Let's say we grabbed thirty thousand. Mickey Diamond would get ten thousand without doin' nothing. He stood in the fuckin' background. Never even came up with a guy [a sucker], in all those fuckin' years.

"When I was in jail I had met this guy who told me about Krugerrands, gold coins, and that they were going to be worth a lot of money. So when I got out, I found out these South African Krugerrands were going for, like, two hundred dollars apiece. They're twenty-four-karat gold, these Krugerrands, it's like owning a twenty-dollar gold piece. But I don't think there's a real twenty-dollar gold piece in the whole country. They're all counterfeit. These other countries make 'em and they put like eleven percent, twelve percent of gold in them.

"But the South African Krugerrand is different—they're pure gold, no alloy. So when I came out, immediately, that became one of my things.

"I bought a couple of them and turned that into three or four hundred thousand dollars. I worked it just like the gold scam and the thousand-dollar-bill deal. I'd get a guy, show him the two coins, and tell him that I knew a guy and a girl whose uncle had just died, leaving a lot of money as well as these South African Krugerrands he'd bought as an invest- ment. But the niece and nephew had stolen the Krugerrands and put them in a bank, in a safety deposit box. They didn't want the rest of the family to know about them and now they wanted to get rid of them. They were willing to sell them for a hundred and fifty apiece.

"Now, you gotta imagine. They were worth two and a quarter [$225], two-thirty. Whatever gold was worth back in the late seventies. I remember paying something like two-twenty-five for them.

"So I would tell the sucker this story and say, 'Listen, I do business in a bank, and if you're interested, we'll do business right in the bank.... How many could you use?' And if the sucker would say, like, a hundred, at one-fifty apiece, that would be fifteen thousand dollars. Sometimes I'd say five hundred. I'd try to get fifty thousand off a guy. Then gold went up. They were worth over five hundred apiece at one time."

It was the $1,000-bill scam all over again. Caramandi took dozens of people to the bank and walked away with hundreds of thousands of dollars. He'd work the Krugerrand scam and the gold-wire scam at the same time, both hustles playing off the current economic recession.

Everybody was into buying, trading, and selling precious metals. As the dollar weakened, the value of gold and silver shot up. All over the Philadelphia area there were shops an- nouncing, "We Buy and Sell Gold." And every week Caramandi would appear at a different one with fifteen pounds of brass wire dipped in gold or a handful of Krugerrands.

With the brass wire he'd work the con right in the shop.

With the Krugerrands it was the bank and the double door.

He'd meet the sucker on Broad Street, walk him up the block, past office buildings, banks, the Academy of Music, and the stately brick-and-brownstone Union League building. In the background was the City Hall tower, on top of which perched a statue of William Penn. The setting was perfect. This was blue-blood Philadelphia. Not a place for con men and flimflam artists.

Caramandi was so busy at these scams that it ended up costing him money. One time, a sting that had brought him $30,000 forced him to blow a $275,000 payoff.

"I had this gold dealer from Jersey, a guy named Peppy, all set up.

"This guy came with two hundred and seventy-five thousand dollars plus two armed bodyguards to the bank on Broad and Walnut. But this guy also had a girlfriend with him. And it turns out I had robbed her. And she recognized me. She had a place in South Jersey. I took thirty thousand off her with the brass-wire deal.

"Peppy didn't know this when I set him up. See, he was a greedy guy. He loved money and he loved shady deals. So after I sold him the deal with the Krugerrands—you know, with the niece and the nephew and the inheritance—he comes to the bank with a truck, like a van, and he pulls up in front. I'm waiting there. Me and my partner. These two guys jump out of the van, and his girlfriend and another guy are in a car behind the van.

"So I says to this Peppy, 'Where's the money at?' So he says, 'The money'll be here. Let me see the stuff.' And I says, 'Look, you ain't gonna see nothin' till I see the money. After all, I ain't got no license to do this. I gotta count your money. I gotta make sure your money's okay, that it's not counterfeit or anything like that.'

"So one word led to another and we're inside the bank talking. My partner is sitting with one of the bank managers, the loan officers, like we do, pretending we're gonna make a loan and all that nonsense. And I wave to him like I'm having problems with Peppy. He wants to see the stuff. See, this guy was a wheeler-dealer himself and he knew some of the moves.

"Anyway, all of a sudden the girlfriend comes in and she starts screaming, 'He's the guy that robbed me. He took thirty thousand dollars from me,' she's telling her boyfriend. So I get a little nervous. I say, 'Listen, you're nuts. Just wait. Lemme go get the stuff.' And so we made some excuse. I says, 'You got the wrong guy. You're mistaken.' But she's saying, 'I remember you.'

"So in the end, we blew the deal because she recognized me. We hadda walk away empty-handed. Sometimes these things happened. See, I had been all over with the scams.

"Anyway, during the first year after I came out of jail I robbed a lot of guys with gold and made a lot of money. I musta made a million dollars with these gold scores. I mean, everywhere I went, it was like bango, bingo. Because gold was the thing. The price of gold was going up. And I had the thousand-dollar-bill move and the Krugerrands. Everything was in the bank.

"I musta robbed four guys in a row, at fifty thousand a crack. Bing, bing, bing, bing, and out the double door. Then I started with the baseball cards, started robbing guys with baseball cards. I made up a list of the cards that were in demand. I went and bought a couple hundred dollars' worth to show as samples. Then I made up a list. 'I got this card, that card. I got it in the bank.'

"One time I had this father and his fourteen-year-old son. They were coming to the bank. The kid had seven thousand dollars. But he wouldn't give me the money till he saw the cards. The father's there telling him, 'Give 'im the money,' meaning me. But the kid kept saying, 'Lemme see the cards.' The kid wouldn't give up the money. I hadda walk away from that deal, too."

Dozens of other older and supposedly wiser "suckers" happily handed over their cash and then sat like idiots in the bank lobby while Caramandi and his partner walked out the side door.

By March 1980, the Crow had been out of jail for several months, but he had fallen back into a familiar routine. He would rob to gamble. He would gamble more than he had. Then he would borrow from the loan sharks to pay off his gambling debts and rob some more to pay back the sharks. Some weeks he would wake up on a Monday morning dead broke following a weekend of gambling and booze at one of Atlantic City's Boardwalk casinos. For the next three or four days you'd find him cruising jewelers' row in Philadelphia with the Krugerrands or hitting the precious-metal shops along Roosevelt Boulevard or Route 38 with his brass wire dipped in gold. It was a heady time for Caramandi. He had few cares or worries. He was living and playing at a much a higher level than he had been before he went to jail, and he was enjoying every moment of it.

He had unlimited sources of income. Whenever he needed money, he went out and robbed someone. He paid no income tax. In fact, at the time of his arrest in 1986 he couldn't remember the last time he had filed an income tax return. He had no dependents. His ex-wife and sons had moved to another part of the country. Home was a small apartment in South Philadelphia, but on any given night he was just as likely to end up in a motel room with some broad or passed out on the couch in an all-night club or mob hangout. With each con he grabbed more money. With each trip to the track or the casino he gambled more away. And all the while he was moving closer and closer to the inner circle of the Philadelphia mob. He was Mickey Diamond's associate, but if he had a padrone, it was Antonio Caponigro.

In fact, Caramandi was now in the shark business as well. Tony Bananas had fronted a deal for Mickey Diamond and Caramandi. He had loaned them $50,000 which they had put out on the street. They were paying Tony Bananas a point— $500—a week. Since they were charging their customers two points, it was a profitable operation. It guaranteed a small but steady weekly income, and it solidified the relationship between Caramandi and the Newark mobster. And although he didn't realize it at the time, it would also provide Caramandi with firsthand knowledge of events that would change the face of the Philadelphia mob. Caramandi became a Tuesday-night regular at Caponigro's 311 Club in Newark. He'd go up there with Mickey Diamond for a weekly banquet that attracted a small but growing group of mob members and associates. Frank Sindone was a frequent visitor. So was Tommy Di-Norsio. Occasionally Santo Idone, who headed operations in Chester, Pennsylvania, and Raymond "Long John" Martorano would make appearances. Caponigro was a gracious host for these casual yet significant get-togethers. A lot of good food and all you could drink. Tony Bananas was clearly setting his own agenda. And at both the 311 Club and during meetings in South Philadelphia, Caramandi began to pick up an undercurrent of unrest within the Bruno organization.

"I started to watch Tony's action," Caramandi said. "He was very close with Frank Sindone. He used to go to Eleventh and Christian a lot, where Sindone had a restaurant with Tommy DelGiorno. At that time Tommy DelGiorno wasn't a soldier, but Sindone was. And I would hear remarks he would pass about Angelo Bruno, like 'This guy wants the money all for himself.'

"He just started to make remarks. Angelo Bruno used to come upstairs at the Annin Street Café, and Tony would turn his back on him while Angelo was talkin' and ask me how did I do for the week. If I robbed anybody. Like, he was unconcerned with what Angelo used to say."

Caramandi wasn't a made member of the mob yet. But he

knew enough about Mafia protocol to know that a member, even the consigliere, had to be concerned with what the boss was saying.

Unless, of course, he didn't expect the boss to be around much longer.

CHAPTER SIX

Defense attorney:	Why or how did you get the nickname Crow?
Caramandi:	It means shrewd bird.
Attorney:	Who gave you that name?
Caramandi:	A fella from the neighborhood.
Attorney:	He must have known you pretty good.
Caramandi:	Probably.

ick Caramandi spent his entire life looking for an edge. He was not, he often pointed out, a college graduate. He didn't even finish high school, for that matter. He had no family wealth or social standing. He was forced to hustle for everything he got, grabbing opportunities wherever they presented themselves. So he would steal whatever he could, however he could, whenever he could. Right and wrong was not even an issue. There was no moral dilemma. Caramandi lived on the other side, always conscious that he had to look out for himself. That was the bottom line. Everyone used him, and he used everyone. It was all part of the cutthroat game of life that he chose to play. Plan, scheme, and anticipate. Take your best shot.

And cover your ass, because nobody else will.

This would eventually lead to his decision to become a government witness. And in that light, the move was consistent with everything else he had done in his life. Those who were shocked and surprised when Caramandi "flipped" really didn't know him. Those who did almost could have predicted it.

But in 1979, fresh out of prison and aligned with Mickey

Diamond and Tony Bananas Caponigro, Caramandi was living the good life. For the first time he had money, well-connected friends, and stature. And all of this led to a fling with a woman who turned out to be a $100,000 Mafia groupie.

She liked the Crow. He liked her cash.

"Me and Mickey met these two broads. They came down to the Annin Street bar one night and we wined and dined 'em. They wanted to be around gangsters. They loved being around gangsters.

"Now, you gotta understand, even though my input and knowledge about the mob at the time wasn't all that much, it was still pretty good. So we meet these girls and it turns out that the girl I'm with had plenty of money and she loved to have sex.

"She's got this beautiful apartment. Elevator. Doorman. Valet parking. She had a '78 Cadillac Eldorado. High-flying broad. So I sleep over there and I find out that this broad's got plenty of cash. I start getting involved with her and I'm wondering where'd she get all this money. This girl's worth a few million dollars. She used to carry ten thousand, easy, in her pocketbook. I thought to myself, I gotta get some of this broad's money.

"Now a couple of weeks go by. She was taking me out and paying for everything. She used to go to Saks on City Line Avenue. She used to buy five-hundred-dollar blouses. She bought me shoes. She was buying me suits. She was paying for my dinners. Long as we could have sex. But I didn't give a fuck, 'cause now I'm looking to make a big score.

"I find out she sells Quaaludes. She had a girlfriend next door who had a connection with a doctor's receptionist on Thirty-sixth and Walnut. The receptionist used to give them ten to fifteen prescriptions. Sign the doctor's name to them and they used to put up a hundred Quaaludes on each script. And in case the druggist would call, the receptionist would say, 'Yeah. The doctor gave her the prescription.' At four dollars apiece, she was grabbing four thousand or five thousand a week with Quaaludes. They were the big thing in them days.

"So I start to see this. Pretty soon, the neighbor starts telling me about my girlfriend's mother, who was dead. Her mother was a woman who had invested a lot of money in stocks and bonds. And this girl stumbled on all this stuff one day after her mother got sick. All these stocks and bonds. So what do you think this broad does? First she found out the stocks were good, then she killed her mother, poisoning her, slowly, with arsenic. Every day, when she would feed her, she would put a little arsenic in there. It took six months before the mother died. Every day she would get sicker and sicker. I know it's the truth,'cause I got the broad drunk one night and she admitted it.

"So now I'm gettin' the whole story. And what do you think she did after she kills her mother? She's gotta get rid of the father. She does the same thing to him. Poisons him the same way. She had a doctor who signed a phony death certificate. And then she had them both cremated so there's no evidence. The only thing left is their ashes.

"This rotten motherfucker. So I get together with a lawyer I know and devise a plan. I told him to give me the names of two FBI agents so I can tell this broad that through my connections we found out these FBI guys are gonna lock her up for the murder of her mother and father. And they know she's in the drug business. When I say their names, she'll try to check it out and she'll find out these guys do exist. And I'll tell her she's gotta come up with a hundred thousand dollars to get them off her back. Because they know she made millions of dollars with the stocks and bonds. That's a cheap figure, a hundred thousand.

"Well, sure enough, I go to her and I tell her the story. I say, 'Listen. You got a *big* fuckin' problem.' I say, 'These two fuckin' agents are gonna lock you up unless you pay them off.' And sure enough, this broad gives me a hundred thousand. She went for the whole okey-doke. The whole nine yards."

The $100,000 score was a jackpot for Caramandi and Mickey Diamond, but it was the beginning of the end of the Crow's fling with the murderess. Things were never the same between them once he took the money, and in the back of her mind, Caramandi believes, she probably knew he was hustling her. He did stick around long enough, however, to pull another $25,000 out of her:

"She had this friend in Pittsburgh. She went out there and robbed her. Her own fuckin' friend. Furs and jewelry. And she came to me to fence the stuff.

"I told her the stuff was too hot and we couldn't get nothing for it. I was giving her the shit. We got about twenty-five grand, and me and Mickey whacked it up. But by then she didn't want anything more to do with me because she knew that I was just looking to take anything I could off her. And I was afraid she was gonna poison me, this mother-fucker."

Caramandi has told this story to federal authorities. It is one of several cases he has given them that have not been—and probably never will be—prosecuted. It is a tale that is almost impossible to verify. The FBI knows who the woman is and has opened an investigative file on her. But even with Caramandi's testimony, there probably isn't enough evidence to make a case.

"It's unbelievable what this broad did," Caramandi says with a trace of admiration in his voice.

"I heard she's currently in the Coca-Cola business. I heard she's dealing coke. She flies to Florida all the time. She's a good mover, this broad."

Caramandi's fling was a brief diversion during a period of building tension within the Philadelphia mob. Even while he was setting up and pulling off the extortion, he was meeting regularly at either the Annin Street Café or the 311 Club in Newark with Tony Bananas Caponigro, who was putting the pieces together for what he hoped would be the biggest move of his career.

Less than two years out of prison and only recently named consigliere, Caponigro was about to become the central figure in one of the bloodiest betrayals in Mafia history. Blinded by greed and ambition, he would be caught in the switches of a Machiavellian double cross that would unleash five years of internecine warfare and, ultimately, bring about the downfall of the Philadelphia organization.

Caramandi watched it all unfold.

By 1980, Angelo Bruno had begun to lose his grip on the crime family he had run so efficiently for more than twenty years. Younger members of the organization were bristling over his apparent indifference to the business opportunities presenting themselves in Atlantic City. They were also angered by what appeared to be his hypocritical stance with regard to the drug trade.

Members of Bruno's sixty-man organization were prohibited from dealing in drugs, yet the boss himself maintained close personal and business associations with some major drug dealers.

Raymond "Long John" Martorano, a federal investigation and successful drug trial would later show, was a major meth-amphetamine dealer in the city. While not a made member of the Bruno organization at the time, he was nevertheless a key business associate of the mob boss. In theory, Bruno "worked" for Martorano's family. The Martoranos, Raymond and his brother John, owned a vending machine business. Bruno's stated occupation was commission salesman for the company. His job was to scout locations where the company might place cigarette machines. Bruno got a two-cents-a-pack commission for each pack of cigarettes sold. He reported a $50,000-a-year salary on his annual income tax returns.

He was, Martorano told the New Jersey State Commission of Investigation in 1977, "the finest salesman we've ever had."

Martorano and his son, George, meanwhile, were establishing themselves as two of the biggest drug dealers in the city. Raymond was deep into the highly lucrative P-2-P trade. George "Cowboy" Martorano, on the other hand, leaned toward cocaine and heroin. He built a drug empire worth an estimated $75 million before he was arrested. Convicted in 1984 under the federal drug kingpin statute, he is currently serving a life prison sentence.

Bruno's connection to the Martoranos, then, seemed to fly in the face of his ban on drug dealing. So did his association with Giuseppe and Rosario Gambino. The Sicilian immigrant cousins of Carlo Gambino moved to South Jersey from Brooklyn in the early 1970s. They opened several pizza shops and, eventually, Valentino's, a fancy restaurant on Haddonfield Road in Cherry Hill.

Bruno was spotted having dinner there with Paul Castellano, at the time the underboss in Carlo Gambino's mob family. Bruno also acknowledged to New Jersey authorities that he was acquainted with Giuseppe and Rosario Gambino. Law enforcement investigators, pointing to the fact that Giuseppe and Rosario were guests for Easter dinner at Bruno's home, were still trying to determine the extent of the relationship between Bruno and the Sicilians when Bruno was killed in March 1980. Federal indictments have now linked the Gambino brothers to a major Sicilian heroin ring, but in 1980, FBI and DEA agents hadn't even begun to sort out the players in the Pizza Connection.

On the night Bruno was killed, detectives found an address book in his pocket that contained thirty-six names and telephone numbers. One of the numbers was for Mimmo's Pizzeria, a Philadelphia pizza shop run by a man named Benito Zito. Four years later an undercover DEA agent would purchase two and a half kilograms of almost pure heroin from Zito, the only drugs seized by the feds during the Pizza Connection investigation.

Given Bruno's stature with the New York families, his standing as a member of the Mafia Commission, and his personal friendship with Carlo Gambino, it is hard to imagine that Giuseppe and Rosario Gambino would set up a drug ring in the Philadelphia–South Jersey area without Bruno's knowledge and tacit approval. Mob protocol would require clearance from Bruno before anyone from another family could set up a business in the area. It would also require that Bruno be offered a piece of the action.

That, in part, explained the resentment that was festering within the Bruno organization. Both Caponigro and Philip Testa, Bruno's hulking underboss, were interested in the thriving drug business. Both had to sneak behind Bruno's back to set up their deals. They were also upset with Bruno's lack of drive. They felt the organization was passing up too many chances to cash in on potential business opportunities, both in the drug world and in Atlantic City. Bruno's laissez-faire approach to the rackets may have worked in the 1950s and 1960s when loan-sharking, bookmaking, and gambling were the principal sources of income. But the 1970s presented bigger and better deals. Drugs and casinos offered a bonanza, and the Bruno family was standing around while others were positioning themselves to cash in.

Atlantic City's first casino, Resorts International, had opened in 1978. Two others, Caesars and Bally's Park Place, were in operation by 1980. And what did the Bruno family have to show for it?

Long John Martorano's vending machine company, according to a report compiled by the New Jersey State Commission of Investigation, had seen its business quadruple in the Atlantic City area following the 1976 casino gambling referendum. A local vending machine company owner awoke one morning to find that a $500,000 contract he had serviced for years was suddenly no longer available. Angelo Bruno had spirited it away through his "salesmanship." That was great for Bruno and Martorano, but it was not something they shared with the rest of the organization.

Other families were moving in on union organizing, junket operations, and the casino service industries. But Bruno, subpoenaed to testify before the State Commission of Investigation, told authorities he wanted no part of the burgeoning East Coast gambling capital.

"I have a pretty good feeling about what my intentions are with Atlantic City," Bruno said in testimony before the commission in 1979. "Would you want me to tell you that?"

Asked what those intentions were, Bruno added, "Stay away from it. That's my intentions. . . . I got nothing to do with Atlantic City as far as gambling's concerned. I'm not interested in any hotels; I'm not interested in any casinos, directly or indirectly."

And he may have been telling the truth. The sixty-nine-year-old mob boss didn't need the headaches that casino gambling would bring. Any move he made in Atlantic City would attract state and federal spotlights. He was already a millionaire. Why bother? He and his wife owned some property in Florida, and he planned to retire there soon. He thought about spending part of each year in Italy and the remainder in the sunny South. His children, a daughter and a son, were grown. He had made a better life for them. His son, Michael, was a legitimate businessman, not part of the organization. His daughter, Jeanne, was married to a successful real estate broker.

Bruno, badly underestimating the depth of discontent within his own organization, thought he could ease into retirement. It was a major miscalculation.

Greed and ambition killed Angelo Bruno.

That and a dispute over a $2-million-a-week bookmaking operation in Hudson County, New Jersey. More than a decade after the Bruno killing, the circumstances surrounding his assassination and the bloody mob war that it spawned have begun to surface. State and federal law enforcement reports and the affidavits and testimony of mob informants like Caramandi, Thomas DelGiorno, and Genovese family member Vincent "Fish" Cafaro have provided pieces of evidence that link Bruno's death to a bloody double cross orchestrated by Frank "Funzi" Tieri, then head of New York's Genovese crime family.

In 1979 Tieri tried to wrest control of a lucrative Hudson

County bookmaking operation from Caponigro, who controlled the gambling racket from his base in nearby Newark.
Tieri took the dispute to the Mafia Commission. Bruno defended Caponigro's proprietary rights, and the Commission
ruled in his favor. Tieri accepted the decision, at least on the
surface. But a year later he saw a way to undo what the Commission had done.

Caponigro had been lining up support in Philadelphia for
a palace coup. He enlisted Frank Sindone, John "Johnny
Keyes" Simone, and Alfred Salerno as willing participants in
the conspiracy. Sindone, a longtime Bruno family soldier and
one of the biggest loan sharks in Philadelphia, was to be the
underboss in Caponigro's rebel regime.

"He was a real barracuda," Caramandi says of Sindone.
"You couldn't trust him at all."

Early in 1980, Caponigro thought he had everything in
place. Then he put out feelers in New York, seeking approval
from the Commission for the murder of Bruno. Word came
back by way of Tieri. It was a go.

On March 21, shortly before 10:00 P.M., Caponigro's emissary—probably Alfred Salerno, although to this day no one
knows for sure—stepped out of the shadows near Bruno's
South Philadelphia home, pulled a shotgun from beneath his
raincoat, and blew a hole in the back of Angelo Bruno's head.

The aging mob boss never knew what hit him.

Thus began the most brutal period of factional mob violence
in Philadelphia's history.

"One night I'm in this private club on Tasker Street. I used to
go there a lot. A guy by the name of Paco owns it. I used
to borrow money off him, too, and owed him, like, thirty
thousand dollars. I used to give him six hundred a week
juice, this Paco. So one Friday night I'm sitting at the bar
talking to him. Now Paco's a neutral guy. He was a bookmaker, a loan shark. He always had a poker game going upstairs at the club. He did all the cooking at the place, the
chicken, the ribs, pizza, clams, and spaghetti. If you spent a
hundred dollars in his joint, Paco would lend you five thousand. Ya know? He was that type of guy, as long as you pa-
tronized his joint.

"We're sitting there talking. I'm drinking at the bar. The
phone rang. Paco goes and answers it. Comes back and he
says, 'Angelo Bruno just got whacked.' This was sometime

around ten. 'Holy mackerel,' I say. It was a shock. I tried to reach Mickey Diamond, to find out what the fuck was happening."

The next day, a rainy Saturday, Caramandi found Mickey Diamond and several other members of the organization at the Annin Street Café. No one knew what was going on. Everyone wondered where the shots had come from and, of more immediate concern, if there were more to come. Long John Martorano arrived, but before he even got out of his car, he stationed an armed bodyguard at either end of the street. The Philadelphia mob had gone for two decades without any significant gunfire; now it seemed the entire organization was an armed camp.

Martorano was not a made member, but was a high-ranking associate. His stature, however, was a product of his links to Bruno. Now Bruno was dead and Long John would have to line up behind someone else. The question, underlined by the shotgun blast of the night before, was who.

"He was worried to death," Caramandi said. "Everybody was paranoid, the whole fuckin' outfit, after Angelo got killed."

Speculation on the street and among police and FBI agents called in to investigate the hit pointed to either Testa or Caponigro, perhaps both working in concert.

Caponigro didn't show up at the Annin Street Café for another three or four days. He apparently had decided the best place to be in the wake of the killing was Newark, where he could watch and listen. When he did appear in South Philadelphia, the message he carried to Mickey Diamond and Nick Caramandi was short and sweet.

"Don't worry about nothin'," he said.

For years the organized crime branch of the Philadelphia police and the FBI squad assigned to track the mob had been building rackets cases against the Bruno organization. Wiretaps and secret listening devices had been planted as early as 1977, and what the electronic surveillance was picking up would eventually lead to a racketeering case based on traditional mob gambits into bookmaking, loan-sharking, and extortion. But now those same investigators had to shift gears. They didn't realize it at the time, but their investigations over the next five years would focus primarily on homicides.

For a month after the Bruno murder, the FBI and Philadelphia police monitored almost every move made by the major members of the Philadelphia mob. They saw both Testa and Caponigro shuttling back and forth to New York where, authorities later learned, they each met separately with Anthony "Fat Tony" Salerno, then underboss of the Genovese crime family.

Philadelphia police were also watching when John Stanfa, the driver of the car in which Bruno was killed, was visited at the hospital by Frank Sindone and John Simone. Stanfa, a Sicilian immigrant who owned a small construction business in Philadelphia, had sustained minor injuries from flying glass and shotgun pellets. A police officer who spoke Italian had been posted at the door of Stanfa's hospital room. When Sindone and Simone visited Stanfa in the hospital, they huddled conspiratorially around his bed, speaking in whispers and in a Sicilian dialect that the police officer couldn't understand. Stanfa was released from the hospital two days after the shooting. Four days later he was spotted getting into a car with Sindone and Simone in Philadelphia. They were trailed by the FBI to Newark, where they met with Caponigro.

Testa, meanwhile, continued to shuttle back and forth between his base in South Philadelphia and New York, where he met with members of the Genovese and Gambino organizations. A burly, gruff man with a pockmarked face, Testa lacked Bruno's polish. But he had the same understanding and respect for the traditions of the organization. He knew he was a suspect in the killing of his boss. And he knew such a suspicion, if not quickly removed, could result in his own death. He had a pretty good idea who had plotted Bruno's murder, and in the weeks following the shooting he laid it out for the leaders of the two most powerful mob families in New York. At least one of those men, Frank "Funzi" Tieri, knew Testa was telling the truth.

About three weeks after the Bruno murder, Caramandi was in Cous' Little Italy, the same restaurant where Bruno had dined on the night of his death. The restaurant was owned by Sindone and Tommy DelGiorno, although the owner of record was DelGiorno's wife. It was a popular spot for members of the Bruno organization and had, in fact, been a mob-connected business for years. It was originally called Piccolo's 500 and was owned by the Piccolo family. Nicholas "Nicky Buck" Piccolo was a capo in the Bruno organization and had brought his nephew, Nicodemo Scarfo, into the mob in the 1950s.

"I go in there with a girl and I'm about to have dinner," Caramandi says. "And who comes in but Tony [Caponigro], Sindone, and Blackie [Ralph Napoli]. Tony sits down and has dinner with me and the girl. We're talking, but he ain't talking business. He's talking to the girl; he was a real ladies' man, this Tony."

After dinner, they moved to the bar, where Caponigro saw a barmaid he had been trying, without success, to get into bed.

"Tony's got a hot nut for the fuckin' barmaid," Caramandi says. "He starts drinking and coming on to her. He used to drink Rémy Martin. Straight. With water on the side."

Caponigro interrupted his play for the barmaid long enough to tell Caramandi he had to go to New York the next day for a meeting. Again, he told Caramandi not to worry about anything, that everything was under control and that Caramandi would soon enjoy new status within the organization.

"Tony says to me, 'When I come back Monday, everything's gonna be under control. You're gonna get down.'"

All the while Caponigro is drinking and trying to move in on the barmaid. She, however, wanted no part of him. Before the night was over, Tony Bananas, drunk and scorned, would be questioning her sexual preference.

"In the beginning of the night he was in love with her," Caramandi said. "Now he's callin' her a cunt and a dike."

Caponigro used booze and bravado to brush aside the barmaid's rejection. In less than twenty-four hours he would have a more serious problem involving another one of his moves.

On Thursday, April 17, 1980, Tony Caponigro and his brother-in-law, Alfred Salerno, traveled to Manhattan, where Salerno—no relation to Fat Tony—owned a jewelry store. There, on the corner of Forty-seventh Street in midtown Manhattan, they were picked up by members of a Genovese crime family crew headed by Vincent "the Chin" Gigante. Caponigro thought he was going to a meeting where he would be installed as the new boss of the Philadelphia organization. It was the last in a series of faulty assumptions. The first was his mistaken belief that Funzi Tieri had gotten Commission approval for the murder of Angelo Bruno.

There are, perhaps, a handful of people alive today who

know where Caponigro and Salerno were taken on that April afternoon. But seven years later, in an appearance before a U.S. Senate subcommittee investigating organized crime, Edward S. G. Dennis, Jr., the number-three man in the U.S. Attorney's Office and the former U.S. Attorney for the Eastern District of Pennsylvania, provided a graphic account of what happened to them.

On April 18, the bodies of Caponigro and Salerno were found stuffed in the trunks of cars about three miles apart in the desolate South Bronx.

Caponigro, Dennis told the Senate subcommittee, "had been tortured, beaten, strangled, and repeatedly stabbed and shot, and his naked body was in a mortuary bag stuffed in the trunk of a car. Approximately three-hundred dollars in twenty-dollar bills was found stuffed in various parts of his body."

The money, stuck in Caponigro's mouth and anus, was a symbolic gesture, signifying that his own greed had killed him.

Salerno's body, also stuffed inside a mortuary bag, was found in much the same condition.

"He had been shot three times behind the right ear and once behind the left ear," Dennis said. "Rope was tied around his neck [and] most of the bones in his face were broken."

Dennis said the brutal assassinations of Caponigro and Salerno signaled the start of "an unprecedented series of murders and attempted murders marking a power struggle within the family for the right to succeed Bruno."

Vincent Cafaro, the Genovese family member who later became a government informant, told the same Senate subcommittee that Caponigro and Salerno were killed because "the New York families had not sanctioned Bruno's murder."

Tieri, who used his position of power within the Genovese organization and on the Mafia Commission to manipulate events, died of natural causes a year later. The Genovese family is now headed by Vincent Gigante, whose crew is suspected of carrying out the Caponigro and Salerno murders. Ironically, one of the major suspects in those killings was John DiGilio, a high-profile Hudson County mobster who controlled the Bayonne waterfront for the Genovese organization. DiGilio, who eventually fell out of favor with Gigante, disappeared in 1988. His body was found floating in the Hoboken River. He had been shot twice in the back of the head. His remains were stuffed inside a mortuary bag.

Philip Testa was appointed boss of the Philadelphia family shortly after Caponigro's body was discovered. While in theory there was supposed to be an election in South Philadelphia, in fact the New York families sent two representatives down to announce that Testa was now in charge. Pete Casella, a longtime Bruno family member who had solid relations with the New York families, was named underboss. Testa picked his friend and ally Nicodemo "Little Nicky" Scarfo as his consigliere. Scarfo, who had a reputation as something of a hothead, had been banished to Atlantic City in 1963 by Bruno.

Now, in 1980, Atlantic City was back. And so was Little Nicky. Teamed with Testa, he would set in motion a reign of terror that would change the face of the Philadelphia mob. For years Angelo Bruno worked quietly in the shadows, avoiding publicity and seldom making waves. You could count on the fingers of one hand the number of murders attributed to the Bruno organization during Don Angelo's twenty-one-year reign. In the Bruno family, murder was a negotiating weapon of last resort. For Testa and Scarfo it became a calling card.

On September 19, 1980, two sanitation department workers discovered the body of John "Johnny Keyes" Simone in a wooded area near a landfill in Staten Island, New York. Simone had been shot three times in the back of the head.

A little more than a month later, on October 30, police were called to a South Philadelphia variety store. In an alley behind the store was the body of Frank Sindone. Like Simone, he had been shot three times in the back of the head. Sindone's hands were tied behind his back. Investigators noticed dirt on the knees of his pant legs, leading to speculation that he had either been forced to kneel down or had voluntarily knelt down and begged for mercy before he was shot.

Sindone had been picked up on an FBI surveillance bug four years earlier complaining about Bruno's old-fashioned ways and moaning about the tight rein Bruno held over his members. Bruno, who drove a Buick and lived in a modest row house, was a conservative boss who abhorred flamboyance in both his own life and the lives of those in his organization.

Sindone had boasted on the FBI tape of having more money than he could ever spend.

Now that was no longer a problem.

Only John Stanfa among the suspected conspirators in the Bruno killing managed to dodge a bullet. Some believe a high-ranking Mafia figure from Sicily interceded on his behalf through the Gambino organization. Others say law enforcement beat the mob to the punch. Stanfa was convicted in 1981 of perjury for lying before a grand jury investigating the Bruno killing. He was sentenced to eight years in prison.

"So what you got was Phil Testa as boss," Caramandi said in recalling that brutal period, "Scarfo as the consigliere, and Pete Casella as the underboss. Pete Casella was in jail with that Valachi guy. He did twenty years in Atlanta [on a federal drug charge] and he made a lot of friends. So he took Phil Testa to New York and told his story. That's when they found Tony in a lie, some kind of lie. And I think the shooter [in the Bruno murder] was Tony's brother-in-law, Alfred Salerno... from what I hear.

"So all the conspirators in the Angelo Bruno hit were killed. Now Phil's the boss."

And, Caramandi said, other Caponigro loyalists scrambled to fall in line behind the new power. Felix Bocchino, a soldier in the organization and a partner with Caponigro in a lucrative loan-sharking business, quickly made his peace, bringing Testa a share from that business and promising to deliver something from each weekly take.

Joseph "Chickie" Ciancaglini, another Caponigro associate, didn't have as much to offer and nearly paid with his life. So did Caramandi's mentor, Mickey Diamond.

"As soon as Tony got killed, this Felix Bocchino went right in and surrendered to Phil Testa. He told him what he had. Later Felix told Pat [mob associate Pasquale "Pat the Cat" Spirito], 'It's a new ball game.' Then they grabbed Ciancaglini. They bring him to a garage and Scarfo, Phil Testa, and Pete Casella put a fucking gun to his head, to see if he was involved with the conspiracy. But he claimed he wasn't and they let him go. Nicky claimed he was a good man and said he was 'innocent of the Barracuda's tricks.' The Barracuda was Frank Sindone. See, Sindone was power-crazy. For years he hated Chickie Narducci, hated Nicky Scarfo. So Caponigro and Sindone had their own fucking hit list. This Caponigro was vicious. They were gonna take Nicky out, Frankie Narducci. Such hatred.... I think Scarfo and Testa ended up using Ciancaglini to set up Sindone. That's how they got him.

"So now Mickey Diamond goes to Phil Testa and he tells him that he paid Tony the fifty thousand dollars we owed from when we started up our shark business. He was trying to pull a hipper-dipper. But they already knew he didn't pay the fifty thousand dollars.

"And one day me and Mickey go to this meeting with Felix and this Tony Ferrante and they really lay Mick out. 'Who the fuck do you think you are? We want this fuckin' money. You're gonna pay this money.' Well, Mickey Diamond was scared to death. Now he had to pay the five hundred a week until he paid the fifty thousand off. So as we were collecting the loan-shark money, we'd give 'em five thousand plus the five hundred every week. We wasn't loaning any more money out. We had to pay the fifty thousand back. We was collecting over five thousand a week at this point, but we couldn't do anything with the money. We had to pay it all back.

"Now Mickey's in hot water. But these guys are great strokers. I went to Virgilio's [a restaurant owned by Testa's daughter] with Mickey. We had dinner and he talked to Phil on the side. After he returned I said to him, 'How you stand, Mick?'

"He said, 'I'm in good standing. There's no problem. There's nothing wrong.' But you could see the way these guys talked there was something wrong. Only Mickey was too stupid to realize it."

By the fall of 1980, Testa had solidified his position as the new boss of the Philadelphia mob. Those suspected of plotting the murder of Angelo Bruno were dead. And Testa, with Scarfo at his side, was ready to expand. One of his first acts was to "open the books." Bruno, trying to maintain a fragile balance between the Sicilian and Calabrian factions of his organization, had put off "making" any new members for years. He was content with the status quo. But Testa and Scarfo had plans, big plans. And they needed new members, whose loyalty would be beyond question, to help carry them out. Among those Testa formally inducted into the Mafia were his son, Salvatore; Scarfo's nephew, Philip "Crazy Phil" Leonetti; two of Scarfo's closest friends, the brothers Salvatore and Lawrence Merlino, and a stocky South Philadelphia triggerman,

Salvatore Grande, who somehow had the very unmoblike nick-name Wayne.

The rise of Testa and Scarfo marked the end of the age of compromise and conciliation in the Philadelphia underworld.

A Bruno friend and longtime associate, tough-talking Phil-adelphia Roofers Union boss John McCullough, would be the next person caught in the switches of that change.

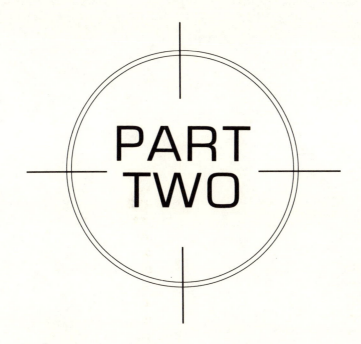

PART
TWO

CHAPTER SEVEN

The first shots in the mob battle over Atlantic City were fired on December 16, 1980, in the kitchen of a modest but well-maintained house in the 2000 block of Foster Street in the Bustleton section of Northeast Philadelphia.

That night a man appeared at the home of Philadelphia Roofers Union boss John McCullough with a delivery of poinsettia plants, the bright red flowers that are a mark of the Christmas holiday season. McCullough was on the phone in the kitchen at the time. The deliveryman placed two plants on the table and said he had to bring several more in from his truck. He left the house, and McCullough, a gruff-talking, thick-necked roofer who wore his hair in a trademark crew cut, signaled to his wife, Audrey.

"Be sure to give him a tip," McCullough said.

"Is two dollars enough?" she asked.

"Make it three," was McCullough's reply. "It's Christmas."

Moments later the deliveryman, wearing a ski cap, heavy jacket, and thick rubber gloves, returned with more plants. He headed straight for the kitchen, put the flowers on the table, then pulled out a .22 caliber pistol and pumped six bullets into the head and neck of the union boss. McCullough crumpled to the floor as the gunman pushed past his horrified wife, jumped into his unmarked van, and fled.

"John McCullough thought he could do whatever he wanted," Caramandi said. "After Angelo got killed, Scarfo and Testa told McCullough to stay out of Atlantic City. That was Scarfo's territory."

McCullough's reply to the new leaders of the Philadelphia mob cost him his life.

"McCullough told Scarfo to go fuck himself," Caramandi said.

For years Johnny McCullough, who headed Roofers Union Local 30 in Philadelphia, had had an accommodation with Angelo Bruno and the Philadelphia mob. Unlike many other cities in the Northeast—New York and Newark, for example—organized crime was not intrinsically linked with organized labor in the City of Brotherly Love. Mob members did not head up locals in Philadelphia. Organized labor was relatively independent and free of mob control.

Most union leaders, however, knew Bruno. And he knew them. And from time to time, when their spheres of influence would overlap, accommodations would be reached. They might both, for example, support the same political candidate. Or they might share an interest in a particular development project, each using the other's influence to arrange the awarding of contracts or the settling of labor disputes. But by and large, Bruno was content to stick with the businesses he knew: bookmaking, gambling, and loan-sharking. He ran a small, loosely knit organization that was a major part of, but did not totally control, the Philadelphia underworld.

Bruno wielded power, but also recognized that with that power came responsibility. Furthermore, he knew his limits. He knew when to push and when to pull back. He preferred to discuss problems and arrive at amicable solutions. He appreciated subtlety. He always worked in the shadows.

Scarfo had a different view. What was the point of having power if you didn't flaunt it? He wanted people to know who he was and what he did. He enjoyed his reputation as the most violent mob boss in America.

"He thought we were the fuckin' Elks Club," Caramandi would say several years later. "He always wanted to have parties. He always wanted a gang of people around him. He thought he was a celebrity, a movie star. With Bruno there was none of that. You didn't even know who all the members were. There were two guys here and two guys over there. Very low-key, low-profile. None of this gangster stuff.

"I remember Mickey Diamond telling me one time that Angelo had said to him that these guys, Scarfo, Testa, Sindone,

[Frank] Narducci, that they would self-destruct. Even back then he knew. And he was right."

During Bruno's long tenure as mob boss, for example, bookmakers were permitted to operate independently of the Bruno organization, provided everyone involved respected everyone else's boundaries and territories. Bruno's bigger operations would always end up taking some of the independents' action. Whenever a bookie needed to edge off some heavy play, he would seek out a larger operator, usually one controlled by Bruno. Bruno also lent money to local bookies, either to help them settle up with customers after a particularly bad week or because they themselves were heavy gamblers. Bruno would usually charge a point a week, maybe two. In time, when a bookie was unable to meet his weekly payment, he would offer Angelo Bruno a piece of his business. In that way, without any strongarm tactics or the use of violence, Bruno would further expand his influence and control over the Philadelphia rackets.

It was a time-honored system that enabled the Bruno organization to flourish. Strictly business.

Even members of the organization were provided wide latitude by the mob boss. Little Harry Riccobene developed a mob within the mob under the broad umbrella of the Bruno crime family. Riccobene, a Bruno contemporary, was from the old school. He was a mobster who preferred to make money rather than make noise. Like Bruno, he became a very wealthy man.

Klaus Rohr, the FBI agent who headed up the Philadelphia office assigned to investigate the mob, said both Bruno and Riccobene epitomized the Philadelphia Mafia member in the pre-Scarfo era.

"These guys were mostly concerned with making money," Rohr said one day as he sat in his office in downtown Philadelphia. "That's one of the reasons Bruno never expanded. He didn't want to have more people who he might have to share with. Harry was the same way.

"It reminded me of that expression that I think came from *Prizzi's Honor*, where they say, 'Sicilians love their money more than they love their children; and they love their children very, very much.'"

Riccobene was barely five feet tall, had a high-pitched, squeaky voice, and was nicknamed Harry the Hunchback or

Harry the Hump because of a slightly curved spine. No one called him the Hunchback or the Hump to his face, however. Over the span of more than twenty years, while Bruno ruled the Philadelphia family, Riccobene had developed his own economic network. He had family members and associates involved in gambling and loan-sharking, illegal video poker machines, and the methamphetamine trade. Riccobene recognized Bruno as boss and would pay him the respect and courtesy required. In return, Harry was free to set up and expand his own business ventures.

Frank "Frankie Flowers" D'Alfonso, a highly placed mob associate, was another man who flourished under Bruno's laissez-faire approach. D'Alfonso was one of the biggest bookmakers in the city. He also was deeply involved in the Atlantic City fight game and was linked with a group of Chicago mob figures in a push to introduce a health and welfare plan to a number of unions operating within the Atlantic City casino industry.

D'Alfonso typified the term "mob associate." He was never initiated into the Mafia, but was closer to Bruno than many made members. In fact, he traveled to New York several times with Bruno when Bruno was called to Commission meetings there. D'Alfonso was never permitted to take part in those sessions, but the fact that Bruno brought him along for the trip demonstrated the high regard in which he was held. Bruno and D'Alfonso became business partners, sharing in the profits generated from illegal card and dice games. D'Alfonso also brought other business ventures to the mob boss. Bruno would get involved with some, pass on others. One deal, according to federal investigators, involved a junket operation to casinos in London. Bruno, D'Alfonso, and members of Boston's Patriarca family were said to share in the business, which involved recruiting high rollers for the casinos and then serving as a collection agency—with a substantial commission, of course—for the credit lines extended by the casinos. The deal was uncovered when police raided a meeting at D'Alfonso's flower shop near the Ninth Street Italian Market in South Philadelphia.

From outward appearances, Frankie Flowers was just another neighborhood guy. Low-keyed in the Bruno mold, he was described by a Philadelphia police investigator as "a genuinely nice guy who happened to be a gambler." But D'Alfonso's gambling operations generated hundreds of thousands of dollars annually. And his other business ventures, legitimate and illegitimate, brought in thousands more. This, coupled with his stature and standing with Bruno, caused some resentment within the organization. For years he made more money than many family members. But as long as Bruno was in charge, Frankie Flowers had a pass in the Philadelphia underworld.

John McCullough, because of his long-standing relationship with Bruno, had a similar arrangement. And shortly after the November 2, 1976, casino gambling referendum was approved in New Jersey, a branch of McCullough's union, calling itself Roofers Local 30B, set up shop in Atlantic City. Local 30B was McCullough's entry into the building trades in the booming casino city, a group whose power and influence was expanding with each new multimillion-dollar casino-hotel project. But McCullough knew the building trades were a short-term bonanza. Eventually casino construction would peter out. The service industries were the key to long-term power, influence, and wealth. So in 1979, some organizers from Local 30B started to move in on the hotel and restaurant employees. These were the bartenders, waiters and waitresses, doormen, dishwashers, bellhops, and maids who staffed the hotels and restaurants.

Until McCullough made his move, all these workers had belonged to Local 54 of the International Hotel and Restaurant Employees Union, an organization headed by Frank Gerace, a longtime friend and associate of Nicky Scarfo.

"Local 54 was Scarfo's union," Caramandi said. "He controlled it. It don't matter what anybody else says or tells you. That was his union."

McCullough's organizers proposed splitting the union, which was commonly known as Bartenders Local 54. One group, which would remain Local 54, would represent all casino-hotel workers except bartenders. The other local, Local 491, would organize casino bartenders and everyone else outside the casino-hotel industry. Since Local 54's jurisdiction at the time stretched across all of South Jersey, McCullough's group was seeking a pretty big piece of the action. The accommodation would leave Scarfo with control over the most influential workers—those who staffed the hotels in the city's big gaming palaces—but it would weaken the overall influence of Local 54 and reduce the size of the union's financial pot. It was an arrangement by which both sides ended up

with something, the kind of deal frequently struck during Bruno's tenure as mob boss. Competition and compromise were
part of doing business in the Bruno underworld.

But the Bartenders Union was a plum that Nicky Scarfo had
no intention of sharing. Local 54 had about two-thousand
members, full- and part-time, when the 1976 casino referendum was approved. Total dues collected from the membership
amounted to about $127,000 that year. Health, welfare, and
pension funds accounted for a similar amount. Twelve years
later, Local 54's membership had swelled to nearly twenty
thousand. Virtually every hotel and casino-hotel worker, with
the exception of dealers and security personnel, carried a Local 54 membership card. Union dues exceeded $2 million an-
nually. Payments to health, welfare, pension, and medical and
dental plans amounted to millions more. The union, which
also represented workers at Garden State Park in Cherry Hill
and Great Adventure Amusement Park in Jackson, New Jersey, was one of the biggest in the southern part of the state.
And it had become *the* major labor force in Atlantic City.

The era of competition and compromise ended in the Philadelphia underworld with the death of Angelo Bruno. The
move to split Local 54 died less than a year later on the kitchen
floor of a home in the Bustleton section of Northeast Philadelphia where John McCullough lay bleeding to death from
six bullet wounds in his head and neck.

The flower deliveryman who shot McCullough drove the rented
van that he used to a shopping center not far from the union
boss's home. There, waiting in a car, were Raymond "Long
John" Martorano and his brother-in-law, Albert Daidone. Daidone was an organizer and officer for Local 54. Martorano,
who feared for his own life after the Bruno murder, was now
working actively for the new mob boss, Philip Testa, and Testa's consigliere, Nicky Scarfo. He took the McCullough contract to solidify his position with the new regime.

But Martorano was a businessman—drug dealer, not a murderer. So he and Daidone hired a street thug named Willard
Moran to carry out the killing. Moran had previously been
convicted of shooting a bouncer in a go-go bar in Westville,
New Jersey. He and his father were low-level South Jersey
racketeers, dealing in the netherworld of methamphetamine
trafficking, adult bookstores, and topless dancers.

"Long John [Martorano] fucked up when he hired that kid,"

Caramandi said. "He wasn't supposed to go outside the family. You never do that. If he needed a shooter he should have gone to Scarfo or Testa and asked for somebody. That was a big mistake on their part. This kid was a nobody."

But "Junior" Moran wanted to be somebody. And he saw the McCullough killing as a way to move up the underworld ladder. He was promised $5,000 and a partnership interest in the meth trade that Martorano was developing in Camden County. As they drove over the Betsy Ross Bridge back to South Jersey after the McCullough killing, Martorano stopped the car and rolled down the window. Daidone took Moran's gun and threw it into the Delaware River. Later that night he and a friend stopped at the Admiral Lounge, a seedy go-go bar on Camden's notorious Admiral Wilson Boulevard strip, an eight-lane highway lined with neon-lit bars, motels, and a warehouse-size adult bookstore that featured nude dancers. Moran, acting the way he assumed a big-time gangster would, ordered up three shots of whiskey. As the jukebox blared and a dancer in a G-string and loose-fitting T-shirt bounced around on a small stage behind the bar, Moran and his friend lifted their glasses in a toast. They downed their drinks in one swift gulp. Then Moran told the bartender to throw the other shot of whiskey in the sink. Later Moran would explain to a friend that the tossed shot of whiskey was for McCullough.

Moran's "Drink for a Dead Man" became a headline writer's dream three years later when he was tried and convicted of first degree murder for the McCullough killing. Poor planning and idle chatter—the rented van was traced to Moran, and the drinking scene and other boasts were overheard by several individuals—led to the hit man's arrest. Sentenced to death in the Pennsylvania electric chair, the would-be mobster quickly rolled over on Martorano and Daidone. The District Attorney's Office promised Moran it would help him get out from under the death penalty and work to win him a pardon and eventual parole. The feds said they'd give him a new identity and a place in the Witness Protection Program. Moran took the deal and became the chief prosecution witness against Martorano and Daidone, who were convicted of first degree murder in 1984. Both were eventually sentenced to life in prison. Martorano's sentence ran currently with a ten-year term for drug dealing that he had started serving by the time of the murder trial.

The December 1980 murder of John McCullough was a turning point in the Philadelphia underworld. The deaths of Caponigro, Salerno, Simone, and Sindone were recognized, even among law enforcement investigators, as acts of retribution for the Bruno killing. While horribly brutal and ruthless, they could be justified by those who accepted a certain criminal code of conduct. You don't kill a mob boss without Commission approval. It simply isn't done.

But the McCullough killing was something else. This was death used to settle a business dispute, murder as a negotiating tool. Testa and Scarfo were changing the rules. Compromise and conciliation were replaced with fear and intimidation.

"It was a message," one New Jersey state police detective said of the McCullough murder, "for everybody to get in line."

Violence was now the way the Philadelphia family would settle its disputes. Three months later, Testa paid the ultimate price for the bloody policy he and Scarfo had put in place.

Around 3:00 in the morning on March 15, 1981, Phil Testa pulled up in his car in front of his home in the 2100 block of Porter Street in the upscale Girard Estates section of South Philadelphia. Unable to find a parking space, he followed neighborhood custom and simply double-parked. The burly fifty-six-year-old mob boss had been out all night with his son, Salvatore, checking on various business interests. One of their last stops was a center city nightclub and restaurant owned by Testa's daughter. Testa had an office in the back of the restaurant out of which he operated his legitimate and illegitimate business enterprises.

The Testas were on top of their world at this point. After years toiling in Angelo Bruno's shadow, Philip, a dour man with a bulbous nose and a pockmarked face, was now boss. And with Nicky Scarfo at his side, he was moving the organization into areas that Bruno had for too long ignored. Money and power were at stake. Labor unions, drugs, and casino gambling offered unlimited possibilities. Testa and Scarfo were ready to cash in.

Testa's son, Salvie, was just twenty-five years old. But he had grown up in La Cosa Nostra and was now a made member. A handsome, athletically built six-footer, he was the next generation of the Philadelphia mob. Schooled by his father in the ways of "this thing of ours," he was already gathering a fol-

lowing among a group of young toughs from the neighborhood. Guys like Gino and Nicky Milano and Joey and Anthony
Pungitore were lining up behind the young mobster whose
father sat at the top of the organization. Together the Testas
had positioned themselves to control the Philadelphia crime
family into the next century.

Philip Testa may have been thinking just such thoughts as
he left his car and walked up the front steps of his modest
twin home at 2117 Porter Street. He had $14,000 in cash in
his pocket. There was another $70,000 stashed in a wall safe
in the house. Money was starting to roll in. He had his own
bookmaking and drug operation, and he had inherited most
of Bruno's big money-makers. He had a trusted ally in Nicky
Scarfo, and Scarfo had a bead on Atlantic City, the East Coast
gambling capital. God only knew how much money they could
earn over the next ten years. Already Scarfo had a hook into
the Bartenders Union, was expanding his influence within the
construction industry, and was lining up a deal that, within
a year, could give the mob the mayor and City Hall. If that
happened, they'd be able to write their own ticket.

For years Bruno had taken a cautious approach. That had
been great for old Angelo, but what about the rest of them?
Testa had struggled. Scarfo had struggled. There were made
members, for Christ's sake, working as tailors downtown.
What the hell kind of mob was this? Now Phil Testa, often
considered a mindless brute, would show them how to really
make money. Testa saw himself as the new Caesar, the man
who would ensure the Philadelphia family its rightful place
in the mob hierarchy. It was all there in front of him, easily
within his grasp. The Bruno conspirators were gone. Mc-
Cullough was out of the way. Things were falling into place.

Then came the Ides of March.

Phil Testa went out with a bang.

Across the street from Testa's double-parked car was a
black Volkswagen van. Inside the van sat Rocco Marinucci, a
local pizza shop operator and an associate and sometime
chauffeur for Testa's underboss, Pete Casella. As Testa's foot
hit the front porch, Marinucci pushed the switch on a remote-
control detonator. Testa's reign as mob boss ended in the
blast that followed. A bomb packed with nails and explosives
erupted from under the porch where it had been hidden, rock-
ing homes and stores within a twelve-block area. Lights began

to flick on up and down the street as neighbors rushed to find out what had happened. For many, their first thoughts were that there had been an explosion at the oil refinery tank farm in nearby Southwest Philadelphia.

Police and medical rescue teams quickly responded. They found Phil Testa writhing in agony amid the rubble of his front porch. The bottom half of his body had been shredded in the explosion. Most of his clothes had been either burned or blown off. The bomb left a thirty-inch hole in the concrete front porch, blew up a section of the house, and rocketed the locked front door—and Testa—into the dining room fifteen feet away. Windows were shattered up and down the street. One police officer sitting in a patrol car four blocks away would report that the blast lifted his car in the air.

Testa was rushed to St. Agnes Medical Center on South Broad Street, but there was little that could be done. The mob boss had been in power less than a year. At 4:15 A.M., as doctors frantically worked to stop the bleeding, Philip Testa died.

With Testa went any semblance of order that might have remained from the Bruno era. Treachery and deceit, always bubbling beneath the surface of an organized crime family, became everyday events as individuals and factions jockeyed for position, vied for power, and attempted to settle old scores. The personal animosities that under Bruno were held in check flashed out in the open.

Caramandi felt himself exposed and in danger. He was an associate, not a made member. His security depended on the people he was "with," the mobsters for whom he worked and made money. His standing and stature were only as good as his last deal. And so he realized that his situation following the March 1981 murder of Phil Testa was precarious at best. He had been close to Tony Bananas Caponigro, a not particularly secure position once Testa became boss. And his primary mentor, Dominick "Mickey Diamond" DeVito, was a guy that Nicky Scarfo considered a two-faced liar and a cheat.

The Crow kept his own counsel, and cautiously watched and waited as developments unfolded.

"Now, when Phil got in he made Frankie Narducci a capo. But Frank Narducci was upset—he thought he would get the post of consigliere. And Pete Casella, who now is underboss, don't have no money. Even though he's underboss, he ain't making no fuckin' money.

"So this new conspiracy is beginning with Narducci and Casella. Pete always had this kid around him, this Marinucci kid. He didn't get down or anything, but he was supposed to have a lot of balls, this kid. Casella just had him around, like a bodyguard.

"It was Chickie Narducci and Pete who planned this fucking thing. The reason they used a nail bomb is they wanted to make it look like the roofers did it. 'Cause they know in the mob we're not allowed to use bombs because then the FBI gets involved. So, Testa gets killed. And right away, Pete Casella, as underboss, tries to take over."

On the night of Philip Testa's wake, Nicky Scarfo and Salvatore Merlino were summoned to a meeting at the Buckeye Club, a private social club in South Philadelphia where Casella and Narducci had set up shop. Merlino, Scarfo's oldest friend, had been initiated into the organization a year earlier by Testa. He and his brother Lawrence became two of Scarfo's most trusted allies. Salvatore "Chuckie" Merlino was Scarfo's man in South Philadelphia. Lawrence "Yogi" Merlino, who moved to Margate, New Jersey, headed up a construction company that literally paved the mob's way into the casino building boom and established Little Nicky as a force to be reckoned with in the organization.

Atlantic City sits atop a barrier island. Construction of any significance requires reinforced concrete. Larry Merlino controlled a company called Nat-Nat that did concrete reinforcement work on several major Atlantic City projects. Then Scarf Inc., which was owned by Scarfo's nephew Philip Leonetti, would pour the concrete that became the foundation of some of the city's gaudiest casinos. Major construction companies, hired by the casino companies to build the Boardwalk gambling palaces, knew that if they wanted a smooth operation in Atlantic City it was best to hire Nat-Nat and Scarf Inc. This message came not only from the mob, but also from the local Iron Workers Union, whose president would later be sentenced to ten years in prison on labor racketeering charges.

This cozy arrangement between the mob, the construction industry, and the union was the focus of a lengthy report issued in 1986 by the New Jersey State Commission of Investigation. The SCI found that Nat-Nat and Scarf Inc. did subcontracting work on nearly a dozen casino and public works projects between 1981 and 1985, including the Golden Nugget, Caesars, Harrah's, Tropicana, Hilton, Showboat, Bally, and Resorts casino-hotels. Ron Chance, an agent with the Organized Crime and Racketeering Section of the U.S. Department of Labor, told the SCI that the mob's involvement in the Atlantic City construction boom was tacitly accepted by everyone involved.

"The reason for this," he said, "is that everybody is happy, everybody is making money. And if Scarfo is making you money and the unions can employ their members and they make money and they are happy and the general contractors are making money, and... everyone knows that to get along you're going to have to do certain things, you're going to have to hire this company to do this and hire that company to do that, and that's an accepted method of doing business in Atlantic City..."

The casino companies, meanwhile, played deaf, dumb, and blind. Their only concern was getting their facility built and open as quickly as possible. Resorts International set gambling industry revenue records in its first year of operation. The former paint company, which opened the city's first casino in May 1978, brought in more than $200 million in its first year. Gamblers lined up for blocks along the Boardwalk that first summer waiting for a chance to get into the gaming hall. Once at a blackjack or craps table, they would stay for hours, refusing to relinquish their spot for even the most fundamental calls of nature. Dealers who worked at Resorts that first summer came away with dozens of horror stories about rude and obnoxious gamblers who fought with casino workers and with each other. More than one dealer was spit upon, and cursed by gamblers who were upset with either their luck or their inability to get a seat at one of the tables. Pushing and shoving matches were everyday occurrences. So was the unseemly sight of a gambler relieving himself at the table rather than giving up his seat to find a men's room.

New Jersey was swept with gambling fever, and the companies that had hesitated while Resorts moved to monopolize play desperately wanted a piece of that action. As a result, they didn't much care what their general contractors did as long as the facility was built on time. Ron Chance went on to explain to the SCI how the mob ripped off both unions and contractors by rigging bids and by refusing to pay standard health and welfare benefits for union workers. Both the contractors and the unions acquiesced. In one typical example, he said, the mob put its man in as timekeeper on a casino construction job. In theory, the timekeeper, who later became an informant for Chance, worked for the Iron Workers Union. His duties included keeping accurate weekly records of who worked and the wages and benefits that were owed to each worker. In fact, Chance said, the timekeeper was there to doctor the records so that Nat-Nat could avoid paying the going union wage and benefit rates. He also had several ancillary services available for the construction workers on the job site.

"This individual spent his time collecting loan-shark debts and football pools and providing hookers at the lunch wagons for the people on the construction site," Chance told the SCI. "He was a criminal himself and he was part of the scheme to defraud the union and the people that they are working for. And so Nat-Nat and Scarf Inc., being companies controlled by criminals, have employees who are criminals and their employees are in influential positions with the union and can permit them to complete the circuit to operate scams."

It was a perfect system. A money-making machine. Scarfo refined his labor racketeering operation in Atlantic City. Later he would try to impose the same control in Philadelphia. This is the kind of thing he and Testa had talked about when they took over from Bruno. The opportunities to make money were unlimited if you had the guts and the instinct to go for it.

Scarfo had guts. He also had instinct. That's why he, and not Pete Casella and Frank Narducci, succeeded Philip Testa.

When Scarfo and Salvatore Merlino were summoned to the Buckeye Club on the night of Philip Testa's wake, Casella, Narducci, and several of their associates, including Casella's young protégé, Rocco Marinucci, were there waiting for them. Casella told Scarfo he had been in contact with New York. The word was that Testa had been killed in retaliation for the McCullough murder. John Berkery, an independent racketeer and well-known Bruno associate, was fingered as the man behind the bomb. The nails were a message from the Roofers Union. Berkery, part of Philadelphia's Irish mob, had longtime links with McCullough and with remnants of the old K&A Gang (named because most of the members came from the area around Kensington and Allegheny avenues). He was also heavily involved in the methamphetamine trade.

Thomas DelGiorno, another mob soldier who became a government informant, later told New Jersey state police about the meeting at the Buckeye.

"So anyway [Casella] gave [Scarfo] some story about how he got a message from New York that [Casella] is the boss, Narducci's the underboss, and that they're supposed to kill Johnny Berkery and bury him because Berkery was the guy that set Phil up," DelGiorno said. "He didn't know that in the meantime Nicky was talking to people from New York and already had an appointment set for the next day.

"So Nicky turned around and said, 'That's not what I heard. I'm going to New York tomorrow and I'll find out.' So when Nicky went to New York and told the story that [Casella] told him, they got the guy that [Casella] was supposed to have got the story from and the guy said it's a lie."

Scarfo, whose connections in Atlantic City had helped him forge alliances with members of the powerful Genovese and Gambino crime families in New York, had outmaneuvered Casella and Narducci. By the end of March 1981, word once again came down to Philadelphia from New York. Nicodemo "Little Nicky" Scarfo was the new boss. Scarfo named Salvatore Merlino his underboss. Frank Monte was appointed consigliere.

Pete Casella left town, "retiring" to his daughter's home in Florida. He was told if he ever showed his face in Philadelphia again he would be killed. Two years later, at age seventy-three, he died of natural causes. His brother Anthony, a soldier in the organization, went underground and was seldom seen around South Philadelphia again. Frank "Chickie" Narducci, however, remained out in the open, operating a major bookmaking and gambling business that had made him a millionaire. A report prepared by the Justice Department's Organized Crime Strike Force in Philadelphia described Narducci, who was forty-eight at this time, as heavily involved in numbers, sports betting, and high-stakes card games. The games, regular weekly affairs that sometimes lasted two days, included hands that "frequently contained as much as $50,000," according to the feds. Narducci took 5 percent of each pot.

One month before Testa was killed, he, Narducci, Harry and Mario Riccobene, Pasquale Spirito, Joseph Ciancaglini, and several associates were indicted in a federal racketeering case that centered on gambling and loan-sharking operations run by the mob. Bruno and Sindone were also targets, but they were dead before the indictments were handed up. The case was based on an FBI investigation called Operation Gangplank and was one of the first built on the Racketeering Influenced and Corrupt Organizations (RICO) Act by the U.S. Attorney's Office in Philadelphia.

Testa became the first defendant unable to make the trial. Narducci would be the second. And like Narducci, Rocco Marinucci, the young pizza shop owner who had pushed the detonator, also was living on borrowed time.

Caramandi's past performance as a money earner for the mob was the one thing he had going for him during this period of upheaval. And when Scarfo—whose lust for power was matched only by his insatiable greed—took over the organization in March of 1981 he recognized that the Crow could be a valuable asset. Scarfo knew Caramandi and trusted him. What's more, he would not hold his past association with Tony Bananas against him. In a twisted way, Scarfo could appreciate and understand Tony Bananas' play. The murder of Angelo Bruno was the kind of move—bold, brash, and violent—that the new mob boss respected. Caponigro failed and he was dead. To Scarfo, that was the way the game was played.

Scarfo was even willing to overlook Caramandi's friendship with Dominick "Mickey Diamond" DeVito, although from the moment Scarfo became boss, Caramandi knew it was just a matter of time for Mickey. He knew that Scarfo had been trying to set DeVito up for more than a year.

"After Scarfo became consigliere he sent for me down the shore one day. I told Mickey Diamond this guy wants to see me. I go down the shore and Nicky takes me to this restaurant, Angelo's, in the afternoon for lunch. Then he says, 'Nick, the reason I called ya down here was I wanted to give you the opportunity that if you want to be with me, you could be with me. Don't worry about Mickey Diamond. I'll handle that.'

"I says, 'No, Nick, I'd rather stay with Mickey. I don't wanna look like I'm a huntin' dog that just goes where the bugle blows.' So I stood with Mickey Diamond.

"Then I started having problems with Chickie Narducci."

Caramandi was a heavy gambler at Narducci's card games and owed him several thousand dollars, always a source of friction within the underworld. But their problems ran deeper than that. Narducci was not a big fan of Caramandi's hustle. In fact, several years earlier he had gone after the Crow in a dispute over one of Caramandi's scams. In addition to his gold and his $1,000-bill routine, Caramandi had become a master of "selling" a $5,000 three-karat diamond ring. The hustle worked this way:

Caramandi would offer the ring to a sucker at a good price. He'd even let the mark take the ring to a jeweler to have it appraised. After the appraisal, there'd be more haggling over a price. During these negotiations Caramandi would replace the real diamond ring with a fake that was identical in size, shape, and design. He had dozens of them made up.

"I musta sold this ring two hundred times," he boasted.

On one occasion, however, he "sold" the diamond to a South Philadelphia restaurant owner who was a friend of both Narducci and Angelo Bruno. Most of Caramandi's victims couldn't or wouldn't bring legal action against him. But the Crow knew that Bruno was a higher court of appeal whose decision he would have to abide by.

"So one day Chickie Narducci comes around the Annin Street Café and hands me the ring, the phony ring, and says, 'Gimme the money.' I says, 'I don't have it.' He says, 'Well, you better get it.'

"So Mickey Diamond intervenes and tells him, 'Listen, go through proper channels.' Because Mickey was a soldier and so was Narducci. So they get in touch with Angelo Bruno and Tony Bananas and we straighten it out. I gave the guy his money back.

"Anyway, I had a lot of problems with Chickie. He used to have a ziganette game—that's an Italian card game—and before I went to jail I owed him some money. I used to borrow big offa this guy, like ten thousand, fifteen thousand at a time. This is back in 1974 when I was rolling high with the counterfeiting. Most of my money went to gambling, and sometimes I used to go to his ziganette game. Then one weekend I lost fifty thousand dollars there. So I had a history of these problems with Narducci. But I was on good terms with Scarfo. He liked me. And I liked him. And I think this helped me.

"I was always known to be a hustler, a good earner, and I had a good rapport with Scarfo. And when he called me down to Atlantic City, he sort of respected that—when I told him I didn't want to look like no huntin' dog. But the order was out for Mickey to be killed. Maybe he was looking for me to set him up. If I woulda said yeah, maybe he woulda asked me to do it. But you know, he figured I was pretty green at the time. I didn't know about this kind of stuff.

"Anyway, then Phil Testa got killed and Nicky became the boss."

CHAPTER EIGHT

Three pictures told you all you needed to know about Nicky Scarfo. They hung on the walls of Scarf Inc., the Atlantic City–based cement contracting company that also served as his personal headquarters.

Two of the pictures were almost identical. They showed a baseball player rounding first base after hitting a home run. Under the first picture were the words "This is NOT a home run." Under the second was the inscription "This IS a home run." Scarfo used to quiz first-time visitors about the two pictures, asking them if they knew the difference. Anybody who understood the rules of baseball would notice that in the first picture the runner failed to touch first base. As a result, he could be called out and his home run wouldn't count.

"Then Scarfo would tell us that's the way it is with us," Caramandi said. "Always touch base, meaning always tell your capo what you're doing. This was real important to him. He didn't like surprises, and he always wanted to know what was going on. If you don't touch base, you're out. That's what he used to say."

The other picture hanging in the office was of one of the men Scarfo admired most. It was a black-and-white portrait of Al Capone, the infamous Chicago mob boss who had been everything Scarfo wanted to be—a bold, brash celebrity mobster who operated above the law.

Several years later, a U.S. Justice Department memorandum would offer a less flattering description of Scarfo.

"[He] is a remorseless and profoundly evil man," the memo read in part. "His life has been committed to the Mafia and all the negative values it represents: greed, viciousness, treachery, deceit, and contempt for the law and the rights of others."

How this profoundly evil man ended up as boss of the Philadelphia mob and Mafia kingpin of an empire that stretched from the Pocono Mountains to the Boardwalk in Atlantic City is an example of the criminal underworld's Peter Principle, that corporate dictum that all executives rise to their own level of incompetence.

Scarfo's early days in the mob in South Philadelphia were largely unremarkable by Mafia standards. A onetime amateur boxer, he gravitated toward the organization under the tutelage of his uncles, Joseph, Michael, and Bruno family capo "Nicky Buck" Piccolo. Scarfo was given a small bookmaking operation, and, like a lot of young wiseguys in the Bruno era, he struggled to make ends meet.

But he had big ambitions. And an even bigger temper.

Scarfo, like his uncles, was a member of the Calabrian faction of the Bruno organization, and in theory at least this should have given him some standing with "Mr. Joe" Rugnetta, Bruno's powerful consigliere. But Scarfo, demonstrating the lack of tact that would plague him for most of his life, insulted Rugnetta by sarcastically spurning an offer to court the consigliere's daughter. It was one thing to politely decline an inquiry in a matter of such a delicate nature, thereby allowing everyone involved to save face. It was something else again to let it be known that the daughter in question was too ugly to even warrant consideration.

Bruno, watching from atop the Philadelphia organization, was not pleased with the quick-tempered and arrogant young nephew of the Piccolo brothers. Two other events in the early 1960s would cement his opinion of Little Nicky.

"At this time Scarfo was hanging with Chuckie [Salvatore Merlino]. He was older than Chuckie by about ten years, but they were hanging out together. Chuckie wasn't a made member then, but he was involved with Nicky in different things.

"Now there were these two brothers, the Marconis [Alfonse and Guerino Marconi]. These guys were from the old school. They were Calabrese. And Chuckie was fooling with their niece, their sister's daughter. This was something you didn't do. So they wanted Chuckie killed. They went to Mr. Joe and had a sit-down. With these two brothers, everything was to the letter. They knew this fucking thing inside out. But who comes to bat for Chuckie but Scarfo. Now it was a big fucking thing. Scarfo represented Chuckie, and Mickey Diamond spoke for these two brothers. Well, Scarfo saves Chuckie. He don't get killed. And although Chuckie denied it, these two brothers knew he was fooling with the niece.

"It was somethin' everybody remembered. I think from that point on Scarfo never liked Mickey Diamond."

Scarfo's role in the dispute further soured his standing with Rugnetta and Bruno. Then, a few months later, Scarfo's hair-trigger temper brought him his first real problem with the law.

On May 25, 1963, Scarfo, Merlino, and a friend of theirs named Louie Matteo stopped in the Oregon Diner, a popular South Philadelphia restaurant near Third Street and Oregon Avenue. According to a police report, they took a booth where moments earlier a longshoreman named William Dugan had been sitting. Dugan had spotted some friends in the diner and had left the booth to talk with them. When he returned and found Scarfo, Merlino, and Matteo sitting in his place, he asked them to move. An argument followed and then a scuffle.

In the melee, Dugan was stabbed to death. Scarfo, Merlino, and Matteo bolted out of the diner and sped away in a car. Ten days after the incident, they surrendered to the police. Ultimately, Scarfo took the rap, pleading guilty to manslaughter. He was sentenced to six to twenty-three months in prison. He served less than a year before being released. Later he would brag about the fight, telling friends how he "stabbed the Irish motherfucker."

While the justice system gave Scarfo a slap on the wrist for the Dugan murder, Angelo Bruno exacted a harsher form of punishment. The stabbing was the last straw. Bruno was fed up with the antics of the skinny hothead. Murder was an option, but the fact that he was Nicky Buck's nephew probably saved Scarfo's life. Clearly, if Bruno had left the matter up to his consigliere, Mr. Joe would have sanctioned Scarfo's murder in the blink of a Calabrian eye. Scarfo realized as much. An FBI electronic listening device would later pick up a conversation in which Scarfo complained about how Rugnetta had tried for twenty years to kill him. The conversation, recorded in 1977 shortly after Rugnetta's death, involved Scarfo, Philip Testa, Frank Narducci, and Harry Riccobene. The topic was speculation on who would be named to succeed Rugnetta and what qualities a consigliere should possess. Clearly, the four mobsters had not been pleased with Rugnetta's tenure. The consigliere, after all, is supposed to be a neutral observer, a counselor who sits at the right hand of the boss and arbitrates family disputes. Ultimately, he has the power to recommend life or death, a point that Testa hammered home in this conversation:

Testa:	He was too vindictive, that guy.
Scarfo:	Too vindictive. Prejudice. And our friend [Bruno] allowed him to go too far, Harry.
Testa:	Christ. Look, look at the hatred he carried for this kid [Scarfo], for Christ sake.
Riccobene:	Right.
Testa:	He tried every way in the world to kill him.
Scarfo:	He tried for twenty years, fifteen years now.
Testa:	Guess what, if I . . .
Scarfo:	He tried to kill me.
Testa:	If I wasn't around a couple of times, you would have went.
Scarfo:	Yeah, sure.

Testa then told Riccobene and Narducci that the "real beef" between Rugnetta and Scarfo was the fact that Rugnetta wanted Scarfo to marry his daughter and that Scarfo refused to even go out with her.

For Rugnetta it had been a matter of honor. But Scarfo felt only disdain. That pattern would repeat itself again and again as Little Nicky survived and, eventually, prospered in the Philadelphia underworld.

Angelo Bruno preferred to avoid bloodshed. He knew violence attracted attention. Murder brought investigations and newspaper headlines. None of this was good for business. And Bruno, above all else, was a businessman. So after Scarfo was released from prison for the Dugan manslaughter in 1964, he was sent packing. Banished from South Philadelphia, he was named the mob's caretaker in Atlantic City.

The Democrats had met in Convention Hall on the Boardwalk that year. It would prove to be Atlantic City's last hurrah. The city had been on the skids for years, and the national political gathering, with the attendant media coverage, turned a spotlight on the decaying resort. The hotel accommodations were poor, the service second-rate; and, adding insult to injury, prices had been jacked up everywhere to gouge more money out of the hapless conventioneers.

Lyndon Johnson got the party's nomination and Atlantic City got a national black eye. The Queen of Resorts had become a bankrupt dowager trying to live off her past glory. And now everybody knew it. For the next twelve years it would be steady decline. Hotels and restaurants would close. Conventions would cancel. Families would take their two weeks at the shore in Wildwood or Sea Isle City. Wealthier visitors who used to stay at the Boardwalk hotels would hop a jet to the Bahamas or the Caribbean. The city's population began to drop and to shift. Once there were nearly eighty thousand year-round residents and a strong middle class. By 1976 the population was down to 46,000, much of the middle class had fled, and the city had become the home for poor blacks and Hispanics and elderly whites, groups who were economically unable to leave.

Things were no better for the mob. Scarfo was Bruno's caretaker, but there wasn't that much to care for. Bookmaking, illegal gambling, and prostitution had flourished in Atlantic City's heyday. In fact, the city was the site, in 1929, of the first major mob summit. Al Capone headed the list of luminaries who came down for a three-day stay at the old President Hotel. Meyer Lanksy was represented at the conclave. So were most of the New York families. Also in attendance were Dutch Schultz, Frank Costello, Lucky Luciano, and Joe Adonis. Well into the 1950s, Atlantic City was still considered a wide-open rackets playground and was the focus of a Kefauver Committee hearing that probed the cozy relationship between local political leaders and the city's racketeers.

Backroom casinos in places like Skinny D'Amato's old 500 Club—where Frank Sinatra would often headline and where Dean Martin and Jerry Lewis first performed together—provided the customers for bookmaking, loan-sharking, and sports betting. Hookers working out of cathouses nearby offered the gamblers a refreshing break from the tables. Cops and politicians winked and nodded while holding out their hands for a small gratuity. What was the harm? People came to Atlantic City to have fun. And the mob was helping the city provide the services that the tourists and conventioneers had come to expect.

But in 1964, when Scarfo was unceremoniously sent to Atlantic City, the lights were going out all over town. He moved into an apartment in a boardinghouse at 26 North Georgia

Avenue in the city's Ducktown section. The building was owned by his mother, Catherine. Scarfo's sister, Nancy Leonetti, and her young son, Philip, also ended up living there. Scarfo married and raised three sons while living in the apartment. One son, Chris, was the result of a failed first marriage. Two other sons, Nicodemo Jr. and Mark, were from his second wife, Domenica, who came to this country from Italy.

"Scarfo was dead out when he was down there," Caramandi recalled. "He was always hustling for a buck, always broke. He had nothing in those days."

Scarfo tended bar, ran a small bookmaking and loansharking operation, and invested in an adult bookstore with a brash hustler named Alvin Feldman.

"This guy used to call himself the King of the Jews," Caramandi said. "Real cocky guy. He and Nicky had this dirty bookstore on Atlantic Avenue. Then in '71 Nicky got cited for contempt [for refusing to testify before the New Jersey State Commission of Investigation] and went to jail. While he was away, Nicky was told the guy was stealing from him in the business. When Nicky got out this guy Feldman disappeared.

"Nicky and Philip [Leonetti] used to joke about this. 'You won't see him no more'—Nicky and Philip used to say that about somebody who got killed. Spike told me one time that Nicky said Feldman was part of a building. Another time they said they dumped him in the bay."

Jim Barber, head of the major crimes unit for the Atlantic County Prosecutor's Office, was a detective assigned to the Atlantic City vice squad in the early 1970s. Barber remembers Feldman well.

"He had a bookstore that Nicky supposedly had an interest in and he was involved in some other things," Barber said. "His name used to come up a lot. Then he just disappeared. The rumor on the street was he had been murdered, but who knows. There was no investigation because nobody reported him missing. He just wasn't around anymore."

Caramandi kept in touch with Scarfo during his early years in Atlantic City, occasionally bringing him a scam or a hustle. Scarfo was struggling to survive at that time, trying to make a living and also hoping to rebuild his reputation within the organization. Ironically, the 1971 SCI contempt citation gave him an opportunity to prove himself not just to Bruno, but to mob figures throughout the state. While other mob figures, like Caponigro, fled New Jersey to avoid the SCI, Scarfo acted like a true man of honor.

He answered the subpoena, but refused to answer any questions. As a result, he was sentenced to a year at the Yardville Correctional Center. Joining him there were Bruno, Genovese family underboss Gerardo "Jerry" Catena, "Bayonne Joe" Zicarelli, Trenton mob leader Anthony "Little Pussy" Russo, and Louis "Bobby" Manna, an up-and-comer from Newark who was part of the Genovese organization. It was heady company for Little Nicky. He and these other top-ranking members of La Cosa Nostra shared a common bond, a link forged by the Mafia's time-honored code of *omertà*.

"Now Angelo got out a couple months before Nicky, he was sick or something. And later, Nicky tells the story when he gets out. He says, 'You know what Angelo gave me when he left?' He gave him some paper clips. Maybe ten paper clips in a box. And that's all he ever gave him. Now, you gotta understand, Bruno was the boss. He had millions of dollars. Scarfo was just a soldier. Scarfo tells that story. But he tells it much later, when he became boss. He don't tell it when he first got out. But he never forgot it. Meaning that Angelo was a cheap fucking prick. He wouldn't give nobody nothin'."

By way of contrast, when Caramandi was jailed on the counterfeiting charge in 1976, Scarfo sent word to him in prison that he had $10,000 and would use it to help "arrange" a reduction in Nick's sentence if possible.

"We always had a good rapport, me and him," Caramandi said. "But I had those counterfeiting charges and there was nothin' anybody could do. But I appreciated the fact."

Paying off judges and lawyers to fix cases or win reduced sentences was a tradition in Philadelphia. Caramandi had helped more than one friend grease the judicial system with $1,000 bills or other things of value. Usually it was money, but on one occasion it was a pair of prostitutes who, at Caramandi's expense, spent some time with a federal magistrate who was involved in a pending court hearing the mob had an interest in.

Scarfo also had some experience manipulating the judicial system, although things didn't always work out the way he planned. In 1972 his good friend Nicholas "Nick the Blade" Virgilio was convicted in a murder case and was looking at a twelve-to-fifteen-year prison sentence. Shortly after Scarfo got out of Yardville, he and Virgilio contacted an Atlantic City lawyer and part-time municipal judge named Edwin Helfant. Helfant said that for $12,000 he could arrange a lenient sentence. The money, Helfant said, was needed to pay off the Superior Court judge who was handling the case.

Scarfo came up with the money and gave it to Helfant. Virgilio walked into court and got slapped with a ten-to-twelve-year sentence, hardly the lenient treatment he and Scarfo were expecting.

Six years later Virgilio was released from prison and headed back to Atlantic City, where the casino boom was about to begin. He got a job as a maître d' in a local restaurant. And on a cold, snowy night in February, he went out and bought a snow shovel and a hooded ski mask.

Eddie Helfant was sitting in a booth in the Flamingo Lounge, a bar attached to the Flamingo Motel on Pacific Avenue. Helfant, a stocky, sharp-featured man with a bald head and hooked nose, was himself on trial at this time, accused of accepting bribes to kick out cases in the Somers Point municipal court where he sat as a part-time judge. In addition, he had an Atlantic City law practice and had begun dabbling in local real estate. Helfant was a typical Atlantic City lawyer, an expediter who did his best work not in a public courtroom, but in private meetings in a judge's chambers or a fellow attorney's office.

But on the night of February 15, 1978, Eddie Helfant ran out of negotiating room. He was sitting next to his wife when a man carrying a snow shovel and wearing a ski mask walked into the Flamingo and headed toward him. It's unlikely Helfant recognized Virgilio. He had other things on his mind. His trial was not going well. He faced the possibility not only of being convicted, but also of being disbarred. Other patrons in the bar took little notice of the man with the shovel until he pulled out a .22 caliber pistol and opened fire. Helfant was hit five times in the face and head. He slumped in the booth, blood pouring from his wounds. His wife screamed. Customers froze momentarily in their seats. And the man with the shovel fled out the door and disappeared.

Police recovered the shovel in a snowbank a block away. But it would be eight years before they had enough evidence to charge Virgilio and Scarfo with the murder.

*   *   *

The Helfant murder was a harbinger of what was to come, a signal that the Little Guy in Atlantic City was on the rise. As mob killings go, it was totally out of character for the Bruno organization. Helfant was a public figure, shot in a public place. And the backdrop was Atlantic City, where, in 1978, state and federal authorities were all over town looking for signs of the mob moving into the nascent casino industry.

This wasn't the way Angelo Bruno did business. But as law enforcement authorities would come to learn much later, by 1978 Bruno had begun to lose his grip on the organization. There was a new order emerging, a new underworld style. And it was personified in Nicodemo "Little Nicky" Scarfo, who in 1981 assumed Bruno's mantle.

Scarfo loved the life of a gangster. He liked the power. He liked the money. But most of all, he liked the celebrity. "He fancied himself a movie star," Caramandi said on more than one occasion.

When Scarfo walked into a restaurant, he enjoyed the fact that he got the best seat in the house. But what he relished even more was the stares and sideways glances of the other patrons. When he went to a boxing match at one of the casinos, he and his entourage always sat ringside, just like the celebrities. When they traveled, it was always first class. And there was always a Rolls, a Caddy, or a Mercedes waiting at the airport. Angelo Bruno had spent a lifetime living in the shadows, quietly earning a fortune. Nicky Scarfo wanted Bruno's wealth, but he also wanted the spotlight.

In March 1981, after Phil Testa was killed, Scarfo moved to center stage. And for a while, at least, he was able to flaunt his penchant for violence in the face of local, state, and federal investigators who tracked his rise to power.

Scarfo was getting away with murder. And he loved it.

To this day, no one knows what happened to Alvin Feldman, Scarfo's partner in the adult bookstore business. Edwin Helfant's murder in the Flamingo Lounge went unsolved for nearly a decade. A year after the Helfant killing, Scarfo plotted the murder of Mickey "Coco" Cifelli, a drug dealer who was gunned down in a South Philadelphia restaurant. Again, it would take law enforcement ten years to solve the case.

And then there was Vincent Falcone.

Scarfo had set up his nephew Philip Leonetti in the cement contracting business in the late 1970s by making him the president of Scarf Inc. He knew at that point that there would be a demand for construction work with the casino gambling boom, and he wanted to assure his family a piece of both the legitimate and illegitimate trade that would be generated. Vincent Falcone was also in the cement business and, for a time at least, worked with Leonetti, showing him the ropes and helping him get started.

"The kid seemed to be genuinely interested in learning the business," said another Atlantic City contractor familiar with those early days.

But Falcone was less than impressed with the quality of the work done by Scarf Inc. And from time to time he would belittle both Leonetti and his uncle. Scarfo took it personally. And on December 16, 1979, he took revenge.

On that day, Scarfo, Leonetti, and Larry Merlino, who was also in the construction business, invited Falcone for drinks at a friend's Margate apartment. It was to be a small preholiday get-together, a chance to talk over business and to socialize. Joseph Salerno, Jr., a plumbing contractor and friend of both Falcone and Leonetti, was also invited.

The five men met at an apartment on Decatur Street. Scarfo was sitting in the living room reading the paper and watching a football game on the television when Leonetti, Falcone, Merlino, and Salerno arrived. The four had driven over together in Merlino's car. During the ride, Leonetti kidded Falcone about old times. They had been friends for several years. Salerno, who is now in the Federal Witness Protection Program after testifying in court about the events that occurred that day, couldn't believe what happened next.

After they got to the apartment, Scarfo asked them if they wanted drinks and told Falcone to get some ice out of the refrigerator in the kitchen. After the drinks were poured, the five men settled in to watch the football game. Leonetti was next to Salerno and behind Falcone. With the game on TV and drinks in everyone's hand, Leonetti calmly pulled out a .32 caliber pistol, pointed it at the back of Falcone's head, and squeezed the trigger.

The blast from the revolver and the sight of Falcone slumping into a lifeless heap on the floor left Salerno momentarily stunned. Almost in a dream he heard Leonetti say, "Joe, this guy was a no good motherfucker." Then Scarfo began to cackle, mocking the body that lay on the floor, calling Falcone a "cocksucker" and "no good motherfucker."

Next Scarfo bent over, opened Falcone's jacket, and put his ear close to his chest. "I think I'll give him another one," Little Nicky said, apparently concerned that all the life hadn't left the body.

"No, I'll give it to him," said Leonetti.

And as Scarfo pointed to a spot where Falcone's heart would be, Leonetti pumped another bullet into the rival cement contractor's chest.

"You're one of us now," Scarfo proudly told the shell-shocked Salerno, who was ordered to help tie Falcone's arms and legs. Scarfo had come prepared. He had a blanket and twine in a box.

"I want you to tie him up like a cowboy," he told Salerno. "Tie his hands behind him. Tie his feet behind him."

After securing the dead man's arms and legs, Scarfo and Salerno wrapped the body in the blanket and tied both ends. Falcone was about five-ten and weighed 185 pounds. His head hung outside the blanket.

"I love this," Scarfo said as they prepared to dump the body. "I love it."

Leonetti and Merlino left the apartment right after the shooting. The late-afternoon sun had set and darkness had fallen when Merlino returned with Falcone's Mercury Cougar. The three men carried the body down the steps from the second-floor apartment and placed it in the trunk of the car. Scarfo got behind the wheel. Merlino and Salerno jumped into Scarfo's black Cadillac, which had been parked in the driveway, and followed. They drove for four or five blocks before Scarfo pulled over, parked the Cougar, and got into the Caddy. They went back to the apartment on Decatur Street and cleaned the place of any trace of Falcone's blood. Then they drove over to Atlantic City. They put the clothes they were wearing when Falcone was killed into a plastic trash bag. They showered and then had dinner at Scarfo's apartment on Georgia Avenue.

Salerno said that during dinner he was told why Falcone had been killed. Earlier that year, Chuckie Merlino and Scarfo had taken a vacation to Italy. During the trip, Merlino told Scarfo that Falcone was criticizing Leonetti's cement contracting work. Merlino also said that Falcone had told him he thought Scarfo was crazy.

"When we get back, I'm gonna kill him," Scarfo replied.

And so he did.

After dinner on the night Falcone was killed, Salerno, Leonetti, and Merlino headed for one of the casinos. On the way they dropped the trash bag full of their bloody clothes in a dumpster and threw the revolver down a sewer. As they walked toward the Boardwalk and dates that were waiting for them, Leonetti said, "If I could bring the motherfucker back to life, I'd kill him again."

Then he told Salerno to put the entire affair out of his mind.

"Forget about it and don't ask me anything more about it," Leonetti said.

But Salerno couldn't forget. He was scared to death. Despite Scarfo's telling him that he was now "one of us," Salerno kept seeing the unsuspecting Falcone, who minutes earlier had been joking in the car with Leonetti, slump forward as the bullet plowed into the back of his head. Salerno thought he might be next.

Vincent Falcone's body was found the next day in the trunk of his car. On December 23—largely on the basis of information provided by Salerno—Scarfo, Leonetti, and Merlino were arrested and charged with the murder. A year later they were tried by an Atlantic County jury and found not guilty. The prosecutor had little evidence other than Salerno's uncorroborated testimony, and the three defendants all provided alibi witnesses.

As he left the courthouse in Mays Landing, New Jersey, after the trial, Scarfo was stopped by reporters looking for a comment.

"Thank God for the American jury system," said the soon-to-be mob boss.

The Falcone trial was a major setback for law enforcement. But the murder investigation had opened a window into Scarfo's operation in Atlantic City. Little Nicky, the punk gangster exiled to the Jersey shore by Angelo Bruno, was no longer a bit player in the organization. It was clear from the pieces of information gathered in the Falcone case that Scarfo was someone law enforcement would have to reckon with. For one thing, investigators noticed that some of the people who put up bail for Scarfo after his arrest were either officials of or relatives of officials of Atlantic City Bartenders Union Local 54. This was one of the first definitive links between Scarfo and what would eventually become the most dominant union in the casino industry. Another major find came when detectives raided Scarfo's Georgia Avenue apartment a few days after Falcone's body was found, looking for evidence that might link him to the brutal killing. They found two items that proved important. One was a two-shot derringer revolver hidden inside an eyeglasses case in Scarfo's bureau. The other was a coded list of names and telephone numbers. Deciphered by investigators, the list contained the names and phone numbers of major mob members and mob meeting places—bars and restaurants—in Philadelphia, Newark, and New York City.

While neither the address book nor the derringer figured in the Falcone case (the derringer, however, later proved to be the basis for a federal gun charge that got Scarfo a short prison stint), what the Falcone investigation did show was that Scarfo was clearly a man on the rise inside the organization. The volatility and penchant for violence that had caused his banishment fifteen years earlier to a then dying resort were coming into vogue in the Philadelphia underworld. By 1981, when Scarfo became boss, murder was the calling card of the Philadelphia mob. Angelo Bruno had ruled for twenty-one years, and during his tenure there had been only a handful of mob murders. By the time Scarfo took over, seven major mob figures had been killed. During his first year as boss, nine more members or associates would die, including Frank Narducci and Rocco Marinucci, who played major roles in the Testa bombing; Johnny Calabrese, a Caponigro associate; Stevie Bouras, a local drug dealer and head of the Greek mob in Philadelphia; and Dominick "Mickey Diamond" DeVito, Caramandi's mob mentor. The murders, like the Helfant shooting in 1978, were public, high-profile affairs. Blood was running in the gutter.

And Scarfo was basking in the spotlight.

CHAPTER NINE

Prosecutor: And how would you get these individuals, the drug dealers or bookmakers or loan sharks, to give you a piece of their profits?

Caramandi: Well, we would threaten them with bodily harm or death, if they didn't pay. . . .

J ohn Calabrese was a high-profile loan-shark and drug dealer. That was his first mistake. His second was his belief that he could ignore the Little Guy, who was now running the mob from Atlantic City.

"They wanted a piece of him and he didn't want to give nothing to these guys," Caramandi said.

And so they killed him.

The hit was set up by Joseph "Chickie" Ciancaglini, one of four new capos appointed shortly after Scarfo took over the organization. The others were Scarfo's nephew Philip Leonetti, Phil Testa's son, Salvatore, and Chuckie Merlino's brother Lawrence. Together with Scarfo and his new underboss, Chuckie Merlino, they formed the nucleus of the bloody criminal organization that was poised to unleash a reign of terror on the Philadelphia underworld.

Calabrese got his shortly after having dinner with Ciancaglini in Cous' Little Italy, the same South Philadelphia restaurant where Angelo Bruno dined on the night of his death. Ciancaglini was walking Calabrese to his car when two men approached them from behind and opened fire. The gunmen, Tommy DelGiorno and Frank "Faffy" Iannarella, were members of Ciancaglini's crew and were on their way up the organization ladder. Both were highly ambitious. And murder was the quickest way for advancement in the Scarfo mob.

"Tommy and Faffy were waiting down the street," Caramandi said. "Chick walked him out and Tommy and Faffy banged him. Pat [Spirito] was the getaway driver. After that they all got made. Tony Meats [Anthony Ferrante] got made then, too, but I don't know what the fuck he did to deserve it."

Johnny Calabrese was gunned down on October 6, 1981. He died of two gunshot wounds to the head and three to the chest. The police report of the shooting said that two gunmen, wearing ski masks and gloves, approached him from behind and opened fire. Police found two pistols, the ski masks, and the gloves in a gutter. The cold-blooded public execution fit the pattern that was beginning to take hold now that Scarfo was in charge.

Five months earlier, on May 27, Chelsais "Stevie" Bouras went in similar fashion. Bouras, leader of a small, loosely knit group of Greek-Americans who operated in the Philadelphia underworld, was sitting in the Meletis Restaurant with several friends, including Raymond "Long John" Martorano, when a gunman walked in, motioned Martorano and the others out of the way, and opened fire. Jannette Curro, Bouras's date, also was killed. Curro's murder was unfortunate. She just happened to be out with the wrong guy on the wrong night. But the wanton killing, coupled with the planned assassinations of Bouras and, later, Calabrese, trumpeted the new scheme of things. The laissez-faire era of Angelo Bruno was over. It was no longer live and let live. Nicky Scarfo was now in charge, and Scarfo wanted a piece of everyone's action.

Frankie Flowers D'Alfonso, Angelo Bruno's old friend and highly successful business associate, was the next to get the message. At about the same time as the Bouras shooting, the *Philadelphia Daily News* had carried an article speculating that D'Alfonso was the new mob boss of Philadelphia. The paper quoted law enforcement sources who said mob members were spotted meeting with D'Alfonso and appeared to be showing him the deference associated with someone in authority. "A New Mob Don Flowers in Philly" was the headline.

D'Alfonso was meeting with mob figures, that much was true. But he was hardly the new boss. He wasn't even a made member. Scarfo was on top, and what he wanted from D'Al-

fonso was the same allegiance—and lucrative business association—that Angelo Bruno had enjoyed. D'Alfonso balked.
Like Bruno, D'Alfonso was largely unimpressed with the little
mobster from Atlantic City. And he did not intend to share
any of his income. He told that to Salvatore Testa, who was
handling more and more of the mob's work in South Philadelphia for Little Nicky. D'Alfonso's attitude, coupled with the
newspaper article, made Scarfo livid.

"There's only one boss," he told associates. "And that's
me."

But D'Alfonso's earning potential was such that Scarfo
ruled out murder. Instead, he told Salvie Testa to give Flowers
a beating. On October 29, 1981, three weeks after the Johnny
Calabrese killing, Salvatore Testa called D'Alfonso from a pay
phone and arranged a meeting near D'Alfonso's home close
to the Ninth Street Italian Market. As D'Alfonso, fifty-one,
walked toward the prearranged meeting spot, Testa and his
bodyguard and close friend Gino Milano popped out from behind a parked van. Milano, a bulky five-foot-ten former high
school football and wrestling star, had an eighteen-inch steel
bar. Testa had a wooden baseball bat, a Cleon Jones Louisville
Slugger model. The two young mobsters proceeded to bash
D'Alfonso to the ground, hitting him repeatedly in the head,
back, neck, and legs.

A Pennsylvania Crime Commission report would later describe D'Alfonso's condition this way:

"D'Alfonso was found lying semiconscious in the 900 block
of South Tenth Street. He had been brutally beaten with a
blunt instrument, possibly a crowbar or a baseball bat. At the
hospital it was found that his skull had been fractured, his
left jaw broken, the bones below both eyes shattered, his left
kneecap shattered, and two bones in the lower left leg broken.
A puncture wound, consistent with the type made by a crowbar, was also found on his lower left leg. Sixty-four stitches
were required to close extensive head wounds. Robbery was
ruled out as a motive in the beating, as authorities found
$1,700 in cash in D'Alfonso's pockets."

When D'Alfonso recovered sufficiently to talk, he didn't.

He told police he had no idea who had attacked him. Some
speculated that he had been assaulted by two local drug dealers whom D'Alfonso had threatened and tried to chase out of
the neighborhood. D'Alfonso was hospitalized for weeks and
was scarred, both mentally and physically, for the rest of his

life. He seldom left his neighborhood after that assault and was much more cautious and circumspect in his business dealings.

Frank Narducci was also unhappy about Scarfo's ascension to the top spot, but he could do little about it. Narducci had two sons, Frank Jr. and Philip, whom he could count on, and there were also a few associates whose loyalty he might be able to put to the test. But Pete Casella had fled to Florida, taking with him any hope of an alliance with New York. Casella had taken his best shot and failed. He managed to survive—if living nearly destitute in Florida with your daughter could be considered survival—but he was no longer a player. Narducci, the other principal conspirator in the Philip Testa bombing, had more at stake. "Chickie" Narducci's gambling and bookmaking enterprises had earned millions for himself and the organization. So he continued to go about his business, trying to avoid crossing Scarfo and, more important, Salvatore Testa, the young capo who was now building and expanding a lucrative rackets operation in South Philadelphia.

Besides, Narducci had other problems. His prosecution under the federal RICO statute had started with jury selection on January 4, 1982. Narducci, like his codefendants, Joseph Ciancaglini, Harry Riccobene, Mario "Sonny" Riccobene, and Pat Spirito, was free on bail. He would leave the courthouse at Sixth and Market streets each day and head home to South Philadelphia. On January 7, a Thursday, the trial broke late in the afternoon. As the defendants were leaving the courthouse, Ciancaglini slipped away from the group and headed for a public telephone. Narducci got into his car and began the twenty-minute ride downtown to his home.

Law enforcement officials can only speculate about whom Ciancaglini called and what was said. What investigators know is that shortly before 6:00 P.M., Narducci was violently and permanently severed from the RICO case.

As he was stepping out of his car less than a block from his home, two men with guns walked up and opened fire. Narducci was hit at point-blank range ten times in the face, neck, and chest. He died bleeding in the gutter. Several years later, Caramandi and Thomas DelGiorno identified the shooters in the Narducci killing as Salvatore Testa and Joey Pungitore. Testa fired the first shot and later bragged to DelGiorno that he waited until Narducci was looking him in the eye before opening fire.

"I wanted him to see it was comin'," said Testa, who had asked Scarfo for the Narducci contract in order to avenge his own father's death. Scarfo was only too happy to oblige. It was a time of vengeance in the Philadelphia mob, a time to settle old scores. And for some it was time to involuntarily part company.

"During this time I was still with Mickey, but I wasn't making any money and I was getting disgusted. I'm burned out in the city, see, with the gold and the other scams. I'm goin' down the racetrack. I'm friendly with Pat Spirito and I start to get friendly with Charlie White [Charles Iannece].

"Pat was from Trenton, but he moved to Philadelphia and went to work for Ciancaglini. He did some bookmaking and he had some loan-shark money on the street. He was just an associate until the Calabrese killing, then he got made, and, see, Pat was mostly interested in making money. Turns out he had long-distance plans. He knew already, like a year in advance, that he wanted me, Charlie White, and Junior Staino [Caramandi's Florida flimflam partner] with him. That's all he wanted. He just wanted to be left alone, with Ciancaglini as his capo, and he would be satisfied.

"So Pat used to tell me things, ask me if I'm happy, if I'm making any money, and so on. We used to go to dinner sometimes at Paco's place around Tenth and Tasker. And I said, 'No, I'm not making any money. I owe this guy [Paco] thirty-one thousand and I'm giving him six hundred and five a week interest.'

"Pat told me just be patient. He said things were going to be different. See, the order was out to kill Mickey Diamond. In fact, I was in the way twice when they were trying to kill 'im. Later I found out that Nicky had said the next time, if anybody's with him, they go too."

The Mickey Diamond contract was an example of the sinister, almost diabolical, way Scarfo's mind worked. He put the contract out on Dominick DeVito for reasons that perhaps only he fully understood. Mickey Diamond had certainly angered enough people. He was constantly trying to get over on somebody, welching on debts, finagling his way into deals. Even

Caramandi was growing tired of his mob mentor. But Scarfo's animosity went back further, back almost twenty years to their early days in South Philadelphia and Mickey Diamond's friendship with the hated "Mr. Joe" Rugnetta, the old consigliere who wanted Scarfo dead. And to the dispute with Angelo Bruno over Chuckie Merlino's improper advances toward the niece of two respected, old-line Bruno mob figures, the brothers Mark and Funzi Marconi.

When Scarfo decided DeVito had to go, he gave the assignment to the very same two mobsters whom Mickey Diamond had stood up for in the dispute with Merlino and Scarfo nearly two decades earlier.

Like some feudal lord, Scarfo was testing the Marconi brothers. Would they be loyal to the Mafia code and blindly follow the orders of their new boss, or would they balk and warn Mickey Diamond, one of their oldest friends? Either way, Scarfo figured himself a winner. If they warned Diamond, then they would become targets as well. And instead of one contract, he could put out three and be rid of them all. If they carried out the killing, then Scarfo would have succeeded not only in removing Mickey Diamond, but also in humiliating the two old mobsters, which in his mind was even better than killing them.

"It was a spite thing for Nicky," Caramandi said. "This shows you that he was a very vengeful, very bitter person."

"So I'm in and out at this time. Hustling. Not making any big money. Playing poker at Paco's place. Living off some loan-shark money we still had out. We started with fifty thousand and had, maybe, a hundred and forty thousand on the street in eighteen months. It took time to collect that money after Tony went and we paid back the fifty.

"Then one day I'm sitting in a car with this guy. We're gettin' ready to go to the racetrack. It's about twelve o'clock. Who comes around but Mickey. He pulls over, jumps in the car. I says, 'Mick, I'm goin' down the track. I got a couple hundred. I'm gonna take a shot.' He was down the track with me the day before. This guy would never leave me alone. Call me fifty times a day. Wanted to know what I was doin'. Where I was at. You know, the party was over. You know what I mean. Tony wasn't around. A new broom sweeps clean.

"Mickey had a car wash at Twenty-sixth and Passyunk, and

he wasn't doing that great. And he says, 'Nah, I gotta meet somebody. I'll see you later tonight.'

"He jumped out of the car and that was it.

"Now, I come back from the track that night. I won. I meet with this girl and we went to Dante and Luigi's [a popular South Philadelphia restaurant] for dinner. Chuckie Merlino's in there, ready to leave. And he says to me, 'Tell Mickey I said hello.' So, knowing Chuckie over the years, I knew that fuckin' remark meant something. So I says, 'Whaddaya mean by that, Chuck? Explain that. Whaddaya mean?'

"'Nothing,' he says. 'Just tell him I said hello.'

"So we go home later that night, about eight-thirty, nine o'clock, and Mickey's girlfriend calls me.

"'Have you heard from Mickey?' she says. I told her no, but I said I'd seen him earlier in the day. I figured he was with this other broad he used to fool with. He had a few broads he was fooling with.

"The next day, Friday night, we go to Paco's. Pat and Charlie had told me to meet them there. 'Your fuckin' problems are over,' they said. 'This fuckin' guy's dead. They didn't find his body yet.'

"Then Pat tells me I'm gonna be with him from now on. He says we're gonna start shaking down bookmakers and anybody else doing anything illegal. He had already told Ciancaglini about it. It was gonna be me, Charlie White [Iannece], Junior Staino, and Pat. Pat says, 'If Junior don't want to do it, you better tell him to get the fuck out of town, because he can't stay here.'"

Dominick DeVito's body was found on the afternoon of February 25, 1982, in the trunk of his own car parked at Ninth and Bainbridge streets in South Philadelphia. His hands and feet had been tied behind him and his body had been placed in plastic trash bags secured with twine. He had been shot in the head. The weapon was a .38 caliber handgun. A police report noted that DeVito, "a heavy gambler who was frequently in debt," had been reported missing the day before by his girlfriend. The woman told police she last saw DeVito on the afternoon of February 22.

No one has ever been charged with the DeVito murder, but few people spent much time mourning Mickey Diamond.

"I hadda collect the loan-shark money that was on the

street," Caramandi said. "I got the books from his girlfriend. And all the money I collected went to them guys, went to Nicky direct. We got nothing out of it. Mickey's girl didn't have no money to bury him, so they gave me six thousand dollars to give her."

DeVito hadn't been buried a week when Pat Spirito set up headquarters in a clubhouse on Bancroft Street in South Philadelphia. He brought Caramandi, Iannece, and Staino in as his associates, eventually elevating their status to "proposed members." Working in a crew under Joseph "Chickie" Ciancaglini, Caramandi became part of what would soon be called the "bomb squad," a group of mobsters who began the systematic shakedown and extortion of the nonaffiliated segments of the Philadelphia underworld.

Scarfo wanted to impose a "street tax" on bookmakers, loan sharks, and drug dealers operating outside the organization. This was in marked contrast to the way Bruno had conducted business. Bruno preferred alliances brought about by mutual needs and influence. He wanted bookmakers and loan sharks to know they could come to him for assistance, financial or otherwise. Maybe they needed to edge off some heavy betting. Maybe they had a scam going that had gotten too big to handle. Maybe they had the inside track on a lucrative construction contract and needed a silent partner to help finance the deal. They'd go to Bruno or one of his people because they knew he'd be fair; that he'd share the deal, and that when it was over, everyone could go back about his business until something else came along.

Scarfo changed those rules. In many ways he was the underworld reflection of the pinstriped outlaws who were terrorizing Wall Street at the same time. Both seemed to subscribe to the same philosophy: Greed is good. Get it all. Get it now. Take no prisoners.

Caramandi adapted perfectly to the new approach. After more than a year of looking over his shoulder, he again felt secure about his mob connections. He survived the bloodletting that had left a dozen more highly regarded mob figures dead. Now he was a step closer to the inner circle. He was a proposed member in good standing. His past association with Caponigro, a possible sore point had Phil Testa remained in power, was no longer a problem. Scarfo knew Caramandi long before he hooked up with Tony Bananas and appreciated his ability to make money. Now the Crow was out on the street every day further proving his worth to the organization.

This time he had some status. More important, he had steady income. And as an added bonus, Pat Spirito told Caramandi he could forget about the $31,000 he owed Paco.

Other people might be impressed or frightened by the wanton and ruthless violence of the mob, but to Caramandi the awesome power of the organization showed up on the bottom line. To be able to arbitrarily wipe out a loan-sharking debt—that was power. Caramandi, who had spent all his life hustling for a buck, who always spent more than he earned, then borrowed more than he could pay, was intoxicated by the strength of those around him.

More than ever, he wanted to be one of them.

"The day after they found Mickey's body I went to Junior Staino's house and told him this is the story. I tell him we're going to be with Pat. We're gonna start shaking down number writers, bookmakers, drug dealers, whatever. I told him it was gonna be him, me, and Charlie White. Now, I didn't know Charlie White too well. He was a bookmaker. I knew him over the years, but we were never close. Junior's scared. Paranoid. I said, 'Junior, you got no fucking choice. Whaddaya wanna do? Let's go over there and talk to them.'

"So me and Junior get in the car and we go over to 1838 Bancroft. That was the new spot. Pat lays it out for Junior the same way he told it to me. So it's the four of us. Now Pat says he's waitin' for the okay from Ciancaglini, but he says we're gonna start a poker game in here. We're gonna remodel the place. And he says, 'You guys ain't got nothin' to worry about. Nobody's gonna bother ya. You're with me.'

"A few days later, Pat gets the okay from Ciancaglini that we could start shakin' down drug dealers. Now we start. Man, we went after those fucking guys. We shook them down, roughed them up. Bookmakers. Loan sharks. Anybody we could reach.

"We were fuckin' terrors. We'd go out and tell people, 'If you don't pay either you get out of business or we're gonna kill ya.' I mean, there was no fuckin' bullshit. We were bringing guys to Bancroft Street, three, four, five at a time. We had bird dogs, guys who would tip us off and tell us who was dealing drugs or who was writing numbers. They'd point the guys out for us and we'd go and get them. We had control of all the shakedowns. We shook down everybody.

"In the beginning, we musta had sixty, seventy guys that were paying anywhere from a hundred to three hundred a week. We were getting packages off of guys, like twenty-five thousand for past performances. Stuff like that.

"We had a guy named Johnny giving us three hundred a week. Another guy, Big Lou, three hundred a week. We got a guy named Slim, who had a bar and restaurant, and who was big in numbers and loan shark. We got ten thousand up front and another three hundred a week from him. With so many guys, we were rolling high. After two months go by, we're collecting, like, five, six, seven thousand a week. Pat told us the deal was that Scarfo got half. This was what they called the 'elbow.' And on that elbow was Scarfo, Chuckie Merlino, Frank Monte [Scarfo's consigliere], Ciancaglini, Scarfo's nephew Philip [Leonetti], Chuckie's brother Lawrence, and Salvie Testa.

"Each week I would take half and put it on the other side for Scarfo and the other half I would chop up. Every day we'd work the shakedowns. Then we started this poker game in there. It would start on a Friday and maybe last to Monday. And over a weekend we would cut eight, ten, twelve thousand. There was a twenty-dollar or forty-dollar limit. Sometimes we'd have no limit. And we used to kill [take 5 percent from] the pots. I was making twelve hundred, fifteen hundred a week between the cuts from the shakes plus the poker game."

Meanwhile, police continued stumbling over the bodies of mobsters and mob associates.

Less than a month after the DeVito murder, law enforcement authorities made another grizzly discovery in South Philadelphia. Rocco Marinucci's body turned up in a parking lot in the 1500 block of South Eighth Street. Marinucci was the thirty-year-old South Philadelphia pizza shop owner who set off the bomb that killed Phil Testa. And although police had questioned him about the Testa contract, they were never able to gather enough evidence to link him to the bombing. Now it didn't matter. The timing and circumstances surrounding his death confirmed his involvement.

Marinucci had been shot repeatedly in the head and chest. His hands were tied in front of his body with clothesline. The first police officers on the scene also noticed that Marinucci's cheeks were puffed out. This turned out to be a message from his killer. Stuffed inside Marinucci's mouth were three large unexploded firecrackers. The date was March 15, 1982, the first anniversary of the bomb blast that had killed Phil Testa.

Salvie Testa had struck again.

CHAPTER TEN

No one could make it into the Scarfo organization without "doing some work." This was the euphemism mob members used to describe taking part in a murder. Killing someone was the final rite of passage. You couldn't be made until you had helped take a life.

At the time Caramandi and Charlie White were assigned to Pat Spirito, they hadn't done any work. But 1982 was a good year for would-be mobsters. There were more than enough contracts out on the street. Salvie Testa was running around ruthlessly avenging his father's death, and Scarfo was solidifying his hold on the organization by settling old scores. The level of violence escalated even further when Scarfo opened an offensive against Harry "the Hunchback" Riccobene, the old Bruno ally who was one of the few mobsters standing in the way of Scarfo's absolute and total control of the organization. Riccobene wasn't anxious to go to war. He would have preferred to be left alone. He had had an understanding with Bruno and probably would have been content with the same arrangement with Scarfo.

"Harry was an independent guy," a Philadelphia police detective explained. "Every year at Christmas he'd send Bruno something and that would be it. For the rest of the year, he was on his own."

And on his own Riccobene did quite well. He had a group of relatives—half brothers and nephews—and associates who worked his loan-sharking, gambling, vending machine, and methamphetamine ventures. It was a mob within the mob, and while Bruno was boss, it didn't seem to matter.

143

But Scarfo wasn't satisfied with a Christmas present and lip service. He wanted a piece of Riccobene's action. And when Harry balked, Scarfo ordered him killed. Thus began another surge of murder and mayhem on the streets of South Philadelphia.

Caramandi began to hear bits and pieces about the Riccobene contract shortly after Mickey Diamond's murder. Chuckie Merlino referred to Riccobene as a "rat" and said he was an "FBI informant" who deserved to die, allegations that Caramandi would later describe as "bullshit." If Riccobene was an informant, that fact probably would have come out during the 1982 RICO trial in which he and several top Scarfo associates, including Ciancaglini and Spirito, were defendants. The trial, put off after the Narducci murder, began in May 1982 and ended with all six defendants convicted. Riccobene sat at the defense table with Spirito and Ciancaglini each day helping attorneys plot their legal defense. At the same time, Ciancaglini and Spirito were plotting Riccobene's murder.

This might seem strange to someone not familiar with the workings of the criminal underworld. But life inside the Scarfo organization was a three-dimensional chess game. Plots and intrigue unfolded on several different levels, and collisions occurred on various planes. So for months during the Riccobene war, protagonists would be in each other's company and, on the surface at least, appear to be getting along famously. They would socialize at weddings and funerals. If they happened to be in the same restaurant, they'd greet each other warmly and buy each other a round of drinks. It was all part of the Mafia machismo that had taken over the Scarfo organization, all part of a battle being fought on Scarfo's terms, a battle of cunning, guile, and deceit. To investigators trying to track the machinations, it was like Kremlin-watching during the height of the Cold War.

"Funzi Marconi used to tell me when I first started gettin' involved with this stuff," Caramandi said, "'You heard of the double cross? In this business you gotta watch for the triple cross.' You gotta always be alert. There's so much jealousy. Guys always trying to set you up, put you in traps. Trying to get ya killed. There was so much viciousness in this thing."

Pat Spirito had gotten the Harry Riccobene contract. He was told to use Charlie White. Eventually Caramandi was brought in to help out as well. For both Iannece and Caramandi, this was a step up. It was their first chance to do some work, to show that they were worthy of the badge. They and other members of the Scarfo mob would spend months trying to nail Harry Riccobene and several of his associates. Sometimes it seemed like a chapter out of *The Gang That Couldn't Shoot Straight*.

"This one time, Pat tells Charlie he's gonna bring Harry around. It's March 1982, just after we opened the club. He says he's gonna take 'im in the back room. Then he tells him, 'When I walk out—I'm gonna ask him if he wants coffee or a Coke or something—you hit him with the pipe.' He had this pipe, about fifteen inches long. 'Then we'll shoot 'im and at nighttime we'll take him out.'

"But Harry never showed up.

"Another time, Salvie and Chick [Ciancaglini] came around. They got a tip that Harry would be on Seventeenth Street between Shunk and Oregon at about six o'clock at night to pick up a girl. So Pat came [to the clubhouse] to pick up Charlie. But the next day, Charlie told me, 'Jesus Christ, we had 'im. He came out of the car. He opened the door on the driver's side. All we hadda do was pull up beside him and I coulda plugged him.' But Pat didn't want to do it. He dogged it. Charlie was disgusted with him.

"But that's the way things were going."

In April, after several attempts to ambush Harry Riccobene had failed, Scarfo decided on a more insidious form of treachery. And so he sent his consigliere, Frank Monte, and Raymond "Long John" Martorano (then a suspect in McCullough murder) to see Harry's half brother, Mario "Sonny" Riccobene. Mario knew Long John. They both were in the methamphetamine business. What Martorano and Monte proposed was that Mario set his half brother up. Mario listened and said he'd get back to them. Then he went to see his brother Harry.

And that, said Caramandi, was what forced the Riccobene war out in the open. For the next year and a half a battle would rage on the streets of South Philadelphia. Harry Riccobene had been cautious and suspicious of Scarfo. He had hoped to avoid open warfare. It was only after Monte and Martorano tried to co-opt his brother that Riccobene decided to act. Once Mario Riccobene was approached, he had just two options. He could either set up his brother or, like his brother, he could become a target. At that point, Scarfo had backed the Riccobenes into a corner.

"It's them or us," Harry Riccobene told his brother. "It is either kill or be killed. Let's get them before they get us."

Mario Riccobene's answer was delivered to Frank Monte outside a service station in Southwest Philadelphia on May 13 by Joseph Pedulla and Victor DeLuca, two Riccobene associates. Pedulla was lying in ambush in a camper mounted on the back of a small pickup truck. The truck was parked across the street from the service station where Monte had left his car. Pedulla had a .22 caliber rifle with a telescopic sight. DeLuca and another associate waited in a bar nearby. Shortly after 9:00 P.M., Monte showed up for his car. Pedulla got him in his sight and squeezed the trigger, and squeezed again, and squeezed again, and squeezed again. Monte, forty-nine, was shot five times in the back and head. There were also bullet wounds in his left hand, right arm, and upper right arm.

The mob consigliere had $600 in cash in his pocket when police found him lying semiconscious in the street near the gas station at 9:30 that night. He was pronounced dead a half hour later.

Monte's name was near the top of a hit list drawn up by the Riccobenes after Mario was approached that spring and asked to set up his brother. The Riccobenes, in turn, were on top of a list prepared by Scarfo and his henchmen. For the rest of 1982 and for all of 1983, squads of gunmen cruised the streets of South Philadelphia looking for targets.

Harry Riccobene, who was nearly seventy years old, would be ambushed twice, but would miraculously survive both attempts. Once he was shot five times while trapped in a phone booth where he had just finished a conversation with his twenty-three-year-old girlfriend. On that occasion, the aging mobster managed to wrestle the gun away from his assailant, Salvatore "Wayne" Grande. Grande was almost fifty years younger and at least one hundred pounds heavier than Riccobene. When police arrived moments after the ambush, Grande was gone and Riccobene was leaning up against the phone booth, bleeding, with an empty revolver in his hand. He told police he had no idea who had shot him.

An investigator then asked Riccobene how he got the gun away from the shooter.

"He was done with it," Harry replied.

On a second occasion, Riccobene was sitting in his car when a man in a jogging suit ran past and opened fire. None of the shots found their mark.

The attempts on Harry Riccobene's life occurred in June and August 1982. Sandwiched in between was a salvo fired in the opposite direction. On a muggy Saturday afternoon in July—the kind of day when half of South Philly heads for the Jersey shore—Salvie Testa sat on a wooden crate outside a pizza shop in the Ninth Street Italian Market eating raw clams out of a bucket. Joe Pedulla and Victor DeLuca drove by in a car, spotted the young mob capo, and made another pass. Only this time Pedulla pointed a shotgun out the window and blasted away. Testa was blown off the wooden crate as shotgun pellets tore away a part of his left arm. He was rushed to the hospital in critical condition, but survived. Within two months he was back on the street heading up a hit squad as the war with the Riccobenes escalated.

Ironically, the federal government provided Scarfo with both an alibi and protection during most of the battle. While Scarfo had beaten the murder rap in the Falcone killing two years earlier, the two-shot derringer investigators found in his home came back to haunt him. He was convicted in April 1981 on a federal gun charge—possession of a weapon by a convicted felon—and sentenced to two years in prison. On August 17, 1982, Scarfo surrendered to begin serving his sentence. He was shipped to a federal prison in La Tuna, Texas, where he would spend the next seventeen months. By the time he returned to Philadelphia, Riccobene and most of his top associates would be in jail. Several of those those who weren't would be dead.

"We were stalking Harry all over the city. I was going to places where he hung at. Where his mother lived. Where he lived. We're trying to set up different spots. One day we followed him down Passyunk Avenue, but we lost him. At this time, we're shaking guys down, we're doing extortions, and we're trying to get Harry. This is going on every day. Now that summer we went down the shore to see one of those heavyweight fights on the big televisions, closed-circuit. Nicky's there. It was right before he went away. Lawrence [Merlino]. Philip [Leonetti]. A lot of guys. Tommy and Faffy. So after the fight, Nicky Scarfo said he wants to talk to Pat. We go downstairs to the bar and Nicky gets him on the side and he tells him, 'Listen, you gotta kill this fuckin' Sonny [Mario Riccobene]. You gotta get this Sonny.'

"So we started with Sonny. Me, Charlie, and Pat. We're stalking him. We go to his house, his job. We're working from seven o'clock in the morning to all hours of the night. Most of the time it's just me and Charlie. We went to Sonny's girlfriend's house up in Huntingdon Valley. He used to sleep there a couple nights a week. But it was a tough place to get him, because there were big, wide streets up there and nowhere to lay an ambush.

"We went to Trenton, where we heard he did business with a guy named Bucky, that he settles on a Sunday night with the numbers. We went and laid there with Reds Pontani [Albert Pontani, a Scarfo soldier who headed up the Trenton rackets]. We had shotguns. But that never panned out.

"And every day Pat would go around to Chick and give him a blow-by-blow description, because you have to report to your capo. In this thing, you gotta tell your capo everything you do. And your capo tries to help you. He tells you to be careful. And if he can, he'll give you a tip, like he's gonna be somewhere or how to get somebody to set him up. But it was pretty frustrating."

"Pat the Cat" Spirito was not cut out for the Scarfo mob. He had come out of Trenton and moved to South Philadelphia at a time when mob members were low-key operators concentrating on gambling, loan-sharking, and bookmaking. He was an associate of Chick Ciancaglini and rode his coattails into the organization. He was greedy and ambitious, attributes that Scarfo could appreciate, but he lacked the killer instinct. He thought he could slide by generating enough money to keep the Little Guy down the shore satisfied. But he underestimated Scarfo's bloodlust. Spirito was a money-maker, but he was also a whiner and complainer.

Nineteen-eighty-two started out well but ended badly for Pat the Cat. He had set up his headquarters at Eighteenth and Bancroft streets and was supervising both the shakedowns and a lucrative gambling operation that police estimated was bringing in more than $1 million a year for the organization.

But his activities were attracting too much attention. Spirito correctly surmised that the feds had placed hidden listening devices in his clubhouse.

Before the year was out, he moved his operation to Camac and Moore streets, just off East Passyunk Avenue. A friend of Caramandi's had rented out an old plumbing supply store, and this became the new center for Spirito's outfit. It was, in fact, a prime location. East Passyunk Avenue, a tree-lined promenade of shops, stores, bars, and restaurants, is the hub of South Philadelphia. The avenue is to South Philadelphians what shopping malls are to suburbanites. Spirito's new headquarters was just a half block away. It was literally in the heart of the city's Italian-American community. And in the petty maneuvering and jockeying for position that would come to plague the Scarfo organization, control of Camac and Moore would eventually become a bone of contention.

But in 1982, Spirito had more pressing concerns.

First there was Ralph "Junior" Staino, a member of the "bomb squad" who apparently didn't know where to draw the line. Even in the underworld, there is a certain recognized code of conduct. But Junior was too greedy to appreciate that, and it nearly cost him his life. Staino, one of Caramandi's oldest friends, was gambling heavily, placing bets with bookmakers whom he, Caramandi, and Charlie White were shaking down. And when he lost, he was refusing to pay. This was bad business. Something Spirito could not abide. If you're extorting bookmakers in exchange for protection, he would say, then you can't abuse them by welshing on bets.

"These guys used to come around to complain because they were paying the street taxes," Caramandi said. "Pat found out about it and was very upset over it.

"In fact, at one time he wanted to kill Junior, but then he just told Junior to get lost, don't come around no more. Me and Charlie just kept on doing what we were doing."

In addition to Staino's shenanigans, Spirito had legal problems. As a result of his conviction in the RICO trial that May, he was sentenced to eight years in prison, but like Ciancaglini, Riccobene, and the others, he remained free pending appeal. Then in September, Spirito was jailed on a contempt charge after a convicted arsonist tied him to a corrupt attorney in a scheme to fix a court case. Spirito was subpoenaed by a grand jury investigating the lawyer and, for a time, refused to testify.

He spent about two weeks in jail, whining and complaining all the while, before agreeing to appear before the grand jury and cleansing himself of the contempt.

And all of this was being played out at the same time the Scarfo organization was going to war with the Riccobenes.

Spirito's personal problems became a constant headache for those associated with him, particularly Caramandi and Charlie White Iannece. Caramandi had spent years dealing with Mickey Diamond, but nothing he had been through before prepared him for the bitching, moaning, and back-biting of Pat the Cat. In many ways it was Caramandi's first exposure to the petty jealousies and bitterness that were always percolating beneath the surface in the Scarfo organization.

"We're gettin' bugged with this guy, me and Charlie. He was a pain in the balls. Always beefing. Always complaining. See, this guy Pat, if he had problems with his wife, we would talk to his wife. Then we had to stay with him from eleven o'clock in the morning till one or two o'clock the next morning. Then he used to call you on the fuckin' phone and he'd have you on the phone for two or three hours, always beefin' about something, beefin' on somebody, guys in the neighborhood.

"While he was away [on the contempt charge], we were handling the shakedowns and bringing his wife his end. In the meantime, me and Charlie went to see Ciancaglini and told him we don't wanna be with this guy no more. We didn't like the way he was talkin' about people. It was all nonsense. But Ciancaglini says, 'You gotta be with him. That's the way it is.' So it was.

"And one day while Pat's in jail, I go visit him and he says that Scarfo's no good, Chuckie's no good, Salvie's no good, Philip's no good, Lawrence is no good. They're all out for themselves. They just leave you hanging.

"This is treason talk. I tell Charlie, 'Hey, I ain't gonna listen to this shit. This guy is nuts.' And we go back and see Ciancaglini again and ask if we gotta be with this guy. Again, he says, 'Yeah.'"

After spending eleven days in jail, Spirito finally agreed to appear before the grand jury, answering its questions in a way that he hoped would not implicate anyone. He was freed on September 14.

Caramandi was there to take him home.

"We drive right to Ninth and Catharine and he tells Chick [Ciancaglini] everything turned out okay," Caramandi said.

"He goes home, but the next day this guy's beefing again."

Spirito had decided that he knew more about running the organization than the people in charge. And he was angered by what he considered the current leadership's indifference to his legal plight. He told Caramandi it was all cutthroat, dog-eat-dog.

"These guys are no good," Spirito said one night as he and Caramandi sat drinking in a Passyunk Avenue bar.

"Who?" Caramandi asked, playing dumb.

"Scarfo, Testa," said Spirito, and then went on a tirade about Salvie.

"I'll pull his other arm off," he said. "I'll cripple him with his other arm."

Caramandi decided he wanted no part of the conversation. "I says to myself this guy's crazy, and I called Charlie up and told him to get the fuck over here," Caramandi recalled. "I don't like the way Pat is talking. This kinda talk can get you killed."

It was about this time that Ciancaglini came up with a tip that seemed to seal the fate of Sonny Riccobene. Instead, it proved to be Pat Spirito's undoing.

"One day Chick sends for us. Somebody had died and Sonny's gonna be at this funeral Friday night. Chick tells us this on a Thursday. He says definitely Sonny's gonna be there at this funeral.

"He gives us the address of the funeral parlor. It was right off [Interstate] 95. Big funeral parlor. So we stake out the joint and we see a good place to park. I'm gonna be the driver. Charlie and Pat's gonna be the shooters. We got a shotgun and a .38. We're all set.

"The next day me and Charlie are up early. Pat comes around around twelve o'clock and he starts drinking. We're sittin' in Marra's [a Passyunk Avenue restaurant] and all day long he's saying, 'You think he's gonna show up? You think he's gonna show up?' I says, 'Well, Pat, we gotta go. Chick told us.'"

At 5:00, Spirito left the restaurant to go home and have dinner. He told Caramandi and Charlie White to drive around to Riccobene's house to see if he was there. Caramandi and Iannece drove past the house and didn't see Riccobene's car.

They headed back to the clubhouse on Camac and Moore and called Spirito at home.

"We said, 'Look, Pat, the car's not there. We better get up to that funeral parlor.' But he says, no, he wants to eat first. So I tell him we'll wait for him in Marra's Restaurant. We'll get something to eat and wait for him. I tell him, 'Hurry up.'

"About quarter to seven, seven o'clock, he calls up. He says, 'Ahh, I don't think that guy's gonna show up.' I says, 'Jesus Christ, Pat, we better go up there. This came from Chick. We just can't ignore it.' And he says, 'Yeah, I'll be around in a little while.'

"Now we're waiting and waiting and he don't come around till after eight. And again he says, 'I don't think this guy's gonna show. There's no sense going up there.' It's like a twenty-five-minute ride. I kick Charlie under the table and I say, 'Look, me and Charlie better go up there. What the fuck, somebody's gotta go there.' Pat was all dressed up, with a tie and sport jacket. He says, 'All right, if you guys wanna go up there, go ahead.' So we get our .38 and Charlie drives to the funeral parlor.

"When we get there, it must be close to nine o'clock. There's a couple guys standing outside. We ask for Chick and they say he left about twenty minutes ago. So we shoot back downtown. Back to the restaurant. Pat's there and he says. 'You don't know what happened. Chick just left. And he's pissed off.' Because Chick caught 'im dead. He says, 'Where's Nick and Charlie?' Pat tells him we went up there. And he says to Pat, 'Why ain't you up there?'

"Little did we know at the time, but Pat told him that *we* didn't want to do it. He lied to Chick. Told him we didn't like it. That was the treachery. Now he tells us that Chick is pissed off. He wants to see the three of us tomorrow.

"It turns out Chick had walked Sonny out of the funeral parlor to the parking lot. Just him and Sonny and Sonny was on crutches. We had him dead. And Chick was so fuckin' pissed off. Because this was eight, nine months that they couldn't get Harry, couldn't get Sonny.

"Me and Charlie talked later and we said it's a good thing we went up there, especially after Pat lied. But he got caught in his own trap. The next day we meet, me, Pat, and Charlie, and he don't even want to go to Chick's, go and face the music. I says, 'Listen, we gotta go. No matter what, we gotta go.'"

*   *   *

About 4:00 that afternoon, Caramandi, Iannece, and Spirito headed over to Ciancaglini's clubhouse at Ninth and Catharine. When they walked in the store, Chuckie Merlino, the family underboss, and Salvie Testa were sitting there. In a back room, Ciancaglini was playing cards. They were waiting for Ciancaglini to finish playing his hand when Merlino called Caramandi over.

"Hey, Crow, come here, I wanna talk to ya," he said.

Off to the side of the room, Merlino lit into Caramandi.

"What the fuck happened last night?" he said.

"Hey, Chuck, I only do what I'm told," Caramandi replied as sweat began to roll down his lower back.

"You fucking guys, your outfit stinks," Merlino screamed. Then he and Salvie walked out the door.

Caramandi was certain Spirito and Iannece heard Merlino, but he decided to say nothing more about it. Minutes later, Ciancaglini called all three of them into the back room and told them they were off the Sonny Riccobene contract.

"Just get off it for a while," he said.

Caramandi and Iannece were beside themselves. Spirito had put them in the middle of something that could cost them all their lives. Later they decided to seek a second, private meeting with Ciancaglini.

"The next morning, Sunday, we went right to Chick's house. It was about eight-thirty. Fuck this Pat. He ain't gonna get us killed. We said to Chick we gotta talk to ya. He says come on in. He makes coffee. And we say, 'Look, Chick, we're not beefing on the guy, but we were ready from eight o'clock in the morning. This guy didn't want to go.'

"He says, 'It's a good thing you guys came here. 'Cause you guys were in trouble. He told me you guys didn't want to go.' So Chick said he would straighten it out with Chuckie. From then on we had our guard up for Pat.

"After the funeral parlor attempt we're off the thing. So one day Gino [Milano] and Salvie [Testa] come around the corner when I'm not there. I come back and Pat says that Salvie was around and he wants me to go take him to Sonny's house up in Huntingdon Valley. I says, 'What, me alone?' Pat says, 'Yeah.' I says, 'Why me?' He says, 'I don't know. He wants you to take him.'

"I'm scared. I tell Pat to come with me, but he says no. Now my antennas are up because this fuckin' Pat, you never know what he might have told Chick. He used to tell him a lot of shit. One day he'd complain about me; one day he'd complain about Charlie. He was goofy, like. I tell Charlie something's up here. Why would Salvie want me to go there by myself? I didn't know Salvie that well, really only to say hello and good-bye. I wasn't a made guy. I was just around Pat. And Salvie's a capo.

"Charlie says don't worry about it and he says he'll go with me. So we get into the station wagon. It's about two-thirty, and we go over to meet Salvie and I try to talk him out of it. I tell him I might not be able to find the place. I hadn't been there for a while.

"He says, 'Come on. Take a ride. Maybe you'll remember when we get up there.' I figure there's something wrong. I'm scared, really fuckin' scared. I figured Pat said something. So I tried to talk him out of it again, but he said, 'Nah, come on. Let's take a ride.' And to top it off, he calls Anthony Pungitore to go with us. Now, I don't know this kid. He's Joe Pung's brother. I'm figuring, what the fuck is going on here? Why would this kid come? And Anthony Pung has a jacket on and you can't tell if he's got a gun inside the jacket.

"Now I know this kid's brother Joe is a made guy and this is the way things are done. The viciousness of it. Put me in the car. Drive up there. Shoot me in the fuckin' head. Now we walk outside. I'm worried about this Anthony Pungitore, fig-uring he's got a gun, and I figured that was it for me.

"So we're walking to the car. Charlie's gonna drive. The four of us walk out. Now I go for the back door. Salvie says, 'No. Sit in the front.' Holy shit. I reach for the front door, but at that point I don't know whether to fuckin' run. I don't know what to do. But I open the door and get in the car. Anthony Pung and Salvie are sittin' in the back. As we're driving, we're talking bullshit talk. I'm turned around. I got my body turned around facing Pung. I wanna make sure. I was paranoid. I couldn't figure out what I did wrong."

They found Sonny Riccobene's girlfriend's house in Hunt-ingdon Valley, and Testa, after seeing the place and the neighborhood around it, was satisfied with Caramandi's explanation that it was not a good spot for an ambush. Ca-ramandi, still keeping an eye on Anthony Pungitore, began to think that maybe that's all the trip was about, that he was not a target after all. On the ride back downtown he began to relax. And after he and Charlie White dropped Salvie

and Anthony Pung off at Ninth and Catharine, Caramandi
breathed a sigh of relief. He had spent an afternoon facing
the prospect of dying, real or imagined. At no other time in
his life had he felt himself in so much jeopardy. He had been
in tight spots before, but he had always been able to plan
and scheme. To anticipate. On this occasion he had been
trapped. He was moving closer to the mob's inner circle, and
as he moved he found it was harder and harder to take a
step back. Murder was now a part of his life.

On the ride back to South Philadelphia, Salvie Testa told
Caramandi and Charlie White that he would now be overseeing
the stalking of the Riccobenes. Scarfo was getting restless in
La Tuna and was sending messages up to Philadelphia. He
wanted to hear "some noise." Salvie Testa hoped to accom-
modate the imprisoned boss.

"After the holidays they gave Pat another chance. Me, Charlie,
and Pat started again with Sonny. Now we had two teams,
Salvie and his men and Chick and his. So they gave out day
shifts and night shifts. We worked the day shift and they would
work the night shift.

"We were stalkin' him again. And Pat started back with the
same fuckin' bullshit. He would say, 'We ain't gonna get this
guy. He's too fuckin' hard.' Now I can't recall what happened,
but another incident came up and Pat started talking treason
again. Me and Charlie went to Chick again. We don't want to
be with this guy no more. We told him about the things he
said about Scarfo and Chuckie and Salvie and Lawrence. It
just wasn't right.

"Now when we made the beef to Chick, we were in fear for
our lives. Because we didn't know what the fuck Pat was saying behind our backs. We know he don't want to kill nobody.
He didn't want to kill Sonny. He was always finding excuses,
and this was making us look bad. But it came to a point where
I think they understood. Chick knew we were serious. We
didn't want no parts of him.

"But, man, you gotta become a stroker in this business.
You gotta know how to stroke, because they look for every
blink of the eye. And I'll never forget what happened next. It
was Johnny Cupcakes' [John Melilli's] daughter's wedding
and we were all there. Ciancaglini. The whole crew. Philip.
Lawrence. The whole mob. Except Scarfo, who was sending
those messages to Salvie that he wanted to hear noise.

"I come in and I sit with Tommy [DelGiorno]. Pat's in the back sitting with Charlie and a couple of other people and their wives. Anyway, I stop and talk to Tommy and Faffy for a while and Pat comes over to the table and says, 'What the fuck. When you gonna come over and sit with us?' I says, 'I'll be right over.' He was pretty bugged. So I go to the table. After a while, Chuckie calls me over and says he wants to see me upstairs in the bathroom. He says he wants to know what's going on with this guy Pat. So I told him. The way Pat talks about him, Nicky, Philip, his brother Lawrence, Salvie. Chuckie just listened.

"I said, 'We can't be around this guy no more. Nothing's gettin' done. It's all nonsense.' You gotta remember. We were spending hours and hours, days and weeks, stalking Sonny. There were a lot of times we coulda had him, but there was always a story. So Chuckie seemed to be satisfied. See, in this business, you always need two guys. You just can't beef on a guy. You gotta have proof. And Charlie was my proof. Everything I said, Charlie confirmed. Charlie had had enough of him, too.

"So when we came down the steps, we go over to the bar and the bartender asks Chuckie what does he want and he says, 'Gimme a .38.' In other words, he wanted to blast him right there."

About a week later, Caramandi and Iannece were summoned to a meeting with Chuckie Merlino and Chickie Ciancaglini at Ciancaglini's clubhouse at Ninth and Catharine. When they arrived, Ciancaglini was huddled in a corner with Ronald "Cuddles" DiCaprio, another mob associate.

Merlino called Caramandi and Iannece over and told them, "Pat's gotta go."

Then he shaped his fingers into the sign of a gun and pointed toward the ground.

"I want you to use this kid over here," he said, nodding toward DiCaprio.

Earlier that year DiCaprio had been linked to the murder of Robert Hornickel, a low-level drug dealer whose body was found in the trunk of his car. Hornickel had been shot and strangled. DiCaprio, who would later be convicted of racketeering charges that included the Hornickel murder, was one of Ciancaglini's associates, and the Spirito contract was a chance for him to move up within the organization.

Ironically, Caramandi and Charlie White were in much the same position. They still hadn't done any work, despite nearly a year of trying. Now they were going to turn their guns in another direction.

Pasquale Spirito would be a much easier target.

"So now the three of us go outside and I ask this Cuddles for his phone number. I tell him we'll be in touch with him as soon as we devise a plan.

"Me and Charlie are talking and we decide the best way to get this guy is to tell him we got a shot at Sonny. We found out Sonny used to go to this place up at Sixty-sixth and Haverford that was owned by a guy who owed Sonny money. We planned to tell Pat that Sonny goes up there on Friday nights.

"Now this was on a Tuesday. The next night me and Charlie drive to this place and we decide it's too far. We'd have to drive all the way up there, blast the guy, then drive all the way back.

"But as we're driving back we devise another plan. We're gonna tell him we're going up there just to stalk it. No guns. Just to see if Sonny goes up there. But en route to going there we picked a spot downtown, on Eleventh Street between Mifflin and Moore. It's pretty dead there. It's near the church. Near Saint Maria Goretti's Church. Pat would pick me up first at my apartment. Then drive down to Broad to pick up Charlie on Wolf Street. Then as we're driving Charlie would pretend, like, he forgot his money and he would ask me if I had any. I'd say, yeah, how much do you want? He'd say he had to give a guy two hundred, and at this point he would tell Pat to pull over. It would be right on the corner. I would be in the front of the car and Charlie would be in the back of the car. Charlie would have his gun hidden under his sport coat over his arm. I would have a little .25 automatic hidden in my back pocket.

"We're set. This is the plan. The next day, early in the morning, we take Cuddles to the spot. We tell him to be there Friday night from nine o'clock on. We made him park facing north on a little street between Tenth and Eleventh on Mifflin. Just to wait there. When he hears the gunshots, we'll run to his car. We had to run, like a block, to the car. We told him don't come around to the clubhouse 'cause Pat might spot him. Just be there Friday. So it was agreed.

"Then on Thursday, Pat takes me into Cravings Luncheon-ette, another place where we used to hang at, around twelve-thirty, one o'clock. He's got me in the booth for three fuckin' hours—see, he had bad vibes, he knew there was something wrong. He knew he was in trouble. He was waiting to go to jail. He got eight years in the racketeering case and he was out on appeal. For three hours he was looking into my eyes and telling me, 'You know you're my best friend. I like you more than Charlie. I'm gonna get you down someday. You're on the verge of gettin' made. It's only a matter of time. We just gotta get this fuckin' Sonny.'

"I'm going, 'Yeah, yeah, yeah.' Now, Pat's trying to work my head. He's trying to look for some kind of reaction. He says, 'You know, if you called me at four o'clock in the morning to meet you, I'd meet you. That's how much I trust you. If I don't trust you, I can't trust nobody.'

"I knew this guy had bad vibes. So I says, 'Are you crazy, Pat? I don't want to hear this shit. You're my best friend. What are you, kidding? You're my best friend. Without you, I wouldn't be here.'

"After I get done talking to him, a couple of hours later, he leaves. Then I go see Charlie and tell him Pat knows something is up."

Pat Spirito spent the last day of his life in about the same way he had been spending most of his time that previous year, drinking at the bar in Marra's Restaurant on Passyunk Avenue and whining about the Sonny Riccobene contract. Spirito got to Marra's a little after noon on Friday, April 29, 1983.

Caramandi and Iannece found him there a short time later.

"All day he's saying, 'I don't think this guy's gonna be there tonight.' I said, 'What the fuck. We'll go see, and if not, we'll have dinner up there. What's the big fuckin' deal?' But he's going, 'Sonny won't show up. It'll be a wasted trip.' But finally he agrees.

"Me and Charlie go home about three or four o'clock. Pat's still at Marra's. Now Pat starts calling me. He says, 'Why don't we go early?' Six fuckin' times he musta called me. Each time I call Charlie and Charlie tells me to give him the shit. See, we can't go early because this Cuddles is not gonna be there till nine o'clock.

"Finally, nine o'clock, quarter after nine, Pat picks me up. He's moaning and beefing. I said, 'Pat, what is the difference?

It's a night out. We'll eat something. We'll drink something. Have a good time.' We get to Charlie's house. He blows the horn. Here comes Charlie with his coat over his arm.

"Charlie gets in the backseat. Pat had a '78 Cadillac. Two-door. Gray. All of a sudden, Charlie says, 'Jeez, I forgot my money. Nick, you got any money?' And I says, 'Yeah, Charlie, how much you need?' He says, 'Two hundred. I gotta give a guy two hundred dollars.' So I reach in my pocket and pull out the money and give it him in the backseat, making it look real. Now we're between Mifflin and McKean. All of a sudden, a fuckin' car is trying to park. It musta took him three or four minutes. Cars are backed up behind us. In fact, they start blowing their horns. We're a little bugged, you know? We finally get moving and get to Eleventh and Mifflin, right at the stop sign. Pat says, 'Where at?' Charlie says, 'Just pull over, Pat.'

"So Pat pulls to the northeast corner on Eleventh Street at Mifflin. There's a fireplug there. Now, I don't know what to do here. There are these cars going by. So I got my hand on the door and I'm hesitating. I wanna turn around to see what Charlie wants to do. I'm hesitating, hesitating. All of a sudden, *boom*. This .38, right in may ears.

"Pat's head—I'm looking at him—his head jerks to the right and just drops down. Then *boom* again. A couple seconds later. Charlie put two in his fuckin' head. No sense me takin' my gun out. It was too late. I jump out of the car. But Pat's got the car in drive and it starts rollin'.

"Charlie's in the backseat. He's burly. He's having trouble gettin' out. I'm pullin' him. And we know everybody heard it, these fuckin' shots. I get him out. The car rolls, about five or six feet, and bangs into a car parked in front of it. We run down Mifflin. This Cuddles pulls out. His lights are on. We jump in the car, me in the front seat, Charlie in the back. We're wiping the guns off with our handkerchiefs. We're both pretty fuckin' nervous. It was our first time.

"I'm screaming at Cuddles, 'Go through the stop signs. Shut your lights off so nobody can see your license tags.' He's got his own car. We get to Ninth and Mifflin, I throw my gun out. Between Eighth and Ninth on Mifflin, Charlie throws his gun out. We go down Seventh Street near Moore and jump out of the car. Charlie goes his way. I go mine. I said, 'Look, I'll talk to you tomorrow.' Charlie was gonna have an alibi with a girl. He was gonna take her to a motel. I would go around the neighborhood. Stay around Passyunk Avenue. So I go take a shower. I use somebody's house. I change my clothes. Put jeans on because I was dressed up. I'm waiting. I figure the cops are gonna come around. I go to this bar on Twelfth and Morris. I'm sittin' there and I'm drinkin', all of a sudden this Big Mike, who used to run the bar, comes around.

"He says, 'Did you hear what happened? They whacked Pat.'

"'Get out,' I said. 'Where at?'

"'Eleventh and Mifflin,' he says. 'Two guys. They don't know who.'

"I says, 'No kidding. Jesus Christ.'

"All of a sudden they break in with it on the eleven-o'clock news—while Mike's talking to me—on television. So now I go back around the corner and, for the corner guys, I pretend like I'm crying. 'They killed my best friend. What am I gonna do? Pat was a good man.'

"But everybody was happy. Everybody hated him. I never seen a guy hated so much. Nobody around that corner liked him.

"The cops never came around. About eleven-thirty, Charlie calls me up from the motel. I'm in Marra's Restaurant. I tell him everything's cool. Don't worry about nothin'.'"

The next day the *Philadelphia Daily News* ran a story about the Spirito murder and the fact that police believed two of his close associates—one of whom had been arrested for counterfeiting and credit card fraud ("That was me," Caramandi said matter-of-factly)—were the key suspects. Charlie White Iannece saw the paper first and called Caramandi in a panic. The Crow told him to just sit tight. All week they expected to get pinched by the cops or the FBI, but they were never charged. Ciancaglini told them to keep a low profile and stay away from his clubhouse for a while. A week after the killing, Chuckie Merlino came around to the corner and took Caramandi and Iannece to Cravings Luncheonette.

"We sat down in a booth and he says, 'You can't get this,' indicating with his thumb and his fingers, you know, the badge, the button, 'because Nicky's away. So just be patient. Here's what we're gonna do. From now on, the elbow money, you guys keep half. Whatever youse two do, you keep half and the other half goes into the elbow. You know, there's seven or eight of us.'

"We says, 'Chuck, whatever way you wanna do it.' He says

he's gonna give us Cupcakes and whoever else Pat had. Pat had a few guys he was makin' a few bucks with. This guy Buster. And Cupcakes, who was a big bookmaker. And all the neighborhood guys became ours.

"We were the two guys on the corner. After that meeting, Chuckie was very happy and pleased with us. You know, they liked noise, these guys. They liked the style and the fashion we did it in. Right out on a fuckin' street corner. In a car. It made a lot of headlines. They like that. It scares people.

"So the neighborhood guys sorta knew we did it. And so did the FBI. But they couldn't prove it."

CHAPTER ELEVEN

uch has been written and said about how New Jersey's gaming regulations are the toughest in the world and about how organized crime has been unable to get a foothold in the multibillion-dollar Atlantic City casino industry.

Forget about it.

While it may be true that mobsters haven't yet found their way into the casino counting rooms—as they once did in Las Vegas—almost anywhere else you look in the city you'll find a wiseguy or one of his associates. The mob is on the floor of every casino in the city. It's in the restaurants and the casino lounges. It controls the labor union whose workers make the big casino-hotels go.

During boom times in the early 1980s, it had a piece—a big piece—of the construction industry. And when things got slow as the decade came to a close, the mob popped up behind the scenes manipulating a stock deal here, taking a rakeoff from a junk bond offering there. All the while it continued to provide drugs for casino patrons, escorts for high rollers, and illegal poker games, sports betting books, and easy credit for gamblers who tired of the neon lights and mind-numbing drone of the slot machines and roulette wheels. It ran junkets into the city from all over the country. It brought food and drink to the kitchens. And at the end of each busy day, it picked up the dirty laundry and hauled away the garbage.

Who needs the counting room and all the government heat that would come with a casino skimming operation? Let corporate America, that other branch of organized crime, run the gambling palaces in Atlantic City. The mob is making millions by simply feeding off their presence. By 1983, six years after Governor Brendan Byrne's grandstand warning to the mob to keep its "filthy hands" out of Atlantic City, there were nine casino-hotels operating in the city, and their gross win for the year was $1.77 billion. Nicodemo Scarfo, from a federal prison in Texas, was one of the most powerful men in town, and mobsters from all over the country were grabbing for a piece of the action.

The New Jersey State Commission of Investigation has documented mob involvement in real estate speculation, the construction industry, and the fight game, in which mobsters controlled fighters and promoters and had a hook into the closed-circuit television rights of certain bouts. Tommy DelGiorno and Frankie D'Alfonso from Philadelphia, Martin and Michael Taccetta from Newark, John DiGilio from Bayonne, and assorted other mob figures and associates showed up in the SCI report.

The SCI also raised serious questions about the brutality of boxing, pointing to numerous instances where fighters had gone into the ring unprepared or ill equipped to handle the legalized mayhem that would follow. Citing those reasons, the SCI recommended that boxing be banned in New Jersey.

That recommendation, of course, was about as effective as Governor Byrne's warning six years earlier. Boxing is big business in the casino industry. And if the mob had a piece of the action—as the SCI clearly demonstrated it did—or if a fighter might be risking permanent bodily injury, nobody seemed to care. Boxing matches bring crowds. Crowds bring money. And that is what Atlantic City is all about.

Even without control of a particular match, the mob benefits from the boxing boom in the city. You don't have to fix a fight to profit from it. The casinos, in promoting and staging prizefights, have created and imported a natural market for the mob's bookmakers. It's illegal to place a bet on a sporting event in New Jersey. There are no sports books in the casinos. In theory, then, these high rollers who come into town to see a heavyweight championship fight are there simply for the sport. But does anyone really believe that while they wager thousands in the gaming halls, they sit cheering at ringside without having placed a bet on the outcome of the fight?

And on Super Bowl Sunday, when the casinos open their amphitheaters for a showing of the football game and provide free food and drinks for their preferred players, does anyone think that no one in the room has any money down on the game?

There are mob loan sharks and bookmakers working each casino in the city, and on a fight night or on Super Bowl Sunday their action is phenomenal. The casinos know they're there. So do New Jersey law enforcement authorities. But the bookies are providing a service, just like the hookers who troll the casino lounges, and as long as everyone is discreet, what's the harm? Who's going to complain?

New Jersey's ever vigilant law enforcement authorities have cracked down in other areas, however. Usually when it is in the casinos' best interest to do so. For instance, in 1982, Las Vegas mobster John Vaccaro and Tony Gallagher, a representative of the North Jersey faction of the Genovese family, set up a slot machine scam that over a four-year period netted millions. Using a slot mechanic who knew how to manipulate the one-armed bandits, Vaccaro and company swooped through town claiming a series of jackpots before they were nabbed. In another case, Bonnano and DeCavalcante crime family leaders were linked to a junket operation that generated an estimated $6 million in kickbacks and payoffs before it was uncovered by the state police.

Politicians and law enforcement authorities point to these and other cases, all successfully brought to justice, as examples of the state's vigilance. But cynics, familiar with the casino industry, say they represent only the tip of the iceberg. Every day, they say, there's a deal going down in Atlantic City.

One of the Scarfo family's best began shortly before Little Nicky became boss and extended through 1983 while he was away in jail. This was the deal that Scarfo had first proposed to Phil Testa, the deal that he said would put the mob in City Hall.

Salvatore "Chuckie" Merlino, Scarfo's underboss, was in charge when the action began to unfold, but Merlino was based in Philadelphia. The real power at the shore was Scarfo's nephew, Philip "Crazy Phil" Leonetti, a handsome young capo and ruthless killer.

Leonetti grew up in Atlantic City, attended St. Michael's Grammar School around the corner from his home on North Georgia Avenue, and was a standout guard on the basketball team at Holy Spirit High School. Lean and muscular with piercing dark eyes and thick black hair, Leonetti had movie-star looks that enhanced his reputation as a local celebrity. By the age of thirty he had already been linked by investigators to three murders, including the Falcone killing and the death of a local tailor who had had the misfortune to get into an argument with Leonetti in a local bar one night. A few days later the tailor was found shot in the head, his car parked near a dump just outside Atlantic City. An eyewitness placed Leonetti near the scene of the shooting, but later recanted his identification. The county prosecutor had no case without the witness. Leonetti's reputation for violence was such that witnesses frequently suffered from memory lapses.

But Leonetti was more than a hit man. He was, like his uncle, a shrewd and calculating mobster. He recognized that Atlantic City was a treasure chest. And he wanted the key.

The first place he looked for it was City Hall.

In November 1981, Atlantic City voters approved a change in the form of government for the city, replacing a five-man city commission with a mayor and nine-member city council. The change was to take effect in May of the following year. Michael Matthews, a state assemblyman and former county freeholder, ran for mayor against James Usry, a former school administrator.

Scarfo and Leonetti became shadow figures in the campaign.

Matthews, whose mother was Italian, had the support of the city's white ethnic communities, primarily the Jewish, Irish, and Italian voters. Usry, who was black, drew the minority voters. Racial polarization and corruption have been two of the hallmarks of the city, and the 1982 campaign brought both of them out. Matthews, who beat Usry by fewer than four hundred votes, spent a fortune to get elected and then ran up enormous legal bills in a court battle over a recount.

By the time he was sworn in as mayor, a federal indictment would later charge, the mob already had him in its pocket. Zoning and planning approvals, variances, and sweetheart contracts were what Scarfo and Leonetti were looking for. They had funneled $185,000 to Matthews's campaign to get it.

Frank Lentino, a former Teamster who had become an organizer for Bartenders Local 54, was Leonetti's conduit to Matthews. The young mobster and the mayor met privately on several occasions, usually at the apartment or office of Kenny Shapiro, a Philadelphia wheeler-dealer who was speculating in Atlantic City real estate and who would later be described by the New Jersey SCI as a Scarfo mob "financier." So active was Shapiro that both the state police and the FBI had set up surveillance of his office on Atlantic Avenue. Shapiro's company was called Seatex. It operated out of a storefront around the block from Leonetti's construction company, Scarf Inc. In 1982 and 1983, detectives watching the office saw a steady parade of wiseguys. Leonetti or one of his associates would drop in. Then the brothers Michael and Martin Taccetta of the Lucchese organization. Then Corky Vastolla, the De-Cavalcante family's emissary to the casino city.

Lentino also introduced Matthews to Jimmy Biaco, another mob associate who was setting up several businesses that were looking for city contracts. Most important of all, Biaco and Lentino were working with Matthews to arrange the sale of a piece of city-owned land zoned for casino development. The mob was willing to pay for the land. But Biaco wanted to be sure that his bid was the one the city would accept. Matthews was offered a hidden interest in the casino development that would follow. Another silent partner would be Leonetti. Each would have a "point" in the casino-hotel.

Mike Matthews was sworn into office on July 1, 1982. He promised unity and progress to the residents of the city. Federal authorities believe he had already promised the Scarfo organization much more.

While Leonetti was busy corrupting the new mayor of Atlantic City, Nick Caramandi was tied up with more mundane mob matters. After the murder of "Pat the Cat" Spirito, Caramandi and Charlie Iannece began working directly with Salvatore Testa in the battle with the Riccobenes. Scarfo, safe in his prison cell at the federal penitentiary, would periodically send up messages through Leonetti or others who went down to visit him.

Scarfo was working in the prison laundry, but the dust and chemicals were bothering his allergies. He was not very comfortable. This made him irritable. So did the fact that neither Riccobene nor any of his loyalists had been killed.

"We kept getting these messages that he wanted to hear noise," Caramandi recalled. "One time we got this wire. He said to ask Salvie how the 'doctor' was doing. 'Doctor' was the code name we had for Harry Riccobene. In other words, he wanted to know why Harry hadn't been killed yet."

The reason Harry hadn't been killed was one Scarfo could appreciate. Late in 1982, Philadelphia police stopped Riccobene's car after some minor traffic violation. They found a gun under the seat. Riccobene, who was free on bail following his racketeering conviction, was hauled into court. His bail was revoked, and on January 10, 1983, he was placed behind bars—and out of the line of fire. In July, the remaining defendants in that racketeering case, including Riccobene's half brother Mario and Scarfo capo Joseph Ciancaglini, were also ordered imprisoned after their appeals were denied. Only Pasquale Spirito managed to avoid going to jail—he was dead.

With Harry and Mario Riccobene away, Scarfo drew up a new hit list and sent it to Testa, who quickly assigned crews of gunmen to work around the clock stalking potential victims. Caramandi, whose stature had improved after he and Iannece completed the Spirito contract, became a major player during this bizarre and bloody period in the Philadelphia underworld.

"Me and Charlie were in this restaurant one day that summer having lunch. Who comes around but Salvie and Gino Milano. Now, I don't know this Gino too well, and neither does Charlie. Gino's Salvie's man. He's a made guy. Salvie's the capo.

"Salvie tells us Chuckie [Merlino] sent him around to talk to us. He says Nicky has a new hit list with, like, eight, ten guys on the list, all Riccobene people. He says, 'I want you two guys to go after Robert Riccobene, Sonny's brother. Gino's gonna do the shootin'. You two guys help out.' Then he said, 'I'll be comin' around here a lot. We gotta get these guys. Nicky wants them.'

"So we go see Chuckie and tell him Salvie was around. He says, 'Whatever Salvie tells ya, you guys do.' So we says, 'Okay.'

"Now we hook up with this Gino. We know he's Salvie's man and we know he was involved in a couple of murders, but we don't know much else. And we start stalking this Bobby Riccobene."

Eugene "Gino" Milano was part of the new breed of the Philadelphia mob. He was just twenty-three years old and was already a made member, brought into the fold by Scarfo on the recommendation of Salvie Testa. Milano had been a standout athlete at South Philadelphia High School, where he starred in football and wrestling. He was also a good amateur boxer. But a knee injury cut short his athletic career and ended any chance he had to go to college. He was one of six children in a one-parent family. His mother, a widow, worked hard to provide all she could for her children, but the lure of big money and the fast life brought Gino—and eventually his younger brother, Nicholas—into the mob.

Milano's loyalty was to Testa rather than to the organization, however, a point that would be dramatically driven home several years later. He didn't really know Scarfo, Leonetti, or most of the other leaders of the family. He was Testa's friend as well as his "associate."

After high school, Milano had worked for a while as a counselor at a South Philadelphia community center. But he began hanging out with the young, charismatic Testa and eventually went to work as a bouncer at a popular center city restaurant where Salvie had some connections. Milano's real job was to stay close to Salvie, who was then in the midst of avenging his father's death. He was formally initiated into the family in 1982 after the beating of Frank D'Alfonso and the murder of Frank Narducci.

Now, despite the fact that Caramandi and Iannece were old enough to be Milano's father and that they each had twenty more years of street experience, they were forced to defer to young Gino in the stalking of Robert Riccobene.

Riccobene was the caretaker of one of his brother's more lucrative operations, illegal poker machines. Caramandi learned that he made rounds weekly to pick up the take from the machines, which had been placed in various stores and restaurants throughout South Philadelphia. One corner store at Seventh and Tasker streets seemed like the perfect spot for an ambush, and so Caramandi set the wheels in motion for a killing.

"Two weeks after we got the order, we're waiting between Morris and Moore streets. We're sittin' in the car. Charlie's got a .38. Gino's got a .38. I'm the driver. We had found out Riccobene used to drop around the store between six and seven o'clock at night. Sure enough, about six, six-thirty, we see him coming down Morris. He makes the left-hand turn on Seventh. We watch him park the car. I say, 'Okay, this is it.' I pull up to the corner. You could see him in the store. His back is to us. They're supposed to go in the store, shoot him, jump back in the car, and then I take off.

"I pull up. Charlie's on the end. Gino's in the middle. All of a sudden, Gino says, 'I don't like it. I don't like it. Let's get out of here.' So we left. He said he didn't like it. We didn't question it. We figured he's got more experience with these things. What the fuck did we know?"

Caramandi let the incident pass. But he learned from it. Slowly the idea began to take shape in his mind. In many ways he was smarter than a lot of the kids Scarfo and Salvie Testa had brought into the organization. Caramandi was not made yet, but he had been around a lot longer than some of the people who were. And as time went on he would come to realize that by using his brain and the instincts honed by thirty years of street hustling, he could move up in this organization. Caramandi knew he was being used. But in his heart he also knew that he could use the organization. Once he had the badge, the button—once he was an initiated member—he could make a fortune. He already knew how to make money. With the mob behind him, he could make it in multiples. That was his goal. And if he had to kill some of Scarfo's enemies to get there, he was willing to do it.

"Now Salvie's hanging around Passyunk and Moore and he's giving out assignments to crews every day. He made this his headquarters. Faffy, Tommy, and the Whip—that was Nicky Milano, Gino's brother. They were breaking him in at the time. They had Sammy Tamburrino. And Joe Pung, Wayne Grande, and Joe Grande had Richie Gunner, another guy on the hit list.

"In the meantime, we're looking for other spots to get Robert Riccobene, other places where he goes. At this time Cuddles DiCaprio got subpoenaed in the Hornickel murder investigation. Me and Charlie felt a little concerned about this, because Cuddles was our getaway driver when we killed Pat. He didn't see us do the shootin', but he heard the gunshots and he knew we threw the guns out. We were concerned because we didn't know him that well and we heard there was all kinds of shit with him.

"We're going to different spots trying to locate Robert Riccobene, and one day Salvie comes around with this guy Joe Rico. He used to be around Chick [Ciancaglini], but he could never get down because he was Jewish. I never trusted the guy. Charlie didn't trust him. But when Chick went to jail, this Rico got close to Salvie.

"So Salvie tells us that the next day Bobby Riccobene would be at Ninth and Catharine to get the machines. Joe Rico knows this is Bobby's day to come around and that he usually gets there around eleven o'clock in the morning. Salvie tells me, Charlie, and Gino to be ready; that there was a back door at this store and that Joe Rico would open it up for us. That would be the signal. So we said okay. We were just doing what we were told.

"Now, we were using an old car with dark windows. The next morning I tell Charlie let's go early and check out this area,'cause I don't trust this Joe Rico. Let's just check out the neighborhood and see what happens.

"We pick up Gino about nine-thirty in the morning and we go around the neighborhood. We see a truck parked with two guys in it. We see a car parked with two guys in it. And I know how the cops work and the FBI. They don't park close to the spot where you're going to. They park three or four blocks away. They don't stay in a big group because they don't want to be noticed. They'll sit with one guy in a car and one guy walking, and they got walkie-talkies and they zero in on the fuckin' spot.

"We just didn't like it. This fuckin' Joe Rico was standing on the corner. There was guys digging construction, all white guys, on Tenth and Bainbridge. I says, 'When'd you ever see white guys using jackhammers? It don't make any sense. These guys are FBI agents. There's somethin' wrong.' So we called it off, and later that day we sent for this Joe Rico. He never came around. So when Salvie came by, we said we didn't want to use Joe Rico for anything, we didn't trust him. I don't know if he was trying to set us up or what. He got arrested later in New Jersey for dealing in hot cars, and then he got charged in the Hornickel killing. I just didn't like the guy.

"The command post was at Camac and Moore. Salvie was there day and night giving out orders, different assignments to crews. And at times when we weren't working Bobby, we were working other guys also. I recall nights when I didn't go home. Three or four days at a time. Didn't even take a fucking bath. We worked around the clock. At this time Salvie was looking to shoot anybody. One time we get a wire that one of these guys is in La Cucina Restaurant. Now Salvie's got a gun. I got a gun. Charlie's waiting outside, and Salvie says, 'Let's go in there. If we see this guy in there we're gonna bang him right in the fuckin' joint.' We looked all over for this guy, but no dice. We didn't find anybody.

"Another time Salvie got a wire that this other guy who was on the hit list was gonna be in a club called Purgatory. So we set up positions, me, Charlie, Salvie, Joe Grande, and Joe Pungitore. Joe Pung was gonna be the getaway driver. Me, Charlie, and Salvie were gonna be the shooters. Charlie had a shotgun. Salvie had the .38 and I had an automatic. We're sitting on the corner, near the club. It's an after-hours club, so it closes at like four in the morning. We're waiting for this guy to show. Three o'clock. Four o'clock. We waited till five-thirty in the morning. He never came. See, these are some of the hazards and the aggravations that we had."

Early that fall, another Riccobene associate named Frank Martines was added to the hit list. Martines was a sometime loan shark and full-time carpenter who had passed the remark that he was neither concerned by nor afraid of Salvie Testa and the people he was with.

"Salvie was fuckin' enraged at this," Caramandi said.

DelGiorno and Iannarella had been assigned the murder contract, but were having trouble carrying it out. Caramandi offered to help. Sitting in a hotel room in Ocean City, Maryland, five years later, he calmly proceeded to tell the story of planning the murder of Frank Martines.

"He was a kid from my old neighborhood," Caramandi said. "I knew the guy."

Then he took out a yellow legal pad and, like Joe Paterno drawing an off-tackle slant, outlined the ambush that he set up, pointing out the strategic use of "blockers" whose cars would seal off the neighborhood until the gunmen had a chance to get away. As an aside and with respectful admiration, Caramandi noted, "They used twenty-seven blocks the time they killed Carmine Galante in New York. They killed him in a restaurant, but they had twenty-seven blockers to keep the streets clear."

Caramandi needed only four. He placed a blocker on each corner around Martines's home at 914 Morris Street. Once they heard the shots, they pulled their cars into the streets, blocking off any oncoming traffic until the getaway car had cleared the area. The plan, Caramandi said with pride, went off without a hitch.

But he was so caught up in the strategy of it all that he

seemed to lose sight of the fact that a man was being shot. It had become business. Just like the scams and the flimflams. Murder was part of what he did now, part of what he was. He accepted that. And he assumed those on the other side of the pistols and shotguns accepted it too. There was no remorse. A guy thinks he's buying hot stuff. He's a crook. You could rob him. A guy becomes part of the mob. He's a killer. You could kill him.

It was like playing hide-and-seek, or cops-and-robbers. Bang, bang, you're dead.

"Me and Charlie met at five o'clock one morning and we spotted the kid's carpenter truck at Ninth and Tasker," Caramandi recalled. "We park so we could see his house. About twenty after six we notice that the light went on in his bedroom. We figure he's just gettin' up, so we position ourselves. Sure enough, he comes out of the house and he's carrying a big carpenter's toolbox on his shoulder. He walks a block by himself to the truck. I says, 'Boy, this guy would be easy.'"

Caramandi reported the findings to Salvie Testa and got the go-ahead for the next day. Joe Pungitore, Frank Narducci, Jr., his younger brother Philip, and Joe Grande were assigned as blockers. Charlie White and Gino Milano were the shooters. Caramandi was to be the getaway driver. The seven arranged to meet at Fifteenth and Castle streets at 6:00 A.M.

It was one of the bloody ironies of the Philadelphia underworld that the Narducci brothers were members of a Scarfo hit squad. Scarfo, after all, had approved the January 1982 murder of their father, Frank "Chickie" Narducci. Yet his sons, Frank Jr.—who was adopted by Narducci when he was just a year old—and Philip, readily put their lives on the line for Little Nicky.

Law enforcement authorities were incredulous when the Narducci brothers were first identified by Caramandi as Scarfo hit men. How, they asked, could they work for—indeed, agree to murder for—a man who had ordered their own father's death? Even some mob members found it hard to believe. "I'll never understand that in a million fuckin' years," Tommy DelGiorno later told New Jersey state police.

But Caramandi said Scarfo had no problem using the Narducci boys because he didn't hold them responsible for "their father's sins."

"He felt these kids were just victims of circumstances,"

Caramandi said. "They wasn't part of no plots. So Nicky made a speech that he will not hold any sons responsible for their father's actions."

As for the kids working for Scarfo?

They probably knew what had happened, he said, "but they'll never bring it up. They want to be gangsters too much."

So it was that in August 1982, just eight months after his own father's murder, Philip Narducci was dispatched to Wildwood Crest, New Jersey, where he pumped a bullet into the neck of Joseph Salerno, Sr., the father of the Atlantic City plumber who had testified against Scarfo in the Falcone murder case. Salerno survived the attack, but another Mafia tradition—one that held that an enemy's family members should not be targeted for retribution—was shattered. Now, in October 1983, here were the Narduccis again preparing to go out and commit murder for Scarfo, working in fact for the very man, Salvie Testa, who had gunned down their father.

This time the target was Frank Martines.

"I give 'em their positions where to park. As soon as they hear shots they're to pull out and just block the streets for a minute until we get away. This morning his truck is parked right on the corner where he lived. They all get in position. They all go to these spots. Here's Joe Pung between Ninth and Tenth on Morris. Here's Joe Grande on Ninth Street facing north. Frankie Narducci is behind me. Gino and Charlie are on foot, hiding. Charlie's around the corner. Gino's across the street near this bar.

"When Martines finally comes, it's quiet. It's a quarter to seven in the morning. He walks to his truck. When Charlie hears him open the truck door, he jumps out from around the corner right in front and starts shooting.

"First shot hits him in the chest, Charlie said, 'cause he hears Martines go 'Ahhh.' Gino comes running and fires five times right into the window. He empties the gun out. Charlie shot three times and thought he got him twice. Gino thought he got him with whatever he shot. Because when they ran back to the car and I picked them up, I said, 'Is he dead?' Gino said, 'Yeah, he's dead. I hit him with every shot.' But he missed him. Charlie got him with a shot and Gino got him once in the arm. But the other four musta missed him because he musta ducked.

"So Joe Grande pulls over here. Frankie Narducci pulls out

behind me and we get away clear. They hold it for a minute, minute and a half.

"That was the first guy of the Riccobene crew that we hit. But he survived it. I don't know how the fuck he did, but he survived it.

"What's funny about it is, Tommy and Faffy were a little jealous. They're bugged with us because even if we weren't successful, at least we did it. This Martines was the first guy since the incident with Harry who'd taken a shot. The kid didn't die, but after a lot of frustrating months with Harry and Sonny, over a year it was, we were happy. Salvie was happy. "Now everybody started coming around Camac and Moore. Like I said, that was the command post. And the stalkings continued."

"One night about eleven we all met around Twentieth and Oregon. Joe Pung. Gino. Myself. Charlie. Nicky Whip. Lawrence. Philip. Salvie. There was a club there, and they start dispersing the crews. Me, Charlie, and Gino, we're looking for Bobby Riccobene. We had gotten a wire that he had a girlfriend on Greenwich Street. Charlie happened to know a guy whose back yard was almost next to the girl's house. We made arrangements to use the house as part of a stakeout.

"Anyhow, we're looking for Bobby's car. Finally, I spot it about one, one-thirty in the morning parked on the northeast corner, popping out. The end car. We said this was a good setup.

"So we went into Charlie's friend's house and set up a plan. When Bobby Riccobene would come to his car, I would pull out and block the street off. He would be behind me. The guys would run out of the house, shoot him in the car, then jump into my car, and we'd take off. We'd just leave him the fuck in the street.

"So, the plan was set. I'm sittin' in the car and I'm waitin'. All of a sudden, about three-thirty, here comes Bobby Riccobene. He starts his car. I'm watching through the window. He pulls out. As he's pullin' out, I pull out. And I got him blocked behind me. I'm stopped a couple doors down so he couldn't see our guys runnin' out of the house. So now I'm sittin' there in the middle of the street and he's behind me. I'm waiting for Charlie and Gino to come out. A minute goes by, a minute and a half, two minutes. No one's coming. Now

Bobby Riccobene starts blowing the horn, but I still stay there. He knows me good. I used to play cards with him. I knew him over the years. But he was a dumb fuckin' kid, though.

"I'm worried about him getting out of the car. I wait a good three or four minutes. These guys don't come out. He's blowing the horn. So I pull away. I ride around and come back to the house. I say, 'What the fuck happened?' Gino says, 'Ahh, I didn't like it. It's too fuckin' dangerous. Three o'clock in the morning, all the noise it woulda made.' You know, some kind of excuse.

"So we dropped Gino off at his house, and Charlie tells me what happened. He says, 'Man, what am I gonna do? I was ready to go. I had the shotgun in my hand, but he just didn't want to do it.' We were gettin' disgusted at Gino. We figured he was another Pat. So we go right over Salvie's house, at four o'clock in the morning. And we tell him, 'Listen, we don't wanna work with this guy no more.' He was a little surprised to hear this, Salvie. We told him what happened. We told him the whole story. And he says, 'Look, I'll take him off the assignment for a while. Gino isn't usually like that.'

"See, Gino was one of his main guys. Salvie bragged about him, and for us to beef on him was a shock. I said, 'Listen, we don't wanna beef, but, I mean, we're tired. We had the guy fucking dead. It was a good spot.'

"I mean, these were maybe awful things, but they hadda be done."

Caramandi figures there were at least a dozen ambushes set for Robert Riccobene over the last six months of 1983. Faffy Iannarella replaced Gino Milano on the hit squad and at one point toyed with the idea of using a motorcycle for a drive-by shooting like the terrorists in Italy. On another occasion Caramandi and Charlie White pulled their car into a small street in South Philadelphia and found Riccobene driving right at them. The street was too small for two cars, but there were too many people around for Caramandi to take advantage of the situation.

"We backed out and let him pass," he said. "He looked right at me."

In addition to Riccobene, Caramandi and Charlie White had also gotten the ticket for Bobby Rego, a Riccobene associate in the methamphetamine business. Caramandi found Rego's house, located on a cul-de-sac in South Philadelphia. Fortunately for Rego, he was seldom home.

"Charlie and me used to take turns," Caramandi said. "One of us would stay in the car. The other would go knock on the door. If he answered, we were gonna shoot 'im. But he was never there. He was a lucky motherfucker, that Rego."

But Sammy Tamburrino, another Riccobene loyalist, wasn't.

"Tommy and Faffy were stalking him. They had this team that included Philip Narducci and Nicky Milano, the Whip. One day Faffy and Tommy are telling a bunch of us that they had a good shot at Sammy Tamburrino. They were stalking a store he had around Sixty-sixth and Dix. It was a candy store or something, with some video machines in it. And they said they were pretty sure they were gonna get him that night.

"So we waited. We met with Salvie that night. We're sitting around and about ten o'clock I spot Faffy coming in the door. He sees me first and he hollers, 'Yo, Crow. Touchdown.' 'Touchdown' meant it was done. Sammy Tamburrino came to the store, and Philip and Whip went in there and shot him.

"Faffy told us what happened in more detail. He says, 'That fuckin' Whip is crazy.' Faffy says they were waiting and waiting and finally they spot Tamburrino going into the store and they tell the Whip, 'That's the guy, going in there now.' 'Cause a lot of our guys didn't know what Harry's guys looked like.

"Tommy and Faffy tell him it's the guy with the green sweater. So they go in the store. They buy some chewing gum or something and they come out.

"They said to Tommy and Faffy, 'The guy don't have on a green sweater, it's a blue sweater.' Tommy and Faffy say, 'That's the fucking guy. Get back in there.' So they run back in and they finally bang the guy. They said the mother was standing there screaming.

"They drove all the way back down to South Philly. Four guys in the car. They parked the car around Twenty-fifth and Wolf. See, in those days we used to get cars. Tommy had a connection, and we'd get cheap cars for a couple hundred bucks and register them under fictitious names. And after a hit, we'd junk the cars, scrap them so the cars wouldn't be found.

"The next day, the Whip comes over my house for something and I congratulate him. And he says, 'Crow, I got him with the first bullet right here.' And he points his finger at his head."

While the Sammy Tamburrino shooting was big news around the mob clubhouse at Camac and Moore, it attracted scant media attention. "Variety Store's Owner Killed by Two Gunmen" read the headline on a short story on page five of the *Philadelphia Daily News* the next day. The *Inquirer* ran an even shorter story on page seven of its metro section with a headline declaring: "Proprietor Is Fatally Shot in Southwest Phila. Store." Neither article mentioned any connection between the killing and the ongoing mob war between the Scarfo and Riccobene factions.

With the next round of gunfire, however, the mob made page one.

CHAPTER TWELVE

After more than six months of stalking, planning, and scheming, one of Salvie Testa's hit teams brought down Robert Riccobene on December 6, 1983.

"Shotgun Blast Kills Half Brother of Mobster Riccobene" read the next morning's headlines. There were also the all too familiar sidebar accounts of the Mafia war that was ripping through the Philadelphia underworld. In those stories, the death of Sammy Tamburrino, which had occurred one month earlier, was given perspective. He was included among the list of more than twenty mob members or associates killed since the assassination of Angelo Bruno in March 1980.

Ironically, both Tamburrino and Riccobene had been shot to death in front of their mothers, another departure from what had been considered mob protocol. But Scarfo had made it clear early on that he had little regard for the traditions of the organization when they did not suit his purposes. Greed and vengeance were what drove him, and even from a federal prison cell in Texas he was able to impose his will—and his ruthless style—on the streets of Philadelphia.

Faffy Iannarella, a forty-year-old up-and-comer in the organization, carried out the hit and later bragged to Caramandi and Testa about the way he used a sawed-off shotgun to blast Bobby Riccobene into oblivion. The shooting occurred after a day of intense stalking that began with Caramandi tailing Riccobene through South Philadelphia as he made his stops for poker machine receipts. Originally, the plan was to ambush Riccobene around Eighth Street and Oregon Avenue, a busy intersection about a mile from the clubhouse. But when Riccobene didn't show there, Iannarella, Charlie White, and Joey Pungitore moved out to Southwest Philadelphia and set an ambush near the home of Riccobene's seventy-four-year-old mother, Jean. Those stalking Riccobene had learned that he frequently visited his mother.

Caramandi and Salvie Testa, frustrated by the failure to make the hit at Eighth and Oregon, returned to the clubhouse at Camac and Moore and waited to hear from the others. Shortly after 10:00 P.M. the phone rang.

"Salvie gets on the phone, then he hangs up and says, 'Come on. We gotta go to Joe Pung's house.' We walk outside. We get in the car and who's pulling up but an OC guy [a detective assigned to the police department's organized crime unit]. He used to watch us all the time. So we make a few turns and we lose him. We go to Joe Pung's house and into the cellar. There's Charlie, Faffy, and Joe Pung. Beautiful home he had. It was his mother's house. Gorgeous home. Big bar down the cellar.

"So, Faffy starts to tell the story. He says, 'I don't know if I killed him.' He said, 'We got up there. We musta beat him by two minutes.' Charlie parked the car maybe a hundred and fifty yards from his house in this cul-de-sac. Faffy got out of the car. When they [Robert Riccobene and his mother] pulled up, it looked like they were gonna go in through the back way, because they had a driveway in the back of the house.

"They got out of the car, the mother and Bobby Riccobene, and started to walk. So as Faffy's coming down the street— he musta been about fifty feet away from him—Bobby Riccobene says, 'Oh, shit,' and starts running.

"Now they had a Cyclone fence in the back of the house. Faffy takes off after him. Bobby jumps over this fuckin' Cyclone fence and Faffy fires the shotgun. Bobby rolls and the mother starts screaming and she's grabbing ahold of Faffy, so Faffy hits her with the butt of the gun. He said he had no choice. And Charlie's screaming, 'Let's get out of here. Let's get out of here.'"

Newspaper and radio accounts the next morning removed any doubt in Iannarella's mind about whether his hit had been successful. Bobby Riccobene, forty-three, was killed by a single shotgun blast to the back of the head while his mother looked on in horror. The gunman fled in a waiting car. The murder weapon had been recovered by police. And unlike the

Tamburrino killing, there was never any doubt that the assassination was related to the power struggle within the Scarfo organization.

"The next morning I'm listening to the radio and I hear, 'Bobby Riccobene Shot,'" Caramandi said. "It's all over the fuckin' news. And who comes over my house but Faffy, at fuckin' eight o'clock in the morning. And he starts to tell me the story all over again.

"Faffy had gotten special bullets for this shotgun—high-powered buckshot. He's tellin' me the story all over again, about hittin' the mother. I said to him, 'Don't worry about it. It's one of them things.'"

Four days after the Riccobene murder, police reported that Salvatore Testa and three associates were ambushed as they were driving in a car near Eleventh and Catharine streets in South Philadelphia. According to police accounts, a car pulled out in front of the late-model Oldsmobile in which Testa was riding, blocking its forward progress. Then shots rang out. Gino Milano, who was driving the Olds, jammed it into reverse and pressed down hard on the gas pedal. Milano tried to maneuver out of the narrow street, but struck a utility pole. He, Testa, Joey Pungitore, and a fourth man scrambled out of the car and fled on foot. They were rounded up later by police. The would-be assailants took off in their own car. Testa and the others were questioned about the shooting. They said they knew nothing.

The aborted attempt on Testa's life was a desperate, last-ditch effort by the beleaguered Riccobenes to turn the tide. With that failure, the hostilities ended. A short time later Chuckie Merlino sent word around to Camac and Moore that the war was over.

There was, however, one postscript to the bloodletting, a macabre twist to the killings. On December 14, Enrico Riccobene, the twenty-seven-year-old son of Mario Riccobene, took a .380 caliber pistol, walked into the safe in the back of his jewelry store on Sansom Street, held the gun to his left temple, and pulled the trigger.

Riccobene was a quiet, polite, and well-mannered boy who had no apparent connection with the underworld in which his father and uncles traveled. The killings had taken their toll, however. After the murder of his uncle Robert, Enrico stayed away from his jewelry store for several days. When he finally did show up, he had a bevy of bodyguards around him. On the day of his death, someone came into the store and said that Salvie Testa, Phil Leonetti, and Lawrence Merlino had been outside looking for him. Enrico Riccobene was literally frightened to death.

"He was a good kid," Caramandi would say later. "He just got scared. He thought they were after him. He never did nothin', the kid. Nobody wanted to hurt him."

The death of Enrico Riccobene further enhanced the street reputation of Salvie Testa. When Testa heard the details he told Caramandi, "Look at this. Now we can kill guys without bullets. They use their own guns. That's how afraid they are of us."

The suicide was also the first in a series of tragic and bizzare subplots that would unfold during the rise and fall of Nicodemo Scarfo. There would be times over the next five years when events surrounding the life and times of Little Nicky would read like the script from an Italian opera, full of passion, lust, betrayal, vengeance, and, above all, irony. But in December 1983, no one could believe that the son of a mobster would want to kill himself. Eventually, Little Nicky himself would come face to face with that reality.

With the end of hostilities in the Riccobene war, the Scarfo loyalists began to collect the spoils. Testa and Merlino supervised the takeover of virtually all of Harry Riccobene's businesses. The vending machine trade went to Joey Pungitore, and most of Riccobene's associates—and their loan-sharking and bookmaking operations—were assigned to the boys at Camac and Moore.

"Salvie assigned most of these guys to me and Charlie," Caramandi said. "By the end of '83, everything was cool."

Tommy DelGiorno hosted a Christmas party at his house that year, a combination holiday and victory party. And for the New Year, Caramandi, Iannece, DelGiorno, and Iannarella headed for Atlantic City. It was time for some rest and relaxation.

Robert Riccobene and Sammy Tamburrino were dead. Frank Martines had been gunned down. Harry and Mario Riccobene were in jail. And the Riccobene loyalists still on the street had lost the desire to fight. After eighteen tense and deadly months of virtually living on twenty-four-hour alert, Caramandi got a chance to slow down, to pause and reflect on where he stood in the organization.

He and Charlie White were both proposed members now. They had killed Pat the Cat. They had been part of the team that wounded Frank Martines. And they were conspirators in the Robert Riccobene murder. What's more, they had developed a good relationship with Salvie Testa, clearly the dominant force in the family in Philadelphia.

Scarfo would be returning from prison soon, but both he and his nephew Philip Leonetti spent most of their time in Atlantic City. Chuckie Merlino was the underboss, but Chuckie had some problems. That summer he had been picked up on a drunken driving charge in Margate. Merlino, who often drank more than he could handle, tried to bribe the police officer who brought him in for a Breathalyzer test. He offered $400 in cash and his gold watch. Merlino made this offer while he was in the police station. The cops got it all on videotape.

No one ever mistook the Merlino brothers for brain surgeons, but this was stupidity of the highest order. Now Chuckie was in real trouble. Drunken driving was one thing. He might lose his license. Attempted bribery was another. Everyone agreed he would have to do some time. There didn't seem to be any way to get him out of the box. And even though that prison sentence was still somewhere down the road, by the end of 1983 it was clear that Salvatore Testa was the heir apparent, if not of Scarfo, then certainly of Merlino.

Testa's position was solidified even more by the fact that he was engaged to Merlino's beautiful young daughter, Maria. The marriage, scheduled for the last Saturday in April 1984, would confirm the Merlino-Testa underworld alliance and enhance the power of both men in South Philadelphia. If Chuckie went away, it would be only natural for Salvie Testa to look after the affairs of his soon-to-be father-in-law.

"I really had a good relationship with Salvie," said Caramandi. "I'm still doing the shakes. Doing what I'm doing. And Salvie's very pleased.

"One night he invites me and this woman I was dating out to dinner with him and his girlfriend, Maria. Took us to this real nice restaurant. But then he gets in a beef with Maria. She's telling him, 'My father bought me all this jewelry,' stuff like that. See, Salvie was a down-to-earth type of guy. He lived on 2117 Porter Street, where his father had lived, and while they're waiting to get married, Maria's having the fuckin' house redone with French toilets and Jacuzzis. And even though it was sorta old-fashioned, that's the way Salvie wanted to live. He wanted to live in his father's footsteps. He didn't like all that fancy stuff. So they got in an argument. My father did this and my father did that. Well, you could see this guy was fed up with her. I could tell then there was no love there. He was just marrying her because she was the underboss's daughter. Little did I know that Salvie had it in his mind to break off the wedding.

"Anyway, we continued to shake down, me and Charlie. We're hanging at Camac and Moore. But now, all of a sudden like, Tommy and Faffy's coming around every day. See, they wanted that fuckin' corner, these two birds. They wanted that corner bad. I could tell there was treachery with Tommy and Faffy. This fuckin' Faffy, he was something. He was always trying to get you in trouble all the time, trying to get you killed.

"And Tommy was like a fuckin' puppet. Faffy used to steam him up and Tommy used to get drunk and he would do all the talking. Faffy just used to lay back."

They were an odd couple, DelGiorno and Iannarella, and through them, Caramandi would discover that the jealousy and intrigue within the organization could be as deadly as anything outside it.

Tommy DelGiorno had the look of a weasel, which fit his character. He was short and thin, with sharp features and a slightly hooked nose. He seldom looked anyone in the eye, and when he talked, it was usually out of the side of his mouth. He lied his way out of the army, pretending to be mentally ill. For a time he drove a truck for United Parcel and ran a small numbers operation on the side. Then he became an associate of several mob members and expanded into sports betting and the restaurant business, and got involved in some boxing deals. But illegal gambling remained his forte, earning him about $100,000 a year.

Tommy Del didn't have much education, but he was good with figures. And, like most mobsters, he was obsessed with money. He always kept a stash on the side for hard times. He was the kind of guy who, during the Bruno era, would have been a career mob associate, never a made member. This was in part due to his character. Even mobsters had trouble trusting him. But character flaws aside, DelGiorno simply didn't qualify. Tommy DelGiorno's mother was Polish. To be a made member, both your parents had to be of Italian descent. DelGiorno, after becoming a government witness, acknowledged that his weren't. From the witness stand he mockingly said that Scarfo had not been aware of his mother's Polish heritage and had initiated him into La Cosa Nostra.

"It was an oversight on his part," DelGiorno said of Scarfo.

Francis "Faffy" Iannarella came from more acceptable stock. His father, a longtime South Philadelphia bookmaker, was a made member of the Bruno family. And Faffy, who had the roguish good looks of a Robert De Niro, acted as if he were born to be a gangster. A decorated Vietnam War veteran, Faffy was a fearless street fighter who seemed to relish confrontation and the chance to prove how tough he was.

Once, in the middle of the Riccobene war, Iannarella was in a bar at the Hilton Hotel in South Philadelphia with Joey Merlino, the young son of mob underboss Chuckie Merlino. The younger Merlino was a target of the Riccobenes. On this night, several members of the Riccobene faction, headed by Sammy Tamburrino, had the Hilton staked out and were preparing to close in.

"Faffy's aunt was in the hotel that night," Caramandi said. "So he sent her home to get a gun and bring it back to him. After she came back, he goes up to Tamburrino, puts the gun to his head, and announces that he and Joey are walking out. 'Anybody tries anything and I'll blow your fucking head off,' he tells Tamburrino.

"Faffy had a lot of balls. A lot of heart. But he was treacherous."

For more than a year, Caramandi's primary concern had been avoiding an ambush from someone connected with the Riccobenes. Now, within his own mob family, he was discovering another more insidious type of minefield. Three years after Bruno's death, the crime organization of the Docile Don was populated by vicious and greedy men who only paid lip service to the so-called code of honor that governed their organization. Caramandi's antennae were up again.

"I had a couple of incidents with Tommy. One of the first incidents was after Pat got killed. In the spring or summer of 1983, we went down to Turnberry, Florida. Me, Charlie, Faffy, and Tommy, on the assumption that we're gonna make a score on this guy who was a friend of Spike DiGregorio's. See, Spike was living down there now. This is years after we did that scam for Scarfo, back in 1971.

"So, we go to Florida. We stay at a nice hotel, two suites. And who's living there but James Caan, the movie star. We met him.

"So me and Spike go talk to this friend of his nicknamed Face of a Dog. He was a druggist who serviced care centers with the medicines and everything. So I try to sell him the thousand-dollar-bill deal. Now we coulda taken ten thousand dollars off the guy. He was that easy. But I said to Spike, 'This fuckin' guy, whadda we wanna rob this guy? By the time we whack it up and everybody gets an end, we're gonna wind up with a thousand dollars apiece.' So I says, 'It don't pay to rob him. I mean, whadda we gonna make out of it?' And Spike agreed and we didn't make the score.

"Then one night we're at the bar in Turnberry, me and Charlie and Tommy. I'm a little drunk. Tommy's a little drunk. And we get into some beef. I'm ready to punch Tommy, but Charlie stops me. He puts me onto the elevator and the next morning Charlie says, 'What the fuck's wrong with you? You crazy? You could get killed.' See, in this business, if you punch another made guy, he could ask for your life. That's a no-no. You could have an argument with him, but if you punch him, he could ask for your life and it's up to the consigliere and the boss to decide whether you're dead or not.

"But when you're drinkin', sometimes you don't know. And after we came back to Philadelphia, they wanna put me on the shelf. They wanna go to Chuckie and tell him. But Charlie spoke up for me. When they say put a guy on the shelf, that means you can't have anything to do with family business anymore and you're just a fuckin' jerkoff. I woulda had to leave town. Luckily, it got smoothed over, though after that we never really got along, me and Tommy.

"See, Tommy used to like to go with crowds, with guys. He used to like to have seven or eight guys with him, go to these bars and terrorize people. I did all that shit twenty years ago. Understand what I mean? I didn't go for that bullshit. Then one night I went out with him. I ended up punching a guy and getting in a fight with the owners of a club on South Street. And these guys, who it turns out were with Philip Leonetti, beefed. But Tommy didn't pick up for me. So I had another fuckin' problem. Philip came and he said, 'Oh, I didn't know it was you. I thought it was Nicky Whip [Milano]. Just forget about it.'

"See, you gotta remember, in this chain of command, you never knew when a guy above you said something about you. It's like politics, this thing. So, I had my problems with Tommy and Faffy. They were looking to zing me in the worst way. In fact, Tommy sent this guy around to me who asked, 'I heard there's meth around this corner. Maybe you know something about it?' I said, 'I don't know nothing about no fuckin' meth.' It was one of Tommy's traps. They were jealous because me and Charlie had that corner tied up. Everybody would come to us. The shake guys were coming to us. And they wanted this corner. And they figured if they could get rid of me, they'd take care of Charlie later. It was divide and conquer. But I always stayed one step ahead of them.

"There was another trap. After Pat got killed, Tommy and Faffy invited me and Charlie to dinner. They took their wives. I went with this Marlene who I was seeing. This posh South Street restaurant had opened up. Upstairs there's a nice club, a really hot spot. Nice people go there and so forth. Anyway, Tommy and Faffy wanted to go there 'cause I used to talk about what a nice place it was. So I musta called five or six times, and every time I called, the guy who ran it would say, 'Well, we're booked up six months in advance. We can't give you no reservation.' And this and that.

"But this is the place where Tommy and Faffy want to go. So I finally get the guy to give me a reservation. Now Tommy says, 'You should tell this guy off. You should really lay it on him. Scare him to death.'

"The four of us couples go. We musta spent a thousand dollars eating and drinking. We ordered eight, ten bottles of Château Lafite at sixty bucks a pop. And we ain't got no money, me and Charlie. These guys are picking up the tab.

"So we're there for a couple of hours, telling jokes, and we're having a lot of fun. After we're done eating we go upstairs. And they start ordering bottles of Dom Pérignon. Now when we were downstairs, this fuckin' maître d' came over and said hello, but he didn't even buy us a lousy drink. So Tommy's talking. He's sizzling me up. He says, 'You know, you oughta tell this guy. You oughta lay the law down with him.'

"But Tommy knew that this fella was a friend of Big Donnie. And Big Donnie was with Russell Bufalino [the mob boss of

Northeastern Pennsylvania]. He's not a made guy, Big Donnie, but he was around Bufalino. So Tommy's saying, 'You oughta tell this fuckin' guy.' And I says, 'You think I should?'

"Anyway, I get the guy and I sit him down. It's me, Tommy, Charlie, and Faffy. The five of us are sitting off to one side. And I tell this guy, 'Listen, you goddam motherfucker, if you ever turn us down for a reservation again I'll kill ya. I'll kill your family.' I says, 'You got any kids?' He said he had three kids. I said, 'I'll kill your kids. And this guy was terrified. I really read him his rights. I destroyed him. The guy was crying. And Tommy and Faffy were laughing. Charlie's laughing. I'm pretty bombed up. This guy was so scared, he sends over a bottle of champagne. He was terrified.

"The very next day, I'm in trouble. Who sends for me but Chuckie. Donnie went to see Chuckie that day. And Donnie told him about the maître d' and what a good friend he is. Chuckie has to show this Donnie some respect because he's with Russell Bufalino.

"I'm not made or anything. This was another one of Tommy's traps. I go see Chuckie. I don't know what it's about.

"He says, 'What the fuck did you do?'

"I says, 'What? What?'

"He says, 'What are you doing threatening to kill guys and kill their families?' I says, 'Jesus, Chuck.' I explained how the guy had kept turning us down and I said I wanted to put a little scare in him. But I couldn't remember very much of what I had said because I was so bombed up. Charlie's with me, but he ain't saying much.

"I go back around the corner, and who comes around, later that day, but Tommy and Faffy. I told them what happened. Little did I know that they seen Chuckie already. And they told Chuckie I acted terrible. I was awful. I shouldn't of did that to this guy. I says to myself, 'How about these motherfuckers. These are the guys that sizzled me up, told me to tell him. And they told Chuckie another story.'

"Me and Charlie have a conference, and I say, 'See, Charlie. It's no use with these guys. They never back you up.'

"What kills me is that now I'm barred from the fuckin' place. These guys could go up there again, but Chuckie tells me I'm barred and to stay out of there. But Tommy and Faffy are going up there all the time, dancing and having a good time. You understand what I'm saying? I paved the way for them and they look like they're the good guys now.

"Then, another time, on the Fourth of July, I get in another beef with Tommy. He's trying to break my fuckin' balls. I get drunk and I jump up, almost throw the table over. Charlie has to pull me out again. The next day, I went to Tommy's house and apologized. See, I hadda do this shit. But they wanted me to throw that first punch just to get me in trouble. Tommy was always jealous.

"Take the time we were in Florida, in Turnberry. After we scrapped the druggist scam, Spike connected with this guy named Craig who owned boats or something. Spike got him up to Philadelphia, and with him is another guy, a retired guy who lives in Florida, who's supposed to have mob connections in Chicago.

"So I told Tommy and Faffy about it. Charlie knew about it. See, when you're doing something, you always gotta register it.

"Spike gets this guy from Florida to stay at the Hilton Hotel on Tenth and Packer. And I sell these guys the thousand-dollar bills. The deal is set for fifty percent. They're gonna buy a hundred thousand dollars' worth of bills for fifty thousand. But he's gotta first fly back to Florida and then to Chicago and then back to Philadelphia.

"So now the day is set. The guy's flying in on an early-morning flight. The meet is at the Bellevue Stratford Hotel. I'm all dressed up in a suit and tie. He thinks my name is Frank. Spike's gonna bring him there around noon. I told him I do business in a bank. The bank is across the street on Broad and Walnut.

"Charlie White's across the street in a restaurant. I'm sitting at a table by myself, waiting for Spike to bring this guy in. At about twelve-thirty they arrive. I says, 'What the fuck took you so long? Jesus Christ, I got this guy waiting in the bank. Are you guys ready?' And I says, 'Who's got the money? You got the money, Spike?' And he says, 'No, he's got the money.' So I says to the guy, 'Give me the money. Wait here. Give me five minutes. Let me get across the street. Then you guys come over to the bank and I'll have your money ready. 'Cause I gotta get it from the vice-president.'

"The guy hands me the money. I look at it. You see, I've had experiences in the past where guys give you an empty fuckin' bag. So I always make sure the money's in there.

"I get the money and I go outside. I give Charlie the signal. I put my right hand to my left chest. I got the money. Now, boom. There's this guy Frankie the Bear waiting for us. He's parked on Locust Street. Now I gotta get Spike away from this guy. Remember, this guy just came in from Florida. So what I do, we go to Broad and Locust, and I make this guy Frankie the Bear call the cops. He tells 'em that four black guys with shotguns just walked into the bank. They're gonna rob the bank.

"Well, that's a distress call. You got cops around that bank in one minute. Now, when Spike walks out of the hotel, all of a sudden there's police cars and sirens and cops coming from every angle. So Spike, just like I had told him to do, says to the guy, 'Oh my God. There's Frank. They're grabbing Frank. Let's get out of here.' We called this sort of thing 'letting the guy see the movies.' We give him the full treatment. He sees all these cops. Then Spike tells him, 'You go that way. I'll go this way. I'll call ya later. Let's get out of here. They grabbed Frank.' The guy's in disarray. The sucker don't know what's going on. He's in a strange town.

"And Spike gets away; he grabs a cab and comes downtown.

"Now I got the fifty thousand, me and Charlie. I got the money at my house and we call Tommy and Faffy to tell them we made the score. They say they'll meet us that night at Charlie White's house.

"Now Spike says, 'How much you think I'm gonna get out of this?' And I says, 'I don't know, Spike. You know, this money's gotta go a lot of ways here. It's up to them.'

"What happens next is the treachery. We're at Charlie White's house. They come over. It's me, Charlie, Tommy, and Faffy. We got the fifty thousand. Now they start dividing the money. First they took five thousand off the top for expenses from when we went to Turnberry. Now they say they get a third. They took fifteen thousand. Chuckie gets an end, fifteen thousand. And they tell me, 'You, Spike, and Charlie cut up the other fifteen thousand.' That's five thousand apiece. So I says, 'Spike ain't gonna be happy with this money, Tommy.'

"He says, 'I don't give a fuck. Let him make a beef.' And I says, 'Well, I'm just tellin' ya, he ain't gonna be happy. You know, it was his man. It's a fifty-thousand-dollar score and he's only winding up with five thousand.' He says, 'Well, that's the way it goes.' Now he says, 'You owe me some money.' I owed him about two thousand. He says, 'I'm takin' a thousand of what you owe me.' So I'm left with four thousand. And I can't say nothing.

"The next morning Spike comes around and we say, 'This is your end, Spike.' And I says, 'Now Spike, whatever you do, don't beef. I ended up with four thousand. Tommy even took out the thousand I owe him.' We even gave him a thousand dollars apiece more out of our money. But he's moaning. He's bugged as a motherfucker."

That night Spike DiGregorio went to a bar and started to drink. The more he drank, the bolder he became. He decided he wasn't going to take the short end of a scam that he had put in motion. He figured his end was worth more than 10 percent of the deal.

"He's in this bar, Frankie Ford's, on Seventh and Kater, and he's drinking. He's with Lawrence Merlino and he starts beefing about Tommy, about how the split went down. Who calls on the phone but Chuckie Merlino. Spike's drunk. He don't know who the fuck he's talking to. And he starts talking about Tommy, calling him a two-bit fuckin' hood. Now Faffy shows up at this bar. Faffy calls me at my house and he says, 'You better come over here. This fuckin' guy's shooting his mouth off. He's beefing.' Now Faffy's a sizzler, understand what I mean? He's stroking. He wants Spike to bury himself. Spike don't know he's talking to Chuckie. He thought he was talking to Philip [Leonetti].

"So me and Charlie get over there and we say, 'Come on, Spike, get in the car.' Now Spike gets scared. He thinks we want to kill him.

"We drive him home, he was staying with his mother, and I tell him, 'You motherfucker, you know what you were saying? You were talking to Chuckie. You got a problem now and we can't help ya.' So I get him home and me and Charlie tell his mother, 'Lock him in the house and keep him there.'

"The next day, who comes around the corner but Tommy and Faffy. 'Where the fuck is Spike?' Tommy says. 'Who's he calling has-beens? That motherfucker belongs to me. I'm gonna get a chain saw and cut his fuckin' heart out.' Now there's a fuckin' commotion.

"Later, me and Charlie go to Spike's house. We sit him down. We say, 'Listen, the only chance you got is to go to Tommy's house and apologize. And you better get on your hands and knees, because we can't help you. We're not in a position to help you.' First of all, we weren't made yet. And Tommy and Faffy had Chuckie's ear.

"So, Spike goes over and apologizes. Says he was drunk and he didn't realize what he was saying. And Tommy lets him go. Later, I said, 'See, Spike, with the kind of guys you're dealing with here, you gotta be very, very careful.' "

DelGiorno and Iannarella also tried to turn the $50,000 score into a problem for Caramandi by telling Merlino that the Crow called the cops. This would have been another violation of the underworld code. One of the unwritten rules of the organization was that you never called the police, no matter what the circumstances. In Caramandi's mind it was petty nonsense. But he also saw it as another example of the treacherous nature of the two mobsters he was dealing with.

"Tommy makes a beef to Chuckie that we called the cops. And Chuckie came to my house and he asks me, 'How come you guys called the cops?'

"I says, 'I didn't call the cops. We gave this guy Frankie the Bear five hundred dollars to make that call.' You know, Tommy said that Charlie called the cops. It was like they were jealous because we made the score. By Tommy saying we called the cops, it looked like we were fuckin' rats. But we gave this guy five hundred bucks to call the cops. So I told this to Chuckie. I said, 'We know better than to call the cops, but we had to in order to get the sucker away from Spike. It's all part of the program. By the time the cops came, I wasn't even there. I'm already downtown. And the sucker can't touch Spike 'cause I was supposedly arrested. That's the way it was done.'

"The thing was, though, that Tommy and Faffy had Chuckie's ear pretty good. And Chuckie also seemed to love the dissension that we had. But I wouldn't tip my mitt too much to Chuckie, because I couldn't trust him. You know what I mean. Because I knew these two guys were his favorites."

Caramandi was discovering that, like any profession, being a mob associate had its ups and downs. There were murder contracts and scams to set up and carry out; shakedown money to collect and whack up; nights of drunken partying and weekends of gambling at the casinos down at the shore. But there was also the constant tension of living on the edge. Scarfo wasn't the only one with a hit list. The Crow knew that throughout 1983, while he was stalking Harry Riccobene's men, they were also out looking for him.

Even more aggravating, however, were the internal sniping,

Partners in crime. "Charlie White" Iannece *(left)* and Nick Caramandi ham it up while vacationing in Florida. Together they became the biggest money-making tandem in the Scarfo crime family, generating several million dollars through gambling, loan-sharking, drug dealing, extortion, and labor racketeering. They were also called upon to carry out several murder contracts as Scarfo consolidated his hold on his underworld empire.

The Docile Don. Angelo Bruno, walking the street in South Philadelphia, avoided the glitz and glitter. A low-key mob boss, his organization reflected his personality during most of his twenty-one-year reign.

The Godfather of South Philadelphia. Nicodemo "Little Nicky" Scarfo loved the spotlight and usually traveled with an entourage. He took over the organization one year after Bruno was killed and molded the family in his own high-profile image.

Phil Testa (left) and Scarfo talk business after emerging from a South Philadelphia diner. Testa succeeded Bruno, but he was blasted from power in the bloody war that catapulted Scarfo to the top.

Fun in the sun. Scarfo *(second row, third from left)* is surrounded by his friends during a day at the beach. "Charlie White" Iannece is to his immediate right with his arm around Nick Caramandi. Scarfo, unlike Bruno, loved to host large gatherings where "family members" and friends would pay him homage.

A day at the beach. Philip Leonetti *(left)*, Scarfo, Caramandi, and Joe Grande bask in the sunshine during another mob get-together on the beach in Fort Lauderdale.

Boys night out. New Year's Eve 1985 was "black tie" for Tommy DelGiorno *(left)*, Caramandi, Frank "Faffy" Iannarella, and Charlie "White" Iannece, who partied at an Atlantic City casino-hotel. Both Caramandi and DelGiorno are now in the Federal Witness Protection Program.

A contrast in styles. In Atlantic City, Scarfo lived modestly. His residence was in this North Georgia Avenue apartment house owned by his mother *(above left)*. The diminutive mob boss did business out of the nondescript storefront next door that served as the headquarters for Scarf Inc., his nephew's cement contracting company *(above right)*. The working-class neighborhood three blocks from the boardwalk could hardly compare with Scarfo's Florida "digs." In Fort Lauderdale, Scarfo lived in a hacienda-style home worth close to $750,000 *(below)*. He docked his forty-one-foot cabin cruiser *Casablanca Usual Suspects* out back. And he parked his Rolls-Royce in the garage.

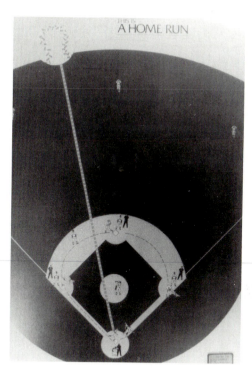

Every member of the Scarfo organization was shown these two photographs, which hung in the mob boss's Atlantic City office. It was paramount for every soldier to "touch base" with his capo. Those who didn't were "out."

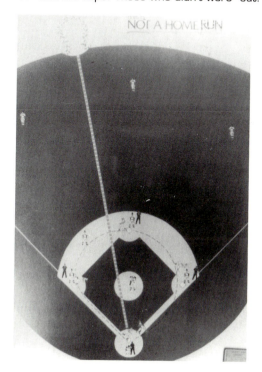

Things change. During happier days, Frank "Chickie" Narducci *(left)*, Salvatore Testa, Phil Testa, and Nicodemo Scarfo share a toast at a South Philadelphia get-together. Only Scarfo is alive today. Narducci plotted Phil Testa's March 15, 1981, assassination. Sal Testa avenged his father's death by killing Narducci on January 7, 1982, and Scarfo ordered Sal Testa's murder, which was carried out on September 14, 1984.

Best of friends. Salvatore Testa *(right)* and Joey Pungitore enjoy themselves at the Jersey shore a year before Pungitore was ordered to lure Testa into a death trap in a Passyunk Avenue candy shop.

For the defense. Attorney Robert Simone *(left)* is greeted by Nicky Scarfo on board the mob boss's cabin cruiser. Simone defended Scarfo through a series of trials that rocked the Philadelphia underworld in the late 1980s.

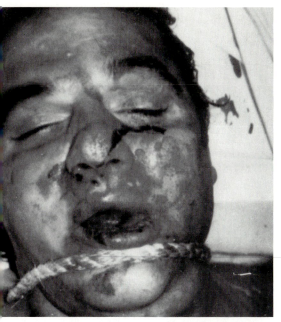

Their services were no longer
required. Scarfo had one way to
deal with his enemies. He
ordered them killed. Sal Testa
(top) was once the crown prince
of the Philadelphia mob. Then
Scarfo turned on him. Pasquale
"Pat the Cat" Spirito *(center)*
balked once too often about
carrying out a Scarfo contract.
The mob then turned its guns his
way. Frank "Chickie" Narducci
(bottom) tried to move up by
murdering Phil Testa. Less than
a year later, he died in the
gutter.

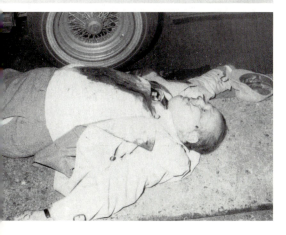

Lord of the manor. Tanned, relaxed, and happy, Nicodemo Scarfo poses in front of the gates of his Fort Lauderdale home. Since 1987, the only gates the mob boss has seen have been in prison. Now serving consecutive terms of fourteen years for extortion, fifty-five years for racketeering, and life for first-degree murder, the sixty-two-year-old mob boss may never again bask in the Florida sun that he loved.

the traps, and the backstabbing. Tommy and Faffy were masters of treachery, and Chuckie Merlino made no effort to rein them in. The Crow walked a tightrope. He was a mobster-in-waiting, but for the first time in more than twenty years, he didn't have a sponsor. There was no one like Tony Bananas, Mickey Diamond, or Mr. Joe around to look out for him.

The one man who appreciated his worth—and who might take an interest in his well-being—was Scarfo. So it was no surprise that Caramandi broke into a broad smile and heaved a sigh of relief when word reached the clubhouse at Camac and Moore that Little Nicky was getting out of jail.

On January 20, 1984, Scarfo was released from the federal prison in La Tuna, Texas. His nephew Philip Leonetti headed a contingent waiting to greet him at the prison gates. From there the Scarfo entourage drove in rented luxury cars to San Antonio, where they spent the night partying in a posh hotel. The next morning they caught a flight to Philadelphia, exiting the airport like celebrities. Reporters and television cameras were on hand to record every move as a tanned and fit Little Nicky headed toward a waiting limousine that whisked him and his murderous band of sycophants to Atlantic City and another celebration.

Scarfo was fifty-five years old. He had been boss of the Philadelphia family for just thirty-four months. He had spent seventeen of those months in a hot, dusty federal prison in Texas. During his brief reign, sixteen mob members or associates had turned up dead, their bodies dumped in empty lots, left in the gutters, or hidden in the trunks of cars all over Philadelphia and South Jersey.

Now Little Nicky was back on the scene. The Riccobene war was over. He had consolidated his power. There were problems, to be sure, but it appeared the era of violence was coming to an end. His enemies were either dead or in jail. As he strode out of the airport, Scarfo was flanked by Leonetti on one side and Salvie Testa on the other. Testa walked just behind Scarfo and to his right, a position that seemed to symbolize his place in the organization.

Not everything, however, was as it seemed.

"The first time I met with Nicky after he came out of jail was up at the Ellsmere Club across the street from the clubhouse at Camac and Moore. He was with Chuckie [Salvatore Merlino], Lawrence Merlino, and Philip Leonetti. And he wants to meet me and Charlie and a couple other guys,'cause now, you gotta remember, the Riccobene war is over and Nicky's trying to get his bearings after being away for so long.

"We meet him and he tells us, 'Wait a little while, till the heat cools down, and you guys are gonna get this' "—rubbing his thumb and forefinger together, meaning the button, the badge.

"So over the next couple of months we're invited to different things. There was a dinner, for instance, at this restaurant a friend of Nicky's owned in Vineland. The guy was gonna cook deer meat. Instead, it was me that almost got cooked.

"A group of us met at, like, one-thirty in the afternoon and we're having drinks. And I didn't know anything about drinking in front of the boss, and on top of that, I had just come from working out on a Nautilus and I was pretty wiped out. And I started drinking vodka on the rocks. Charlie says, 'Go ahead. Drink. Don't worry about it.'

"So we're all drinkin', talkin', laughin' about nothing. Then we sit down to dinner and there's a big spread—wine, deer meat, salad, hot peppers. The whole works.

"So, Nicky's talking but I can't keep my fucking eyes open. I'm bombed drunk. Joey Merlino, who's across from me, is giving me the eye and kicking me under the table, trying to keep me awake. Nicky's talkin' and I'm just, uhuh, uhuh. I'm ready to pass out. Sure enough, as he's talking, bango, I pass out. I fall right from the chair onto the floor.

"Holy Christ. They get me up. They try to get me awake. And I say, 'I don't know what hit me. This whiskey just got me.'

"Anyway, the next day I go around to see Chuckie and I say, 'Hey, Chuck, man, I don't know what happened last night. I hope Nicky's not mad at me. You gotta tell him that I'm sorry. Apologize for me. Please, do me this favor.'

"He says, 'All right. I'll tell 'im.'

"So, about a week later, Chuckie sends for me. And he says, 'I gave Nicky that message that you told me.' And I says, 'Well, what did he say?'

" 'He said if you fall down a hundred times, he's gonna pick you up a hundred times. So don't worry about it.' Phew. I was relieved. That was an awful thing to do, to pass out in front of the boss.

"See, Nicky knows how to drink. He drinks Cutty Sark. And what he does, he'll get a glass of water and he just keeps waterin' it down. He knows how to pace himself. Eventually, we all learned this, how to drink in front of him and pace ourselves. We all learned how to use drinking. We might get a guy drunk while we stayed sober. I mean, you could work a guy pretty good when he's drinking because he gets a little loose. Things that are on his mind come out because the whiskey makes him talk.

"That's one of Nicky's tricks with people, to get things out of them when he wants to. He knows how to work a guy. He looks like he's drinkin' socially. He'll pour his glass and say, 'Come on. Let's have another drink.' But he's not gettin' drunk. That's one of his tricks, and he uses it to find things out. He'll make a guy get drunk.

"Anyway, we went to a couple more social events, and things were looking pretty good. We were just looking to get made and we weren't looking for no problems. Then the Testa thing came up."

CHAPTER THIRTEEN

Defense attorney:	If you were ordered to do violence, would you do it?
Caramandi:	It was either kill or be killed.

When Scarfo was released from prison early in 1984 he was the undisputed king of the Philadelphia underworld. And Salvie Testa was the mob's crown prince. Testa, who at twenty-eight was the youngest mob capo in America, had learned the ways of La Cosa Nostra from his father, but he had come into his own during the bloody reign of Little Nicky.

"He'd never ask you to do something he wouldn't do himself," Caramandi said with admiration. "He was right out there with you."

But in 1984, after risking his life to solidify Scarfo's hold on the underworld, Testa badly miscalculated his status within the organization. He thought he had proved himself. He figured that his loyalty was beyond question. In Bruno's day, that certainly would have been the case. But Scarfo played by a different set of rules. The very attributes that made Salvie Testa such an asset during the Riccobene war—his leadership and his fearlessness—turned him into a threat after the war was over.

"Salvie was all for 'this thing.' Knew it inside out. Knew it better than guys who were sixty years old and who'd been in it for forty years. Because of his father. He'd been a good teacher. Salvie had nerve and he didn't care who he killed. Sometimes we used to go [on a contract] and we'd come back and tell him, 'Well, the kids were in the car, the family's in the car.'

"'I don't care who's in the car,' he'd say. 'Everybody goes.' That's the kind of guy he was.

"One Thanksgiving Day he wanted us to go into Sonny Riccobene's house where Robert Riccobene was havin' dinner with his family. 'Shoot everybody in the house.' But me and Charlie and Faffy made up some story that he didn't show up. Just to appease Salvie. 'Cause we didn't go for killing kids. It was something we drew a line with, but he was just so full of venom that he didn't care.

"He was a guy made for 'this thing.' He loved it. He lived it. And he was very bitter about what happened to his father, about the way his father got killed, blown up with nails in him."

Testa personally killed the two men responsible for his father's death, Frank "Chickie" Narducci and Rocco Marinucci, and made no attempt to hide his satisfaction in those bloody acts of vengeance.

"Salvie used to say to me, 'I wish that motherfucker was alive so I could kill him again,' meaning Chickie Narducci," said Caramandi. "This is how much he hated this man. He had no mercy on anybody. Business was business, and killing to him was business."

Salvatore Testa quickly moved up the organizational ladder after the Narducci killing. He "inherited" most of his father's business, including a loan-sharking operation in South Philadelphia. He also developed a lucrative financial arrangement with several local drug dealers, including a black organization that supplied parts of the North and West Philadelphia ghettoes.

The Philadelphia branch of La Cosa Nostra, like most of the New York families, paid lip service to the ban on made members dealing in drugs. But Testa, like many of his cohorts, found a way around the prohibition. Caramandi explained the somewhat distorted logic:

"You couldn't deal drugs, but you could shake down drug dealers or you could loan them money. You could do anything you wanted with them. Steal from them, rob them, make them pay a street tax. They tried to say Salvie was dealing drugs, which he wasn't. But he was financing some drug dealers and he was making a lot of money with them."

Testa had a house at the shore near Atlantic City. He kept a boat in a nearby marina. He made more than $1 million selling a piece of Atlantic City real estate to casino developer Donald Trump. His legitimate and illegitimate businesses had made him a millionaire. In April 1984 a front-page article in the *Wall Street Journal* described him as the most feared Mafia figure in Philadelphia and cited a law enforcement report that called him the "fastest-rising star" in the Scarfo organization. He was a ruggedly handsome, 6-foot-1, 210-pound Mafia prince, a charismatic leader, and, without question, the field general for the Scarfo organization during the brief but bloody Riccobene war.

Salvatore Testa loved it all, the stalkings, the murders, even the Enrico Riccobene suicide. He was the South Philadelphia equivalent of a Main Line blue blood. He was born to be a wiseguy.

When Scarfo came out of prison, he and Testa were, respectively, the king and the prince of the Philadelphia underworld. But in less than a month, Scarfo would turn on his young capo. And in less than a year, Salvatore Testa would be dead.

The reason?

Just before Scarfo's release from prison, Testa broke off his engagement with Maria Merlino, the pretty young daughter of underboss Chuckie Merlino. Caramandi, recalling their bitter argument in the restaurant several months earlier, was not surprised.

"Salvie really didn't love Chuckie's daughter. But being the underboss's son for twenty-five years, he was used to being close to the top. So one day he goes to Chuckie Merlino, who now was the underboss, and says, 'I would like to go out with your daughter, take your daughter out.' Before long, they were engaged, but they had decided to wait for Scarfo to come out of jail before they married.

"By that time Salvie was in love with another girl and he didn't want to marry Maria. And he thought when Nicky came out of jail, Nicky would take the brunt of his not marrying Chuckie's daughter because of what a good job Salvie had done during the Riccobene war. But he didn't know Chuckie the way I knew Chuckie.

"Me and Charlie White knew Chuckie all our lives. He's a

very bitter guy, and he took the broken engagement as a personal insult. I'll never forget the night when Salvie and Joe Pung came into this club that we used to hang in. I'm sitting at the bar and Joe Pung tells me, 'Salvie just told Chuckie that he isn't going to marry his daughter.' From that moment on I knew he was a dead man.

"In the next few months, they built up things against him, saying he was going to start his own gang, he was fooling with drugs. Chuckie got allies to convince Nicky that this fella had treason in his mind, that he was starting his own gang. But all these things weren't true. He was dedicated to Scarfo. He worked twenty-four hours a day.

"That's the way it is. See, we believe the organization comes before your family, before your kids, before life itself. The badge is first, this thing of ours, La Cosa Nostra, comes first, before anything. And when it comes to problems like the Riccobene war, where somebody wants to hurt our mob, it's all out. And that's the way it was for Salvie."

But Salvatore Testa, as schooled and savvy as he was about the ways of La Cosa Nosta, badly miscalculated when he figured Scarfo would back him in a dispute with Chuckie Merlino over the canceled wedding plans. Whether Scarfo truly sided with Merlino in an affair of honor, however, remains an open question in the Philadelphia underworld. There are those who believe that Scarfo, like some tribal chief, feared a Testa-Merlino alliance and was only too happy to hear that the marriage plans were off. And, seeing the young Testa as his eventual rival, Scarfo had no problem being convinced by Merlino of the need to avenge his daughter's embarrassment.

"Nicky didn't take the brunt. What happened was that Chuckie started recruitin' Faffy and Tommy to help him tell Nicky about Testa's wrongdoings. He's doing this. He's doing that. They were creating stories. This is the viciousness within. Now, there's something in it for Faffy and Tommy. Get rid of Testa and they would become capos. So they start telling Nicky stories. 'Salvie's dealing with black people. Salvie's dealing drugs. Salvie's trying to get a gang together.' They had to come up with something to show Nicky that Testa should be dead.

"I had many conversations with Chuckie. He used to come over my house to drink wine. He'd say, 'You know, I'm not mad because he didn't marry my daughter. If he would just take himself down and start all over again, he would be forgiven. You know, this thing comes first. If he didn't wanna marry my daughter... he coulda did it a different way.'

"You see, the wedding was all planned. Salvie canceled out two months before it was supposed to go. They had bought gowns and they had the church. They even bought special tablecloths. There were going to be over seven hundred guests."

But despite Chuckie Merlino's protestations, despite his argument that all Salvie Testa would have to do was "take himself down"—relinquish his title as capo and become a mob soldier again—Caramandi knew Philadelphia's mob prince was about to be permanently and fatally dethroned.

"We knew it was only a matter of time for Salvie," he said.

Salvatore Testa's fall from grace in the spring of 1984 did not go unnoticed within the Philadelphia underworld. The first sign came during a benefit dinner for a local charity at Palumbo's Restaurant in South Philadelphia in April, around the same time the *Wall Street Journal* was heralding Testa's rise. Nicky Scarfo took a table for himself and his top associates at the affair. Salvatore Testa was told to sit somewhere else. Then, about a month later, Scarfo and his entourage took a trip to Puerto Rico. Salvie wasn't invited.

By then, Caramandi said, Salvatore Testa realized something was amiss. "He sorta got vibes," said the Crow.

The order for the hit came down about that time. Caramandi and Charlie White got the ticket.

"One morning," recalled Caramandi, "Tommy comes around and says, 'You don't know what happened last night. We had dinner with Nicky. Chuckie, Philip, Lawrence, me, and Faffy. Faffy buried Salvie Testa. He's gotta be killed.'

"Me and Charlie looked at one another and we knew. It was no surprise to us."

Later that day or the next, Chuckie Merlino came around to see the Crow and Charlie White. Merlino was standing out in the middle of the 1800 block of Camac Street. Caramandi, Iannece, DelGiorno, and Iannarella walked up and gathered around him. There they were, the mob underboss of Philadelphia and four of his top soldiers, standing in a huddle in the middle of the street in the middle of the afternoon. They met like that because, in the wake of the Riccobene violence, they feared police surveillance and hidden listening devices. They knew that even their own clubhouses could be bugged, so when important business had to be discussed, they would take a walk down the block or around the corner. They figured while they still could be seen, they wouldn't be overheard.

"Chuckie's standing by himself and we get in a circle. He says, 'Salvie's gotta be killed,' and puts his fingers toward the ground with the sign [right hand with forefinger and thumb in the shape of a gun]. Salvie's gotta go. Nicky wants him dead. Too much treason. He's gettin' too big for his britches. He's fooling with drugs.' Then he turned to me and Charlie and says, 'You guys got any ideas?'"

At that meeting it was decided that Testa's code name would be Brownie, that Caramandi and Charlie White would be responsible for carrying out the hit, and that DelGiorno and Iannarella would supervise.

"Chuckie told us, 'Try to come up with a good plan. Be careful and let's get this guy as soon as we can.'"

This was early in the spring of 1984. Summer would be nearly over before Salvatore Testa was dead. Part of the problem was Testa. He was a difficult target, always on the alert. And those stalking him knew that he'd be willing to shoot back. But another cause for the delay was Scarfo. The blood-thirsty little mob boss preferred to see his contracts carried out in public.

"Nicky liked cowboy-style. See, he didn't like walk-ins, where you take a guy in his house. He liked broad daylight, restaurants or busy street corners, anything cowboy-style. He liked a lotta noise to scare people. He figured that way there would never be any witnesses because nobody would ever come forward and testify against us. And after, he liked to see a lot of publicity of the murder. Headlines and television.

"Salvie knew this. He always said Nicky liked Wild West. The more noise the better. So Salvie was very cautious. He just felt bad vibes. Every time you shook his hand, he'd bring ya in close with his right hand and just pat ya down with his left hand from behind just to see if you were carrying a gun. Now, with the warm weather coming, it was pretty hard to carry a gun. We'd just have to stash it somewhere and bushwhack him, sneak it on him.

"And it's a little tough for us, because we couldn't station ourselves in front of Salvie's house and wait for him to come out—he's gonna know we're the guys that's gonna do the shooting. It was going to have to be a spot he wouldn't expect, because he was very, very alert by this time. He's doing his regular business, but he knows there's something wrong. He suspects he's gonna be killed. He just can't figure out who's going to do it to him.

"And as he looks the field over, the guys around him, he sees Joe Pungitore, his best friend, and Gino Milano. But these fellas weren't told about it. The only people that knew were Nicky, Chuckie, Philip, Lawrence, Charlie White, Faffy, Tommy, and me."

At that point, Caramandi said, the only way Salvatore Testa could have saved his own life was to disappear. But that, apparently, wasn't in the kid's makeup.

"He coulda just taken the fuck off," Caramandi said. "Me and Charlie used to talk about that. We don't know why this fuckin' guy don't take off. We woulda loved to have told him, but we couldn't tell him. You know what I mean?

"He was the type of guy who, if he knew for sure, woulda went after Chuckie or Nicky and tried to kill them. This kid woulda went down in a blaze of glory. But he wasn't sure. He was aware. He was alert. But he wasn't sure."

For the next five months, Caramandi, Charlie White, and eventually several other members of the Scarfo organization stalked Salvatore Testa, looking for the right time and the right place to whack the mob prince.

Caramandi considered the Pier 30 Tennis Club down by the Delaware River waterfront where Testa played on a regular basis. But he rejected that spot as too risky. Heavy traffic in the area would make a getaway difficult. And because of the way the tennis courts were laid out, Testa would be able to spot someone before he could get off a good shot.

He looked at Testa's girlfriend's apartment and the neighborhood around it, at a vacant store at Ninth and Christian in South Philadelphia where Testa was building a new clubhouse, and at a hair salon owned by Testa and frequented by many mobsters.

"Nicky, Philip, and Lawrence used to come up from Atlantic City every ten days or so to get their hair cut and get a manicure," Caramandi said. "Tommy thought about luring Salvie there. Me and Charlie had guns and a car ready. We were supposed to walk in and blast him. But they couldn't get him there."

The first serious opportunity presented itself that summer when Faffy Iannarella's wife, who was pregnant, was going to be feted at a baby shower.

"Faffy's wife was going to be given a big shower, in the Italian custom. People come and bring gifts. It's like a party. So Faffy runs into Salvie on the street and Salvie says, 'Are you gonna be home tonight? I wanna bring ya a gift.' Faffy says, 'Yeah.'

"So now we see a golden opportunity. Me, Tommy, Faffy, and Charlie get together. But now Chuckie intercedes and he says he wants Tory [Salvatore Scafidi] to do the shooting, to be at this house. Because if me or Charlie were there when Salvie pulls up, he might not want to come in. But being that Tory Scafidi hangs with Faffy it would look normal, because Faffy had bought a house and he was remodeling it. It used to be Pat Spirito's house. And they would be outside.

"Anyway, Tommy says, 'Look, I got two .22 pistols with silencers. You got a place where we could practice?' I says yeah, my house, in the cellar. So he says, 'Okay, I'll be there at six o'clock with Tory. We'll practice, because sometimes the guns jam. You gotta watch the way you pull the triggers.'

"At six P.M., Tommy and Tory come to my house and we practiced. We were using homemade silencers, but they worked pretty good. After we shot awhile, we decided the guns were okay. So right then and there we told Tory what to do. We knew Faffy was waiting. We said to go over to the house and stash the guns. Put one upstairs and one downstairs, but make sure they're accessible. We told Tory and Faffy to hang outside the house and pretend like they're working. Once Salvie gets out of the car and onto the porch, Faffy would say, 'Let me show you the house.' Then when they get him inside, Faffy would distract him and Tory would get the gun.

"So that night Tory goes to Faffy's house and they're waiting outside. Me and Tommy go pick up Charlie, because we got to take the body away if he does get him in the house. We were waiting in the neighborhood, about two blocks from Faffy's house. We waited until it got dark. Salvie never showed up. We decided we'd do it the next night. We waited again, but Salvie never showed up.

"The following day, Salvie bumps into Faffy on the street and gives him the baby gift on the street. So that was the end of that plan."

After the opportunity offered by the baby shower didn't pan out, the shooters shifted their attention in the opposite direction. Joey Pungitore's aunt had died, and everyone, including Salvie Testa, was expected at the wake, which was to be at the Cato Funeral Home on Broad Street in the heart of South Philadelphia.

"Joe Pungitore was Salvie Testa's best friend out of all the fellas. He's also a made guy and was one of Salvie's top guys. So there's no way Salvie's not going to come to the funeral parlor. But Salvie knows about funeral parlors, because we were gonna shoot Sonny Riccobene in one.

"Anyway, two days before the wake we made our plans. Me, Tommy, Charlie, and Tory and Faffy. Chuckie wanted Tory to do the shooting and for me and Charlie to be blockers inside the funeral parlor just in case anybody tried to interfere with Tory's escape. We'd push into them and help him get away clean. He would just drop the gun in the funeral parlor and walk out.

"So the day of the wake comes. Eleven o'clock that morning, we receive a phone call to go to Chuckie's house, me and Charlie. Tommy and Faffy are there, too. Chuckie says, 'Tory got arrested this morning. He won't get outta jail until late tonight.' He says, 'Nicky's gonna be mad. I don't know what we're gonna do.'

"So we're just listening. And he's waiting for Nicky to come up from Atlantic City. Finally, Scarfo comes in with Phil Leonetti and Lawrence Merlino. We sit at the table. Chuckie starts to tell Nicky the story of how Tory got locked up at five-thirty in the morning after being drunk and that he's still in jail and that they'd hold him till maybe late tonight.

"So Nicky said, 'Look, these fucking kids are irresponsible. The plan goes on as we said it would.' He looks at me and Charlie and says, 'You two guys ready?'

"We said yes. He said, 'Okay, that's it.'

"That night Faffy picks me up. I got a .380 magnum. Charlie's got a .38. Tommy picks up Charlie at his house. Faffy picks me up at my house. About twenty-five after seven, Salvie's outside of the funeral parlor with a couple other members milling around while waiting for Nicky to come. Me and Charlie got our guns. We had jackets on. We're trying to stay away from Salvie, because we know about the frisks and we want to be careful. So we're talking to other members and trying to stay away from him.

"About eight o'clock, Nicky pulls up with Lawrence Merlino, Chuckie Merlino, and Phil Leonetti. We're standing on the top of the steps. He greets some people when he gets out of the car, shakes hands with people. He walks up to the top of the steps. He looks at me and Charlie and he says, 'Youse ready?' We said yes.

"We go inside the funeral parlor. We pay our respects to the dead. Now we're looking for a spot and we're looking for some kind of signal. Charlie's on one side of the room. I'm on the other side of the room. We notice Salvie looking all around, constantly looking. And we're waitin' for some kind of signal from Tommy or Faffy to tell us, 'Go ahead.'

"A short time later I was told to go upstairs. There's a lounge area there in the front of the room and a bar. It's got twelve, thirteen stools. Salvie's sitting at the end of the bar talking to somebody. I walk right next to him and I get in position right behind him. And Nicky and Chuckie and Philip are ten feet away from me. I'm looking directly at them. They're against the wall. Chuckie's standing there and I motion to Chuckie with my head, up and down, like, let's do it right now. But he waves me off.

"So when he does that, I go to the lounge and sit down. We were all tense and I couldn't understand what happened. I was right behind him, ready to shoot him—he's talking to a guy at the bar. All I hadda do is go bing, right in the back of his head. Then about ten minutes later Tommy and Faffy come over and they tell me there's too much law outside. Too many cops.

"I mean, here's Nicky, here's the boss, who wants you to do it right in front of him. It's unheard-of. But these fucking guys were so crazy that it even goes further. When we leave the funeral parlor, we all go downstairs outside and we're saying goodbye to everybody, members and nonmembers. I'm standing with Nicky, Chuckie, Philip, Tommy, Faffy, and Charlie. Now, when Salvie says goodbye, he shakes hands with all of us. Chuckie Merlino shakes his hand, grabs his head, and kisses him on the lips...for like ten seconds. Tommy, Charlie, Faffy, and me, we looked at one another. We said, 'What the fuck. This guy's nuts. [Salvie's] gotta know now.' It was the kiss of death.

"We looked at the expression on Salvie. He was sorta stunned. He just couldn't figure out what the fuck was going on. But this is how crazy they were. I mean, they wanted him to know."

If Testa suspected he had problems before the Pungitore

wake, Merlino confirmed them with his kiss. Now it would be even more difficult for Caramandi, Iannece, DelGiorno, and Iannarella to set up and carry out the hit. So, with Scarfo's approval, they decided to recruit Joey Pungitore, one of Salvie Testa's oldest and best friends.

"Joe Pung is completely unaware of the situation, which has been going on for months by this time. Now Tommy, Joe Pung, and Salvie are in the numbers business and the sports business together. The plan is they're going to get Joe Pung to take him to Tommy's house, where I would be hiding behind the cellar door and would come out and shoot Salvie at the kitchen table. When we told Joe Pung about the plan, he said, 'I don't know if I can get him here, but I'll try. He's been acting funny.'

"You see, Joe Pung was all upset because here was his best friend and this thing with Salvie was all new to him. But he had no choice—if Joe had said no, he would've been dead. This was an order, you know what I mean? Who's he gonna go beef to? And if he even said one fucking word to Salvie, one iota, he woulda been dead. He knows that. He knows this game. So what was he gonna do?"

A few years later, in a debriefing session with New Jersey state police on this same topic, Tommy DelGiorno told how he recruited Pungitore on Scarfo's orders and how Pungitore had only one request.

"He said he would set him up, but he didn't want to pull the trigger, do the shooting," DelGiorno told New Jersey investigators. "I told this to Scarfo and he laughed.

"'What the fuck's the difference?' he said."

So Pungitore got a partial dispensation. If he set up his best friend, he wouldn't have to be the triggerman.

The plan to lure Testa to DelGiorno's house failed, as did several other attempts that summer to set him up. But Pungitore was now part of the plot, and the circle was tightening around Salvatore Testa. Throughout that summer the schemes continued. As Testa traveled back and forth between his home in South Philadelphia and his place at the shore—often with Pungitore serving as driver and bodyguard—Caramandi, Iannece, DelGiorno, and Iannarella kept devising new plans to carry out the hit.

Maybe it was dumb luck. Or maybe it was his guile, cunning, and innate sixth sense about the ways of La Cosa

Nostra. Whatever the reason, Salvie Testa outmaneuvered those plotting his death. He didn't show up for meetings. He skipped dinner appointments. He varied his routine. At one point Caramandi had a pharmacist friend from Florida ship him knockout drops. There had been stories in the papers about hookers in Atlantic City robbing their johns after knocking them out. The hookers would secrete a drug in their mouths, then slip it into the mouth of their customer. The papers were calling them the kissing bandits. Caramandi and DelGiorno figured they'd drug Testa. The new plan was to lure him to DelGiorno's boardwalk condominium in Ocean City, New Jersey.

"Me, Charlie, and Tory go down the shore to Tommy's. We put some of the liquid in a glass and some in a cup. Joe Pung is supposed to get Salvie there. When he gets Salvie there, Tommy's gonna offer him some coffee or soda. He had the glass ready and the cup ready.

"So we were waiting on the boardwalk at a pizzeria. Once this was done, we were supposed to take Salvie out, shoot him, and leave him on a highway somewhere. See, the way Tommy's building was set up we coulda got him right out the door, pulled the car right up alongside the door. Practically nobody woulda seen us.

"We waited most of the day. After a while, Joe Pung showed up and said, 'I couldn't get him here.'"

The plotting and scheming had begun to take its toll. Pungitore lost thirty pounds over the course of the summer as one after another plan was set up and abandoned. Caramandi, Iannece, DelGiorno, and Iannarella, who were supposedly in charge of the hit, were getting constant complaints from Merlino, Scarfo, and Leonetti.

"One time I'm down the shore and Leonetti tells me, 'This motherfucker, I'm getting sick and tired of looking at him.'

"It was constant tension. There were a lot of fucking attempts on this guy," Caramandi said as he ticked off several other plots, including one night when he and Charlie White waited at the bar in an Atlantic City casino where DelGiorno was supposed to bring Testa.

"We were in the casino, either the Playboy or the Sands. Me and Charlie were sitting there with our fucking guns, looking to shoot him right there. Right in the fucking casino. That's how desperate they were near the end. Tommy was supposed to bring him in. But he didn't show. This guy, he didn't trust no place."

And nobody.

Except his best friend, Joey Pungitore.

Then, on September 14, 1984, the crew that had been stalking Salvie Testa for months finally got it right.

"This was the plan. Joe Pung was gonna pick up Salvie at his house at 2117 Porter. And when he went there he was gonna act very, very disturbed because he's gonna say that Wayne Grande messed up ten thousand dollars of his money and he's very upset about it. And he wants to get it straightened out now and let's go see him now. And Grande would be at this sweet shop on Passyunk Avenue.

"So at twelve o'clock that day, Joe Pung goes by Salvie's and tells him what happened. Wayne Grande messed up his money and he wants it straightened out right away. Salvie falls for the whole story. 'Let's go get him,' he says. 'Let's go talk to him.'

Testa and Pungitore arrived at the sweet shop shortly before 1:00 P.M. The store, which was about two blocks from the clubhouse at Camac and Moore, was being renovated. The owner, a friend of several of the young mob figures, planned to open in a few months. Wayne Grande and his brother Joe were there when Testa walked in. Salvie shook hands with each of them, patting them down in the way that had become his custom. Then he started to walk toward a back room where he, Pungitore, and Wayne Grande would meet to discuss the money problem. At that moment, Wayne slipped behind Testa, reached under a pillow on the sofa in the front room, pulled out a pistol, and pointed it toward Testa's head.

Outside on Passyunk Avenue, a crew from the streets department was busting up a section of the sidewalk with jackhammers. No one heard the shot that ripped into the back of Salvie Testa's head. He dropped like a rock to the floor. Wayne Grande stood over the fallen mob prince and pumped another bullet into his brain.

Testa's head jerked on impact, but the life had already left his body.

Wayne Grande and the others dragged the body behind the sofa, covered it with a sheet, and took off, locking the door of the sweet shop behind them.

Joe Grande headed back toward the clubhouse, where he met Caramandi.

"It's done," he said. "It's over. He's dead."

"So now me and Charlie call Chuckie Merlino. We say, 'Chuckie, we gotta see ya.' Boom, five minutes later Chuckie comes around and we says, 'Salvie's dead.'

"He says, 'All right, you guys know what you gotta do. Get in touch with Tommy.' We call Tommy and tell him we're gonna go to Jersey and find a spot to dump the body that night.

"We drive to Jersey. We get off at Sicklerville Road in South Jersey. We find what's like a sand trap about four or five miles up the road. We said this spot was as good as any. This is where we'll bring him tonight."

On the way back, Caramandi and Charlie Iannece stopped at a Penney's, where Caramandi bought a king-size blanket to use to wrap the body. Iannece had already arranged to borrow a van from a friend. Tory Scafidi would be going with them when they dumped the body.

"We drive the van right in front of the sweet shop and park. That night, I pick up Tory and Charlie in my car and take them to the store. I ride around to make sure everything was okay and then wait for Charlie to give me the signal. Twenty, twenty-five minutes later, Charlie comes out. He waves to me. I pull up behind the van and they come out and throw the body into the back of the van. We drive over the Ben Franklin Bridge and head to the Sicklerville Road.

"My job was to drive the crash car in case the van got stopped on the way. In case a cop car stopped them, I was to smash into the cop car so that they could get away."

After dumping the body in New Jersey, Caramandi followed the van back to South Philadelphia, where it was parked in a prearranged spot. Iannece had arranged to have some associates clean out the inside of the vehicle the next day. A separate crew would clean up the sweet shop.

"Later, Charlie said to me, 'Nick, we never coulda lifted him up. It's a good thing Tory was with us. The body was stiff. We couldn't straighten the legs out. We tried to pull 'em. First of all, we couldn't find him. He was behind the couch and he was covered with blood. We couldn't get the blanket around him. We just had a big, big problem in there.'

"The body was sitting from, like, twelve to nine. Rigor mortis musta set in. And you know he's a big guy, he was like six-one, six-two, and he weighed two hundred and twenty-five pounds. So he musta been just dead weight.

"After we made the drop, I drove everybody home. We were supposed to get changed and meet around the corner in half an hour. Then we drove down to La Cucina.

"Nicky's there with about ten or fifteen members. Joe Pung. Wayne Grande. Chuckie, Nicky, Philip, Lawrence. Gino. Joe Grande. We're all getting congratulated. Congratulating one another. Nicky had ordered a buffet dinner for us, and he had some of his friends from Mexico there with him. It was like some great big party."

As Scarfo wined and dined his guests, Salvatore Testa's body lay wrapped in a blanket along the side of a lonely road in southern New Jersey. Testa had been Scarfo's right arm. Now the mob boss was throwing a buffet dinner at one of Philadelphia's fanciest restaurants to celebrate his murder. Nothing better captured the treachery and deceit that had become the trademarks of the Scarfo organization.

During the celebration at La Cucina, Scarfo walked up to Caramandi and offered his personal congratulations.

"I heard there was a lot of blood," he said.

"Yeah, it was pretty messy," said Caramandi.

Caramandi remembers one other thing about that night at the restaurant. Charlie White apparently didn't do a great job cleaning himself up after disposing of Salvie Testa's body. Tommy DelGiorno was the first to notice: "Tommy says to Charlie, 'You got blood on your neck.' So Charlie goes to the bathroom to wash it off."

Then they all headed back to the buffet table.

The next day, September 15, 1984, police in Gloucester Township, New Jersey, found Testa's body dumped along the side of a rural road. He was wearing sneakers and tennis shorts and, according to one preliminary report, a red Temple University T-shirt. Only later did investigators realize the shirt was white. Blood streaming from two bullet holes in the back of his head had first soaked the shirt a deep crimson, then dried it to a brownish red.

Two or three weeks later, Caramandi was on the corner near the clubhouse with Wayne Grande. The Crow said he was curious about how Grande had avoided the frisk greeting that Salvie Testa used on everybody.

"You know, I always wondered how you got over on Salvie with that handshake," he said.

"Oh, I knew about that handshake," Grande replied. "I was ready for that. I was sitting on the couch when he came in. I had the gun under the couch pillow. When he came in, I shook his hand. And as soon as he turned around, I grabbed the gun. I shot him in the head. As soon as he went down I gave him another one in the head and it was over.

"I knew about that handshake," he said again proudly. "He gave me the frisk. When I shook his hand, he patted me down on the back, but I was hip to the handshake."

With Testa's death, the mob moved in to split up the spoils. Wayne Grande got 25 percent of Salvatore Testa's business. DelGiorno and Iannarella were named acting capos and eventually became capos. Scafidi got a $500-a-week job making numbers pickups.

And Charlie White and Caramandi, proposed members since the Pat Spirito murder in 1983, were formally initiated into La Cosa Nostra.

CHAPTER FOURTEEN

The initiation took place on a Sunday afternoon about a month after the Testa murder. It was a formal ceremony, an unholy rite of passage. For Caramandi it was also a confirmation. He was now more than just a hustler and a con man with connections. The kid who used to hang on the South Philadelphia street corner admiring the wiseguys was now one of them. He had the badge, the button.

Four years later, after he had become a government witness and shattered *omertà*, the Mafia's time-honored code of silence, Caramandi still seemed to display a sense of pride at having once been a member.

"Remember," he said as he sat sipping a cup of coffee in a hotel room in Ocean City, Maryland, "you don't choose to join the mob. The mob has to choose you. Out of all the millions of people in Jersey and Pennsylvania, there were only sixty of us. It's something you can't choose, you can't join. You gotta be chosen."

"When you go to a making, you're not supposed to know that you're going to be made. It's supposed to be a secret thing. But usually you do know. So Chuckie [Merlino] came over my house one Saturday and he says, 'Tomorrow's your day. You, Charlie, and Joe Grande.' He says, 'Nicky'll help ya. It'll be easy. Just don't be nervous. Don't worry about nothin'. It's your time.'

" 'Cause we waited pretty long. Usually when somebody gets killed, it's a month or two before these guys get made. When you hear somebody's gettin' made and you know somebody's been killed, you know these guys did it. The new guys. That they participated in some way.

"So, the next day I'm told by Tommy and Faffy to be with Charlie at a McDonald's at Twenty-sixth and Passyunk at one o'clock in the afternoon. That morning I get ready, all dressed up. Suit-and-tie affair. Now we don't know where the place is going to be. It's supposed to be a secret spot. Me and Charlie's nervous. We get in Tommy's car and we're driving. We go on the expressway and we head over to Montgomery County somewhere. We still don't know where we're going. Finally, we get to the house and it's Sam the Barber's house." Salvatore "Sam the Barber" LaRussa, a Scarfo associate, was the owner of La Cucina, the popular Philadelphia restaurant. "A beautiful house in Whitemarsh. He built the house himself and later he was offered, like, nine hundred thousand for it. It's got this winding driveway up on a hill. It's a gorgeous home.

"So, anyway, when we get to the house, there's some other members there. And Sam the Barber's there. He's got a big dining room, with a long table and, like, forty chairs, twenty-five feet long, something like that. And Sam's got all kinds of food set out in chafing dishes to keep it hot. Like a catered affair. And we're waiting for Scarfo to come. There's like thirty, thirty-five members there.

"A short time later, here comes Nicky, Philip, Chuckie, and Lawrence. We're standing around talking, drinking coffee. After about ten minutes, Tommy and Faffy tell Charlie, Joe Grande, and me to go into one of the bedrooms.

"The three of us go in and we're talking among ourselves. I wonder what's gonna happen. Who they gonna call out first? And we're kinda nervous. So the first guy they call out is Charlie. We don't know what happened, because me and Joe Grande stay in the room and we can't hear what's bein' said. Then thirty minutes or so later they call me out.

"Nicky's at the head of the table. Everybody's sitting down. Everybody's very solemn. They all got straight faces. Nicky tells me to stand next to him at the head of the table. And he says, 'Well, Nick, do you know why you're here?' I says, 'No.'

"He says, 'The reason why you're here around this table with these fellas is because we would like you to become one of us. We want you to belong to this thing of ours. I want you to look around the table. Do you know all the people who are here?'

"I says, 'Yes, I do.' Then he says, 'You don't have any hard feelings against anybody here, do you?' I says, 'No, I get along with everybody that's here.' So he says, 'We want you to become one of us.'

"Now I notice there's a gun and knife on the table. In fact, I got the knife and Charlie got the gun. But Nicky doesn't know that, because we gave 'em to Tommy and Faffy. It was a dagger-type knife and a .38 handgun. So he says, 'Now look, if you don't want to join and become one of us, you can leave now and you'll have the same respect from us. There'll be no hard feelings and you'll have the same favors granted to you.' Then he says, 'You want some time to think about it?'

"I says, 'No, I don't want no time to think about it. I wanna belong.' Now, if I woulda said, 'No, I wanna think about it, I don't wanna belong,' I woulda never made the fuckin' door.

"I woulda been stabbed, shot, mutilated. Because once you're at that table, there's no turning back."

So with thirty-five members of the Philadelphia mob looking on (Salvatore LaRussa had left his house prior to the start of the ceremony), Nick Caramandi stood at the head of the table as Nicky Scarfo administered what a federal prosecutor would later aptly describe as the bloody oath of loyalty. But first the mob boss went out of his way to praise him, acknowledging that his initiation was long overdue.

"I feel, and some of these members here feel, you shoulda been here a long time ago," Scarfo said. "Ten years ago. We really appreciate what you've done for this thing of ours. The way you helped us against our enemies. The way you've been loyal. We truly believe that you belong here and we really want you to be one of us."

With that, Scarfo reached for a piece of tissue paper and placed it in Caramandi's cupped hands. Then he took a match and lit the paper. As it burned he told Caramandi to repeat after him the words that a Mafioso lives—and dies—by.

"May I burn like the saints in hell if I betray any one of my friends."

Scarfo then pointed to the table.

"He says, 'You see this knife and gun on the table. Would you use it for any one of your friends?' I says, 'Yes.'

"Now he looks around the room and calls Faffy to the head of the table. There's a pin on the table and Faffy grabs the pin and pricks the index finger, the shooting finger, on my right hand and some blood comes out.

"Then everybody gets up and joins hands and Nicky says a few words in Italian. We all put our heads down. I can't make out what he's saying, since I don't understand Italian, but I hear the words *amico nostro* and *cosa nostra*. After that, he tells me to go around the table and shake everybody's hand. And as I do this, each member wished me luck. Who kisses you on the cheek. Who kisses you on the lips. I shake their hands, all the way around the table, till I come back to Scarfo. Then I shake his hand. Kiss him. Then we all join hands again and he repeats a few things more in Italian and tells me to walk around the table again.

"I shake hands. Everybody wishes me luck again. I come back to him and he says, 'You are now one of us. These are all your brothers here.'"

The ceremony was repeated again for Joe Grande. Then Scarfo pulled a pair of small reading glasses from his pocket and placed some notes he had written earlier in front of him on the table.

"He says Blackie Napoli is going to retire and Patty Specs [Pasquale Martirano] is going to be the new capo in Newark. He says, 'Blackie is gettin' old and it's too much for him to handle. My choice here is Patty Specs.' So the announcement is made and we all clap for Patty.

"Then Nicky says, 'I'm going to make Tommy and Faffy acting capos.' Well, their faces dropped, because these two birds thought they were gonna get the slot immediately. But Scarfo said, 'I'm gonna have them acting capos. If they do well, then we'll see what happens in the future.' Then he says for the time being me and Charlie were going to be with Tommy and Faffy and Joey Grande was going to be with Nicky's nephew, Philip [Leonetti].

"Then he told us the dos and don'ts. He said we couldn't fool with counterfeit money. We couldn't fool with bonds. He said no kidnapping. And no drugs. But he says it was all right to shake down drug dealers, which I was already doing. And he says, 'You could loan 'em money. You could rob them.' But nobody could protect them. You could more or less have your way with them. If they wanna pay ya, okay. But if they resist, they gotta face this."

And then Scarfo stuck out his finger and cocked his thumb, making the sign of the gun.

Scarfo also said that any member could borrow up to $999

from another member without reporting it to his capo. But if you borrowed $1,000 or more, it had to be reported. He also explained how a made member would introduce another made member to a third member.

"If I'm introducing a made guy to another made guy, I say, 'This is a friend of ours,'" Caramandi said. "If it's not a made guy, I'd say, 'This is a friend of mine.' And, see, there always has to be a third person. I couldn't walk up to another guy who was made and introduce myself as a made member. Somebody else who was in the mob had to make the introduction. This is the way it was done."

It was all part of the family protocol that Scarfo outlined that afternoon. Rules to live by. Rules, Caramandi soon found out, that governed almost every aspect of his life. Any trip out of the Philadelphia area, other than to Atlantic City, had to be reported to your capo. And every business venture, legitimate or illegitimate, had to be cleared first. Always touch base, he was told repeatedly.

By four o'clock that afternoon, the ceremonies were over and the drinks and food were served. It was a crisp autumn afternoon in Whitemarsh Township, an upper-middle-class Waspish community a half hour's drive but light-years away from the South Philadelphia where Caramandi had spent virtually all of his life. This was the land of manicured lawns, hidden driveways, BMWs, and Volvo station wagons. It was where the Philadelphia Cricket Club made its home. And the posh Whitemarsh Valley Country Club. And there in the middle of it all sat Caramandi, who certainly would never qualify for membership in either one of those organizations, but who on this afternoon had been granted membership in an even more exclusive club. So he and the rest of the mob ate and drank and shared hearty good fellowship. They laughed and joked and congratulated each other.

"We were on cloud nine," Caramandi said.

They were men of honor.

No one mentioned that three years earlier Salvatore Testa, in a similar ceremony, had taken that same bloody oath. No one asked whether the loyalty that Scarfo demanded went both ways.

That was a question for another time.

PART
THREE

CHAPTER FIFTEEN

nce they were formally initiated into the organization, Caramandi and Iannece effectively took control of the corner at Camac and Moore. It was their neighborhood, their clubhouse. They were the kings of Passyunk Avenue.

At about this same time, the Crow experienced another major change in his life. On a Friday afternoon early in November, two weeks after he was initiated into the Mafia, Caramandi and his girlfriend, Marlene, went to City Hall and were married. Marlene had two teenaged daughters from a previous marriage. She lived with them in a stylish brick row house on Pierce Street just around the corner from the clubhouse at Camac and Moore. The house had a fancy wrought-iron gate across the entryway.

Caramandi moved in and established a routine that would carry him through the next two years. On most mornings, he got up around 7:00 and met Charlie White. They'd drive down to The Lakes, a park in South Philadelphia, where they would jog two or three miles. Then they'd head back to Charlie's house for coffee. Caramandi would then go home to shower and shave. By 10:00 A.M. he and Iannece were on the corner in front of the clubhouse at Camac and Moore ready to start the day.

"It was a good spot," Caramandi said of the clubhouse. "In the front was a coffee machine and in back were a couple of card tables. We'd hang out there and guys from the neighborhood would come around. We even had a guy who used to take care of the place. People would drop off the street tax in the morning and then in the afternoons I might go out and do some business."

Caramandi liked the routine of the corner. And he liked the feel of the neighborhood.

"People loved us there because we treated them right," Caramandi said. "See, some of these guys, like Tommy and Faffy, thought they were gangsters, but they didn't really understand about this thing.

"You need the people. I remember one time somebody from the police department came down to talk at a neighborhood community meeting about street crime. And he passed some remark about the 'gangsters' over at Camac and Moore. The people started screaming at him about how we help the neighborhood. How we keep out troublemakers. See, that's what this thing is about."

Helping your neighbor and caring for your family. As 1984 drew to a close, the Crow was becoming domesticated. And he loved it. Although during more than two years of interviews he always shied away from any in-depth discussion about his wife and her family—"We don't need to bring them into this," he would say—it was clear that he enjoyed being married. He was almost fifty years old and he was tired of the nightclub and bar scene. He might spend his "workday" lying, cheating, robbing, stealing, and threatening people's lives, but he preferred to spend his evenings watching television with his wife or puttering around the kitchen putting together a meal. In that respect he was different from most of the other members brought into the mob around this same time.

Scarfo had surrounded himself with a bunch of young kids. Joey and Wayne Grande, Gino and Nick Milano, Salvatore Scafidi, Frank and Philip Narducci, and Joey and Anthony Pungitore were all made or proposed at about the same time as Caramandi. And all of them were under thirty years old. It was almost unheard-of. In Bruno's day they would have had to spend another ten years on the street as associates before they'd even be considered for membership, and then only one in ten might get the button. They lacked experience and maturity. They didn't know how things were done—not necessarily mob things, just street things. Caramandi had been on the hustle for thirty years, and it showed. He knew the importance of planning. He was patient. He was cautious.

And his brains weren't in his pants. Some of these younger guys were Passyunk Avenue Romeos. They were more interested in chasing broads than stalking Harry Riccobene. They were at home in the trendy nightclubs on South Street or at the casinos in Atlantic City. They killed time hanging out in neighborhood taverns dressed in designer sport shirts, $80 slacks, and highly polished $200 Italian loafers. You'd find them drinking a beer and watching a ball game on the big-screen television, preening in front of a mirror while Frank Sinatra sang "New York, New York" on the jukebox. Then Scarfo or Testa or Leonetti would hand them a gun and tell them to go out and shoot somebody and they'd be on their way. And they thought that's all there was to being a mobster, that that was what the Mafia was all about.

Caramandi knew better.

"All my life I knew made guys, but until I got made I never knew what the fuck they were. And then you learn what life is all about. What people are all about. Who you can trust and who you can't. What fortunes you can make. And what doors open for you. You become like a god. Your whole life changes. You have powers that are unlimited. You got a secret army behind you. But you gotta know how to use this.

"Take a guy like Chickie Narducci. He died a millionaire 'cause he knew how to use his power. He knew how to create things. He knew how to be a success.

"See, it's up to you to create and develop things. That's one aspect of being a made guy. And there's no limit to what you can do, as long as you do the right thing. As long as you touch base. You'll have the strength and the army behind you and the doors and the keys to do anything you want.

"But not too many guys can handle it. Some people, it goes to their fuckin' head. The people you could be around, the people who acknowledge you. From all walks of life. Movie stars love to be around made guys. So it's power. Some people use it wisely. Some people don't know how to use it and don't want to use it. And when they do get it, they get scared of it. It looks like peaches and cream, but it can be fuckin' devastating, too.

"For one thing, you're not a regular guy anymore. You just can't go in a bar and get drunk with the guys and kid around. You gotta watch yourself. You gotta keep your composure all the time. There's a certain makeup you have to develop. You put this coat of armor on. Sometimes you think you're fuckin' bulletproof."

For Caramandi, being Mafioso was a career achievement. It was his Ph.D., his listing in the blue book. Being a member of the mob gave him status, clout, a chance to be somebody.

"Look, I grew up on the streets," he would say. "I didn't go to no college. I wasn't born with no silver spoon in my mouth. What did I have?"

So he robbed and he stole and he cheated. And eventually he killed. But this was simply the way things were. His victims were crooks too—"You can't cheat an honest man," he'd say. The suckers, the victims he stung, were greedy people looking to get over on either their competitors in business or the tax man.

Caramandi operated in this netherworld where there were no rules, where cheating, lying, and stealing were accepted, even expected. He figured the people he dealt with knew this as well as he did. He applied the same logic to murder. He didn't kill any "innocent" people. His victims were mobsters or mob associates. They knew what the life was. They had crossed over that line the same way he had. They understood just what Caramandi meant when, discussing the wanton and ruthless killing during the Riccobene war, he had said, "These were crazy things, but they had to be done."

You graduate from Harvard Business or the Wharton School and the degree opens doors for you. You get a job with a big Wall Street firm, you join a fancy health club, you buy a co-op on the Upper East Side.

Caramandi graduated from the streets. Membership in the mob was his ticket to the good life. So he welcomed it, but not because he enjoyed killing people. Scarfo, Leonetti, Salvie Testa—they were the ones who seemed to get a rush from blowing somebody away. For Caramandi, murder was just a business proposition, something he had to do. But being a Mafioso, that was more than being a murderer. That was being somebody. That was being recognized and respected.

"You see, it's like word of mouth, and it just feeds on itself. In the neighborhood, let's say, you go to a wedding and you're greeted by different people and they know your status. And they feel that macho respect you're getting, and they want to be with you. Now when we say a person is 'with us' it means that we're responsible for them. They know they've got the power of the mob behind them. They've got clout, and in case they have any problems, we fix them.

"Let me explain what I mean about people being with you.

This is the biggest thing that the mob has, the people that are around us, and you can have as many people as you want. You could have two guys with you, or ten thousand. It doesn't make any difference, as long as you register 'em with your capo and tell 'em they're with you. You could have a grocery store guy, a politician, a union guy, a judge, a lawyer. You can have anybody from any walk of life. As long as you register him, he belongs to you. In other words, like I explained, you're responsible for him.

"Now, most of the guys, you make a buck with. Maybe some people you can't make a buck with, but they can benefit you in other ways. Some people you like and you want to protect. This is what makes this thing of ours so strong, having people with you from all walks of life. I had doctors with me, lawyers, union officials, loan sharks, drug dealers, flimflam guys. I had so many people with me, and with a sixty-member Mafia family in Philadelphia, you gotta figure we controlled like twenty million people in Philadelphia, Jersey, and upstate Pennsylvania. That was our territory. Twenty million people you're talking about. Just in our territory.

"So this is a powerful, powerful thing. You might have a guy, say, that's with you that has a problem. The guy comes to me, say for instance, he's got a daughter and somebody's bothering her. Well, now I have to protect that guy. I'll grab ahold of whoever it is that's bothering his daughter and say, 'If you don't leave this girl alone, you got a big problem.' Now if the guy doesn't respond, if he doesn't want to do the right thing, he'll get hurt. And in some cases, he might get killed. Or one of our union guys is having trouble getting work. We would go to the union president or the union's business agent and say, 'Make sure this guy's working. Keep this guy working.'

"This is one of the things that makes this thing of ours so effective, and why it has so much respect and impact. You have to understand that. Because they know we don't play no games. The gun is our power. That's always been the power of the mob. You have to realize, and people don't understand, that the respect that we have is because we build it and we keep it firm. We keep the policies firm. We keep the chain of command strong. And we take care of our own.

"See, the people are with us because we protect them. And it works both ways—they do for us, too. They stand by us. They protect us. During the war with the Riccobenes, for example, when we were looking to kill all these people, we used neighborhood guys that were with us. They wasn't made members. But we borrowed their cars, they held guns for us in their houses, they took all kinds of chances. We made 'em do different things. We would go to a person's home to change clothes after a shooting. See, after you fire a gun, you have to wash down with vinegar and take a shower so the gunpowder don't stay on you. And you have to get rid of your clothes. So you would use people that are with you. I mean, that's a biggie. 'Cause you need these things. And this relationship is the strength and the backbone of the mob. They come to us, we go to them.

"Because, you know, the other law, the police law, is the police law. But our law is a law that you know is gonna get results. They know when they come with a problem and they sit down and they explain their problem, no matter how difficult, we're right there to help them.

"So, if you're a member and you've got the ability, there's no telling how far you can go and how much money you can make and how strong your position can become. You could have a loan-shark business and be partners with a guy without putting up no money. You could be in the construction business—you got a piece of a contractor because when he has problems, you take care of them. And periodically, the guy will throw you money. Politicians. Judges. It's like one hand washes the other.

"This is the hidden second government that we talk about. The people that are with us. These are John Q. Citizen. These are good people, people who wouldn't hurt a mouse. But they need the strength of the mob. They depend on it. They depend on their jobs and their businesses because of us. But it also goes beyond that—they might have problems with their mothers gettin' into nursing homes, for instance. We even solve that problem for them. I mean, anything you can think of, no matter how big, no matter how small, we can help them.

"And elections. If a guy wants to run for an office in the city and he comes to us, we'll put him in office. If he wants our support, you understand? We'll go to unions, presidents of unions, and tell 'em to vote for this guy. And this is what makes it powerful. This is how you control things.

"You get somebody elected and he's indebted. And he makes friends with other politicians and judges. And this is how we become powerful. People are just tools to benefit us, to benefit our strength, to benefit our power, to benefit our structure nationwide. In every, every avenue there is in life, we benefit. You understand?

"And the more you learn as you're in the Mafia, the more you make. It all depends on how much you want to gain. It all depends on how much ambition you have. It's up to you. It's up to each individual member how they want to do things.

"This is the way it goes. It's the way this whole fucking thing exists. By people being with us, being around us. I mean, who else is there to go to? Look at the unions. These guys are not killers, they're workers. Understand? It's always the power of the gun. And they know the guns will come up. People respect that. They fear the gun."

Following the Testa murder, Caramandi had few other occasions when he would even have to consider using the gun. He and Charlie White were now ensconced at the clubhouse on Camac and Moore. They were reporting to Faffy and Tommy, who were acting capos, but they were pretty much on their own.

And as mobsters, they were the perfect complement for one another. Iannece liked the traditional mob gambits, loan-sharking, gambling, and bookmaking. Caramandi was an expert on scams, labor racketeering, and the construction business. Together they became the Scarfo family's most consistent money-making machine. From 1984 through 1986, they were in the middle of quasi-legitimate and illegitimate business propositions that brought the organization close to $5 million. The money just kept rolling in. And each month they would whack it up, Caramandi and Charlie White keeping half of what they made. The other half was set aside for the "elbow." They'd keep a record of what was coming in, and each month they'd send cash down the shore to Little Nicky. Caramandi, by this time, had reached out into the construction industry in Philadelphia, helping local developers to get contracts—arranging to rig bids when he could—and taking care of any union problems. In exchange, he got a kickback or a cut from the business. If the deal was big enough, he'd spread the work around, often arranging cement or concrete work for companies controlled by Larry Merlino or Nicky Scarfo, Jr.

But while 1984 proved to be a good year for Nick Caramandi, it was full of problems for Nicky Scarfo, who was struggling to get his house in order after returning from prison. The Salvie Testa situation had taken up a lot of time and was the cause of substantial aggravation. There were also several other nagging problems. Cracks had begun to appear in the once impenetrable organization, warning signs that Scarfo chose to ignore.

The Atlantic City deal with Mayor Mike Matthews, for example, had blown up in everyone's face. Jimmy Biaco, who was touting the corrupt land deal in which Leonetti and Matthews were to hold a hidden interest, turned out to be an undercover federal agent whose real name was Jim Bannister. Matthews, Frank Lentino (one of Scarfo's contacts inside Local 54), and, eventually, Leonetti were indicted. The charges were subsequently dropped against Philip, but Lentino ended up copping a plea and, at age seventy-three, was sentenced to ten years in prison.

Matthews, after dancing on the fence for almost a year (for a brief period, the FBI says, he agreed to cooperate), pleaded out to one count of accepting a $10,000 payoff from Biaco/Bannister. He got fifteen years, but to this day continues to deny the broader allegations that he sold his office to the mob. In pleading guilty, however, he did offer a partial explanation that Caramandi could appreciate.

"Greed," the mayor told a federal judge, "got the better of me."

Also in 1984, Raymond "Long John" Martorano and Albert Daidone, another Local 54 official, were convicted of first degree murder for ordering the assassination of John McCullough. Willie Moran, the wannabe mobster who carried out the hit, testified for the prosecution in the case, becoming the first in a long line of Scarfo family members or associates to turn.

Mario "Sonny" Riccobene, Victor DeLuca, and Joseph Pedulla—major players in the shooting of Scarfo family consigliere Frank Monte—also made their debuts as government informants that summer, testifing against Harry Riccobene and two other associates in the Monte murder trial. Harry and Sonny were in jail on racketeering charges when Sonny decided to cooperate in the Monte investigation. Distraught over the wanton use of violence that had brought about the deaths of his brother, Robert, and his son, Enrico, Sonny pleaded guilty to a third degree murder charge in the Monte case and took the witness stand against his half brother Harry. This testimony, coupled with that of Pedulla and DeLuca, two of the hit men assigned by Harry to kill Monte, gave the government an airtight case. Harry Riccobene, now seventy-four, is currently serving a life prison term and is likely to die behind bars.

In September, just two weeks after Sal Testa was finally killed, Chuckie Merlino pleaded guilty to the bribery charge resulting from his drunken driving arrest and videotaped attempt to pay off a Margate police officer. Scarfo was not pleased. It was one thing to get pinched for committing a crime. Hell, that could happen to anybody. But this was stupidity, and Scarfo was coming to the end of the line with Merlino, who happened to be his oldest friend.

"See, Chuckie didn't really want to be underboss," Caramandi said. "He just wanted to stay in South Philly, drink his wine, and have a few businesses."

Merlino couldn't handle the responsibility. He drank too much. And then when the pressure built, he drank some more. There was one occasion, Caramandi recalled, when Scarfo took Merlino up to New York for a meeting with some ranking members of the Gambino organization. Scarfo, over the years, had forged ties with both the Genovese family and with one branch of the Gambino organization. Bruno had been tight with old Carlo Gambino and his brother-in-law Paul Castellano. By 1984, Gambino was dead and Castellano was the boss. But Scarfo's connections went in another direction. His links to the Gambinos were through Aniello Dellacroce and a young up-and-comer who reported to Dellacroce—a man named John Gotti.

"So Nicky and Chuckie go up to New York for a meeting. I think it was about the video jukeboxes," Caramandi recalled.

Scarfo and the Gambinos were discussing a business venture involving jukeboxes equipped with video screens, a new pay-for-play technology aimed at the MTV generation. And the mob was ready to cash in. In addition to placing and servicing the jukeboxes, the deal involved selling advertising space. Typed commercial messages could be flashed across the bottom of the screen during the video performance. Scarfo was angling to set up distributorships up and down the East Coast.

"At this meeting in New York, Nicky went upstairs to meet with some guys, and he told Chuckie to wait down in the bar with some other people," Caramandi said. "By the time Nicky comes down, Chuckie's drunk, he's made a pass at somebody's wife, and he's in an argument with somebody at the bar. Now Nicky's embarrassed in front of these New York guys. I mean, how's it look, your underboss drunk?"

Adding to Scarfo's annoyance, the New Jersey Casino Control Commission finally succeeded in forcing Frank Gerace out as head of Atlantic City Bartenders Union Local 54. Like the former mayor, Gerace insisted right to the end that he was not running his union at Scarfo's behest. New Jersey authorities felt otherwise, however, and in a legal battle that lasted nearly five years and went all the way to the U.S. Supreme Court, they succeeded in defending the state's right to intervene in union activities involving the casino industry.

Gerace lashed out at both the state and the media, claiming he was a victim of guilt by association and anti-Italian bias. To state and federal law enforcement authorities, however, Gerace was merely being held legally accountable for his connections to Nicky Scarfo, a man they wanted desperately to keep away from the casino industry.

As 1984 drew to a close, no one realized how many others would soon find themselves forced to pay an even steeper legal price for their dealings on behalf of the most violent Mafia boss in America.

CHAPTER SIXTEEN

There wasn't much that Nick Caramandi was afraid of at this point. Except airplanes. And it was the Crow's misfortune that in 1984 Nicky Scarfo decided to expand his operations to southern Florida. Over the next two years, Scarfo would spend almost as much time in Fort Lauderdale as he would in South Philadelphia. And he always wanted members of his organization around.

"I just don't like to fly," Caramandi said, "so I used to drink before we got on the plane. One time I got so drunk they wouldn't let me on. I hadda wait till the next flight."

Scarfo began traveling to Florida shortly after he got out of prison. At first, law enforcement authorities thought the trips were nothing more than vacations. Scarfo had spent almost two years in Texas, and his blood had thinned. Winters in Atlantic City are cold and damp. At Turnberry, outside of Miami, where Scarfo stayed in a condominium, it was sunny and warm. But then Scarfo showed up in a lavish home in Fort Lauderdale owned by a Philadelphia-area developer named Leonard Mercer. And eventually documents would be filed indicating that a Scarfo company, Casablanca South Leasing, was "renting" the home from Mercer. Later Scarfo's forty-foot Silverton cabin cruiser would dock behind the home. The boat was registered to Jerry Blavat, a Philadelphia disk jockey of some renown who billed himself as "the Geater with the Heater." Scarfo, according to the Geater's attorney, had entered into a lease-purchase deal for the boat and was paying off the loan Blavat had negotiated when he bought it. Scarfo christened the cabin cruiser *Casablanca Usual Suspects*, a reference to one of the more memorable lines from the classic Bogart film that he loved.

It was a great way to tweak the noses of police and federal agents, who now had him under almost constant surveillance. Scarfo would take a dozen or so of his Mafiosi out on fishing trips whenever they were in Florida. The FBI cameras would be clicking away as they set off. Here would be some of the most notorious mobsters in Philadelphia history, tanned, smiling, and standing on the deck of this luxurious cabin cruiser hamming it up for the hidden cameras they knew were out there. Federal and New Jersey authorities would later unsuccessfully try to seize both the boat and the home, arguing that they were, in fact, Scarfo's property and had been obtained with ill-gotten gains.

The Broward County Sheriff's Department, which joined in the Scarfo surveillance, began to record the comings and goings of other mob members and associates who turned up on the doorstep of the $650,000 hacienda-style house that became Scarfo's southern headquarters. Not just Philadelphia family members, but mobsters and associates connected with the Lucchese, DeCavalcante, and Genovese organizations were making appearances. Southern Florida had become a haven for mobsters from the Northeast. Many had homes and business interests there. And in late 1984, with talk of legalized casino gambling for Miami and its environs, Scarfo's appearance on the scene began to be viewed as more than mere coincidence. The feeling in law enforcement circles was that Scarfo wanted his organization in place to cash in if another casino boom developed.

"My rapport was good with Scarfo. He never forgot what I did for him back in the seventies. He knew what kind of guy I was, and he liked me. He just liked me. Later, when he came out of jail, he had to have a job, so he started working for a shirt-maker named Gennaro. Scarfo said he was a salesman, selling shirts. Custom-made, two hundred dollars each. I was in charge of selling these shirts for him.

"Charlie and me started to get real close to Nicky at this time. We'd meet him for dinners, we started going to his house. Then he got the place in Florida and we started going there. He would make me stay with him, while the other guys had to stay at a hotel. And he had parties at the house. We used to go out to a lot of restaurants wherever we were. And he always paid. He always picked up the tab, for ten, fifteen, twenty guys, like nothing."

During one of their stays in Florida, Caramandi first broached a plan to tap into the health benefits fund of Bartenders Union Local 54 in Atlantic City. These were the kind of deals the Crow dreamed about, multimillion-dollar deals that could last a lifetime. Caramandi, following the established chain of command, had tried twice to get DelGiorno to bring the idea to Scarfo.

"But Tommy didn't understand it, he didn't absorb it, and I don't think he explained it right to Nicky," Caramandi said. "When I told him about it, he saw right away what I was talking about."

Caramandi had a doctor friend who, he said, would be willing to set up clinics all over South Jersey, which was the area Local 54 covered. Then, for a set fee, these clinics would provide medical service for all the union members.

"It didn't matter whether he saw one person or a hundred people, he'd get the same amount of money," Caramandi said. And in exchange for setting him up with this contract, the doctor would agree to kick a portion of his money back to Caramandi and Scarfo.

By 1985, Local 54 had more than fifteen thousand members. The union's contract called for the casinos to contribute $1 per hour per worker into the health, welfare, and pension funds. It didn't take a financial genius to figure that even with seasonal employment variations and some part-time workers, this created a pot of millions of dollars. This was better than the Krugerrands or the $1,000 bills. It was the kind of quasi-legitimate scam that you could milk for years. It was what Caramandi figured being a mobster was really all about.

"Nicky liked the idea a lot," he said. "So I started to put the deal together. It was one of the things I was working on when I got pinched. I was also setting up a deal to organize the casino dealers. See, in Atlantic City the dealers don't belong to a union. I had a guy, worked at Caesars, who was gonna get everybody to sign union cards. We woulda had a vote and I think we woulda got in there. Then we woulda organized the other hotels."

Scarfo liked this kind of grandiose planning. It played to his vanity and demonstrated his power and control. Most of all, however, he liked the money that was involved. He loved to discuss "his end" of a deal, his take. For Scarfo, this was his entitlement. This was what came with being mob boss.

He and Caramandi fed off each other's dreams when they were together in Florida. Little Nicky even talked about what he would do when he retired, demonstrating a confidence that seemed somewhat misplaced, given the way his two predecessors had left the job. Scarfo said he wanted to get a ranch in El Paso, Texas. He had made some Mexican connections while he was in La Tuna, and he saw opportunities south of the border. He talked about sending Caramandi down to Mexico to organize some unions and about setting up deals with some Mexican drug dealers he had met in prison. Scarfo had two heroes, Caramandi said. One was Al Capone. The other was Emiliano Zapata, the Mexican revolutionary whose life was captured on film in a movie starring Marlon Brando.

"Every time that fuckin' *Viva Zapata* came on TV, he used to watch it," Caramandi said. "Certain guys he glorified."

Scarfo was not a student of Mexican history. He wasn't a champion of liberty for the oppressed. But he was fascinated with men of action. And in his mind, he would mix the real with the reel. Capone and Bogart. Zapata and Brando. He liked tough guys, hard drinkers, hard livers; guys who knew how to handle a gun and knew how to handle a broad. In many ways, Nicky Scarfo was a caricature. Here was this five-foot-five 130-pound fifty-five-year-old playing at being a gangster. It was almost funny, until the bullets started flying and the bodies started dropping.

Scarfo adhered to this macho style, and he expected those around him to do the same. On almost every trip to Florida, he was accompanied by his new girlfriend, a former cocktail waitress whom Caramandi and everyone else in the outfit knew simply as Chicago. Scarfo had set her up in an apartment at the shore. And while his wife stayed home in Atlantic City, Little Nicky would fly to Florida with Chicago for a vacation. Like almost everything else in his life, however, Scarfo's extramarital relationship was tinged with violence. Periodically, Caramandi said, when Chicago "got out of line," Little Nicky would "tune her up a little bit."

"Me and Spike [Anthony DiGregorio, who was now working as the caretaker of the Florida home] used to be in the house, and we'd hear Nicky giving her a beating upstairs," Caramandi said. "Then he'd come down and say, 'Every once in a while you gotta bang 'em around to keep them in line.'

"He could be a very vicious guy, turn on you in a fuckin'

second. He had these sayings. 'I could forgive, but I could never forget.' 'I'm like the turtle. I always get there.' 'Sooner or later I'll get there.'

"And once he turned on ya, forget about it. You might as well go to fuckin' Russia, because nothing could help ya."

It was impossible to tell what would set Scarfo off, Caramandi said. His moods changed quickly, and he frequently found fault with those around him. One memorable Scarfo tirade occurred on board his cabin cruiser during a party he threw to celebrate the annual Night in Venice festival that was held in Ocean City, New Jersey, each summer.

The affair is staged on the intracoastal waterway, a back-bay area that separates the South Jersey shore communities from the mainland. Every year, usually on the third or fourth Saturday night in July, people with homes and docks along the waterway put out fancy lights, lanterns, and decorations as the city invites anyone with a boat to join in what amounts to a regatta. Hundreds of boats, big and small, take part each year. It's a slow-moving parade on water. The Coast Guard seals off the area to all but those involved.

This proved to be a major problem, Caramandi said, for Tyrone DeNittis, a Philadelphia entertainment agent who had promised to provide a band for Scarfo and about thirty friends who were on the cabin cruiser.

"What happened was that all the boats had to follow a certain path. And at some point, Tyrone DeNittis was supposed to have a three- or four-piece band play for us on the boat. We had plenty of food. Drinks. A big affair. The boat was over forty feet.

"But when we get to the spot where Tyrone and the band were supposed to meet us, it's blocked off. They were supposed to come in on a speedboat and meet us. But the speedboat couldn't get in. Well, Scarfo blew his fuckin' top. He'd been telling everybody that morning about the band we were gonna have and all this stuff. So when the band doesn't show, he told Philip [Leonetti], 'You tell Tyrone to stay the fuck out of Atlantic City for a fuckin' year. I don't want to see him.' Fifteen minutes go by and Nicky screams, 'Make that a year and a half. I don't wanna see him for a year and a half.' An hour goes by. 'Make that five years. In fact, I never want to see him for the rest of my fuckin' life. You do business with him, meet him in fuckin' Chicago or somewhere. Keep him away from Atlantic City. Don't even meet him in Philadelphia.'

"I mean, he just carried on something awful."

Caramandi saw that same violent and irrational temper a few months later in Florida. This time, Scarfo's ire was aimed at a pharmacist and mob groupie whom Caramandi and several other members of the organization had nicknamed Face of a Dog.

Face of a Dog was always trying to ingratiate himself with Scarfo and had promised to give Scarfo's girlfriend, Chicago, a car. "It wasn't even an expensive car," Caramandi said. "He had it up in New York. It was worth about fifteen hundred." But Scarfo decided he wanted it and was pressing the Dog on the issue.

"But the guy couldn't leave his job, he was operating this pharmacy in Miami and he couldn't get any time off to go up to New York to get this car. So instead, this poor guy buys Nicky like a thousand dollars' worth of whiskey for a house-opening present when Scarfo got the house. And he'd get medicine for him and anything else that he needed. I mean, the guy was worth his weight in gold. But one day Scarfo got his horns up and he says, 'This motherfucker thinks he's jerking me off. Nick, I want you to go down there'—he was working at a place on Collins Avenue, downtown Miami—'and tell him he better never come around here. He better stay the fuck away from this house. I never want to see his face again. And tell him if I ever see his face he's gonna wind up floating in the fuckin' ocean.' He says, 'I want you to go there *now* and tell 'im.' Me and Spike look at each other and we say, 'Okay, Nick. If that's what you want.'

"We get in the car and drive to the pharmacy. The guy's behind the counter. I go back there and I tell him, 'I got bad news for you. This came from the top.' And I go with my hand [in front of his chest]. 'You know, the Little Guy.'

" 'You better not come around the house anymore. Forget about him. This guy's pissed off about the car, and he says you're lucky you ain't dead.' Well, this guy turned all kinds of colors. He says, 'What did I do? Is this what I get for being good?' There was tears in his eyes. He was so scared. He didn't know which way to turn. So that night, he comes around, the goof. But me and Spike walk him down the street and we say, 'Listen. Stay away from here. This guy is on the warpath with you. There's nothing you could do. Give us some time and we'll try to cool him off. He don't want the car no more. He's just fuckin' bitter, so just stay away.'

"See, this was the way Scarfo was. Once he turned, he got bitter. I mean, it wasn't the guy's fault. Because the car was in New York and there was no way he could get up there and drive it back. The guy was just too busy working, trying to make a living.

"But with Scarfo, you can't fuck up. There's no room for mistakes. 'Cause when Scarfo turns on you, you ain't got a Chinaman's chance. Even Spike says that. He said, 'I'd rather have trouble with fifty tough guys than with Scarfo, because he ain't gonna let you off the hook.'"

That was the way Scarfo was. Everything had to be precise with him. And everything had to be his way. Scarfo, Caramandi said, got intoxicated with power once he became boss.

"He had been held down all those years. But he made it to the top, and he got carried away there. You see, Scarfo wanted to be like a movie star. He fancied himself a fuckin' movie star. You know, he had his nose fixed. He used to wear built-in shoes [shoes with lifts] to make himself taller. He had a complex about his height.

"He was the kind of guy who never let anything pass him. He had big expectations. Nobody counted but us. You had to be a member to count, and certain members counted more than others. So long as Scarfo didn't turn on ya, you were solid. But if he turned, then you had a problem."

Caramandi now believes that the weeks he spent with Scarfo in Florida between 1984 and 1986 saved his life. It was during that period, he says, that he really got to know the volatile mob boss, that he learned how he thought and how he operated. The Crow, drawing on the instincts that had served him so well as a con man and hustler, became adept at reading Scarfo's moods and anticipating his actions. This proved to be very advantageous while he was a member in good standing, and was even more of a boon after he had fallen from grace. Survival depended on understanding Scarfo. The streets of South Philadelphia had been littered with the bodies of those who didn't. Some, like Caramandi's old friends Mickey Diamond and Pat Spirito, never even saw it coming. Caramandi did not intend to go out that way. So whenever Scarfo talked, he listened. Whenever Scarfo moved on someone, he watched.

"One time we were sitting around the patio at the house in Florida. We're drinking, and Scarfo starts talking about his oldest son, Chris. He was very down on the kid, who was his child by his first wife. And he starts saying, 'This fuckin' kid, he don't want to be with us. He's good with his hands, but he's no good with this,' pointing the finger in the sign of the gun. This really bothered him. He kept saying, 'This kid could have everything,' and he couldn't understand why this kid didn't want no part of being in the mob.

"But the kid, you know, was working for the father. He worked for him in the construction business for a while. Good kid. Nice kid. I worked with him. Got him some concrete work. He didn't show any kind of attitude. I mean, he never knocked the mob. He just didn't want no part of it for some reason. Pretty straight kid. Pretty honorable kid. That's the way it was. But Scarfo carried on about him. He was displeased and disappointed. But there was nothing he could do about it."

Nor could Scarfo—or Caramandi, for that matter—do anything about a situation involving Little Nicky's second son, a situation that was at first ticklish and later potentially lethal.

"One morning I'm at the house and Scarfo walks out and tells me, 'Nick, you know, my son Nicky is going out with your stepdaughter.' So I says, 'Yeah, I know,' which I did. But then he says, 'Well, I don't want him to go steady with her. I want him to have a lot of girls. He's young yet. I don't want him to get serious.'

"So I turn around and, I don't know what made me say this, I says, 'Hey, Nick. I didn't condone this. But your fuckin' kid's got a hard head like you do.' Well, he just looked at me and he turned around and he didn't say nothin'. Spike and Philip, who were there, both gave me a look.

"See, I didn't mean to say it that way, but what the fuck. I hadn't put them together. His son, Nicky Jr., met my stepdaughter in Atlantic City. I was with my wife and her two daughters at some party and he was there, too. Now he starts dating her and it gets serious. She's a very, very pretty girl. And then Nicky found out about it. And see, he don't like girls from downtown [South Philadelphia].

"He always said, 'These fuckin' girls from downtown, Italian girls from downtown, are no good. You go out with them for a couple of years, you wine 'em and dine 'em. You give 'em things. Then you have a beef with 'em and the next thing you know they're out with your best friend and you gotta bust the guy's head.' He didn't like girls from downtown. For some reason, that was in his brain.

"But by then it was was too late. It was six or seven months later and Nicky Jr. was head over heels in love with my stepdaughter. I didn't condone it. I never even invited him over the house. He came to me one day and he said, 'Listen, is it all right if I go out with your stepdaughter? I wanna do the right thing.' And I said to him, 'That's your business.' But I didn't like the idea, you know what I mean? 'Cause other guys might think I was condoning it to get points with Nicky. And that wasn't true."

Of Nicky Scarfo's three sons, Nicky Jr. was the most like his father. He had the same quick temper and carried himself with the same macho bravado. He was taller than his father, but there was no mistaking the sharp-featured, angular face. His hair was brown rather than black, but Nicky Jr.—like dozens of other young members and associates of the mob—combed it in the same straight-back, slightly teased style that Little Nicky had adopted. Nicky Jr., like his cousin Philip Leonetti, grew up around the mob and naturally gravitated toward it. He theoretically worked for Scarf Inc., the Atlantic City cement contracting company, but he most often served as a gofer for his dad.

Not a particularly bright kid, Nicky Jr. lived off his father's reputation, a risky proposition, given the ever-changing makeup of the Philadelphia underworld. Although Little Nicky hoped to eventually initiate his son into the organization, Nicky Jr. had not done any "work" by the time the Scarfo crime family began to collapse. He did have several minor brushes with the law, however, most involving pushing-and-shoving matches set off by his volatile temper.

"He was a fresh kid," Caramandi said. "And he wasn't very well liked."

But Caramandi's stepdaughter Vicky was caught up in the glamour of it all. Despite the Crow's lack of enthusiasm for the pairing and Marlene's warnings against it, Vicky and Nicky became an item. It was another one of those bizzare subplots that played itself out against the rise and fall of Nicodemo Scarfo. Nicky Jr. continued dating Caramandi's stepdaughter throughout the three-year period that Caramandi was in federal custody helping to build cases against Nicky Sr. and the rest of the mob. And by the time Little Nicky and the others were sentenced to lengthy prison terms, the couple were living together. It was the South Philadelphia version of *West Side*

Story. It was *Romeo and Juliet* on the Boardwalk in Atlantic City.

For the most part, though, Scarfo's life in Fort Lauderdale proved amazingly free of contention and worry. He could be a gracious host, and he loved to show off the house, often opening it for parties at which dozens of mob members and associates—and their dates, but never their wives—would gather. They'd eat, drink, and swim in the pool, dance and laugh into the early hours of the morning.

"One time, Nicky decided he wanted to have this big home-made dinner for maybe forty or fifty guys who were down there. Spike was supposed to do the cooking, and I winded up making three hundred meatballs. It took me five hours to roll three hundred fuckin' meatballs. And you see, the way they eat, where Nicky comes from, they eat the meat first, then the pasta. And the salad last. It was a little different than my custom, 'cause we ate the pasta first, then the meat. But I'm telling Spike, 'You want me to put the macks on now,' meaning the macaroni, the spaghetti. And he says, 'No, no. He eats it different. They eat the meat first.' So we hadda serve the meat first. We had maybe a hundred pounds of beef, pork, and veal. We had all kind of pots going with the pasta. And he likes them *al dente.* And the gravy hadda be just right. I cooked the gravy that whole day. And Scarfo loved it. He loved them kind of gatherings."

Federal and local authorities who had the Fort Lauderdale home under surveillance got a glimpse of just how Scarfo entertained during a big mob confab on January 4, 1986. Later Joseph Moran, a Pennsylvania state trooper assigned to the organized crime division, testified at a parole board in New Jersey about what he had seen that day. Moran had been sent to Florida to assist local police and the FBI in identifying the participants. Police had set up surveillance from a home across the street. Early that afternoon, Moran noted, Scarfo had had to pull his Rolls-Royce out of the garage to make room for the caterer. Now Scarfo and his underboss, Salvatore "Chuckie" Merlino, stood in the driveway. It was about 5:00 P.M., and a parade of guests—virtually every major member and associate of the Scarfo organization—began to arrive. Each passed through a receiving line, paying his respects.

"Nicky was in the doorway and Chuckie Merlino was in a walkway which led from the garage area to the front door,"

Moran said. "And as each of the members of the family walked by Chuckie Merlino, they would kiss him and they would walk up and they would kiss, also, Nicky.

"It was on the cheek.... It was a greeting.

"It's a known showing of respect for persons that are higher up in the organization, just like you—like I would salute my superior. They, in turn, rather than salute, they kiss."

Then, just to make sure no one would get the wrong idea, Moran went on to explain, "It's more or less a hug-type kiss. They don't get involved in anything. Just, maybe, a peck, a little hug."

It was classic testimony—an Irish cop explaining a Sicilian custom to a bunch of Wasps sitting on a parole board.

Yet what police never got—until Caramandi—was the all-important view from inside the home. The New Jersey state police managed to place bugs in Tommy DelGiorno's Ocean City, New Jersey, condominium, and the feds wired mob clubhouses in South Philadelphia and the Roofers Union headquarters in Northeast Philadelphia. But in five years of intense investigation, the authorities were never able to get a bug close to Scarfo, never able to pick up the Little Guy's high-pitched voice, never able to catch Scarfo playing the role he loved.

This was Scarfo as padrone. Little Nicky as the Godfather. Dispensing favors and solving problems. Feting his loyal subjects with a lavish dinner at his estate. Offering advice and counsel. Issuing orders and ultimatums.

Marlon Brando couldn't have played the part any better.

Or De Niro.

Or Pacino.

CHAPTER SEVENTEEN

Defense attorney: Do you only steal from one another or hurt one
                    another?
Caramandi: No. Crooked politicians, crooked judges, crooked
                    union officials, anywhere there is corruption we
                    penetrate. That was our thing.

Caramandi figures he earned the Scarfo organization anywhere from $5 million to $7 million between 1982 and 1986. This, like virtually all the
mob's earnings, was tax-free. Cash. Usually wads
of it. Wrapped in rubber bands and stashed in any
number of places until it was time, at the end of each month,
to send the "elbow" money down the shore.

There was the loan-sharking and the bookmaking and the
sports betting and the shakedowns. These were the staples
of the organization. And there were dozens of other scams,
flimflams, and swindles, including the mob's first serious
forays into organized labor in Philadelphia. Each deal got bigger. And each deal looked better. At the time he was arrested
in June 1986, Caramandi said, he was setting up a $2 million
drug deal and a $1 million extortion scheme. The "shakes"
were generating about $200,000 a year. He, Charlie White, and
a gambling partner named Johnny Cupcakes Melilli were handling $60,000 a week in bookmaking action and had a sports
betting business that, during the football season, took in
$300,000 a week. In addition, Caramandi and Charlie White
had $500,000 in loan-sharking money on the street earning
two points a week. They had $150,000 in cash from the shark

business, and they had a piece of a private methamphetamine deal that netted $375,000.

"I had a lot of things going," Caramandi said. "We were going to make a lot of money. I thought it would never end."

Making money became routine for Nicky Crow. It was no longer a question of finding a scam or setting up a hustle. He now had regular sources of income. He was not averse, however, to supplementing his cash flow with free-lance deals. And these, too, he shared with the organization. One of his first big scores after becoming a made member came from a local guy named Richie Disco, "a half-assed hustler," said Caramandi, who dabbled in several businesses and occasionally "bird-dogged" for the Crow.

"In between 1984 and 1986, I was always busy, hustling different things. I knew this Richie for years. He's got plenty of money, this kid. His father had left him a lot of money, and although the kid was in pretty good shape, he fooled with drugs, credit cards. He was a kind of hanger-on guy.

"One day he tells me a story about a guy who owned an auto body shop."

The story involved the murder of an investment broker who had embezzled a ton of money. The auto body shop owner became friends with the broker, filled him up with booze one day, took the money, and then poisoned him, making it look like suicide. He used a guy from the neighborhood named Tony to help out. Now this auto body shop owner had all the money. And this Tony was angry because he hadn't been given a cut. Caramandi listened to the story and saw the possibilities.

"According to Richie, there was no telling how much money might be involved. So I says to Richie, 'All right. Bring this Tony around. We'll work it out.' So Tony comes around and he says, 'Yeah, I was supposed to get a lot of money. We took the guy to Delaware County and we got him drunk in a motel.' He said they bought paint thinner, made the broker sign a suicide note, and then made him drink the paint thinner, like he poisoned himself.

"I says to myself, this looks good. But first I hadda get the okay—I hadda clear it with Scarfo. A week later I get the word from him. 'Go ahead. Do what you want.' Now I grab ahold of this Tony and Richie to set up the split. They were gonna get a third of the money. I was gonna ask for three hundred thousand. They said it should be no problem, because this guy took millions. But they didn't know how I was gonna go about this thing.

"I asked 'em both does this auto shop guy know any gangsters. They said a few wiseguys, maybe, but nobody really. That was good. So I said to Tony, ' I want you to be there when I move on this guy, because after I leave, I want you to say to him that you know who I am and that I'm with the mob. That makes it easier.' So the plan is set.

"The next day I go to his shop and I start to ask him about the guy he killed. I said, 'You motherfucker. You poisoned him. I want three hundred thousand dollars by tomorrow or else I'm gonna kill you. You'll be dead.' And I grabbed him by the throat. Well, this guy is stunned. I said to him, 'This guy had friends.'

"What happened, this guy shit his pants, he was in such a panic. I said, 'I'll be here tomorrow, and you better make sure that fuckin' money's here.' So I leave, and about an hour later Richie comes around and tells me that after I left, Tony threw up. I was so fuckin' convincing he wanted to back out of the deal. See, just to make it look good, I had said to Tony, 'Do you know me, motherfucker? You got anything to do with this?' And Tony didn't say nothing. He just froze.

"So anyway, now Richie says, 'You got this guy so scared, Tony wants to back out of the deal.' I says, 'You tell him he better do the right thing or else we're gonna hurt him. There's no backing out of the deal.' He says, 'All right. But the guy is petrified, and he's gonna try to reach out for people.'

"I reported what happened to my capos. You know, always touch base. And we all laughed. This next day I go to the auto body shop and who's there but this number writer by the name of Three Fingers Marty, and I know he's associated with certain people. As soon as he sees me, he says, 'Nick, I wanted to see if it was you, that you were authentic.' And he says, 'I'm out of this thing. I ain't got nothin' to do with it.' And he's gone.

"So I grabbed the guy at the auto body shop and I say, 'Where's my fuckin' money?' He says he needs some time to get it. I says, 'I'll be back at three o'clock, and you better have it.' Richie comes around the clubhouse and says we got this guy really shook up but he's still reaching out for people."

Through the South Philadelphia grapevine, the auto body shop owner was able to reach another Caramandi associate, Tony Blinds. Blinds called Caramandi early that afternoon and asked if he could come around and talk to him. They met very briefly at the clubhouse at Camac and Moore.

"Tony Blinds says to me, 'Do me a favor.' But I says, 'Tony, mind your business and tell the guy to pay the fuckin' money. This came from the top. Just forget about it.' So he says, 'Okay, Nick. No problem.' So now Richie comes back and reports that, finally, the guy's gonna pay, but it can't be three hundred thousand. He says, 'He wants to cut you in half.' So I says, 'I'll keep pressing for the three hundred thousand. Let's see what he comes up with.'

"Anyway, the next morning I go there and he's got seventy-five thousand. He says he could only pay half. I tell him this shows he's on the right track and ask when he could have the rest. And he tells me it's gonna take a little time.

"I tell him I want the money tomorrow. So I take the seventy-five thousand and go back around the corner. I meet this Richie and I gave him one-third. I gave him twenty-five thousand. He's gotta give Tony twelve five. And the other twenty-five thousand goes into the elbow, and me and Charlie cut up the rest, twelve five each. I tell Charlie, 'Tomorrow we'll get the rest of the money.'

"But this cocksucker was still stalling. I go back the next morning and he says he's having a hard time. He don't have this kind of money. And Richie's stepping back and forth into it. He says he'll talk to him. See, he looked like the good guy 'cause he cut the shake down to one hundred and fifty thousand.

"Eventually the guy comes up with the other seventy-five thousand. But what happened first was this guy's father-in-law went to Richie and asked if we would leave him alone after this. 'Cause he was worried about me shaking him down for more money later. And I said to Richie, 'You tell him my word is my bond and he'll never have any problem.' So the guy paid the other seventy-five thousand. And when he paid this, I told Richie, 'Your guy Tony doesn't get another end. You tell him to go fuck himself, because he didn't do what he was supposed to do and he didn't help in this thing in any way.' Richie says, 'Okay. If that's the way you want it.'

"I get the rest of the money. I cut it up, and now the deal's done. But a couple days later this Tony comes to my house to talk to me. He says, 'Well, Richie says that you cut me out on my end.'

"I says, 'Yeah, you don't deserve anything. How the fuck could you say you deserve anything when you didn't do anything? You didn't do what you were supposed to do. You're lucky you got the first piece.'

"He says, 'Well, I just wanted to know. I wanted to see if Richie double-crossed me.' I says, 'He didn't double-cross you. It was my fucking thinking, and that's the way it is.' And he says, 'Well, I might have another score for you. I might have a drug dealer.' And I tell him, 'Listen. Keep your fucking scores. I don't like the way you do business. You're supposed to do what you're supposed to do. This is a deadly game here, kid. You can't fuck with this shit.'"

Like the shakedown of the mob groupie who had killed her mother and father, this scam and the murder connected to it have become part of an FBI investigative file. Federal authorities and the Pennsylvania state police are probing the "suicide" of the investment broker and have questioned several of the principals involved. A grand jury heard some testimony, but, as in the case of the earlier double murder, no charges have been brought. Caramandi said the auto body shop owner has admitted paying him $150,000, but said he did it out of fear, not because he killed anyone.

"They gotta dig up the body, and they haven't done that yet," Caramandi said.

This shakedown also reflected a shift in Caramandi's style. It wasn't like his earlier scams. It had a harder edge. Less finesse. The Crow was now a made member of an organization whose only negotiating tool was a gun. Consequently, it was no longer a question of tricking someone out of his money. Now Caramandi could just scare it out of the "sucker." He would use the same tactic again and again over the next two years in dealing with drug dealers, bookmakers, contractors, and union officials.

"I'll kill you, I'll kill your wife, I'll kill your family," he would say. "This ain't no fuckin' game we're playing here."

It was easier and far less complicated than the elaborate scams he used to work out. But it also dulled the senses. All his life, Caramandi's greatest weapons had been his wits and his instinct. Now it was muscle and a gun. He'd make several million dollars doing it this way. But it would eventually cost him—and Scarfo—everything.

*   *   *

At about this time, Caramandi met John Pastorella, a convicted drug dealer and gambler from upstate Pennsylvania
who had recently relocated to South Philadelphia and had
started a small construction business. Back in 1980, Pastorella had funneled $5,000 to the Crow to help a friend get a
reduction in a prison sentence. Caramandi used a lawyer who
had some influence to appeal for the reduction. He let Pastorella
believe, however, that the $5,000 went to pay off the judge.
Now Pastorella was back in the area and looking to do some
business. He first approached Caramandi through "Cuddles"
DiCaprio, the driver in the Spirito murder. Pastorella had some
money he wanted to put on the street in a loan-sharking operation. It was a small-time deal, $10,000, but it opened the
door to bigger things. Pastorella was going into the construction business, and Caramandi offered to become his "partner." They began bidding jobs around South Philadelphia and
center city. One of their first contracts was with a developer
named Harry Devoe who was renovating an apartment building
in the 900 block of Spruce Street, a neighborhood where urban
gentrification was in bloom. The contract, calling for the construction of an eleven-unit condominium complex, was for
close to $1 million.

Pastorella and the Crow also hooked up in a gambling scam
that proved that even with the mob behind him, Caramandi
did not always come out ahead. The mark this time was one
of the most famous white-collar bookmakers in the city, Joseph Vito Mastronardo, Jr. Joe Vito, as he was sometimes
called, operated out of Northeast Philadelphia and the suburbs, handling big-money sports bets from yuppies and other
business types. He was from a highly respected middle-class
family, and his younger brother had been a standout football
player at Villanova University. Joe Vito, described as a "gentle-
man gambler" by his own defense attorney, was eventually
convicted of running a multimillion-dollar gambling operation. One police raid turned up betting tally sheets that
showed action totaling more than $5 million. A Pennsylvania
Crime Commission report later estimated that Mastronardo's
operation grossed $50 million annually. Mastronardo was a
fascinating figure in his own right. What's more, he was married to the daughter of Frank L. Rizzo, the tough-talking, conservative, law-and-order former mayor and former police
commissioner of Philadelphia.

"Pastorella knew him [Mastronardo], and so we started betting with the guy, fifty thousand, sixty thousand on ten or fifteen football games each weekend. But I was also trying to smoke this guy out, because I wanted to get tribute money off of him, shake money, because we'd heard this guy did real well, taking one hundred, two hundred thousand a game. I figured once we lose I'll meet this guy and read him his rights, that he has to pay.

"Well, the first week we win, like, fifteen thousand. Pastorella picks up the money. But the second week we lose fifty-two thousand. And Mastronardo's on the phone looking for his money. So now I switch everything around and I tell him that he owes *me* fifty thousand. I tell him Pastorella made a mistake betting the games. I says Pastorella was betting with my money and that Mastronardo's responsible and I wanna meet him. He says, 'I don't wanna get involved with no gangsters.' And he would never meet me. He musta gone underground or something, 'cause we could never find him. And so eventually we boxed a draw there and forgot about it."

Despite that minor setback, Caramandi's partnership with Pastorella proved a success. The Crow got more deeply involved in the construction industry. He started brokering deals with both city and union officials and became Scarfo's point man in the building trades. With the city in the midst of a multimillion-dollar development boom, Caramandi had his fingers in a dozen deals, both big and small.

One deal, involving the old Benjamin Franklin Hotel at Ninth and Chestnut streets, is a textbook study of how the mob operates, a classic example of labor racketeering. The Ben Franklin had been shuttered for five years, but now was undergoing a $45 million renovation and rehab job that would turn it into the Benjamin Franklin House, a swank center city apartment complex topped with penthouse duplexes. Plans called for a total restoration of the eighteen-story Georgian Revival building, with shops and stores on the ground floor and 416 luxury apartments above. Caramandi had a friend, Big Ralph Costobile, whose construction company had the demolition and asbestos-removal contract. Big Ralph's job was to gut the building before the renovation and rehab could begin. But Costobile was not happy with the way things were going. He complained that the Laborers Union wasn't sending reliable workers and that its pay scale and benefits were murder. Big Ralph asked the Crow for help. Caramandi was only too happy to oblige.

"I know Big Ralph all my life. He was a Vietnam War hero. He was born and raised around Passyunk and Dickinson. He owned this bar [Big Ralph's Saloon] at Passyunk and Dickinson.

"So he comes to me one day and he says, 'If you could help me with this union, here's the deal I'll make with ya.' And then he says for each man he could hire who was nonunion, he'd give me half of the health and welfare benefits he'd save, which would be, like, seventy-five dollars a week per man. The way I figured it, this would mean about a hundred thousand over the course of the job, which was gonna take more than a year. Well, I said I'd see what I could do. I get ahold of Tommy [DelGiorno], and Tommy goes to Scarfo, who says it could be handled. I tell this guy Ralph, 'You got yourself a deal. It's gonna take a week or two. It takes a little time to make communications.'"

Caramandi said Scarfo reached out for Stevie Traitz, Jr., the Roofers Union boss who had become the mob's liaison to the labor unions in the city. Whenever there was a problem, Scarfo would call on Traitz to intercede, to make the right connection, or, in this case, to set up a meeting to straighten out Big Ralph's problem.

Within two weeks, Caramandi said, a business agent with the Laborers Union came downtown for a meeting at Big Ralph's bar. It was not a collective bargaining session. Caramandi said when the union official left the bar that day, he had a half pound of cocaine in his pocket, Costobile had a bunch of phony union cards to give his workers, and Caramandi and the Scarfo mob had a piece of the action. As an added bonus, Caramandi promised to "take care" of a union member who was planning to run against the business agent in the next union election.

"We were either gonna pay him off or kill him," Caramandi said of the potential rival.

Four years later, Costobile was charged in a thirty-three-count federal labor racketeering indictment that included the payoffs surrounding the Ben Franklin job, bid rigging in several other construction projects, and a $5,000 bribe to a dissident union member who agreed not to seek union office. He eventually pleaded guilty and was sentenced to three years in prison.

"Big Ralph didn't even have to give him the drugs. The deal was already set. But that's the way Ralph was. He was always doing extra stuff to make sure. I told him, 'Don't worry. You got the deal.' But he gave the guy the cocaine just to be sure.

"See, everything goes through Stevie Traitz. Once Stevie Traitz told somebody to do something, they knew it came from Scarfo, and everybody would have to back off.

"Now kids are coming to me for jobs. Young fellas, twenty-one, twenty-two. All the neighborhood kids, I'm getting them jobs for fifty, fifty-five dollars a day and they're making three hundred a week. And if they're working on a Saturday they're grabbing, like, another seventy-five.

"Big Ralph's happy because the union wage rate was about twelve dollars an hour, and he's paying these kids half of that. Plus he's saving on the benefits. Each week I would go to his restaurant and he would show me a list of how many guys worked that week and we'd count them up and he'd pay me. My end was averaging about two thousand a week. And this went on the elbow.

"So Ralph's running good and I'm doing good. I'm getting involved with unions and construction, and in the meantime, I run into Beloff."

This was Philadelphia city councilman Leland Beloff, whose legislative district included a portion of South Philadelphia as well as center city. Beloff had been a state representative, but in 1984 he decided he'd rather serve on the council. He won the Democratic Party nomination, which was tantamount to election, and then was swept into office that November in a special election for a vacated council seat. At forty-two, Beloff still had the taut body of the amateur boxer he had once been and the Paul Newman good looks that always attracted the ladies. He also had a modest family fortune behind him.

"He was a millionaire," Caramandi said. "But in his heart he was a crook. He liked to be around gangsters."

Beloff, who grew up in the same South Philadelphia neighborhood as Scarfo, was already well acquainted with Little Nicky. In fact, investigators for the New Jersey State Commission of Investigation had once tailed Scarfo and Leonetti to a meeting at Beloff's posh summer home in Longport, an exclusive shore community just south of Atlantic City. At the time, Beloff was still a state representative, and although he dismissed the visit as a "social" call, he seemed to enjoy the notoriety that came with the media reports about the contact. Beloff liked to live on the edge. He had a much younger wife, a thin, dark-haired woman with fashion-model features. And he had a girlfriend, a brassy strawberry blonde whom he placed on the city payroll working in a judge's office.

Beloff wanted to be a player, which is why the city council was more attractive than the Pennsylvania house of representatives. Harrisburg was just that, a burg. You could get lost there among all the senators and representatives. But there were only seventeen city councilmen, ten elected by district and seven at-large. And each councilman ran his district like a fiefdom, exercising total veto control over anything planned or proposed within its boundaries. Anything that needed city approval had to go through the councilman's office. A councilman had impact. He could get things done...and he could have things done for him.

When Beloff took office, he brought in one of his South Philadelphia constituents as his legislative aide. The guy was short and sort of stout, with a slightly receding hairline and a round, pudgy face. Caramandi couldn't quite place him, but he knew he had seen him before. His name was Bobby Rego.

"I used to go to the Bellevue Stratford a lot, to the Versailles Room. And Beloff and Rego would go there a lot. Beloff used to buy me a drink. I used to buy him a drink. I would go there at five o'clock at night and meet guys there for different things.

"So he knew who I was. And one night we get talking, me, him, and Rego. I tell Beloff I'm in the construction business, and he says, 'Yeah? You know, I could do you a lot of good. You know what I own? You know what I'm in charge of?' I says, 'No.' So he makes Rego explain everything to me. Bobby explains that they're in charge from Allegheny Avenue to Oregon Avenue, from Broad Street to the river, and that everything that gets done has to go through him. That's his area, his district. Construction. Buildings. Bids. It's all gotta meet his approval.

"He says, 'We could do ya a lot of good.' And I says, 'Yes, you could.' But first, he says, 'I gotta do what I hafta do.' And he says, 'You know, I'm with this guy.' And he puts his hand out, indicating the Little Guy. So I says, 'All right, you do what you gotta do and I'll do what I gotta do.'"

About a week later, Caramandi got clearance to begin doing

business with Beloff. Scarfo sent word up from the shore that it was okay. He also ordered that Rego, Beloff's legislative aide, would now be "with" Caramandi.

Caramandi met with Rego in the Versailles Room shortly after all this was approved. The Versailles Room, just off the lobby of the posh Bellevue Stratford, was a meeting place for pols, businessmen, and various movers and shakers in the city. It was the place to stop for a drink after work. The Bellevue was only three blocks down Broad Street from City Hall and almost around the corner from Democratic party headquarters. Rego, now connected politically, and Caramandi, posing as a construction company consultant, sat there with the rest of the deal makers, smoking, drinking, and talking about old times.

"Don't you remember me?" Rego asked.

"No, I don't," said Caramandi. "Who are you? You look familiar."

"I used to be with Harry."

Caramandi made the connection immediately. Rego had been on the hit list during the Riccobene war. He was one of Mario Riccobene's associates, a guy who dealt in methamphetamine for the Riccobenes and who had been marked for death by Scarfo. In fact, Caramandi and Charlie White had Rego's ticket. He was the guy whose door they used to knock on. If he answered, they were going to kill him. But Bobby Rego was never home. So he survived the Riccobene war. And now he was ensconced on the fourth floor of City Hall wheeling and dealing for Leland Beloff.

"You was on the hit list," the Crow said. "Now I remember. I used to go to your house. You lived at 513 Saint James Street, around Fifth and Oregon."

"Right," Rego said, happy to be recognized.

"How many times I used to bang on your fuckin' door," Caramandi said.

They sat there drinking for a while, reflecting on where they had come from and where they were going. It was a strange pairing of the hunter and the hunted. Then Caramandi looked at Rego and said, "You're very lucky."

CHAPTER EIGHTEEN

ormer mayor William Green once called the seventeen-member Philadelphia city council "the worst legislative body in the free world." Most people found this an apt description for an organization whose history is replete with examples of arrogance, incompetence, and corruption. Two members once ended a floor debate during a council session with a fistfight. Three others were sentenced to prison for taking money for a zoning deal requested by an Arab potentate. They were the only municipal officials in America caught in Abscam's web.

Two Philadelphia congressmen were also nabbed in that infamous FBI sting, and one was filmed and recorded uttering what is perhaps the most succinct description of how politics and government work in the City of Brotherly Love.

"Money talks," he said. "Bullshit walks."

Nick Caramandi spoke the language of the politicians. That's one of the reasons he hit it off so well with Beloff and Rego. The city councilman and his legislative aide were already in the shakedown business when they started dealing with the Crow. They had their hooks into a developer named John Bennett who needed legislation to clear the way for a project he had proposed downtown. With Rego as his point man, Beloff sucked close to $50,000 out of Bennett, trading off the legislation for cash and about $8,000 worth of home improvements. A federal indictment and the successful prosecution of Beloff and Rego would later lay this all out for public scrutiny.

At the time Caramandi began meeting with Rego, developer Harry Devoe, for whom Caramandi and Pastorella were already doing work, was looking for legislative assistance. Devoe had two yuppie apartment projects underway on Orianna Street in center city, and he wanted a small cobblestone street vacated so that he could make it a private passageway. This would give the potential residents of his buildings more privacy and security, thus enhancing the projects' value. He also wanted some street lights installed around another one of his apartment projects at Front and Arch streets.

Beloff thought he and Devoe could do business. Devoe owned several apartment buildings in the city. And Beloff's girlfriend needed an apartment. This was the first deal Caramandi helped pull off for Beloff. And although no one knew it at the time, it was the start of a relationship that would bring down the mob. It can be argued, in fact, that Nicky Scarfo is in jail today because back in 1985 Leland Beloff had a little something going with a woman who wasn't his wife.

"Beloff asks me one time if I know a guy by the name of Harry Devoe. I says, 'Yeah, I know him. We're doing some work for him, 918-920 Spruce Street.' Beloff says, 'I got something on my desk from him.' And then Beloff tells me the deal. So I grab ahold of Pastorella and tell him, 'Go to Devoe and tell him you could get him the street and the lights and that we'll throw in free trash pickup for his apartments on Front and Arch. And what my friend wants is a free apartment at that Front and Arch location or twenty-five thousand in cash. Either one.'"

Over the next few months, negotiations, with Pastorella relaying the offers and counteroffers, went back and forth. Then, on October 10, 1985, Beloff introduced Bill Number 715 into city council, calling for the vacation of Orianna Street. Now it was time for the payoff. This was standard operating procedure for Beloff and Rego. They'd strike a deal, then they'd introduce the necessary legislation. But before the bill came up for a final vote and approval by the entire council, the payoff had to be made.

Shortly after the bill was placed in council, Caramandi sent Pastorella to Devoe with a simple message: "Do the right thing." Caramandi also added a warning from Beloff.

"Tell him that Beloff said if he don't go along we'll make a fuckin' vending mall on Orianna Street," he told Pastorella. "We'll have hot-dog vendors all over the place. It would be, like, a looney-tune street."

Devoe agreed to the deal. He said Beloff could have an apartment in the Smythe Stores Apartments, the Front and Arch street complex where Devoe was to get the street lights.

"This is our first transaction, and Beloff loves it. Devoe's got the street and the lights. And he's got free trash pickup, which means a lot, because it costs about four hundred apiece to haul away them containers [by private pickup]. If you use ten containers, say, it's four thousand a week. So Harry was very pleased. And we're doing the job at 918-920 Spruce Street. Now we got Big Ralph doing the demolition, and everything's going good and we're starting to build.

"All of a sudden, John [Pastorella] calls me up. 'We got a problem.' I go see him and he says we got a problem with this guy Dougherty, who's the business agent for the Carpenters Union. At that time we had five nonunion carpenters on the Spruce Street job. Dougherty wanted us to pay the union benefits, which would come to something like a hundred and fifty a man a week. No fucking way. I says to Pastorella, 'You tell Dougherty I want to see him.' So I tell Tommy about this guy on my back, and he says he'll talk to Nicky.

"So I meet with this guy at the Bellevue Stratford. Tommy had told me to tell this Dougherty that he'll be reached and somebody will tell him to back off.

"Dougherty's young and gung-ho. He says, 'Listen, nobody came to me yet. You gotta pay or I'm gonna strike the job. I'm gonna throw a picket around the job.' I says, 'You just wait. It may take a week or so, but somebody will talk to you. Just hold your horses. Do you know what I represent?' And he says, 'I don't know. Seeing is believing.'

"I says, 'You just wait. I'm not here to play games with you. If you want to have problems, you'll have all the problems you want. Wait.' So we shake hands, and about ten days later, Tommy says everything is straightened out.

"Now don't this guy Dougherty come back! He starts screaming at Pastorella that he's gonna strike the job. I go to Tommy, and he says, 'Nick, the guy was told.' Tommy goes to Scarfo, and Scarfo tells him, 'The guy was told.' The guy was supposed to have been told three times. So I says, 'What am I supposed to do with this guy?' Tommy says, 'The word is, you do whatever the fuck you want to do with him.'

"So I tell Pastorella, 'Get this guy. Make a meet with him. And don't be there. Just make a meet with him in the building, and don't be there.' Now we were gonna set him up. When he came in, we were gonna say Pastorella was on the fourth floor and we were gonna throw this guy Dougherty right out the fucking window."

But Jim Dougherty, for reasons that Caramandi would learn later, never showed for the meeting. Caramandi and Pastorella never had any union problems again at 918-920 Spruce Street. The Crow figured Dougherty had finally gotten the word to back off. It was all, Caramandi thought, part of the growing power of the organization.

"This goes to show you how the fucking unions hadda pay attention to what Scarfo said," Caramandi said. "At this time we got the connections with the unions, we got the connections with the city. We got connections all over. Rego's giving me tips on different jobs. I'm meeting people from the Redevelopment Authority. Everything's going good."

Caramandi was in his element, wheeling and dealing on several different levels. He would spend mornings at the clubhouse at Camac and Moore attending to the shakes. Afternoons he would head out to several construction job sites. He and Pastorella had a decent little business going. They were bidding on jobs and, in most cases, subcontracting the work out. The concrete work went to Scarfo, either through Leonetti or through Scarfo's son Nicky Jr., who was helping run Scarf Inc. If they needed rebar work, Lawrence Merlino and his son Joey had the business. Other work they'd pass off to Big Ralph—who was heavily involved in kickbacks and bid rigging with Caramandi—or Tony Blinds, associates who could be trusted. Scarfo had done this in Atlantic City during the casino boom. Now Caramandi was paving the way for the organization to exercise the same control in Philadelphia.

It was, federal authorities would later said, a blueprint for mob control of the construction industry throughout the city.

"Caramandi was the chief architect of all of this," said Special Agent Dave Gentile, who was assigned to the FBI's labor racketeering squad and who later spent hours debriefing Caramandi. "Nick saw the mob as a way to make money. He was a classic entrepreneur."

And when the city was involved, Rego and Beloff would make sure Caramandi and his associates had the inside track. If, for example, Pastorella bid a city job and, for some reason, another contractor underbid him, Beloff would come up with some pretext to throw out all the bids. When the job came up again, Pastorella would rebid, usually at the lowest price. The bid itself was immaterial. Kickbacks, bribes, payoffs, and, if necessary, extortion would guarantee that whatever work was done was done on the mob's terms.

If it was a private deal, Caramandi would "reach out" for help, arranging to rig the bid so that his company got the award. Since they'd never have union problems, they could usually low-bid the contract anyway. And if the developer they were dealing with needed help in City Hall, Caramandi had the connections. It was a perfect situation. And it just seemed to keep getting better.

"See, I was involved in so many things," Caramandi boasted. "Things were really booming for me and Charlie. I mean, we were on our way. We had some good guys around us, real live guys. Cupcakes. Tony Blinds. Big Ralph. I had this Frank Aiello who was making big drug deals. In another two years I woulda been worth ten million with no problem. And who knows what Scarfo would have been worth. He was on his way, too. He probably would have become the richest boss ever in Philadelphia. Richer than Angelo [Bruno]. I mean, Angelo musta been worth between thirty and fifty million."

Control of an organized crime family in a city like Philadelphia meant power and influence. It meant shadowy business arrangements with union leaders and politicians. It meant access, directly or indirectly, to the lawyers and judges who ran the judicial system. And it meant money. Millions of dollars annually.

Angelo Bruno, who reported an income of $50,000 a year as a commission salesman for a cigarette vending machine company, was a millionaire when he died even though his estate listed less than $100,000 in assets. Federal and state law enforcement sources said at the time of his death the Docile Don owned apartment buildings in center city, real estate in Florida, an interest in a Caribbean casino, a piece of a casino junket operation in London, and dozens of other business ventures, none of them listed in his own name. And a rumor inside the family, Caramandi added, was that "Angelo made a big kill with Resorts stocks [Resorts International, the company that opened the first casino in Atlantic City]. He had a tip and bought early. They figure he made himself millions."

Scarfo once listed his job as caretaker and maintenance man for his mother's small apartment building in Atlantic City. After his parole, he was a shirt salesman. Still another venture was as an entertainment consultant and booking agent. He apparently did very well in these endeavors, given his Florida home, his cabin cruiser, and his Rolls-Royce and Cadillac. He always flew first-class, dined in the best restaurants, and dressed in $500 suits and $100 silk shirts.

Scarfo had inherited Bruno's mantle and the source of much of his wealth. Now, with the casinos, the construction industry, the unions, and the drugs, he was in a position to earn even more, maybe ten or twenty times what Bruno had earned in his best years.

But Scarfo was no Angelo Bruno. And while he left Caramandi and Charlie White alone as long as they were making money, there was constant turmoil within the organization. This was caused, in part, by Scarfo's personality—his paranoia, mistrust, and penchant for violence. Little Nicky didn't understand compromise or conciliation. He demanded total and complete loyalty from the members of his organization, and subservience from everyone else. He had become a Mafia potentate, a despot. He would sit in Atlantic City or Fort Lauderdale and issue orders about who would live and who would die, about who could do business and who should go broke. Even after he had defeated the Riccobenes, even after most of his "enemies" were either dead or in jail, Scarfo continued to lash out with random and seemingly illogical acts of violence.

Fred Martens, executive director of the Pennsylvania Crime Commission, captured the essence of the problem in a report issued in 1987. Whereas Bruno's leadership "evolved into a benevolent dictatorship," Scarfo was, Martens said, "an ineffective and bumbling leader" who had "demonstrated few managerial skills other than the ability to kill people."

Nowhere was Scarfo's arbitrary hand so chillingly in evidence as in the July 23, 1985, murder of "Frankie Flowers" D'Alfonso, Angelo Bruno's old ally and business associate. The murder took place near the Ninth Street Italian Market. D'Alfonso had just walked to a corner store to pick up some cigarettes when two men came up on him from behind and shot him five times in the head, face, and back. He slumped to the sidewalk while the two gunmen ran to a waiting car and fled. D'Alfonso had survived a brutal beating administered four years earlier by Salvie Testa and Gino Milano. This time he wasn't as lucky. He was pronounced dead at the scene.

"Sometime early in 1985, Tommy came to me and put his finger to his nose—this was the sign we had for D'Alfonso, because he had a big nose—and he says, 'This guy is gonna go.'

"A few days later he tells me it's off for a while. Then in February, Chuckie comes to me and says there's this neighborhood guy named Mike who deals with hot stuff. He might be dealing in junk. He says, 'This guy's been doing stuff for twenty years and never gave nobody nuttin'. Go get him.' I say, 'All right.' Then Tommy and Faffy come around and they say Chuckie wants this Mike bad, and do I know why. I says no. They say, 'Because this guy is around Frankie Flowers.'

"You gotta understand, Frankie Flowers wasn't a made guy. But he was very well loved by Angelo Bruno, and he made tons of money. So I said, 'When's the hit on?' Tommy says not yet. He says, 'Go shake this guy Mike. I want to see what Flowers is gonna do.'

"I go around to this store Mike owned around Ninth Street, but he ain't there. I leave a message with his brother to have him come and see me.

"He comes around to the clubhouse at Camac and Moore, and me and Charlie take him up the street. We say, 'We want fifty thousand or we're gonna kill ya.' This guy's face coulda dropped to the ground. 'Fifty thousand? I got a stand on Ninth Street.' I says, 'Listen, you motherfucker, everybody pays. You been making tons of money for years. Now it's fifty fucking thousand dollars or we're gonna fucking kill ya. And I'm tellin' ya now, we don't want no for an answer. Now you go where you gotta go and do what you gotta do, but you better pay this fuckin' money.' Now we knew he was gonna go to Flowers. Charlie had said, 'You really shook this guy up.' I says, 'Well, they told me to lay it in, so I did.'

"A couple days go by, and who comes around the corner but Frankie Flowers. But we're not around, so later we go see him. 'Yeah, Frank, what is it?' He says, 'I wanted to talk to you guys about Mike. Jesus Christ. He's hiding in his house. He don't want to come out. He's scared to death.' He says, 'Nick, you know, he don't have this kind of money. He would be glad to pay, but he ain't making no money.' I says, 'Listen, Frank, this thing came from the top. Do you understand this? You want me to go back and tell this guy what you said?' And I make the sign with my hand, you know, the Little Guy.

"He says, 'No, no.' Right away his colors changed. And I says, 'By the way, how do you stand with this guy?' 'Well, I stand good with him,' he said. 'I'm on good terms with him.'

So I says, 'Frank, you wanna do yourself a favor? You want to stand on better terms? You tell this Mike to pay the fifty thousand. I'll make it even easier for him. He could pay twenty-five thousand in the front and five thousand a month for the next five months. I'll go out of my way and do that for him.' See, I know that Flowers coulda gave him the money. They'd done business for years. Flowers was a millionaire. So Frankie says, 'I'll talk to him.'

"I told him I'd be back in a week. Tommy and Faffy wanted to know what Flowers had to say, and we told them that he was gonna try to make the guy pay the money, that he was being very helpful.

"A week later we go back. Flowers says this guy Mike wants to pay 'but he just don't have the money at this time.' I says, 'Frank, save the conversation. Tell him that the guys that come after me are not gonna ask him for money. It's this.' And I put my finger down in the sign of the gun.

"He says, 'Okay. I'll tell 'im.' We go and tell Tommy and Faffy, and they say they'll let us know about the hit. First they gotta go talk to Chuckie. A couple days later they come back. 'Go get this guy and press him. Keep pressing.' I says, 'Tommy, Faffy, how the fuck could I do this? I just got done telling Flowers what we're gonna do to the guy. I can't go around there. We're gonna have to hit him. We're gonna have to give him a fucking beating or we're gonna have to shoot him. I just can't say you gotta pay, you gotta pay.' But they said just keep putting the pressure on."

For three straight weeks, at least once a day, Caramandi and Charlie White would travel over to Ninth Street looking for Mike. They went to his store and they went to his house. They left messages and warnings each time. Mike stayed underground.

"Then one day, Tommy comes around and he says, 'We got this guy,' and he puts his thumb and his index finger to his nose, meaning Flowers. He said he was gonna assign Gino [Milano], Nicky Whip [Milano], and Frankie Narducci the contract. I says, 'All right. Good.' He sends for them, and I seen them in a huddle. They walk up the street. I know they're on the hit.

"But me and Charlie knew this fuckin' hit wasn't gonna go down, because Gino's the type of guy who likes to come from behind. And this fuckin' Frankie Narducci ain't gonna run up on the guy himself. This is gonna wind up to be a blank. We said, 'We're gonna have to wind up doing it.'"

Caramandi and Charlie White were right. For nearly four months the Milano brothers and Narducci stalked Frankie Flowers in vain. At one point, DelGiorno would later testify, he asked the three would-be hit men if they had everything they needed.

"Yeah, everything except the guns and a car," Narducci said.

"Well, if you ain't got the guns and a car, what the fuck have you got?" DelGiorno angrily replied.

Milano got the keys to a fruit store on Ninth Street near D'Alfonso's home and set up surveillance. They knew one night when Flowers had to go to a wake in New Jersey and they planned to bang him when he got back.

"But he was with his wife," Gino Milano said. "And we didn't want to do it in front of his wife."

Another time they followed D'Alfonso to a Sunday dinner in the suburbs, but the wide, open streets made an ambush too risky.

Eventually, Milano and his brother were pulled off the contract. They were known around the Ninth Street Italian Market, and their constant presence might attract too much attention. At another planning session attended by Scarfo, Lawrence Merlino, Chuckie Merlino, and Tommy and Faffy, it was decided that Frank Narducci's younger brother Philip would be assigned as one of the shooters along with Joe Ligambi, a local bookmaker and longtime associate of Chuckie Merlino. Frank Narducci would drive the getaway car.

It was Ligambi and the Narduccis who finally ambushed D'Alfonso on the night of July 23.

"It took, like, five or six months," Caramandi said. "See, with these hits, some teams are good, some teams are bad. It takes time. Eventually, they'll get the guy. It all depends on how bad they want 'im. They're not gonna jeopardize a couple of good men to go do something crazy. But at this time Nicky was hollering about when were they gonna get it done. And he likes it cowboy-style in front of fifty people. He figures the more noise, the more scared people are gonna get."

Several people were on the street that summer night when Frankie Flowers was gunned down, but few were able to provide police with any specific details about the shooting.

The word in South Philadelphia was that Frankie Flowers had gotten killed for the same reason he had been so brutally beaten four years earlier—his failure to pay "respect" to

Scarfo. And in part, that was true. But Caramandi learned it was more than that. It was business. D'Alfonso, he said, was putting together a big real estate deal and was once again keeping everything to himself. Scarfo was fed up. Here was a guy who made a ton of money with Bruno. Now he was hoarding all his action.

The attempted shakedown of Mike was just a way to smoke D'Alfonso out, Caramandi said. In a twisted sort of way, Scarfo was offering Frankie Flowers one last chance. Flowers could have used Mike to offer Caramandi—and therefore Scarfo—a piece of the real estate proposition in lieu of the $50,000 that had been demanded. He had that option, but he didn't take it.

Now he was dead. It was business.

Everybody pays.

CHAPTER NINETEEN

I n the underworld controlled by Nicky Scarfo, nobody paid more than the drug dealers.

They were fair game, targets for shakedowns, extortion, and, if they didn't pay the street tax, murder. It didn't matter how big or how small their operation. Caramandi boasted about several scams he pulled on hapless drug dealers, taking their money and, in one case, commandeering a car.

"This guy owed us some money and he couldn't pay," the Crow said. "He had a nice car. He was leasing it. An Oldsmobile, I think. I took it. Used it for about six months. He couldn't do nothing about it. Where was he gonna go to complain?"

Drug dealers were the lowest of the underworld lowlifes. But for Scarfo, they were also a ready source of big money and had been since 1983, when Tommy DelGiorno first brokered two major methamphetamine deals—loaning drug dealers money for the purchase of phenyl-2-propanone, the "oil" that is the precursor in the manufacture of speed. Scarfo's people were making piles of money in the drug underworld. And Little Nicky was only too happy to share in the action.

Joey Pungitore, picking up where Salvie Testa had left off, was also deeply involved with a group of meth dealers. Like DelGiorno, Pungitore skirted the prohibition on dealing drugs by playing the role of financier, backing an operation and skimming off the profits.

Caramandi, on the other hand, was out on the street shaking down whomever he could find, assessing a $2,000-a-gallon street tax on the P-2-P that a bunch of neighborhood dealers were bringing into the country. The tax became the cost of doing business. But a guy who was wholesaling oil—which could be purchased for from $200 to $2,000 a gallon in Europe and could be sold for about $20,000 here—could afford to pay.

One of Caramandi's best "clients" was Angelo "Chick" DiTullio, who was using a garage and repair shop in South Philadelphia as a front for a multimillion-dollar P-2-P smuggling operation. Caramandi got the word from Chuckie Merlino to begin shaking DiTullio down shortly after he and Charlie White were formally initiated into the organization. They used the straightforward approach with the drug merchants. "Pay us or we'll kill ya," they said.

DiTullio had a fifty-gallon shipment on its way from Germany. Caramandi said the mob wanted $2,000 for each gallon brought in.

"He was selling it for twenty grand a gallon, so I told him to start charging twenty-two grand," said Caramandi, already looking out for his new client's interest. In return for the payments, Caramandi and Charlie White promised DiTullio he wouldn't have any problems, that he would have the protection of the Scarfo organization and that "no one would bother him." Over the next twelve months, from the summer of 1985 through the spring of 1986, Caramandi said he collected about $500,000 from DiTullio. Half the money went to the elbow. The other half he and Charlie White split.

The Crow was also collecting from several low-level drug dealers whose weekly or monthly payments ranged from a few hundred to a few thousand dollars. Most of the dealers he approached readily agreed to pay. One who balked was a young kid named Louie Turra. And on August 8, 1985, Turra found out how Scarfo negotiated with recalcitrant business associates.

"I had a problem with this Louie Turra. About a year earlier, Faffy had been pressing me to go in on [shake down] Tony Turra, the kid's father. Louie and his father were working together. Tony Turra had a brother, Rocky, that I knew all my life. And I knew Tony Turra all my life. I knew their family. I was in jail with Rocky Turra. And he was no fucking punk. He was willing to go to war with Chickie Narducci and Little Harry [Riccobene] years before. Rocky Turra was no slouch, but he was not a made guy. He was just a neighborhood guy who didn't like to get involved with our kind of people. But I knew him real good.

"Anyhow, I go see this Tony and he says, 'Nick, I'm selling. I'm making a living. I grab a thousand, twelve hundred a week, me and my son. Nothing on a big scale.' I says, 'Tony, you gotta pay. You gotta fuckin' pay.' So he says, 'Let them loan me money so I could buy stuff and maneuver.' I says, 'That could be arranged, but you gotta fuckin' pay.'

"I says, 'Every time you do something, throw me ten percent of what you do. Okay? Just to save the peace.' He says, 'Okay. Good.' Now his son's there and he starts to get a little cocky. 'What the fuck we gotta pay you guys for?' the kid wants to know. I said, 'Listen. There's only one fuckin' mob in Philadelphia, and you guys ain't gonna make all the fucking money and think we're assholes. Youse are gonna have to pay. And I'm tellin' ya something, kid, you got a big mouth. I heard bad stories about you, and you just better close your fuckin' mouth. 'Cause you're gonna cause a problem for yourself *and* your father here.'

"So he gives me a few payments. A couple hundred one time. A couple of hundred another time. But see, this Louie Turra had a friend named Dutchie. Nice-looking kid. Used to go out with Faffy's girlfriend, Cheryl. So this fucking Faffy was jealous of Dutchie because Cheryl always used to throw him up to Faffy. And Dutchie and Louie Turra were the best of friends. Faffy was crazy about this Cheryl. He left his wife for her.

"Now the reason why Faffy is putting the heat on Louie Turra is to show his girlfriend who the strength is. Because they hung together, this Louie Turra and this Dutchie. They were like brothers. So he can't give a beating to Dutchie, 'cause it will look too phony. He didn't have nothing on the kid. So he decides to give the beating to Louie Turra to show this broad Cheryl.

"So he starts pressing me to go get this Louie Turra. And I says, 'Faff, they're paying me.' And he says, 'No. They're making money. I heard they just made a move,' and bop, bop, bop and on and on he goes. And what he does is, he goes over my head to Nicky with it. He says that this Louie Turra says that he don't give a fuck about us guys. Now Nicky says, 'Go give him a beating.'

"Six guys go beat him up. Charlie White. Faffy. Philip Narducci. Wayne Grande. Gino. And I think Tory [Salvatore Scafidi]. On South Street. This was in the summer. I mean, it was ridiculous. Six fucking guys.

"The next day Tony Turra wants to see me. He says, 'How could you do this to me, Nick? It's my son. I been paying ya. I mean, what the fuck.' He says, 'You know, when Charlie came out of jail, I was the first guy to go over his house and say, "Charlie, you need anything?"' Charlie went away in 1976 on a gambling charge. He did a year. And when he came out this Louie Turra went right over his house. This guy, we knew him all our lives. He was a neighborhood guy. I felt real bad. Then his brother came over, Rocky. I said, 'Look, Rocky, stay out of it. I know it's your nephew, but it's over drugs.' He says, 'Well, if it's drugs, I don't want to get involved.' I says, 'There's nothing I can do. Just tell this fuckin' kid to keep his mouth shut. I mean, he was lucky it was just that.' And Rocky says, 'But six guys?' I says, 'What are you gonna do?'

"I mean, the kid was like a sissy. He kept saying, 'Don't hit me. Please don't hit me.' And they gave him a good tuning, all at Faffy's instigation, because he wanted to show off to Cheryl. Me and Charlie talked about this and broke it right down. I said, 'Charlie, why didn't you try to stop it?' He says, 'What was I gonna do? Nicky said go do it.'

"I says, 'You seen the way the guy was paying me. I mean, the guy lives in an apartment here.' I says, 'What the fuck are we becoming?'"

It was a question that would remain in the back of Caramandi's mind for the next fourteen months as he watched the Scarfo organization slowly disintegrate. Tommy and Faffy kept maneuvering, spending more and more time around the clubhouse at Camac and Moore and, whenever they got the chance, fanning the flames of internal discontent. And the younger kids, big shots now that they had Scarfo behind them, used to flex their muscles in nightclubs and bars all over South Philadelphia and center city. They'd go clubbing and get into fights, intimidating patrons and bar owners alike, daring anyone to challenge them.

After the beating of Louie Turra, a federal sentencing memorandum later noted, "Grande, Iannarella, and DelGiorno 'bragged how all South Philadelphia' was shaking because of the beating, which was done in public view on a street corner in a busy section of Philadelphia."

"See, they were all gettin' too cocky," Caramandi said. "This wasn't the way it was supposed to be.

"Tommy and Faffy had a bar at Twenty-second and Crosskeys. That was the corner they were hanging on. But they wanted Passyunk Avenue. They maneuvered that they got on Passyunk Avenue. But you ain't supposed to have ten, twelve, fifteen made guys hangin' on one fuckin' corner. This ain't no Boy Scout club. And, I mean, when Charlie and me operate, we do it quietly. But Tommy wanted a big scene. Every time there was always some kind of beef. Somebody got drunk and caused problems. They were always 'motherfuckin'' somebody. And people were scared. This gang terrorized a lot of people, a lot of nice guys. You know, neighborhood guys. They took a lot of abuse.

"Now, Passyunk Avenue, that was our corner. Actually, it was Charlie's corner. He grew up in that neighborhood. And as far as we were concerned, the neighborhood guys were with me and Charlie, we protected them, showed them some respect. That's the way it is. You just can't terrorize people that can't fight back. But this is what these guys used to enjoy. Especially Tommy and Faffy loved to abuse every guy that hung on our corner.

"You gotta understand about corners. That was our corner, our headquarters. I'd collect the shake money there. Guys would come around and we'd play cards. We played hearts or we played gin. Me, Tommy, Faffy, Junior [Ralph Staino], a couple of the neighborhood guys. And sometimes the neighborhood guys would get a little scared to play because they were afraid of us. But we used to make them feel good. I'd say, 'Come on. You could take our fuckin' money. We got plenty of it.' Understand? I used to kid them so they wouldn't get scared.

"But these guys, Tommy and Faffy, used to say, 'What are youse, hustlers?' And these neighborhood guys used to get scared. Tommy and Faffy, though, didn't give a fuck. They disregarded everybody. Everybody was shit to them. I never thought like that. I always gave the neighborhood guy an even shake. They came to me for a favor, if it was in my power, I did it. Same thing with Charlie. Charlie was good-hearted that way, too. We were very, very liked by the neighborhood. But these birds, Tommy and Faffy, wasn't. But Nicky never knew this, see. And we had to keep things back because you can't beef. You can never, never beef."

Scarfo's leadership—or lack of leadership—was beginning to take a toll, even on Caramandi and Charlie White. They just wanted to be left alone to do their deals and make their money.

But there was always something, or somebody, trying to mess things up. The Crow had a dozen different business propositions going at this time, and the money was beginning to roll in. If he could just concentrate on that end of things, he thought, everything would be fine. But there were constant distractions. Bickering and petty jealousy became commonplace within the organization, and Caramandi was always on the lookout for "traps" that Tommy Del and Faffy might be laying for him. Chuckie Merlino, the underboss, was supposed to be in charge of the Philadelphia end of the operation, but Tommy and Faffy were exerting more and more influence in their roles as acting capos. Merlino was scheduled to turn himself in February 1986 to begin a four-year bribery sentence over that drunken driving incident in Margate. As 1985 drew to a close, Merlino spent days at a time holed up in his house drinking homemade wine and bemoaning his fate. He had become a lame duck, and Tommy and Faffy were only too happy to fill the power vacuum that his absence would create.

Phil Leonetti and Lawrence Merlino were also capos, but they were both down at the shore. And Little Nicky was bouncing back and forth between Atlantic City and Florida, issuing orders and counting his money.

Then, that fall, Caramandi found himself in the middle of another sticky internal situation. This time it was Salvatore Scafidi, one of the arrogant young turks of the organization, and Big Ralph Costobile, the construction company owner who was doing the Ben Franklin deal with Caramandi and who had also brought a couple of other construction projects and kickback schemes the Crow's way.

"Big Ralph was always a headache to me, to be honest. He always had problems. It was one thing after another. But he got pretty lucky in the construction business, and I was making money with him, so I persevered.

"Now Big Ralph could drink a lot. He'd drink a whiskey, Jack Daniel's, straight, and chase it down with a bottle of Heineken's. And he drank all day long.

"One night he goes to Louie Irish's bar on Twelfth and Morris. And who's in there but Tory [Salvatore Scafidi] and his girlfriend. Big Ralph comes in with his wife, Adelene. Now Big Ralph's a big-hearted guy. He's buying drinks. And all of a sudden Tory starts talking about Adelene and her family, insulting them. Just being a real wiseass. This is in front of Big

Ralph. Ralph knew that this guy was around us. He didn't know Tory that well, but he said, 'Why don't you stop it, Tory?' He tried to be friendly. He even offered to take him and his girlfriend to Puerto Rico. But Tory wouldn't stop. So Adelene gets up and Tory punches her.

"Now he and Big Ralph start fighting, and Big Ralph coulda killed Tory, 'cause Tory can't fight with his hands."

Indeed, recognizing Scafidi's standing with the mob, Costobile did more pushing than he did punching. The fight moved from inside the bar out onto the street. Then Tory and his girlfriend took off, heading for her mother's home. Coincidentally, the woman lived right up the street from the Crow. Costobile, upset over the confrontation, headed in the same direction. He wanted to meet with Caramandi and explain what had happened. Big Ralph was banging on Caramandi's door when Scafidi came out of his girlfriend's house and went at him again. Only this time the young mobster had a kitchen knife in his hand. Caramandi caught the end of the action.

"It's two o'clock in the morning. I'm home sleeping and my wife wakes me up and says, 'Big Ralph's downstairs. You got the key to the gate?'

"So now I go downstairs and the first thing I see is Ralph throwing something. He hollers, 'Ahh, take this with ya.' I say, 'Come on in, Ralph. What's the problem?' And he says, 'I'm gonna kill this fuckin' Tory. Look what he did to me.' He takes off his jacket and he shows me on his shoulder. I think it's a scratch, about an inch and a half. So I says, 'Sit down. You ain't gonna shoot nobody.' He's pretty bombed up. I said. 'Just take it easy. This kid someday is gonna become something.' And he tells me, 'Yeah, but Nicky, I offered to take him to Puerto Rico. Why the fuck is he talking about my wife? He's making me look bad.' Now I'm just sittin' there. I'm barefoot and I got my robe on. All of a sudden I see the fuckin' floor's wet. I look down and I see my kitchen floor is filled with blood. I look at him and all of a sudden the blood squirts out of his shoulder and it hits the ceiling. I mean, it shot straight up to the ceiling. Holy Christ. This guy was so bombed out he didn't even feel the pain.

"I say, 'Hey, man, you're dying. Look at this fuckin' blood.' At that minute, who's banging on the door but Louie Irish, the guy who owned the bar where the fight started. I says, 'You gotta help me get this guy out of here. He's dying.' At the same time Big Ralph's wife pulls up with the car and we get her to take him to the hospital. I phone Charlie White and he comes over. Blood is all over my kitchen floor. It took us two, three hours to clean it up.

"About six o'clock that morning, I'm laying in bed and the phone rings. It's Adelene. She says she just got home and she has some bad news. The priest was just at the hospital and they gave Big Ralph his last rites. I says, 'Don't tell me that, Adelene. I'll be right over.'

"I call Charlie and tell him he better come with me. I say, 'We got a problem here.' This Tory's a treacherous kid. He put a kitchen knife in Ralph that musta been twelve inches long. He hit him on top of the shoulder. And Ralph was so bombed he didn't even feel it. He just pulled the knife out and threw it at Tory. So I tell Charlie what happened and we go over to the house.

"Adelene's telling us what she remembers about the fight. I says, 'Look, Adelene, let's forget about that for now. These things happen. You're gonna have to tell the cops that you were walking home and a couple black guys tried to jump you for money and they stabbed your husband.'

"Me and Charlie leave, and the next day, who's around the corner bright and early and wants to see me but Chuckie Merlino. I get in his car and he says, 'What happened?' I says, 'What happened? Chuckie, I don't know what happened.' See, I'm not gonna knock Tory because Tory was one of Chuckie's main guys and him and Chuckie's son were best friends. They hung together. Chuckie practically raised Tory. I said, 'Look, you know the way Big Ralph is.' And he says, 'Yeah, but he's with you and he's supposed to respect Tory cause he's with us.' I says they were drinking. Chuckie wanted to see my reaction, to see if I had any malice toward Tory, but I was too smart for that. I said, 'As far as I'm concerned, it's Big Ralph's fault. He's not supposed to go in these places drunk.' I made it look like Tory was right.

"If I woulda knocked this kid, it woulda done me no good. You can't knock nobody in this business. Chuckie acted like he was pissed off, but he was jerking me off. He was a good stroker, that Chuckie.

"Around twelve o'clock I called up Adelene and she says Ralph's making a recovery. She said she was going to the hospital. I'm tellin' ya, this Ralph's got nine lives. He was shot a couple of times in Vietnam and in his house one time by a guy he'd beaten up. So I go to the hospital and see him and he's telling me that he wants vengeance.

"I said to him, ' You better forget about fuckin' vengeance. You're better now and just forget about it.' But he tortured me about this Tory in the months that followed, and I had to calm him down all the time. He never took shit from nobody, but I'd say, 'Look, this is the way it is.'

"It took a lot of time for him to swallow it. You know, he just couldn't swallow it. See, I know he coulda killed Tory with his hands that night, but he didn't want to hit him. While Tory was hitting him Big Ralph was saying, 'Why are you doing this to me?' And eventually, he stabbed him. Tory had no reason to hate him. We gave everybody in the neighborhood construction jobs. I musta given out two hundred jobs. Kids were coming from all over to get jobs with this guy. I mean, they were making sixty dollars a day, going home with three hundred a week clear. Nineteen, twenty years old. It kept 'em off the street and they were seeing good money. So Big Ralph was very bitter about this, and he always said that someday he would get even. But I said to him, 'You better forget about even. There is no fuckin' even.'"

A Philadelphia police report indicates that Ralph Costobile, white male, age forty-two, was admitted to St. Agnes Medical Center following an "aggravated assault" at approximately 2:30 A.M. on the morning of October 26, 1985. Police were told that Costobile was riding in a car with his wife when he was attacked in the vicinity of Twelfth and Morris streets.

Costobile, according to the report, was stabbed in the back and on the right side. He also had a "laceration over his right eye." He was transported to the hospital by his wife.

Police had no other details.

No arrests were ever made.

CHAPTER TWENTY

or almost twenty years and through several different administrations, the city of Philadelphia had tried without success to develop a stretch of Delaware River waterfront at the foot of Market Street. City officials and business types hung their heads in disgust and embarrassment as one plan after another faltered while other cities turned a valuable resource—a once industrial but now stagnating waterfront—into a viable commercial center. New York's South Street Seaport and Baltimore's Inner Harbor were the two most prominent examples.

One of the crowning accomplishments of the administration of Mayor Bill Green was the adoption of a new development plan for Penn's Landing, as the waterfront site was known. The proposal, unveiled with much ballyhoo, called for a massive commercial, residential, and recreational project, a "festival marketplace" in the words of the urban planners touting the plan. Towering office buildings, luxury hotels, and fancy condominiums would create a waterfront community. And an open-air amphitheater, a broad promenade along the river's edge, and dozens of shops, restaurants, and boutiques would make Penn's Landing a tourist attraction as well.

In May 1985, Green's successor as mayor, W. Wilson Goode, announced that Willard G. Rouse III had been selected as the developer of Penn's Landing. Rouse was the young, tweedy general partner of Rouse & Associates, a development company with an excellent track record both in Philadelphia and along the East Coast. Rouse said Penn's Landing would be a $700 million development project.

Leland Beloff only wanted a million.

*   *   *

Beloff first mentioned Rouse to Caramandi at about the same time he asked about Devoe. Beloff said Rouse had the Penn's Landing project, which was in his district. And he told Caramandi that one of the things the city intended to do was turn the Port of History Museum, a white elephant of a building that sat in the middle of Penn's Landing, over to Rouse so that it could be incorporated into the development project. This would be done as one of those nominal-fee deals, a ninety-nine-year lease for $1 a year.

Beloff figured Rouse ought to pay a little more than that.

"He asked me if I could find somebody that knows this guy and talk to him," Caramandi recalled later. "Beloff said, 'Nobody gets nothing without me. It's my territory. Ain't no way this guy is gettin' this thing for a dollar a year.'"

Caramandi put some feelers out, and word came back: The deal was already done. Rouse had the Port of History Museum guaranteed from the mayor. Beloff had no leverage.

In the meantime, things were heating up inside the organization. Yet another round of Machiavellian intrigue and deceit was about to be played out. Caramandi had seen Scarfo turn on Salvie Testa. He had watched the way Scarfo dealt with Frankie Flowers. He knew his boss was volatile and unpredictable. But he never anticipated what happened next. Scarfo's ire was now directed toward one of his oldest friends, Salvatore "Chuckie" Merlino.

Merlino had been with Nicky Scarfo for over twenty-five years. They went back to the neighborhood together. Merlino was with Scarfo in 1963 when he stabbed the longshoreman in the Oregon Diner. He had remained his friend through the lean early years in Atlantic City, and he had risen to the top of the organization with him. When Scarfo went away to jail in 1982, Merlino was his caretaker boss. Then they plotted the Salvie Testa murder together.

"Chuckie was about ten years younger than Nicky, and Nicky always took him under his wing. Now, I go back with Chuckie like I go back with Nicky, twenty, twenty-five years. Nicky always liked Chuckie. Nicky was the outcast then because of that problem with Mr. Joe [Rugnetta]. And, remember, Nicky stuck his neck out for Chuckie in that incident with the Marconi brothers.

"After Salvie went, things were still good with him and Nicky, although I tried to stay away from Chuckie, because

he used to come around our corner drunk. He'd stay all fuckin'
day and say all kinds of crazy things about wanting to shoot
this one and wanting to kill that one. We always worried about
eavesdropping equipment. We knew we were being watched
very closely. We had done all these murders, and the cops
were always watching us.

"Chuckie's headquarters were at Sartain and Shunk. He
used to like to play gin in the afternoon, but this guy also
used to stay home and drink for weeks at a time. Didn't come
out of the house. Whiskey and beer. Whiskey and beer. Get
drunk. Go to sleep. Get up again. We used to go over the house
when Nicky was away and we would see this. He was the boss
when Nicky was away.

"So for twenty-five years he and Nicky had been friends,
and he had Nicky's ear. His problems started around the
Christmas party of '85. Nicky's having this big thing [at La
Cucina, the South Street restaurant] and everybody's gotta be
there about two o'clock. The Newark guys, Patty Specs [Pas-
quale Martirano]... everybody was there. It was filled with
members, forty, maybe fifty of them. Later, after four o'clock,
invited nonmembers would start arriving. Nicky, Chuckie,
Philip, and Lawrence came in a limousine together from down
the shore. And Chuckie's dead fuckin' drunk. He's a mess.
He got in all kinds of trouble.

"First he pushes this Joey from Newark who's with Patty
Specs. And this Joey is very upset. Then who comes in but
Sal Avena."

Avena is a respected criminal defense attorney from New
Jersey whose clients had included Angelo Bruno, Rosario
Gambino, and John Stanfa, among others. His legal work, Caramandi said, was highly regarded by some of the older members of the Gambino organization who had earlier forged
alliances with Angelo Bruno. Three days before the Christmas
party, on December 16, 1985, Paul Castellano, the head of the
Gambino organization, was gunned down outside a steak
house in Manhattan. The word within the organization was
that the murder, which paved the way for John Gotti's rise to
power, had been sanctioned by the Commission. Chuckie Merlino, drunk but hardly full of Christmas good cheer, made a
point of mentioning it to Avena as soon as he walked in the
door.

"Chuckie says to him, 'What are you gonna do now, Sal?
Your buddy's gone.' So that was another insult. He's bothering

everybody. I mean, he's drunk and he's all over the fuckin' table. Stevie Traitz is there talking to Nicky at the bar for a couple hours. I had Big Ralph and other people that I had invited. Guys from the neighborhood. The hangaround guys. It was packed. We had everybody there. Even Stanley Branche [a former Congressional candidate and onetime civil rights leader who was later convicted of extortion]. Everybody in the city was there.

"Chuckie bothered so many people. He couldn't even stand up. During the course of the night I'm talking to this doctor friend of mine and he's got a cousin in California with the same last name as Chuckie, Merlino. So I call Chuckie over to introduce him and to tell him they've got a mutual cousin. Chuckie says, 'Fuck you and him. I'll kill youse both.' So I laughed and then I apologized to the doctor.

"Eventually, they took Chuckie home. That night went on till about four in the morning. But this was the beginning of the end for Chuckie."

Caramandi said Merlino remained on a binge for most of the holiday season. On Christmas Eve he and Charlie White paid their respects by visiting Merlino's home in South Philadelphia. The hapless mob underboss greeted them in his bathrobe, unshaven, with a bottle of homemade wine in his hand. They stayed for over an hour while Merlino babbled almost incoherently about the mob, his pending jail term, and the treachery within the organization.

Scarfo had headed south for the holidays. He was staying in Fort Lauderdale, where a big New Year's party was planned for the first week in January. Little Nicky summoned the entire regime—including the soon-to-be-deposed Merlino—to his Florida retreat, which now had a large plaque on the wall next to the front door that grandly proclaimed the residence "Casablanca South." In all, about one hundred people, mob members, associates, and their girlfriends, would head south to help Little Nicky welcome in 1986.

"The party was set for January 5th. It started at six-thirty. Now Chuckie comes to the party drunk. And he's telling Nicky that he's gotta go away. He's gonna get four years. That was his sentence. So he's crying to Nicky and he's disgusted. And Nicky's just sort of passing it off.

"Then Chuckie starts talking with Junior [Ralph Staino] after that conversation with Nicky and he's, like, ignoring Scarfo. Now Joey Merlino, Chuckie's son, tells Philip Leonetti,

'I want to show you my car,' which was in the front of the house. We were in the back of the house, by the swimming pool. And to get to the front, you hadda walk through, like, an alleyway. So when Philip starts walking behind Joey, who goes behind Philip but Faffy.

"Nicky's watching all this, and you could see that his set is really on. He's really bugged about something. They go out to the front and I don't know what the hell's going on. Later I would find out Nicky suspected some treason from Chuckie.

"The next day all the guys are supposed to come over and go on the boat. They was all staying at the Diplomat Hotel down in Hollywood. It's about ten, ten-thirty. Nicky comes down and we get him some coffee and shredded wheat. Nicky was on a big health kick then.

"While he was having his coffee, I was out in the courtyard with Spike [Anthony DiGregorio] and Philip, who was gettin' the boat ready in back of the house. I'm sweeping these leaves from the tree next door. These leaves used to drive Scarfo nuts. He wanted to strangle the neighbor. He wanted him to cut the tree down. He used to say he was gonna cut the tree down himself. So I start kidding around with Spike. I says, 'Hey, Spike, you gotta watch what you say.' Philip turns around and tells me, 'Hey, Nick, he don't have to worry about nobody but my fucking uncle, do you understand that?' I was shocked. I says, 'Yeah, Philip. I didn't mean nothin'.' And he says, 'He never has to worry about anybody. The only guy he worries about is my uncle.'

"So I looked at Spike and I go, with my hands, like, what's going on here. And Spike says, 'Shhh, I'll talk to you later.'

"Now all of a sudden here comes Scarfo. He looks at me and he says, 'You see that guy in there,' and he points to the room where Lawrence Merlino, Chuckie's brother, was still sleeping. He says, 'You see that motherfucker in there. He'll fuck your mother, your sister, your daughter, your grandmother. He'll fuck anybody.' Viciously, he said this. Now I ain't seen this color on Scarfo for a long time. He walks back in the house. I look at Spike and he gives me a signal—don't say nothing.

"Five minutes later, here he comes out again. And he says the same thing again. Now, I don't know what to think."

Caramandi spent the rest of the day staying out of Scarfo's way and trying to get Spike aside.

"Something's going on," Spike said at one point, "but I don't know what it is. When he's this way, you can't get it out of him."

Adding to the tension in the house that day was the failure of anyone to show up for the scheduled boat trip. Tired from the late-night party of the day before, most of the mobsters ended up sleeping in. By late afternoon, Scarfo had Caramandi call the Diplomat Hotel to see where everyone was. Caramandi called for three hours before reaching anyone.

"Finally, about seven o'clock, I get Charlie on the phone. 'Charlie, there's something going on. Why didn't you get over here?' Charlie says, 'I couldn't get away. This guy wouldn't let us go.' I says, 'What guy?' He says, 'Chuckie. He wouldn't let none of us go.' I says, 'Charlie, I gotta talk to you. There's something wrong. You better get over here tomorrow. You better tell somebody and get those guys the fuck here.'

"That night me and Spike made dinner. Spaghetti or something. After we finished eating, me and Scarfo are sitting outside, we open up a bottle of wine and he starts talking. Philip's inside playing cards with Spike and we're outside drinking. But he still didn't tip his mitt to me about what was going on. He wanted to see where I was coming from.

"We finally go to bed, and the next morning I get up. Spike's got it all planned. He told Nicky he wants to clean up the house and he needs me around. So I didn't have to go on the boat—I used to hate those fuckin' boat rides. Now, here comes everybody. Faffy, Tommy, Joey Grande, Joey Pung, Wayne Grande, Gino, Nicky Whip—about fifteen guys. And Charlie's pissed off because I'm not going on that boat. I know that boat's a fuckin' all-day trip.

"So I got Spike alone and I asked him what's going on. He says something with Chuckie. He says the other night when Joey asked Philip to go out front to see his car, Nicky thought it was a move on Philip. That Chuckie's got some treason in his mind and Nicky wants to see just where it's going. Holy Christ almighty, I thought. This is bad. This is real fucking bad. Once this guy puts something in his head, nobody could get it out of him. He's stubborn as they come.

"They come back that night. We had ordered, it must have been, six hundred dollars' worth of Chinese food. We took five cars to the restaurant to go pick it up. We had other people, associates, coming over that night. Later, I told Charlie what was going on. He said he knew there was something up."

Charlie White told Caramandi that Chuckie Merlino had

clammed up after the New Year's party in Fort Lauderdale. He stopped drinking and he stopped talking to virtually everyone staying at the Diplomat Hotel. When several of the members went out drinking the night after the party, Merlino stayed in, locking himself in his room.

The Crow and Charlie White then began speculating on the reasons for Scarfo's tirade and Spike's suspicions. They agreed to stay alert and to avoid Merlino if possible. A week later, back in South Philadelphia, Caramandi told Charlie White, "There's something up and I'm not trusting nobody. The only guy I'm listening to is Scarfo. I don't know what this Chuckie's got in his brain, but he's gotta be crazy. I'm not fucking with Scarfo." It was important, Caramandi knew, to stay nonaligned. If Scarfo suspected treachery, the Crow didn't want to be perceived as one of the conspirators. Neither did Charlie White. Perceptions, as they both well knew, could get you killed.

Two days later, Caramandi got a call from Spike DiGregorio. Scarfo wanted to see him. He had to hop on a plane and fly back to Florida right now.

"I said, 'Spike, you know I don't like to fly.' Spike told me, 'You better get on that fuckin' airplane.' So once I'm back down there, Nicky gets me alone and he says, 'The reason I want you here is that I think there's a conspiracy. Chuckie's got something in his mind. He made a move at the New Year's party with my nephew Philip. What the fuck did he think he was gonna do? Faffy was gonna kill my nephew?' Jesus Christ, I'm stunned. I says, 'Well, Nicky, I told Charlie whatever's going on, I'm with you. And Charlie said the same thing.' Well, he says, 'this cocksucker...' Now he starts opening up. It was two o'clock in the morning. He musta talked till six. All about the things that Chuckie's done.

"He told me about the time he was at the Sheraton Hotel in New York for a meeting with these two people. Chuckie was downstairs waiting for him, got drunk, and started flirting with one of their wives. Now they were all supposed to have dinner that night after the meeting, with their wives. Nicky was bringing Chicago. But these two guys canceled out. It was an embarrassment to him. He says, 'This motherfucker's been embarrassing me for years with his drunkenness. Now he thinks he's gonna overthrow me? I'm gonna take up arms. I'm gonna protect myself.'

"He says, 'I wanna know who's involved in this conspiracy.' Now this is in his head... and he says, 'This motherfucker thinks he's gonna overthrow me. We'll see about that. I'm gonna take him down. And he might get this. I might kill his whole family, his wife, his son.'

Caramandi flew back to Philadelphia a few days later and again met with Charlie White, warning him both about Scarfo's paranoia and Merlino's either real or perceived treachery. They decided to maintain the same posture that they had taken earlier. They weren't going to trust anyone.

"The reason I didn't want to get mixed up in this thing was I knew these two birds had been friends for so long that I never dreamed he would turn on Chuckie. I figured he would get pissed off at him, reprimand him, but I never thought it would go this far. Then a couple of weeks later, Charlie and me go back to Florida and meet with Nicky one night. I talked to him for two hours. I told him, sure, this Chuckie's got some peculiar ways. I told him about the incident with my friend, the doctor. But I said, that's Chuckie. I said, 'How could I bury this guy? My loyalty to you is first, but I just can't go beefing on a guy.' Charlie's sitting right next to me and he's saying the same thing. 'Chuckie's Chuckie.' But Nicky's staying firm, saying, 'This guy's up to no good. I'm gonna get to the bottom of it.'

"One by one, Nicky starts to get guys. Joey Pung. Anthony Pung. They tell him about the abuse they got from Chuckie. A little at a time he gets everything out of everybody, and everybody beefs on Chuckie, especially Tommy and Faffy, who know with Chuckie out of the way, they'll be in charge of the city. So everybody's telling Scarfo stories about Chuckie. He's a pain in the ass when he's drunk. He wants to kill ya.

"And Nicky's really, really disgusted. Now he's got such a hatred not only for Chuckie, but for his son, Joey. He wants to kill his son.

"About a week later we're all back in Philadelphia and he calls another meeting. A place in Jersey, outside of Atlantic City. He had a friend who had a restaurant. It was snowing, I'll never forget. At this meeting were me, Charlie, Philip, Nick the Blade, the Whip, Frankie Narducci, Wayne Grande, Joe Grande, Gino Milano, Faffy, and Tommy. They give us a back room. We have dinner, and after dinner Nicky starts talking.

"He says about Chuckie, 'From now on we call him cocksucker. That's what he is, a no-good cocksucker.' And 'The situation can only get worse with him. He's crying like a baby. He's gotta do ten months in jail [the likely minimum for the four-year prison term] and he's crying like a fucking baby. He's a disgrace. He's a drunk. He's a cocksucker. He's always drunk and embarrassing me.' He said he was ungrateful. He said he made Chuckie over two million dollars. Now he starts talking about Chuckie's son. He says, 'My nephew wants to kill him. My nephew is for killing the son immediately. *But*, I'm gonna give him [Chuckie] a break. I'm gonna give him ten months. Ten months to sober up, go to jail and sober up. If he does this much, just a hair, I'll kill him and his whole fucking family. His wife, his daughter, his son.'

"He was really crazy. You gotta see the craziness come out of him. So we're all listening. He says, 'I know he's gonna fuck up, but he's got ten months. And if his son does one thing, we're gonna bang his fucking son.' He says he's gonna go get the clearance [from New York] and he's gonna take Chuckie down and his brother Lawrence, too. 'I'm taking them both down. I'm protecting myself. I'm gonna keep this thing in my family. A guy like this controlling the city? A drunk? Something happens to me, if I get killed on an airplane, I'm gonna make this guy the boss? No fucking way.'

"It's now sometime in late February 1986. Chuckie and Joey Merlino go to Charlie White's house, and Chuckie asks Charlie, 'What the fuck is happening? I called Nicky up and he don't want to answer my phone calls. What did I do?' And so Charlie tells him the whole story, that Faffy and Tommy beefed on him.

"The next day I go to the clubhouse and who's there but Chuckie. I go and shake hands with him. Then he calls me to the back of the store. He says, 'Nick, what happened? He took me down. He don't wanna see me no more.' I said, 'Hey, Chuck, I didn't beef on you.' He says, 'Charlie told me everything last night.' He said, 'I'm going to jail tomorrow.' He takes out the paper and shows me the notice.

"He says, 'Nick, all I ever wanted to do was be left alone, stay around the corner. But he wants to go on these fuckin' boat trips, to act like a movie star. I don't wanna be bothered. I don't want to be around all these assholes, have all these problems. I just wanna stay on the corner. This thing is supposed to be low-key. I don't have no treachery in my mind.' I says, 'Well, Chuck, you know who buried ya.'

"Now me and Charlie figured Chuckie had a gun and he

wanted to kill Tommy or Faffy. But they didn't come around that day. And Chuckie's telling me to stay and drink with him, but I say, 'Chuck, go to jail. Forget about it. It don't mean nothing. You know the way this guy is. You been his friend all his life. You'll find a way to get around it. You know the name of this game.'

"This game is so unpredictable, you never know what's gonna happen. Today he's your friend, tomorrow he wants to kill ya. You can't trust nobody. Look at Chuckie's best friends, Tommy and Faffy, the two guys he put where they're at. They were running the city.

"I said to Chuckie, 'Just go to jail.'

"The next day his son comes around the corner. He's scared to death. Me and Charlie grab him and say, 'Listen, Joey, you better not do one thing wrong. You got a bad problem, buddy. Just stay off this corner. Don't show yourself. You got a problem and nobody could help you.'"

Salvatore "Chuckie" Merlino surrendered to New Jersey authorities on February 21, 1986, to begin serving a four-year prison term for attempting to bribe the Margate, New Jersey, police officer who had arrested him for drunken driving. Two weeks later, his fall from grace was formalized at a mob making ceremony presided over by Scarfo and attended by about thirty-five members of the organization. The affair was held in a private room on top of a pizza parlor at Fourth and South streets, not far from La Cucina. Scarfo initiated Philip Narducci and Nicky "the Whip" Milano into the family. Both had taken part in the Frankie Flowers murder. Little Nicky held off on making Joe Ligambi, the other shooter in the Flowers killing, because he still wasn't certain about Ligambi's loyalty: Ligambi was clearly a friend of Chuckie Merlino's, and Scarfo wanted to see how he reacted to what was about to unfold.

After the formal induction ceremony, Scarfo made several announcements. He said he had gotten Commission approval to demote both Salvatore and Lawrence Merlino. Both men were dropped to the rank of soldier. And again he warned that the demotion might just be the beginning of their problems. Scarfo appointed his nephew, Philip Leonetti, the new family underboss. And he said that both Tommy DelGiorno and Faffy Iannarella would move up from "acting" capos to capos in the organization. With Chuckie out of the way and with Philip

Leonetti based in Atlantic City, this meant that Tommy and Faffy would be running the city for the Scarfo mob. Caramandi and Charlie White looked at one another and shrugged.

For the Crow it was another lesson in the way Scarfo operated.

CHAPTER TWENTY-ONE

A few weeks after the making ceremony and formal demotion of the Merlino brothers, Caramandi got a pair of telephone calls that would change his life. One of the calls came from Chick DiTullio, the methamphetamine merchant whose payoffs to the mob were now approaching $500,000. The other was from Bobby Rego. Both would lead to million-dollar scams. And in both cases Caramandi would uncharacteristically misjudge the "sucker" he thought he had on the hook.

Brute force and muscle were beginning to take their toll. The Crow was losing his edge; his instincts were not as sharp as they used to be.

DiTullio told Caramandi he had a problem and wanted to see him. A hundred-gallon shipment of P-2-P had been stolen from him in Germany. He suspected one of his partners, a guy named Joe Kelly. And he told Caramandi he also thought Kelly was acting in concert with Junior Staino, Caramandi's long-time mob associate. This could prove to be a major headache for Caramandi, because he and Charlie White had promised DiTullio protection in exchange for the street tax he was so readily paying.

Rego's message was more positive. Willard Rouse was going to need special legislation passed in city council in order to go forward with the Penn's Landing project. The first phase of the multimillion-dollar waterfront deal hinged on Rouse's ability to obtain $10 million in federal financing. Rouse had applied for an Urban Development Action Grant (UDAG), and part of the application called for a commitment from the city and from two quasi-governmental city funding agencies. City

council would have to pass two ordinances. And time was
running out. The legislation would have to be approved by
June if Rouse was to qualify for the federal funds.

Rego told Caramandi that Beloff was beside himself when
he heard about this. "Now we got this guy by the balls," the
city councilman said.

Caramandi told Rego he would meet with him shortly to
discuss the details. In the meantime, he told DelGiorno that
he might have a big score working with Beloff. He gave his
capo a brief sketch of the deal and asked DelGiorno to get the
go-ahead from Scarfo. He didn't mention DiTullio and his
problem.

"Chick DiTullio calls me up sometime in March or April of
'86 and he says he had a hundred gallons in Germany in an
apartment. He had a guy named Joe Kelly who used to go get
the stuff. He tells me Kelly came in to him, threw the keys [to
the apartment] on the table, and said DiTullio owed him a
hundred thousand for the work he had done and he didn't
want to work for him no more. After this happened, DiTullio
got another guy and sent him over to Germany. The guy gets
there and the apartment's cleaned out. There's nothing there.

"Now he tells me that he thinks Junior had something to
do with this. I says, 'Listen, I don't know about Junior.' But
he says, 'He's friends with Joe Kelly, and Joe Kelly ain't got
the balls to do it on his own.'

"I tell him to wait. I says I want Charlie White to hear every
word he's saying, because you want a witness when a guy
talks like this. I go back around the corner and I grab Charlie
and tell him we got a problem. I tell him the story of what
happened as we're driving to Chick's place. This Junior, we
just knew that he had something to do with it."

Ralph "Junior" Staino, fifty-six, had been a mob groupie for
most of his adult life, working various scams and shakedowns.
His biggest claim to fame was his involvement in the "Pottsville Heist," a 1959 burglary of the home of an upstate Pennsylvania coal baron. Burglars made off with $478,000 in
jewelry. Staino, a young, handsome, dark-haired Passyunk
Avenue Romeo at the time, was dating Lillian Reis, a Philadelphia showgirl and local celebrity.

Staino and Diamond Lil, the good-looking mobster and the
sexy showgirl, could have walked right out of a Damon Runyon
short story. And the newspapers loved to tout their exploits.

The late Tom Fox, once the preeminent newspaper columnist in the city, used to write about Reis's "limousine legs" and her running battle with old Captain Clarence Ferguson, head of the city's vice squad. Reis owned a nightclub called the Celebrity Room where "hostesses" were suspected of offering customers more than drinks. Ferguson would periodically raid the joint, and headlines in the next morning's papers would trumpet the event.

Reis, Staino, Irish mobster John Berkery, and several other local hoods were suspected of the Pottsville heist. Both Reis and Staino were eventually convicted. But those convictions were overturned on appeal in 1970 on technical grounds, and the case was never again brought to trial. The publicity made underworld folk heroes out of the lovely Lillian and her South Philly paramour. There was even some discussion of making a movie about the caper. But that, like so much else surrounding Junior Staino, never got beyond the talking stage.

Staino, always living on the edge, beat a counterfeiting rap three years later. And then in 1976 he was sentenced to a year in jail after hooking up with Caramandi in the credit card scam while both were flimflamming in Florida.

All the while, Staino remained an associate of the South Philadelphia wiseguys, which gave him added stature in the neighborhood. For a time he was part of the "bomb squad," the shakedown team that Pat Spirito put together in 1982. But Spirito never trusted Staino around money and eventually accused him of stealing petty cash from the register in the store/clubhouse they had opened on Bancroft Street. After that came the complaints from bookmakers who said Staino was welshing on bets.

On another occasion Staino got into a beef with Giuseppe Gambino while both were playing blackjack at Resorts International in Atlantic City. Gambino, nephew of the late Carlo Gambino, was a friend of Angelo Bruno's. He was living in Cherry Hill at the time and was setting up, police would later learn, a piece of the Sicilian heroin-smuggling operation that became known as the Pizza Connection. Staino, Caramandi said, was oblivious to all this. He didn't even know who Gambino was. But he knew the guy didn't know how to play blackjack.

"Junior kept getting upset because the guy was asking for a card when he shouldn't have or wasn't asking when he should have," Caramandi said. "He ended up calling him a stupid motherfucker, and they got into a big beef.

"Junior was always screwing up," is the way the Crow explained it.

This time, if DiTullio was right, Staino might have screwed up on a grand scale.

Caramandi drove Charlie White back to Chick DiTullio's garage, and the drug dealer repeated the story about the missing hundred gallons of P-2-P. What's more, DiTullio told the two mobsters, the stuff belonged not only to him but to Stevie Vento, a notorious South Philadelphia drug dealer who was then serving time in Lewisburg Federal Penitentiary. Vento, despite his incarceration, was continuing his drug dealing, using his young son, Stevie Vento, Jr., as his liaison with DiTullio.

"I said, 'Look, Chick, I'll get back to you. Give me a day or two. Just let me talk to this Junior.' Charlie's convinced that Junior ripped the stuff off and I'm convinced. And Junior's gonna have a big fucking problem if he did.

"We go back around the corner and run straight into Junior. I say, 'Junior, come here. We want to talk to you. You know a guy by the name of Joe Kelly?' He says, 'Yeah. He was over at my house last night.' So I tell him about Chick and how Chick is paying us. Now Junior's not a made guy yet. Tommy's got him hanging around and he's got him proposed. But in our hearts me and Charlie knew he wouldn't be no good for this thing because he was too greedy.

"So Junior tells us that Joe Kelly came to his house last night and he's got the hundred gallons and he don't know what to do. He stole it from Chick and he would like help from Junior. So Junior says, 'I told him I don't want to get involved in this thing, but I'll go see somebody and I'll let ya know.' We said, 'Look, Junior, you gotta tell us the truth, because this is bad shit. This guy pays and we're supposed to protect him.'"

Staino said that's why he was coming around the corner. He said he was coming to report the incident to Tommy DelGiorno. Later that morning, after Staino had left, Caramandi and Charlie White discussed the situation. Both of them had come to the same conclusion. Staino was lying through his teeth.

"Me and Charlie figured this guy, Joe Kelly, wouldn't do this on his own, knowing DiTullio is with the mob. Junior had to okay this thing. We decide to go to Junior's house and lay it on him. We say, 'Junior, you gotta tell us the truth, because the truth is gonna come out here and you're gonna have a big fucking problem. And we cannot help you. We cannot save you in any way. We cannot even talk for you. It's up to you. You gotta tell us the truth.'

"Well, he breaks out in a sweat. 'I'll tell ya everything,' he says. 'We took a hundred gallons. I already sold fifty gallons. What am I gonna do? What am I gonna do?' I says, 'Junior, how the fuck could you do something like that knowing the guy is paying us?' See, he did this on his own, and now he says, 'How am I gonna get out of this?'"

Caramandi and Charlie White decided Staino's only option was to go to DelGiorno and tell him what had happened. They told him, however, not to mention that he had already sold any of the oil. Staino told them there were still fifty gallons at another apartment in Germany. He said Kelly had brought half the shipment into the country and left the other half behind.

The plan was that Staino would tell DelGiorno some of the truth. He would say that Kelly took the oil because Kelly felt DiTullio owed him money. And he would say that Kelly came to him for help in getting rid of the stuff.

Caramandi figured correctly that the lure of one hundred gallons of P-2-P with a street value of about $2 million would be too much for Tommy Del to resist.

"Tommy was looking to make a score so bad," Caramandi said. "He had just been made capo."

Staino did as he was told. And DelGiorno did as Caramandi expected.

"The next morning Junior comes around the corner, big smile on his face. He said, 'He went for it hook, line, and sinker.' And he told Junior to tell us that he would be around that afternoon to talk to us.

"Junior's happy, but now we gotta rob this stuff to save his fucking neck. In the meantime, I got a problem with Chick DiTullio. I gotta go explain to him that Junior didn't take the stuff, that Junior wasn't involved. That we're gonna look to kill Kelly.

"We go see Chick and tell him there's no way Junior took the stuff. We said we know Kelly was with another guy and we're gonna find out who it is and that we got the okay to kill Kelly and the other guy. Then I says, 'What kind of money did it cost you to get this stuff?' He's crying, 'It's a lot of money,

two million dollars. Stevie Vento's screaming bloody murder.'
I says, 'What's this stuff cost ya [in Germany]?' I don't think
the stuff cost him twenty thousand. The oil is cheap in Germany. You make a connection, you might be able to get it for
five or six hundred a gallon. Then you gotta put it in these
stoves [to smuggle it into the country], that's another couple
hundred. So it might cost ya a thousand dollars a gallon between costs and expenses. It's not that much.

"We calm this Chick down, but he says we gotta talk to
Stevie because he thinks Junior ripped him off. And he says
Vento didn't know that he was paying us the street tax. And
his son's giving DiTullio a hard time, saying he ain't paying
no fucking gangsters and making all kinds of threats. So we
tell Chick we'll handle Stevie Vento's kid and we'll handle Joe
Kelly and not to worry, I'll talk to Vento."

Back around the corner on Camac and Moore that afternoon, Caramandi and Charlie White met with DelGiorno. As
expected, Tommy Del told them he wanted to keep the P-2-P
that Kelly and Staino had stolen. He said he was going to go
down to Atlantic City and get the approval from Scarfo.
DelGiorno said they would sell the stuff to John Renzulli,
another meth dealer who was on the mob pay list.

Caramandi asked DelGiorno how he would get Scarfo to go
along with what was clearly a drug deal, given the ban on the
mob dealing in drugs.

"I'll just tell him it's a score," DelGiorno said. "I won't give
him all the details. I mean, you ever see this guy turn down a
million dollars?"

Over the next week, Caramandi, Charlie White, DelGiorno,
Faffy Iannarella, and Junior Staino laid the groundwork for
what DelGiorno had told Scarfo would be a $2 million drug
deal. Scarfo was going to get $1 million. Tommy, Faffy, the
Crow, Charlie White, and Junior would split the other million.
The five drug-dealing mobsters put up $5,000 each to finance
a trip back to Germany for Kelly and an associate. They also
arranged for the oil to be shipped to a local warehouse hidden
in wood-burning stoves and barbecue grills.

Junior said it would take a month or two to get the stuff
into the country. In the meantime he privately agreed to sell
five gallons of P-2-P he already had in the country to Caramandi and Charlie White for $100,000. The Crow and Charlie
White had a meth dealer lined up who would cook the stuff,
turn it into speed, and sell it on the open market. Caramandi

and Iannece figured to split about $800,000 once the drugs were sold. The ban on drug dealing had become a joke within the Scarfo organization.

"Now I'm telling Tommy I'm having problems with Vento and with Vento's kid. I talk to Vento on the phone. He called from prison. I tell him, 'Look, we're trying to help you with your problem. Just be patient and don't talk on this phone.' He says, 'All right. We'll see.' In the meantime, I get a guy I know to go see Vento in Lewisburg. I want him to tell Vento that he's got a fucking son out here and to stop beefing that he ain't gonna pay. He's gotta pay like everybody else.'

But the Ventos, father and son, proved to be a major headache for the Scarfo organization. Neither man was cowed by the threats and bully tactics of the mob. Instead, Vento Sr. from prison and Vento Jr. from the streets of South Philadelphia began to issue threats of their own, threats that Caramandi and Charlie White took seriously.

"He was a very vengeful person," Caramandi would say later of the older Vento. "He's the type of guy who would pay somebody to throw a bomb in your house."

The message Vento Sr. sent back to the Scarfo mob was that he had no intention of paying a street tax to deal drugs: "Tell 'im I said go fuck himself and everybody connected to him. I don't give nothing to anybody."

Vento's phone conversations from Lewisburg prison, which were being secretly recorded by the FBI, included several other threats aimed at Iannece, Caramandi, and Scarfo. When a Vento associate asked him if he was serious, Vento replied, "I'm serious as fucking cancer."

For the first time since the Riccobene war, Scarfo and his mob were running up against somebody who might be willing to shoot back. Vento Sr., who had been an associate of Harry Riccobene, had earned a reputation over the years as a ruthless and hardhearted narcotics dealer who asked and gave no quarter in the drug underworld. He was sentenced to seven years in prison in 1974 on income tax evasion charges and ten years later got eighteen years for drug dealing. He would later tell a federal jury that he continued to deal drugs from prison, earning "better than a million, better than a million and a half dollars" while in Lewisburg. He and his son gave a new meaning to the term "crime family." Just eighteen years old in 1986, Steven Vento, Jr., was awaiting trial on one drug-related murder and was a suspect in a second at the time he and his father clashed with the Scarfo mob. In July of that year, both father and son would be charged with attempting one of the boldest prison escapes in Pennsylvania history. Vento Jr. paid a helicopter pilot to land in the yard at Lewisburg, where his father and another inmate would be waiting to hop aboard and literally fly the coop. But the FBI and Drug Enforcement Administration agents learned of the plan, and armed guards were waiting when the hapless pilot touched down in the prison yard.

Little Nicky Scarfo responded to the Vento threats in predictable fashion. He ordered Vento Jr. killed. The contract was issued on April 12, 1986. Federal authorities have been able to fix that date exactly because Caramandi remembered the time and place when the order came down. Almost the entire regime was at La Cucina that afternoon for a big celebration, the Crow said. Scarfo sat at a table in a private room that had been set aside for the festivities. Periodically, different members would stop by to discuss what they had going. Tommy DelGiorno brought up both the Penn's Landing deal and the Vento problem. Scarfo decided that day to go ahead with Beloff's scam and to have Stevie Vento, Jr., killed.

Only a few members at the private party that day got the word. Most of the other mobsters, their girlfriends, their wives, and their children had no idea what was going on. The murder and the extortion were planned while almost everyone in the room was celebrating and toasting Salvatore "Wayne" Grande, his wife, and their little girl, who had just made her First Holy Communion.

Junior Staino, Anthony Pungitore, and Tory Scafidi got the Vento contract. DelGiorno told Caramandi he was assigning them because he wanted them to "get down," that is, become full-fledged members of the organization. After about a month of planning and several missed opportunities, Pungitore and Scafidi trapped Vento Jr. as he sat with his girlfriend in a parked car in front of her South Philadelphia home. Scafidi fired through the open car window and Vento Jr. went down in a hail of bullets.

"Tory put the gun right to the kid's head," Caramandi said. "But he didn't die. Tory couldn't understand it. He was pretty upset. He shot him right in the temple. Anthony Pung threw a couple shots in the window, but the kid didn't die.

"They figured the bullet might have been bad and stuff like that."

A day later, Caramandi got word from Lewisburg Prison. Steve Vento, Sr., was holding him and Charlie White responsible for the shooting of his son.

Vento Jr., meanwhile, was making a rapid recovery from a gunshot wound to the head. He was in a semiprivate room at Methodist Hospital. In the bed next to his was an older man from South Philadelphia. The man was Tory Scafidi's grandfather.

This presented a problem for Scafidi, who was supposed to visit his grandfather the next day.

"He asked me my opinion, what I thought about him going up there," Caramandi said. "I said, 'He ain't gonna remember you. How is he gonna remember? He probably didn't even see you anyway.'

"A short time later, the next day or two, Tory comes around the clubhouse at Camac and Moore. He says he visited his grandfather in the hospital and made friends with Vento Jr. The kid had no idea who Tory was. In fact, Tory says, 'He's gonna come around the corner after he comes out of the hospital.'"

Caramandi couldn't believe it.

Maybe this really was *The Gang That Couldn't Shoot Straight*.

CHAPTER TWENTY-TWO

The FBI, the Philadelphia District Attorney's Office, the Philadelphia police department, and the Pennsylvania state police had spent tens of thousands of man-hours and hundreds of thousands of dollars investigating the Scarfo organization during the bloody reign of terror that began with the March 21, 1980, assassination of Angelo Bruno.

But by the summer of 1986 there were still more than a dozen unsolved homicides on the books and Scarfo was sitting pretty atop a multimillion-dollar mob organization whose power and influence stretched from the corridors of City Hall in Philadelphia to the Boardwalk casino strip in Atlantic City.

Sure, investigators had a pretty good idea who had been behind most of the killings. They had confidential informant reports detailing the when, where, and how of almost every hit. But they had very little proof that they could bring into court. No witnesses who would testify. No hard evidence.

Anthony Gatto helped change all that by doing his job. It was one of those little things that months later prove to be a turning point in a major investigation. Gatto didn't realize the significance of what he had done, and for nearly a year, neither did anyone else.

Around 1:00 P.M. on June 16, 1986, Gatto, a detective sergeant with the New Jersey state police, stepped out into the bright afternoon sunlight in front of Bally's Park Place Casino Hotel. Gatto, an eighteen-year veteran of the state police, was assigned to the New Jersey Division of Gaming Enforcement. He was part of the security detail attached to the casino industry.

As he walked out onto the Boardwalk in front of the casino, Gatto looked toward the ocean. And there, on the other side of the famous walkway, standing up against a railing, were Nicky Scarfo, Phil Leonetti, and two other men whom Gatto could not identify. The four men appeared to be deep in conversation, oblivious to the beach, the blue sky, and the blue-green ocean that provided a postcard setting behind them.

Gatto went to a nearby public phone and called the gaming enforcement security room inside Bally's. Each casino-hotel is equipped with highly sophisticated "electronic eyes," surveillance cameras hidden in the ceiling of the casino and on the outside of the building. The cameras inside are used to ferret out suspected cheating. Monitors, banks of television screens connected to the surveillance cameras, are used by gaming enforcement officials to scan the action on the casino floor, looking for anything out of the ordinary—dealers who might be palming cards or stacking the deck, players who might be marking cards or rigging slot machines. Thousands upon thousands of hours of videotape are maintained by each casino. It might be weeks before the count, numbers, and payouts at a particular baccarat game, for example, raise the eyebrows of investigators or casino executives. If they suspect something isn't kosher, one of the first things they do is call up the tapes and examine the play.

A sophisticated cheating scam set up by a group of professional card cheats from Hong Kong was documented in just this way. The players, backed by the leader of a Chinese Triad, popped Caesars and the Sands for a total of $2.7 million during two days of gambling at the baccarat tables in August 1984. By the time investigators got onto the scam several weeks later, the gamblers and their organized crime leader were long gone. But the casinos had it all on tape, and eventually New Jersey authorities were able to track down most of the participants.

The cameras on the outside of the casino-hotels are there to provide more traditional protection. Like spotlights and burglar alarms, they are part of an elaborate security system that rings each of the glitzy gaming houses.

Gatto told one of his subordinates in the security room to train a camera on the four men leaning up against the Boardwalk railing. There was no way to pick up the conversation. Eavesdropping is not a part of the casino's security network. But the videotape did clearly show Scarfo, Leonetti, and two other men engaged in a lengthy conversation. Periodically, Leonetti would look up and scan the Boardwalk, and on at least two occasions, the four-man party moved farther along the railing after a passerby stopped within apparent earshot.

After ordering his cameraman to focus on the Scarfo party, Gatto went back into the casino to look for a pair of binoculars and a spot where he could spy on the mob boss. Later he took the videotape of that Boardwalk meeting and had it duplicated. He put the original in a file cabinet next to his desk in the Division of Gaming Enforcement's office at Bally's Park Place Casino Hotel. Nine months later he would turn it over to the FBI. It became a crucial piece of evidence, allowing prosecutors to independently corroborate a key piece of Nick Caramandi's testimony. It would be used in four different federal trials.

Sometimes there is no substitute for luck. This was one of those times. Thanks to an alert New Jersey state police detective sergeant, law enforcement investigators who were trying to build a case against the Scarfo organization rolled a seven.

Nick Caramandi and Charles "Charlie White" Iannece were the two men Gatto was unable to identify that afternoon. They had gone to Atlantic City to meet with Scarfo because they were upset with the way things were going in Philadelphia.

First there was Steven Vento, Sr., who they were certain would attempt to avenge his son's shooting. And while the Crow had been able to temporarily shift the blame for it to two local drug dealers—"We told DiTullio we were gonna kill them"—Caramandi was still concerned. One of the things he and Charlie White wanted to do during this visit to Atlantic City was convince Scarfo to call off the contract on Vento Jr. If the New Jersey Division of Gaming Enforcement had had listening devices as well as hidden cameras, investigators would have heard Scarfo do just that as he leaned up against the Boardwalk railing.

The other item on the agenda that day was Penn's Landing and the extortion of Willard Rouse. Things were moving forward. The application deadline for the federal $10 million UDAG grant that Rouse desperately needed to move the first phase of the project off the drawing board was rapidly approaching. The city council would have to act within the month if the funds were to be obtained. And without the city's commitment to support his application for the federal funding, Rouse had told city officials, private financing for an additional $40 million would disappear and the project would founder.

Beloff and Rego saw the situation as the perfect setup. They quickly brought Caramandi into the deal. As Caramandi stood on the Boardwalk that afternoon recapping events for Scarfo, he was in the middle of a $1 million shakedown and a $2 million drug deal. Scarfo told him he was one of the best "earners" in the organization.

Bobby Rego had set the Rouse extortion in motion on June 2 when he met with two representatives of the developer for drinks after work at DiLullo Central, a posh center city restaurant a few blocks from City Hall.

Rego told Peter Balitsaris, one of Rouse's top associates, that Beloff favored the Penn's Landing project and saw no problem in introducing the two ordinances that were needed to pave the way for the UDAG grant. Beloff and Rouse were supposed to sit down for a face-to-face meeting on June 5, and the ordinances would be introduced the following week and brought up for a final vote before the end of the month.

"We are in favor of it," Rego told Balitsaris. "We will introduce the bills. No problem."

Balitsaris was surprised at Rego's almost casual attitude. These were not simple pieces of legislation. He wondered why Rego and Beloff didn't have any questions. He was also concerned about community opposition. Residents of Queen Village, an upscale residential neighborhood, had long opposed development along the waterfront that might bring traffic congestion and swarms of tourists through their streets.

"Is there anything we can do in connection with this?" he asked. "Is there any information you need? Do we meet with the community groups?"

"No," said Rego. "We support the legislation and we'll handle the community groups."

When the waitress brought the tab for the drinks, Rego reached for the check, but Balitsaris beat him to it.

"I didn't think Bill Rouse would pay for anything," Rego said.

Balitsaris thought Rego was referring to Rouse's long-standing policy of not making any political contributions.

"Bill won't make any campaign contributions," he replied,

"but as far as I know, he doesn't have any objections to a drink."

The Rouse company picked up the tab for a second round of drinks, and then Balitsaris and Rego parted company. Balitsaris, the point man for Rouse on the Penn's Landing project, figured he had done his job. It appeared the legislation would move forward. Rego, the point man for Leland Beloff, had also done his job. He had opened a line of communication into the company.

The next day at work, Balitsaris was puzzled. The rumor floating around the office and through the development community was that Beloff was opposed to the Penn's Landing project and did not intend to introduce the legislation. In fact, Beloff had told Rouse's secretary there really was no reason for him and Rouse to meet because the project was "dead."

Balitsaris picked up the phone and called Rego at City Hall. The conversation, he would say later, was rather bizarre. He started out by telling Rego that he had just heard that Beloff wouldn't support the legislation and wouldn't introduce it in city council.

"Yeah, that's true," Rego said.

"But we just had a conversation last night where you said you had no problems with the legislation and would introduce it and support it," said a puzzled Balitsaris.

"Yeah, that's true," said Rego again.

"But these two things are completely contradictory," said the developer.

"Yeah, that's true," replied Rego.

Balitsaris tried for several more minutes to get an explanation out of Rego, but the politico was inscrutable. The next day, however, Rego called back and asked Balitsaris to meet him for drinks again. This time at Marabella's, a trendy bar and restaurant just across the street from DiLullo's, where their first meeting had occurred. When Balitsaris arrived, Rego was already there, sitting at one of the small conversation tables just off the bar. A man Balitsaris had never seen before was sitting next to Rego.

"He looked like a gangster," Balitsaris would later tell a federal jury. "He was sitting in a dark bar with his sunglasses on, talking out of the side of his mouth."

Rego introduced the man as his "friend" and then he told Balitsaris, "I'm going to finish my coffee and then I am going to leave and you talk to him."

That is how Peter Balitsaris first met Nick Caramandi.

And that is how the seeds were sown for the destruction of the Scarfo crime family.

Caramandi, Rego, and Beloff had badly miscalculated. Neither Peter Balitsaris nor his boss, Willard Rouse, could be corrupted. But the script, with dialogue from a second-rate gangster film, still had to be played out.

"They are not against the project," Caramandi said, pointing to the vacant seat where Rego had been sitting. "They want it to happen. But for it to happen, it will take this."

Then Caramandi rubbed his thumb across the tips of his four fingers several times.

Balitsaris asked Caramandi just what he had in mind.

The Crow held up his forefinger and said, "We want one."

"Would you tell me a little more what you are talking about?" asked Balitsaris, trying to draw Caramandi out while his mind raced over the events of the past two days.

"We want one," Caramandi repeated.

"May I assume there are some zeroes to go behind the one?" said Balitsaris, picking up the macho rhythm of this equally bizarre conversation.

"Yeah," said the Crow, "all the zeroes there are."

"We didn't use the word 'million' because he understood what I meant by all the zeroes. He said he would go talk to Rouse. I explained to him that nobody could help him. The fellows in City Hall can't help him, the mayor can't help him. It has to go through me. So he sort of looked at me and he says, 'Okay, I will give him the message.'

"So we left and made an appointment for the next morning. Ten o'clock. Broad and Walnut, on the corner of Broad and Walnut. That night I met with Rego and Beloff in DiLullo's and I explained to them what I told [Balitsaris], that it is going to cost a million dollars. And then they were happy about it. I says, 'We'll get an answer tomorrow.'

"They asked me what I told him. And I said I told him he can't get nothing without me, without my approval. Rouse has to go through me. The money has to pass through me. I told Beloff and Rego that Balitsaris said it was hard to get a million dollars at one time out of the company without the IRS or anybody, you know, somebody seeing it. He said that was a large sum of money. And I told him, 'We will work out the terms because this is a long-range plan.'"

Beloff and Rego's euphoria was short-lived. Balitsaris failed to appear for the meeting the next morning with Caramandi. The Crow waited on the corner for nearly an hour, then headed up the street for City Hall and Beloff's fourth-floor city council office. He and Beloff huddled in the hallway, a mobster and a city councilman meeting in the corridor just a few hundred feet from the ornate city council chambers where representative government is practiced in the City of Brotherly Love.

"I said, 'Look, this guy was playing games. He didn't show up. If he tries to get in touch with you, refer him back to me. Tell him you can't help him, you are not in a position to help him.'

"So, anyway, I think a few days went by before Rego got in touch with me again. And he told me Balitsaris had been calling, and that he don't want to do business with me. He would rather do business with him, Rego. Rego said he would have to go back to me; he would have to talk to me. So Rego made another meeting for me at Marabella's again. Rego brought Balitsaris into Marabella's. We had a cup of coffee together, the three of us. We didn't discuss any business. Then Rego got up and left.

"And I started to talk again and Balitsaris said, 'It's a lot of money.' He says his boss just can't come up with this kind of money all at one time. He wants to pay it, but there would have to be some kind of arrangement. I said, 'Well, this guy has got money. He has friends. Let him hock his wife's jewelry if he has to.'

"The next day the bill was supposed to be introduced into city council. So I said to Balitsaris I would meet him tomorrow and that if he didn't come with any money tomorrow, forget about it. I told him, 'You ain't gonna get nothin'. In fact, you are gonna have problems with the unions. You are gonna have all kind of problems.'

"So we agreed. He agreed he was going to come with the money the following day. And I made an appointment with him at the Hershey Hotel on Broad and Locust. He was supposed to bring close to a hundred thousand. I told him, 'Don't come with a hot dog,' meaning don't come with little money. 'Come with money that is good-faith money.' So he said he was going to do the best he could.

"The next morning Balitsaris showed up with another fellow, who he introduced as Jim Vance. He said, 'Look, this thing is too big for me. This fellow is going to take charge now.' I was a little hesitant, because I didn't know this Jim Vance. I said, 'I don't know you. I don't know if I want to talk to you.' And he said, 'Well, look, I am the guy that is going to take over. This is a little too big for Pete. Let me talk to you.'

"So he tried to explain that this kind of money, you know, was a great deal of money and it would have to be worked out. You just can't be taking this kind of money outta a company. Everything is on computers. And he sort of went through the same story that Balitsaris had.

"Anyway, he says, 'I'm prepared to give you some money now. I'm here to do business but I want to see what you could do.' So he took out a package. It was a white envelope and he says, 'I have ten thousand in this package to start the ball rolling. Let's see if the bill gets introduced.'"

And so on June 12, 1986—less than two hours after Caramandi's meeting with Jim Vance—Leland Beloff introduced bills number 990 and 991 into city council. The bills ensured the city's participation and support for the first phase of the Penn's Landing development project. They were scheduled for a final vote on June 26, the last council meeting before the summer recess. Beloff and Rego were cutting it close to the wire, a tactic they assumed would put maximum pressure on Rouse.

After giving Rego and Beloff the okay to push the legislation, Caramandi took the $10,000 to South Philadelphia, where he met with Charlie White and whacked up the cash. They put $5,000 aside for Rego and Beloff. They put $2,500 into the "elbow" for Scarfo. And they each took $1,250. As an added precaution, Caramandi got one of his "neighborhood guys" to take the $5,000 he had set aside for Beloff to a bank and exchange it for different bills—in effect laundering the money so the Rouse payoff could not be traced back to the councilman. Later that night the Crow met Rego in Marra's Restaurant on Passyunk Avenue and gave him the $5,000.

Caramandi told Rego that Vance was supposed to come up with another $90,000 in good-faith money before the bill was passed. Four days later, standing on the Boardwalk in Atlantic City, he told Scarfo the same thing. He outlined the $1 million extortion while Little Nicky leaned up against the railing and the New Jersey state police filmed the meeting.

"The only thing that bothered Scarfo was why Beloff and

Rego were getting so much. And I said, 'Well, I made the deal for them for half.' And he says, 'Naw, that is too much money.' See, the deal was, fifty percent of whatever I collected would go to them and fifty percent would go to me and Charlie White. And half of what we got would go to Scarfo. But Scarfo says, 'I think that is too much. I want to give some other fellas some of this. There are only two of them and there is a lot of us.' I says, 'Nick, whatever you say.' So Scarfo says, 'Give them thirty-three percent. If Rego doesn't like it, I want to know about it.'"

Over the next week and a half, Scarfo would cut Beloff and Rego even further. He sent word to Caramandi to reduce their take to 30 percent. And then revised it again to 25 percent. Beloff and Rego balked briefly when Caramandi brought them the bad news during a meeting over drinks in the Versailles Room of the Bellevue Stratford Hotel. But both men knew there was no room for negotiation with the Little Guy. Beloff did, however, extract a promise from Caramandi about his upcoming reelection to the council.

Caramandi later recounted the incident from the witness stand:

"I go back into the bar and I tell Beloff and Rego, I said, 'I have some bad news for you.' They say what kind of bad news. I said, 'Nicky said he wants to cut [the] thing down to 25 percent. They says, 'Jesus Christ, we're doing a lot here. We're sticking our necks out.'

"I said, 'Listen, I can't argue with the boss.'

"Beloff says, 'Well, what did he say about, you know, me running again? Is he going to back me up?' And I said, 'He told me to tell you don't worry about it. Whoever runs against you, the night before [the election] we will kill them and you won't have any opposition.' And with that he said, 'Heh, heh, heh,' and he was happy about it. He said, 'I don't care about nothin' now.'"

During this same period while Scarfo was cutting the take Beloff and Rego were to share, Caramandi kept up a dialogue with Jim Vance, the Rouse representative who was supposed to come up with the additional $90,000. Vance told the Crow on two separate occasions that his boss was balking at the shakedown and wanted some "proof" that Beloff was in on the deal. He said Rouse was concerned that Caramandi and Rego were simply cooking up a scam and using Beloff's title and power as leverage.

At one point Caramandi set up a meeting for the hallway outside of Beloff's City Hall office. He told Vance to have Rouse there. The plan was that Caramandi would walk up. Beloff would acknowledge his presence and they would shake hands. That would be the signal that Beloff was in on the deal. At the last minute, however, Caramandi was called away and couldn't make the meeting. Scarfo had scheduled a making ceremony in a restaurant outside of Vineland, New Jersey, for the same day, and the Crow had to be there. After years as a hanger-on, Junior Staino was finally getting the button. But he'd have little time to enjoy it.

After the aborted City Hall meeting, Caramandi and Vance met again in private and worked out another scenario in which Beloff would signal his involvement. He told Vance to be at the Hershey Hotel at Broad and Locust streets at 1:00 on Wednesday afternoon, June 25. The two bills needed for the Penn's Landing project were on the council calendar for a final vote the next day.

Caramandi had arranged for Rego and Beloff to be around the corner at Marabella's Restaurant at the same time. The Crow didn't want to blow a chance for $1 million, but he also was beginning to feel uneasy about this Jim Vance. He wanted too many assurances. He was too concerned about putting Beloff in the middle of the deal. He was acting strange. Acting, the Crow thought, a lot like a cop.

Meeting Vance at the Hershey was the first part of Caramandi's fail-safe system. If Vance was a fed, the FBI would be setting up surveillance for the Beloff signal. But nothing was going to happen at the Hershey.

Caramandi met Vance there, but said as little as possible. In fact, he communicated most of the information by writing notes on pieces of paper. After Vance read the note, Caramandi would take a match and set it on fire. He and Vance sat at a table in the bar of the Hershey Hotel "talking" this way for several minutes. Then they walked over to Marabella's.

"When we went in, Rego and Beloff were at one side of the bar and we stood at the other. So I walked over to Rego and Beloff and I shook Beloff's hand. When I shook his hand, I told him, 'Look, scratch your shoulder, just go like this,' because I had told Vance that he would do this.

"I wrote him a note when I was in the Hershey about what Beloff was going to do. I was going to shake his hand and he was going to scratch his shoulder. Would this be satisfactory?

And Vance said, 'Yeah,' and I burned the note. I didn't know if he was wired up. I wasn't sure if he was legitimate or what.

"So we walked in. I walked over to Beloff and Rego. I shook Beloff's hand. He scratched his shoulder. Then I says, 'Look, it looks like a pole is in the way. Maybe he didn't see it. Do it again.' So I shook his hand and I says, 'Scratch your shoulder.' He scratched his shoulder again and he says, 'What do you want me to do, bark like a dog?' I said, 'No. That's good enough.'

"So after this I walked over to Vance and I took him outside. I says, 'Are you satisfied now?' He says, 'Yeah.' So I asked him how long it would take to get the money, and he said it would take a couple of hours and to meet him at four o'clock at the Hershey Hotel."

Caramandi went back to Marabella's, where he told Beloff and Rego what had happened. He then walked the two politicos back to City Hall before heading downtown to wait for his afternoon meeting with Vance. At 4:00 P.M. he was back at the Hershey Hotel.

"Vance didn't have no money. I said, 'What happened?' He says his boss still ain't satisfied. He wants the thing done before he gives up any money. I said, 'I can't do that.' So he says, 'Or I could bring the ninety thousand but you have to stay with me in the hotel until the bill is passed. Then I will give you the ninety thousand.' The next morning the bill was supposed to be [brought up for a vote].

"'Look,' I says, 'this is no deal.' By now I figured he was a cop. So I decided to stroke him. Let him believe I'm gonna come the next morning and pick up the ninety thousand. So I says, 'All right, I'll tell you what I will do. We'll meet tomorrow morning. You make two packages up of forty-five thousand and forty-five thousand. I'll give forty-five thousand to somebody and I'll stay with you until the bill is approved. Then I'll take the other forty-five thousand. He agreed. But I knew I wasn't going to show up. I just wanted to win his confidence, to make him think that I was going to show up. I says, 'If you don't come with no money, this thing is dead. The bill is dead.' And he says, 'Don't worry, I'll be here with the money.'

"So I left. I walked to Marabella's. It was about four-thirty. I had to meet Rego and Beloff at five o'clock at DiLullo's. So I stood at Marabella's till five. When I walked out of Marabella's at five I saw what I thought was a cop, in a car. I went into

DiLullo's. Beloff, Rego, and Bobby Simone [Scarfo's defense attorney] were there. And we went downstairs to the lounge area where they have the rest rooms. And I told them I don't like this thing, that I thought this guy was a cop. And Bobby said he thought he saw some FBI agent that he recognized. He says, 'Let's get out of here. Let's break this conversation up.' And Bobby left.

"I had a brief conversation with Beloff, and I told him, 'Hey, you ain't got nothing to worry about. There is nothing they can prove you did. You wasn't even involved. It is just one of those things. Let's just chalk it up. I'll talk to you later."

The next morning Caramandi was at City Hall taking care of some business for a neighborhood girl who had a problem in municipal court. As he was leaving the building he met Rego and explained again that he thought Vance was a cop and that he did not intend to keep their noontime appointment.

"Kill the bill," Caramandi told Rego. "Just don't introduce it. Just knock it out. If these guys are not cops, they'll come back. We can always refile it."

"Okay," said Bobby Rego.

At the city council meeting later that morning, city councilman Leland Beloff quietly withdrew bills 990 and 991, effectively scuttling the financial plans for the first phase of the Penn's Landing project.

The next morning, Caramandi, Rego, and Beloff were arrested by the FBI.

CHAPTER TWENTY-THREE

"Jim Vance" was really James Vaules, an FBI agent. Right after Caramandi's first meeting with Balitsaris, Rouse officials called the U.S. Attorney's Office in Philadelphia and reported the extortion attempt. The feds had the case wired, and when Caramandi failed to show for the second payoff and Beloff pulled back the two bills, they closed in.

Caramandi was arrested on June 27, 1986, at Charlie White's house. He was not surprised. He had gone to Iannece's that morning to tell him that he expected to be pinched. The day before he had sent some people around to the Hershey Hotel, where he was supposed to meet with Vance. "They spotted agents all over the place," he said. "There was no way I was gonna show up. I knew he was a cop and that I was gonna be arrested."

Caramandi and Iannece were drinking coffee before heading for the clubhouse at Camac and Moore when the FBI knocked on the door. Beloff and Rego were arrested that same day. All three defendants were released on personal recognizance bonds pending trial. Newspaper, radio, and television stories screamed about the mob and City Hall. It made for a lot of media sound and fury, but proved to be little more than a thundershower in the storm that was building over the Scarfo crime family.

Eleven days after the arrests, all the charges were dropped. It was a procedural move, the U.S. Attorney's Office announced. There wasn't enough time for a grand jury to hear testimony and return an indictment within thirty days as required by law. The feds decided to back off in order to shape the case properly. Caramandi, Beloff, and Rego were already in the net. The question was whether the case could be expanded. Scarfo was the guy the feds wanted.

Caramandi headed for the shore to tell his boss there was nothing to worry about. The Crow figured he might have a problem, but he doubted the feds could make a case against Beloff and Rego. Nor was there any way, he said, that the government could put Scarfo in the scam. Under the worst circumstances, Caramandi figured he might have to take a fall. But he'd been in jail before and he knew he could do the time. It came with the territory.

In fact, he was somewhat relieved when the agents who picked him up at Charlie White's said the charge was attempted extortion. For more than a year he and Iannece had worried about the Spirito murder. Ronald "Cuddles" DiCaprio, the getaway driver for that hit, was constantly in trouble for drug dealing, and Caramandi and Iannece were concerned that he would give them up to get out from under some narcotics charge. Attempted extortion seemed almost petty in comparison to a first degree murder charge that could get you life in prison or a death sentence.

"I wanted to go down the shore to tell Nicky it was all bullshit. So about a week after they drop the charges I go to his office on Georgia Avenue. Johnny Palumbo, who used to do some carpentry work for Scarfo, was there and he says, 'Nicky's upstairs. I'll go call him.'

"So he goes upstairs and he comes down and he says, 'Nicky says where you gonna be at. Leave a phone number and he'll get in touch with ya.' I thought this to be a little strange. So I give him the phone number at the hotel I'm staying at and I go back and wait. About three o'clock I get a phone call from Joe Grande. He says, 'Come on downstairs to the Boardwalk. The guy's here.' Meaning Nicky. Nicky's downstairs. Whip's with him. Anthony Pung. Joe Grande, couple other guys.

"The first thing he tells me is, 'Nick, the reason I didn't receive ya in my office is because they mighta wanted to put me in this Rouse extortion.' So I looked at him and I thought it was kinda funny, him saying that. I felt like saying, 'What the fuck. I'm not gonna mention you, Nick.' So he says they're watching his house. Well, I knew all this. But this was the first fucking time I ever seen any trait in Scarfo about worrying about something. I mean, he's the gangster. Understand what I mean?

"Now he starts to tell me a story about Tommy [DelGiorno]. He's gonna take Tommy down. He says, 'I'm gettin' too many complaints. The guy's fuckin' around.' See, Tommy was doing the same thing Chuckie was doing. Getting drunk. Abusing people. And Scarfo got each of these guys, like Whip [Nick Milano] and Joe Pung and Wayne Grande, to beef on Tommy. Everybody did. So he said to me, 'I'm gonna take him down.'

"So I said, 'Nick, I knew he couldn't fool you.' And we discussed this for about an hour. Before I left I told him Charlie was coming in the next day. Charlie had a summer home that he used to rent in Longport. So he said we would meet there the next day around noontime. He said he had some other things he wanted to discuss with us.

"The following day I go over to Charlie's. I take my wife. Charlie's wife is there and his kids. Our wives leave after Nicky and Philip [Leonetti] arrive. We're in the house alone and he starts tellin' us the reason why he's taking Tommy down. He says, 'I'm not gonna kill him, but he just better be on his p's and q's. His fucking drunkenness has got to stop. We can't have that.'

"See, he says he wants to straighten the regime out. This regime just wasn't right, and he knew it. The guys were either indifferent to each other or there was hard feelings. Joe Grande and Anthony Pung. Tommy had hard feelings with me and Charlie. So many fuckin' things. Tommy abused a lot of guys. He took advantage of the badge. This capo shit finally went to his head.

"Now Nicky brings up another subject. There was this guy, Forlini, they called him JR. He got killed in August of 1985. They found him at nine o'clock in the morning in a shopping center up in Delaware County. Right in his own truck. So whoever killed him had to know him. Nicky wanted to know who we thought did it."

Frank "JR" Forlini was an associate of Joe Ciancaglini, the mob capo who was then in prison on racketeering charges. He had had a run-in with Caramandi when he tried to "protect" a restaurant owner whom the Crow and Charlie White were trying to shake down. There was also bad blood between Forlini and DelGiorno that Caramandi said grew out of the drug trade.

The Forlini murder has never been solved. Neither the authorities nor Scarfo was ever able to confirm who was behind the shooting, although Scarfo—along with Caramandi and Iannece—strongly suspected Tommy Del.

"Me and Charlie say we kind of think it was Tommy. But we don't know if Tommy would have had the balls to do it himself. He hadda have somebody else, like maybe Faffy. Anyway, Nicky says, 'I'd like you guys to try to find out. If I find out that Tommy did it, I'm gonna kill him.' See, you gotta have permission to kill anybody in this business. We had a suspicion that Tommy was involved in drugs with this guy and that he was trying to cover something up. And Nicky had the same suspicion. He had one of these gut feelings.

"But Nicky's also saying different things. He says, 'The reason I don't want to kill him is we can't be killing each other every day. I'll give him a chance and let's see how he conducts himself. He'll go down to a regular soldier and if he conducts himself right, who knows.' But we knew in our hearts he was gonna get killed. It was only a matter of time."

DelGiorno also knew it. He had been around Scarfo too long to be fooled by the mob boss's phony diplomacy. Being taken down was the first step. Being gunned down would be the next. The question was when.

Like Caramandi, DelGiorno decided not to wait around to find out.

Through the summer and early fall of 1986 the Scarfo crime family sat on the edge of a legal precipice. The Rouse extortion case hung over everyone's head. While the charges had been dropped, there was little doubt the U.S. Attorney would have them reinstated once a grand jury had been empaneled and given the time to hear the evidence.

"Jim Vance," Pete Balitsaris, and Willard Rouse knew enough to make a prima facie case against Caramandi, Beloff, and Rego. And John Pastorella—Caramandi's construction company partner—would be able to fill in any of the blanks. Although it had not yet been disclosed publicly, Pastorella had been working with the FBI for more than a year, ever since his return to Philadelphia.

His 1984 drug bust in Baltimore had brought him into the federal fold. He had cut a deal in exchange for a reduction in the charges and had agreed to infiltrate the drug underworld in Philadelphia. This eventually led him to Caramandi. It also led away from drugs and into the construction industry. While this was not the original intent of his undercover work, Pastorella had struck a rich vein inside the South Philadelphia mob. The feds decided to let him play it out. He got Caramandi on tape discussing labor racketeering, shakedowns, and extortions, including the Devoe deal and the apartment lease for Beloff's girlfriend. It was Pastorella, in fact, who had warned the FBI of the plan to throw Jim Dougherty, the Carpenters Union business agent, off the roof at the Spruce Street project. This was the real reason Dougherty failed to show up for that meeting. Pastorella was also aware from early in 1986 of the attempts to shake down Willard Rouse, first with the Port of History Museum lease and then with the UDAG bills.

Pastorella and his tapes gave the feds an added dimension in the case against Caramandi, Rego, and Beloff. The tapes also offered a glimpse of the way Caramandi's mind was working. In a conversation recorded in May, just a month before the Rouse case blew up, the Crow complained about his lost independence and looked back fondly on his days as a street hustler:

Caramandi:	See, you can get in a fuckin' plane and go. I can't. If I do, I gotta go say I'm going here.
Pastorella:	There are little deals here and there that you can't [do because] you know, you don't have . . . you're too busy.
Caramandi:	For two years, I hadda take a bath once a week.
Pastorella:	I can see, uh, day-to-day bullshit going on and [that it] makes you sick and you know it takes all your time, and you got no time for nothing else. Right?
Caramandi:	Yesterday . . . I was supposed to meet you for something. They say wait . . . I hadda hang around till four o'clock.
Pastorella:	Bullshit, right? What can I tell ya?
Caramandi:	I was always independent. I used to do my own fucking thing even. These guys hadda bug me 'cause I don't socialize as much as I should, but I can't. I just can't . . .
Pastorella:	Have the time.
Caramandi:	I always been, like, a loner. Did my own fucking thing.

Six months after that conversation, while sitting in a cell in the Philadelphia Detention Center, Caramandi would decide to strike out on his own again, to become a loner, an independent whose first and only concern was his self-preservation. The pressure that led Caramandi to that decision built throughout the summer and early fall of 1986. Scarfo belatedly tried to get his crime family back in order, but his hair-trigger temper, volatile mood swings, and almost gleeful delight in the use of violence mitigated against any attempts to stabilize the organization.

And while DelGiorno's demotion was hailed by almost everyone in the regime as the right move, it left Faffy Iannarella in charge. And neither Caramandi nor Charlie Iannece was especially enamored of Faffy's management style.

"Nicky said he was gonna make Faffy run the regime. He said, 'I'd rather have a guy drag his feet a little bit. Faffy's not the fastest guy in the world, but he gets the job done.' He sort of liked Faffy. So we can't say nothing. We're just listening.

"Then me and Charlie say to him, 'Look, Nick, we just got one request for you. We ain't got nothing against Faffy. But we would appreciate if we could be with you direct.' Now we're jerking him off when we say this. We're lying. Because Faffy's the most treacherous of them all. He made Tommy fall on his face. He shoulda pulled his coat. He shoulda told Tommy, 'What the fuck are you doing? Straighten up here. You're a capo. Don't do this fucking shit.' But Faffy let Tommy bury himself. Faffy wanted control.

"Now he's boss of the city. Scarfo's in Atlantic City, remember. Philip's in Atlantic City. And the only guy we could go to in Philadelphia is Faffy. He had all the guys. So we talked to Nicky and he said he'd think about it."

In August, Caramandi and his wife left with Charlie White and his wife for a vacation in Florida. They stayed at the home of John Pastorella, whose undercover work for the FBI had not yet been discovered. Several members of the organization, as well as Scarfo himself, were leery of Pastorella. But Caramandi insisted that he never discussed family business with him. The only things Pastorella knew concerned the construction industry, and Caramandi was willing to take his chances on that because they were making money.

The mob also scored big that summer with the P-2-P deal that Staino had worked out through DelGiorno. Chick Di-Tullio's loss was the mob's gain. While in Florida, Caramandi got word that the stolen shipment had made it into the country. While there were forty-seven gallons—not the one hundred Scarfo had been expecting—the deal still brought in over $1 million. Scarfo got half and DelGiorno, Staino, Caramandi, and Charlie White split the other half, each ending up with about $150,000.

Eventually DelGiorno and Caramandi would have to come up with some story to cover for Staino. But the $1 million score seemed, at least temporarily, to settle everyone down. There were already plans in motion to bring in another shipment, to send over a buyer and set up a brand-new deal that, Tommy Del was saying, could generate $2 million. Scarfo loved it. DelGiorno had been taken down, but on the surface at least, the demotion appeared to have little effect on the day-to-day operations of the organization. And for a time, talk of a contract on his life subsided. Even the Rouse extortion faded into the background as the feds moved slowly with the grand jury.

Caramandi was cautious, but Beloff and Rego were buoyed by the government's failure to act.

The two politicos, demonstrating a level of audacity that seemed to strain even Philadelphia political standards, had reestablished contact with John Bennett, the developer they were shaking down prior to their Caramandi connection. Bennett had another project going, and Beloff and Rego were looking for their piece.

"We're back in business," Rego told Bennett.

"We got this thing beat," boasted Beloff.

After vacationing with their wives for about two weeks, Caramandi and Iannece headed over to Fort Lauderdale for a late-August summit at Scarfo's Casablanca South. It would be the last time members of the South Philly regime would break bread together in the Florida sunshine.

"I stayed at Scarfo's house for ten days. After the [drug] score, he was happy. But I heard two weeks later that he wasn't happy, that he'd been expecting a million dollars for himself and he ended up with only five hundred thousand. Then we were hearing Junior wasn't happy. He got a hundred and fifty thousand but he had to give fifty thousand to Joe Kelly and fifty thousand to Kelly's partner. Junior felt he should have got a hundred and fifty like each of us. I said, 'Junior, you robbed all the fuckin' stuff. How could you complain? You're lucky you're alive.' See, Nicky thought the other five hundred thousand was gonna come. So we stalled and then we said it was lost, the other fifty gallons.

"The whole mob came in that week down in Florida. And Nicky, every night, would take us out to restaurants. Now I had asked Nicky if he minded if I brought Pastorella down there. And he said all right, he could come to a party, but he said he didn't want to meet him or anything. Then one morning, we go to the beach. All these guys are down there. We get there late. There are all these guys there and who's on the beach with everybody but Pastorella. Nicky sees him and he gets bugged.

"Charlie tells me, 'What the fuck did you make this guy come here for?' So I get John on the side and I tell him he's gotta go. See, Nicky had just made a speech the night before about this informant in Atlantic City who had tried to trip up his lawyer, Bobby Simone. So I says to John, 'Look, you gotta go back. Everybody's beefing that you're here. It's not good.'

"John took off. Right away. He said, 'Oh, I understand,' and bingo, he's gone. See, in conversations I had had with him I told him there were always some jealous guys. I always had a gut feeling about John being an informer, but I didn't want these guys to think I was paranoid. And I didn't want them to think I could make a mistake like that."

Through the rest of the summer, Caramandi and Charlie White continued to maneuver within the organization, hoping to get their status changed, to get out from under Faffy's regime and be with Scarfo "direct."

It was a status position, Caramandi said. Better, even, than capo. It would give them direct access to Scarfo. There would be no more passing messages back and forth and taking orders secondhand. They would get their assignments directly from the boss. More important, they would have the boss's ear. In a family where Machiavelli would have found keen competition, this was the safest place to be. To survive, you had to know what Scarfo was thinking. To succeed, you had to be able to influence his thoughts.

Early in October, Caramandi and Charlie White got the word. They were to be "with" Little Nicky. It happened at one of the strangest mob meetings in history. Scarfo and a half-dozen of his key associates sat down to discuss family business over coffee at a McDonald's at Broad and Vine streets in the heart of Philadelphia.

Scarfo had gone for his annual medical checkup at Hahnemann Hospital that morning. The hospital was right across
the street from the fast-food restaurant, and he set up a meeting there to announce the new positions of Caramandi and
Charlie White within the organization.

"Now you gotta understand this position. This is a high,
top-ranking position in the mob, being with the boss direct.
That means nobody could tell you anything. Nobody could say
one fucking word to you about anything. You could do anything you want. You don't have to get permission from nobody.

"Everybody would be scared. The boss could tell me,
'Whack this guy.' I don't have to tell these other guys nothing.
We don't have to say nothing. You're like a ruler. You're better
than a capo. The capos don't know what you're doing. Nobody
knows what you're doing with the boss. It's just between you
and the boss. This is how strong of a position it is.

"Now, Faffy doesn't know this yet. So Nicky gets him aside
to one table and he calls me and Charlie over. And he says,
'Faffy, I'm gonna put these two fellas with me. I'm still a young
guy and I want guys to be with me. You got plenty of guys with
you. It's nothing against you, but I want some guys with me.
I want to stay active.'

"So, what the fuck could Faffy say? But you could see the
venom in his face. But we were very, very happy. We discussed
it later. We said, man, who the fuck is going to fuck with us
now? See, this meant we could go to different towns and see
different people as the boss's representative. Like, he might
send us to New York or Chicago or anywhere in the United
States and we'd go talk to people for him. And if they knew
you represented the boss, they knew you were good men. I
mean, you gotta be a top-notch guy to be with the boss direct.
Direct means nobody could say a fucking word to you. You
can't stress enough how big this position was."

For Caramandi it was a career achievement. He had come
just about as far as he ever thought possible. From a street
hustler who started out holding up a candy store with his
son's toy gun he was now a representative of one of the top
Mafia bosses in America, a man who ruled the underworld
from the Poconos to the Boardwalk, a man who sat on the
seven-member Mafia Commission that set the agenda for La
Cosa Nostra across the entire United States.

It had taken almost thirty years. Caramandi had lied, stolen,
and shot his way to this position of power. He had risked his

life and, when asked, he had betrayed his friends. He had passed Tony Bananas, Mickey Diamond, Pat Spirito, Salvie Testa, and dozens of others along the way. Now he was in a position that even they—people he had looked up to—would admire.

Nicky Crow was sitting on top of the world as he knew it. He had less than a month to enjoy the view.

CHAPTER TWENTY-FOUR

Prosecutor: Tell the jury about the [Scarfo] organization.
Caramandi: Once you are admitted into this mob and you take this oath there is no way you can quit. The only way you can go out, you get killed. There is no retirement.

O n Sunday, October 26, 1986, almost two years to the day from the afternoon when he was formally initiated into La Cosa Nostra, Nick Caramandi's world began to crumble.

At 8:00 that morning the phone rang. It was John Pastorella. He wanted the Crow to stop at his house. Caramandi had lent Pastorella $50,000 a few days earlier to finance a drug deal. He was promised $100,000 in return. But 8:00 on a rainy Sunday morning hardly seemed the time for a payoff. Why couldn't it wait until Monday? Pastorella just said he had to see him.

Caramandi got dressed and headed out. Before he left, however, he told his wife, Marlene, "If I'm not back in an hour, call Charlie White and tell him I got arrested."

"I just had bad vibes," he said of that Sunday morning.

Outside Pastorella's apartment, Caramandi saw a couple of cars that "didn't look right." His street instincts were beginning to kick in again. There definitely was something wrong here. Caramandi pulled his car into the driveway in front of Pastorella's place. He walked up to the door and rang the bell.

"The door opens and it's [FBI agent] Jim Maher. He grabs me by my shirt collar and pulls me in with a gun to my head. With him is Mike Leyden, another agent, and I could hear this other agent, Bob Brown, in the back, in the kitchen, talking to Pastorella.

"Now they start talking to me, Maher and Leyden. They had some tapes that Pastorella made. He was wired up. And they're telling me if I would cooperate things would go easy for me. They got me dead with this Rouse extortion. 'Listen to these tapes,' they say. They had the tapes with Jim Vance and Pete Balitsaris. He taped me with the shakedown. They said I didn't have a chance. They said I talked about putting bullets in guys' heads and they said Scarfo would be pissed off at me. That I'm gonna go to jail for a long time and it would be better if I turned. All fucking nonsense.

"But they let me go that morning. They followed me back around the house, but they didn't arrest me. And then I met with Charlie and told him what happened. I said, 'I'm gonna get arrested, Charlie. It's only a matter of time. This fucking Pastorella is a rat and now it's confirmed.' But I said, 'What the fuck do they have on me except the Rouse thing? I never told Pastorella anything about shakedowns. I never told him who we killed.' So I said I'd just have to take it on the chin. I was gonna take off for a while, but then I thought, where the fuck am I gonna go? So the next day I went around the corner and I was playing cards when these [FBI] agents from Squad One come in. They said, 'Nick, you're under arrest. Get up. Put your hands behind you.' And they locked me up."

The Caramandi arrest was the second major blow for the Scarfo organization in less than a week. On Thursday, October 23, Stevie Traitz, head of Roofers Union Local 30, was indicted in a federal racketeering case that included charges of payoffs to municipal judges and extortion. Eighteen other defendants were also named in the indictment, which for the first time outlined the links between the Roofers Union and the mob. The charges clearly detailed how the tough-talking union leaders had become underworld pimps for the very man who had orchestrated the murder of John McCullough, a man still a hero to most rank-and-file members of the local.

Caramandi was booked and fingerprinted and sent over to a holding cell in the Police Administration Building at Eighth and Race streets. A preliminary hearing was set for October 28. The charges had been expanded to include the Devoe shakedown. In addition, Beloff and his wife, Diane, were indicted in an unrelated election-fraud charge having to do with an old South Philadelphia political practice of stuffing the ballot box.

At the detention hearing, federal officials disclosed that Pastorella was a government informant and that part of the case was based on 150 secretly recorded conversations he had had with Caramandi over an eighteen-month period. Caramandi was also named as a suspect in the Pat Spirito murder and as a major operative of the Scarfo organized crime family in Philadelphia. A federal magistrate ordered him held without bail pending trial.

Beloff, his wife, and Rego, all insisting they were innocent, were arraigned ten days after the indictments were announced. They were all released on bail.

Caramandi, however, sat squirming in the overcrowded Philadelphia Detention Center, physically and emotionally cramped. He learned through the prison grapevine that Scarfo was blaming him for allowing Pastorella to get too close to the organization. To Caramandi it didn't make sense. He didn't see this as a big beef. Sure, he had talked to Pastorella about the mob, but he had never said anything that could hurt the organization. Most of it was ancient history. He had told some stories about Tony Bananas Caponigro. He had talked about Scarfo, but only in a general way, about how Nicky could help them in the construction business. The only specifics Pastorella knew concerned the Rouse extortion, because Caramandi planned to use him as a go-between once the payoffs started. But there was no way Pastorella could link Scarfo to the shakedown.

All of this was going through Caramandi's mind as he sat in jail in the days immediately following his arrest. His plan was to make bail and fight the case in court. A trial and the appeals process could take more than a year. There was plenty of time to worry about the long-term repercussions later. For now the issues were getting him out of jail and, to borrow a phrase from the politicos, damage control. That, at least, was initially the way the Crow saw things from behind bars. He soon learned, however, that Little Nicky had a different view of the situation. Scarfo's damage control came out of the barrel of a gun. And this time it was pointed at Caramandi.

"The day they arrested me, every hour on the hour—I was in Eighth and Race [the Police Administration Building]—they kept moving me from cell to cell so I couldn't sleep. Through the whole day and the whole night, they just kept moving me from cell to cell. The following day, they took me to the Detention Center, and that was a mess. There was no beds. We slept in the gym for three days. It was freezing.

"I finally get situated in the Detention Center and I'm waiting for a lawyer. And I meet Long John [Raymond Martorano, the former Bruno associate who was convicted of ordering John McCullough's murder] in there. And I had discussions with Long John. He's been in there for four years and he's telling me, 'Do I look crazy?' And who's in there but his son, Georgie. Georgie's down on a writ, he had to work with his lawyer on some appeal. And he was in the same block I was in. But his father used to get him out and he would stay with his father all day. I used to see him at night.

"Georgie said he had once celled with John Gotti in New York. And he was telling me, making innuendoes that the people in New York didn't like the way Scarfo did things because he was too wild, Wild West. That he put too much heat on the town of Philadelphia. But he couldn't say too much.

"So Long John and me would talk. He was in the hospital ward and I used to meet him at the fence that separated the hospital patients from the regular inmates. He says, 'You know, my son's gonna be with the New York people if everything gets straightened out.' Well, this guy had life without parole for drug dealing, so I don't know how anything was gonna get straightened out.

"Anyway, I'm in jail and I'm trying to get a lawyer and Charlie White sends word to me, just wait, they're gonna send a lawyer. But while I'm in jail, I don't like the way Charlie White is acting. I got a couple of problems in jail."

One day, for instance, Caramandi ended up in a room with Harry Riccobene, the mobster he had tried to kill for nearly two years.

"A guard put us in the same room in the doctor's office. I look at Harry. Harry looks at me. He's got a long beard. I said, 'Harry, how did things get this way?' He said, 'I don't know. I don't know.' He had this high, screechy voice. We chatted a bit, maybe fifteen minutes. I asked how his brother, Sonny, was doing. I asked how he was doing. Harry was doing life, see. But he used to come down to the Detention Center to get checked by the doctors.

"When I get out of that room I tell the guard, 'Hey, don't you ever fucking do that to me again.' He knew what he did, he knew he shouldn't leave me alone in a room with Harry.

"When Charlie comes to visit me, I tell him about Harry and then I asked him, 'Did you go see Nicky?' And he nodded and I said, 'What did he say?'

"And he said, 'You ain't got nobody to blame but yourself.' And I says, 'Well, who the fuck knew about this Pastorella?' So Charlie starts talking, but Charlie's supposed to be my partner, and he don't offer me no money. He don't say, like, 'Whatever it is, whatever it costs, don't worry about it. We'll take it out of the business.'

"I mean, he was involved just as much as I was. He was involved right down the line with me. For five years, everything that I did, this guy got a piece of. So I thought that was kind of funny.

"But he says, 'Just be patient. They're gonna get a lawyer for ya.' And he leaves. But he just bugged me that day. Then one Sunday night he took my wife and his wife to dinner at Louie Irish's place and my wife is telling him she'll mortgage the house and he's saying, 'You don't have to do that.' But he's still not offering no money. Now I can't understand this. This fucking Charlie.

"Now we had this guy that had to give us three hundred and seventy-five thousand dollars each. For drugs. We gave him oil [the five gallons of P-2-P they had bought from Junior Staino]. And Charlie had asked me what I wanted him to do with my end. And I said, 'Just give it to my wife.'"

That drug money became a sore spot between Iannece and Caramandi, who, even after he became a cooperating federal witness, attempted to collect his share of the payoff.

After sitting in prison for about two weeks, Caramandi got word that Robert Madden, a former assistant U.S. Attorney, would be his lawyer in the Rouse case. Madden visited him in prison, set a fee of $25,000, and, at Caramandi's urging, began researching ways to fight the no-bail order.

"One Saturday afternoon they call me and say, 'Your lawyer is here.' Now in the Detention Center, you meet your lawyer in the library. When I go in, Stevie Traitz is there along with this other kid. They're waiting for their lawyers.

"Now Madden comes in and we talk. I agree to give him ten thousand of his fee up front and the other fifteen as we go. We're sitting there and I start discussing this bail reform act which I want him to use to get me out on bail. And he said, 'I'll look it up.' You know, I'm talking about just going in front of the judge and going home, even if I gotta be under house arrest. I says, 'All I want you to do is concentrate on that. Don't concentrate on the case now.'

"Now, while we're talking, who comes in but [defense attorneys] Ron Kidd and Charles Peruto, who were representing Traitz and one of his codefendants. We say hello and I shake hands with Peruto, who I knew for a couple of years. And as I'm shaking hands, he says, 'You got a problem?' I says, 'What do you mean, in here?' He says, 'No, anywhere.' I says, 'What are you talking about?'

"Now I'm sitting down with Madden and the others go to the other side of the room to discuss their case. But as I'm talking to my lawyer, this thing is bothering me. So I says to Madden, 'Do me a favor. Excuse yourself. Go over there and ask this Peruto what he meant by do I have a problem.' Madden don't know what's going on. He's in another world. He goes over and calls Peruto on the side and Peruto tells him he didn't mean nothing. So I says, 'All right. Good enough.'

"After he leaves I go outside in the yard and run into Long John. I says, 'Long John, I want ya to do me a favor.' I told him what Peruto said and I asked him if he knew anybody who knew Peruto well enough to ask him, to find out from him, what kind of problem I got without Peruto knowing that I would know about it. Long John thinks for a second and he says, 'Yeah, I got the right man. Give me some time and I'll let ya know.' "

Peruto, one of the top defense attorneys in Philadelphia, has testified that all he did that Saturday at the Detention Center was say hello to Caramandi. Caramandi, from the witness stand, has insisted that the defense attorney mentioned a "problem." That encounter, coming on the heels of Charlie White's indifference and Scarfo's distance, set in motion the chain of events that would eventually bring down the Philadelphia mob.

A few days later, Martorano and Caramandi met in the prison yard. Long John said he had gotten a response to the query he sent out.

"He tells me, 'Bobby Simone [Scarfo's defense attorney] and Nicky Scarfo sold you down the river. They're gonna go with Beloff and Rego.' And he says, 'You know what that means.' And he jumps onto the ground like, 'You're dead.' I says, 'Are you sure?' He says, 'Look, I shouldn't be telling ya this, but this is the way it is. If I was you, I would get a different lawyer. Nobody's gonna help ya.'

"Jesus Christ. This was a blow. I'm a little stunned here. I don't know what to think. My head's confused. Everything is building up. The thing with Peruto. The thing with Harry. And Charlie with no money and Nicky no messages.

"Then Charlie gives my wife five hundred dollars for the month when I know I'm due over eight thousand. He told her everything got confused. What the fuck was he bullshitting her for? Understand what I mean?

"So I go back to the cell and there's a million things going through my head. And I say to myself, let me wait for this Georgie Martorano to come back and I'll talk to him. I waited. About nine o'clock he comes back to the cellblock. George's celling four or five cells away from me. He's gonna leave the next day. He's going back to New York. So I says to him, 'What your father says, I mean, could I take stock in it?' He says, 'Brother, you could take it to the fuckin' bank.'

"I says, 'Are you sure?' He says, 'You listen to my father. He'll never steer you wrong.'

"You know how you get a sick feeling all over ya? You feel weak. You feel like nothing. I just felt low, down to the fuckin' ground. I didn't know what to think. I says, 'I'm done. I'm dead here. I can't win.'

"And then everything started flashing back to me about Scarfo. About Testa and all this shit about how Scarfo turns on ya for every little fuckin' thing. And then that incident on the Boardwalk when he was afraid he was gonna get pinched. Sure, he figured, he'd rather sacrifice me than put on more heat by killing Beloff and Rego.

"The next morning about seven o'clock I used the phone in the kitchen area. I called the FBI and I asked for Jim Maher or Bud Warner. I got Jim Maher and told him I thought I was gonna be hit and wanted to cooperate. Him and Mike Leyden came and got me out.

"So, if you judge me as a rat, I'm a rat. Look, I didn't intend to hurt these other guys. My beef was with Scarfo and Bobby Simone, Charlie, Faffy, and a couple of other guys. It was never my intention to testify against all these other guys. I was scared to death. I was surrounded by FBI guys. I didn't know what day it was. They didn't have nothing on me except the Rouse case. And they had absolutely nothing on nobody else.

Nothing about no murders. Nothing was solved."

The first document in the FBI's file on Nick Caramandi as a mob informant is a record of that November 14, 1986, phone call. Caramandi, the file notes, "telephonically contacted" agent Maher at 6:50 A.M. and "said he feared for his life and wished to cooperate with the FBI." The report went on to note that Caramandi requested that his lawyer, Robert Madden, not be notified because "Madden had been retained for him by the LCN [La Cosa Nostra] since Madden was regarded as an attorney the LCN 'could trust.'"

From prison that morning, the file states, Caramandi "was taken to a secure location where he was provided with a written waiver of his right to have his attorney present." He was then brought before a federal judge and "remanded... to the custody of the FBI."

Mike Leyden and Jim Maher were part of the FBI's Squad One, the squad assigned to investigate the Scarfo mob. Both were veteran agents who had been chasing local mobsters since the Angelo Bruno era. They were hardworking, no-nonsense investigators who over the years had built up a wealth of knowledge about the local organization. But without an insider, most of that knowledge would never figure in a criminal prosecution. Caramandi was that insider. He was the guy who could help the feds make more than a gambling and loan-sharking case against the mob. He brought a history of murder and mayhem to the table. Names. Dates. Places. Motives.

With that phone call, Caramandi crossed over the line. There would be no turning back. The consummate con man and flimflam artist had run out of moves. Defense attorneys, of course, would argue just the opposite. They said that Caramandi's pitch to the government was the ultimate scam, that he was selling out his friends to save himself and that what he brought to the prosecution was no different from the "colored" television sets, the $1,000 bills, or the gold Krugerrands he had "sold" on the street. Caramandi, they would argue, was trying to double-door his way to freedom. The Justice Department, they contended, was his final sucker.

Although he didn't know it at the time, Caramandi's defection came just three days after Tommy DelGiorno had reached a similar arrangement with the New Jersey state police.

On November 11, 1986, an unmarked state police van and two chase cars pulled up behind DelGiorno's home on South

Broad Street. DelGiorno and his wife and sons threw their belongings into plastic trash bags. Tommy grabbed a stash of money. The van was packed and the DelGiornos left South Philadelphia.

DelGiorno's defection capped a two-year state police investigation that included wiretaps and hidden microphones in Tommy Del's summer condominium at the Ocean Colony in Ocean City, New Jersey. For two summers, state police investigators listened to DelGiorno and his associates discuss gambling and loan-sharking deals and privately grouse about one another and Scarfo. The conversations began to change toward the end of the second summer. DelGiorno, who was frequently drunk, was becoming more and more critical of Scarfo. Investigators heard that Tommy Del had been "taken down," but at that point no one in law enforcement knew what that meant. They also heard two of DelGiorno's mob associates discuss the problems Tommy Del was having with Scarfo. From the gist of their conversation it was clear to the police that DelGiorno was going to be killed.

Edward Johnson, a ruddy-faced detective sergeant with the New Jersey state police, visited DelGiorno in August to warn about the murder contract. Johnson, a veteran investigator, didn't mince any words.

Standing in the doorway of DelGiorno's Broad Street home, Johnson said, "You're going to be murdered, and the contract's coming from your boss."

DelGiorno asked for proof, and Johnson said he had some tapes. DelGiorno did not appear to be impressed.

"We're damn serious," Johnson said. "We're not here to play the bogeyman."

Then, as he was leaving, he looked DelGiorno in the eye and said, "Have a nice day."

Johnson continued to work Tommy Del over the next two months. Federal agents also passed the same warning along to the former mob capo. On November 3 the New Jersey Attorney General's Office announced a racketeering indictment in which Scarfo, DelGiorno, and twelve others were named. The charges, largely related to gambling and sports betting, grew out of the secret wiretaps and conversations picked up on the electronic bugs in DelGiorno's condo, state officials announced. The tapes, Tommy Del knew, would eventually become public. His drunken criticism of Scarfo and Philip Leonetti could come back to haunt him.

Ed Johnson paid another visit, and this time Tommy was more receptive. They arranged to meet at a motel near the Philadelphia International Airport. Johnson played some tapes. Tommy Del listened. Like Caramandi, he decided that unless he made a move, he was a dead man. Within a week, under cover of darkness, he and his family slipped into state police custody. They would remain with New Jersey authorities for about five months, just enough time for the state police to shoot themselves in the foot.

Flipping DelGiorno was a major coup for the state police, one of the high points in its long and storied battle with the mob in New Jersey. A special squad of troopers was assigned to guard DelGiorno and his family as they were moved from safe house to safe house around the state. DelGiorno was debriefed at length about the mob and also was ferried to various court appearances where his testimony was required.

Then one afternoon, while returning from a hearing in federal court in Philadelphia, Tommy Del and his trooper guardians stopped at a cocktail lounge in New Jersey. There was a woman at the bar. She liked Tommy. Tommy liked her. For $100 she showed him how much she liked him. Eventually, as they always do, defense attorneys found out about the brief interlude. When it was brought out in court, the three troopers assigned to escort duty were suspended without pay for a year. They, however, got off easy in comparison to one of their fellow officers, a trooper named Raymond Caramanna. Caramanna was arrested and eventually convicted of stealing $57,000 of Tommy's money while serving as part of the guard detail assigned to the DelGiorno family.

It was also later established that the state police took the DelGiornos to expensive dinners in New York City, took Tommy's two oldest—but still underage—sons drinking at bars, and financed ski trips to relieve the boredom and tension of life under constant security.

The misadventures and extravagances sullied what had otherwise been an outstanding job by the New Jersey state police. But adding insult to injury, the state racketeering charges that grew out of the DelGiorno investigation—and that were later expanded to include a series of murder charges—were never brought to trial. DelGiorno was turned over to federal authorities in April 1987, and he and Caramandi became a pair, testifying together in a series of trials, including a federal RICO case that echoed most of the same charges still pending in

New Jersey. So while it is unlikely that the New Jersey state attorney general will ever get Scarfo in the docket, it is irrefutable that the New Jersey state police played a major role in bringing the Scarfo organization down.

Caramandi and DelGiorno, while hardly bosom mob buddies, became a dynamic one-two punch for federal and Philadelphia prosecutors. Each tended to corroborate the other. And while a jury might question the credibility of one mobster-turned-informant, the fact that two mob members from the same organization were standing up and pointing fingers at their former associates strengthened their individual testimony and the cases that were built around it. So it was that after years of bickering and backstabbing, the Crow and Tommy Del finally found a place where they were compatible: the witness stand.

On December 23, 1986, Nicholas Caramandi appeared before U.S. District Judge John P. Fullam and, under the terms of an agreement worked out with federal authorities, pleaded guilty to one count of attempted extortion in the Rouse case and one count of RICO conspiracy contained in a separate federal information that had been drawn up against him. Caramandi faced a maximum of twenty years for each offense. Sentencing was delayed pending his testimony in a number of as yet unspecified cases.

Organized Crime Strike Force attorney Ron Cole told Judge Fullam that Caramandi had agreed to testify truthfully and honestly and that if he failed to do so, he could be prosecuted for all the charges listed in the agreement as well as for perjury.

Cole, who would later handle the first Rouse trial, said that Caramandi "acknowledges that he is a member of an organization known as La Cosa Nostra" whose purpose was "to produce income through various illegal activities, including murder, extortion, loan-sharking, gambling, and the infiltration of legitimate business." He said the agreement Caramandi had signed "sets forth categories of crime and some specific murders and/or conspiracy to murder that Mr. Caramandi participated in." These included the Pat Spirito, Robert Riccobene, and Sal Testa murders and the attempted murder of Frank Martines, the Riccobene associate who had survived the early-morning South Philadelphia street corner ambush Caramandi had so meticulously planned.

"Mr. Caramandi acknowledges he participated in...con-spiracy to murder, extortion, collection of what is known as a street tax from individuals engaged in criminal activity, loan-sharking, gambling, and narcotics," Cole said. Nick Cara-mandi stood silently through most of the twenty-seven-minute hearing. "Yes sir" and "no sir" were the extent of his testimony on that day.

But over the next two years, during several dozen highly publicized court appearances, the Crow would have much more to say.

CHAPTER TWENTY-FIVE

icky Scarfo was arrested on January 8, 1987, as he got off a plane at the Atlantic City airport. Scarfo and his girlfriend were returning from a New Year's holiday stay in Fort Lauderdale. Sporting a deep winter tan, his dark black hair neatly combed, his suit impeccable, Scarfo smiled and nodded as he was driven off in handcuffs by the FBI to face charges of conspiracy to commit extortion in the Penn's Landing shakedown. The charges were contained in a sealed federal indictment made public earlier that day. Charlie White Iannece was also named as a defendant in that case, along with Leland Beloff and Robert Rego. Caramandi's name was dropped from the indictment. He was now a cooperating government witness.

With the arrest at the airport, law enforcement's battle with the Scarfo mob shifted from the streets of South Philadelphia to the ornate federal and Common Pleas courtrooms of the city's judiciary. Between 1987 and 1989, every ranking member of the Philadelphia Mafia and dozens of top mob associates, including Beloff and Rego, Roofers Union boss Steven Traitz, Jr., and drug kingpin Angelo "Chick" DiTullio, were convicted and sentenced to prison in a series of trials that rocked the Philadelphia underworld.

During roughly this same time period, mob leaders had been convicted in several other cities. The Mafia Commission trial in New York, for example, resulted in three top mob bosses' receiving hundred-year prison terms, and RICO cases in Boston, Cleveland, Kansas City, and Los Angeles ended with lengthy jail terms for major Mafia figures. But in no other city had a mob family—and the infrastructure of associates that supports it—taken such a beating.

In all, Caramandi would testify at eleven trials resulting in the convictions of fifty-two people. Scarfo would be tried five times and convicted on three different occasions. He got fourteen years for the Rouse extortion conspiracy and fifty-five years for a federal RICO conviction (which included a charge that he was the head of an organized crime family and had ordered nine murders and four attempted murders), and he was sentenced to life in prison for a first degree murder conviction in the death of "Frankie Flowers" D'Alfonso.

No other American Mafia boss—not even the legendary Al Capone, the ruthless Albert Anastasia, or the despotic Vito Genovese—had ever been convicted of first degree murder. It was a fitting distinction for Philadelphia's petulant little mob boss, who, at almost every level, chose blood over honor.

For Scarfo, the battering was not only legal, however. It was also highly personal. The convictions and the public testimony that led to them provided an inside look at his reign as mob boss. And the picture that emerged was that of a greedy, small-minded, and violent terrorist who climbed to the top over the dead bodies of onetime associates and who solidified his hold by killing anyone he considered a potential rival. There was no sense of charisma; not even a hint of the old Mafia mystique. Scarfo was a bully with a gun. And his organization was a band of venal and corrupt street hustlers—like Caramandi—who would do anything for a buck. Maybe there had never been any true men of honor. Maybe that was just in the movies. Or maybe any organization in which a man like Scarfo could rise to the top was fatally flawed.

For Caramandi, life as a government witness was a string of safe houses and a series of court appearances. He was constantly traveling back and forth to Philadelphia, where his testimony was required first at a number of preliminary and bail hearings, then before various investigative grand juries, and finally on the witness stand in several highly publicized trials. In many ways, it was a game. The trials seemed to run into one another. Many involved the same defendants, the same witnesses, and the same defense lawyers. Very often they asked the same questions. Caramandi, who had spent a lifetime adapting to his surroundings and surviving on wit and guile, adjusted accordingly. He had been a con man and a hustler, then an extortionist and a murderer. Now he was a government witness. With each appearance his delivery and demeanor improved. And after a few go-arounds in the court-room, he became adept at deflecting the often barbed thrusts of defense attorneys, trading quips and asides, parrying in-sults with epithets of his own.

By the summer of 1988, there was only one major trial left for Caramandi, the federal RICO case that would end with Scarfo and all his codefendants found guilty. The Crow and his FBI keepers were living in the condominium in Ocean City, Maryland, at the time. And periodically, federal prosecutor Louis Pichini, a veteran Strike Force attorney and head of the prosecution team in the RICO case, would drive down from Philadelphia for debriefing sessions. Pichini, whose meticu-lous preparation and eye for detail are part of Philadelphia courtroom legend, left nothing to chance. So for hours on end and for days at a time he and Caramandi went over the case—the murders, the shakedowns, the drug deals.

"He used to make me nuts," Caramandi said. "Day after day going over the same stuff. Every detail. Every question. He was a real pain in the ass."

Pichini was the perfect choice as prosecutor. The grandson of Italian immigrants, he exuded pride in his heritage and brought to the courtroom an almost palpable disdain for Scarfo and his organization. It was clear to every member of the jury that Pichini found Scarfo and all that he stood for offensive, that he considered the Mafia an affront to every Italian-American, and that this was his chance—and the jury's chance—to do something about that.

It was during a lull between one of Pichini's Ocean City visits that the mob missed its best, and perhaps last, chance to silence Caramandi. At an earlier hearing it had been dis-closed that there was a contract out on the Crow's life. Infor-mants said the word on the street was that there was $100,000 available for anyone who could make Caramandi permanently disappear. The first step, obviously, was to locate him. And late in August 1988, just about a month before the RICO trial was to begin, Caramandi's cover was blown. As he was walking past the pool near his condo he heard someone shout his name. He turned and saw two women whom he recognized immediately; one was the mother and the other the sister of mob hit men Philip and Frank Narducci.

By a strange twist of fate, the two women had come to spend

a week's vacation in Ocean City, Maryland, and had booked a
suite in the condominium complex where the feds had stashed
Nicky Crow. Of the hundred thousand vacationers in Ocean
City that week, three people from the same small corner of
South Philadelphia crossed paths. Adeline Narducci, whose
sons were languishing in the Philadelphia Detention Center,
began to taunt and berate Caramandi, screaming insults that
shattered the lazy summer afternoon. Her daughter joined in
the verbal assault while more than a dozen suntanned tourists
looked on in shock and amazement. Caramandi tried to ignore
the women as he quickened his pace and headed for the safety
of his FBI-guarded condo unit. But there was little doubt the
Narducci women had recognized him. Their anger and hos-
tility, however, probably saved his life. If they had not shouted
out, Caramandi might not have been aware that he had been
spotted. Their screams set off a federal alarm. Within hours,
the FBI had closed down the Ocean City condo and spirited
Caramandi to another, more secure location.

In a brief phone conversation the next day, Caramandi
passed on this cryptic message, "I hadda get out of Dodge,"
he said. "I got spotted."

The federal racketeering trial of Nicky Scarfo and his mob
family began on September 28, 1988. Over the next seven
weeks, Pichini and his three co-prosecutors called more than
two dozen witnesses, introduced several hundred pieces of
evidence, and played hours of secretly recorded mob conversations. Skillfully using DelGiorno and then Caramandi to
weave it all together, Pichini built his case block by block.
The murders, the extortions, the shakedowns, the ritual initiation, the Rouse–Penn's Landing scam, the drug deals. All
became part of the fabric, part of the life and times, of Nicodemo Scarfo and his bloody organization.

And even as Pichini built his case, Scarfo's world continued
to crumble. Unexpectedly, in the middle of the trial, a recess
was called. The jury, sequestered and sitting anonymously,
had no idea why. But reporters, attorneys, and the scores of
people who jammed the federal courtroom each day to hear
the testimony in the historic case soon learned.

On November 1, Nicodemo Scarfo's youngest son, Mark,
who was just seventeen, had walked into the offices of Scarf
Inc. on North Georgia Avenue in Atlantic City and hanged
himself. Discovered by his mother, he was rushed to a hospital
in Atlantic City. He was alive, but comatose. No one may ever

know for certain why Mark Scarfo tried to kill himself, but reports in the days following the incident indicated that he was unable to cope with the taunts and jeers of schoolmates who repeatedly called his father a gangster and a killer. Like Enrico Riccobene before him, Mark Scarfo had only one tie with the mob, the blood running through his veins.

Mark Scarfo was transferred from the Atlantic City Medical Center to Hahnemann Hospital in Philadelphia. On November 2 the RICO trial was recessed early and Nicodemo Scarfo, handcuffed and guarded by federal marshals, was allowed to visit his son. A month later Mark Scarfo, still in a coma, was transported to a nursing home near Atlantic City. He has been there ever since, his condition unchanged.

When the trial resumed, Caramandi spent close to five days on the witness stand, detailing his own life of crime and his wheeling and dealing for the Scarfo mob. It was his longest and, perhaps, best performance, and it effectively nailed shut the door on Scarfo and the others.

Pichini, calling the initiation rite a "criminal baptism" and labeling those who took it ruthless killers, iced the verdict by verbally dismantling the Scarfo organization in a summation that extended over two days. While the jury listened in rapt attention, he described how Scarfo "took the mob that he had inherited from Angelo Bruno . . . and molded it in his own image. And the image and the reality, as this evidence shows, is that of a cold-blooded, paranoid killer. What Little Nicky lacked in height, he more than made up for in viciousness."

On Saturday night, November 19, 1988, the jury returned its verdict. Scarfo and sixteen codefendants were found guilty of every charge in the multicount RICO indictment. Caramandi had little to say when he was informed of the verdict. In fact, the enormity of what he had done had subdued the usually loquacious mobster. "All guilty, all charges," he said in a brief phone conversation that night. "I guess that means I'm credible."

The RICO convictions signaled the end of the Scarfo organization. There was, literally, no one left to run the family. The leadership and half of the active soldiers in the sixty-member mob were in prison. And the prosecutors weren't finished.

Four months later, the Philadelphia District Attorney's Office provided the *coup de grâce* by winning murder convictions in the D'Alfonso case. For Caramandi, who wasn't even called to testify, the convictions were anticlimactic.

"It's over," he said, even before that trial had begun.

For Scarfo and his organization, that was probably true. But for federal investigators, what had happened in Philadelphia between 1987 and 1989 was much more. The story of the rise and fall of Little Nicky Scarfo was the prototype for an assault on mob families across the country. Their next targets, not surprisingly, would be the powerful mob organizations in New York. Part of the ammunition for that assault would come from a surprising source in Philadelphia.

Joe Valachi was the first and most notorious Mafia songbird. He turned in 1963 and provided federal authorities with the first detailed account of La Cosa Nostra. Since Valachi there have been ten "made" members of the American Mafia who have testified against their former brothers in blood, ten who have broken the once sacred code of silence, ten who have shattered *omertà*. Six of those ten have been members of the Scarfo organization. That is the legacy of Little Nicky.

And that, even more than the trials and convictions that destroyed his crime family, could have the greatest impact on the mob.

Caramandi and DelGiorno were the first and most important. Without them, what followed would not have been possible. The total results, however, shocked even the most cynical mob watchers. In underworld terms, it was comparable to the dismantling of the communist bloc in Eastern Europe. Nothing would ever be the same again.

On March 14, 1989, in the midst of jury selection for the D'Alfonso murder trial, Eugene "Gino" Milano struck a deal with the federal government and the Philadelphia District Attorney's Office. Milano was allowed to plead guilty to a third degree murder charge in the D'Alfonso case. In exchange he agreed to testify for the District Attorney's Office and also for the federal government in any subsequent cases that might develop. For more than a week, Gino Milano, convinced that Scarfo was taking everyone down with him, had been maneuvering for the deal. The major delay was his futile attempt to negotiate a plea for his younger brother, Nicky Whip, as well.

"Gino had a better deal worked out for his brother than he did for himself," one federal official said later. "But Nicky Milano is dumb as mud and didn't realize it."

Nicky Milano refused to budge from the defense table, and

so when the D'Alfonso murder trial began on March 16, he was sitting there along with Scarfo and the others. He was still there on March 28 when Gino Milano walked into the hushed Common Pleas courtroom and took the witness stand.

There had been much debate prior to the start of the trial about whether the defense should move for a mistrial and demand a new jury. The argument in support of that tactic was that since Gino Milano was part of the defense during jury selection, his decision to "flip" and appear as a government witness would be prejudicial. Countering that argument, however, was the defense concern that with more time the DA would be better able to prep Gino. The defense opted to go ahead with the trial and simultaneously to launch an attack on the prosecution's new star witness. With Scarfo's lawyer Bobby Simone leading the way, defense attorneys publicly berated Gino Milano in the local press, asking how anyone could turn on his own brother.

"What kind of crumb is he?" Simone asked.

"See, they didn't know Gino," Caramandi later explained. "Gino wasn't close to any of them. He didn't like Scarfo or Philip [Leonetti]. He was always with Salvie [Testa]. And he was a pretty sharp kid. I think he realized what was happening, and that's why he decided to do what he did. He had no love for Scarfo or this thing. He was loyal to Testa. And they had killed Testa. He knew that."

It was a final piece of irony, an event that read like the script from a tragic Italian opera. Salvie Testa was reaching out from the grave to avenge his own death through the testimony of his best friend, Gino Milano.

The defense badly miscalculated the impact of Milano's rushed court appearance. The fact that he did not appear rehearsed made him a much more effective witness. And, in a way, so did the fact that he was testifying against his own brother. His appearance on the witness stand lasted less than half a day. His voice cracked on only two occasions, each time he mentioned his attempts to get his brother out from under the charges. But he was unshakable in his description of the planning and stalking that led up to the murder of Frank D'Alfonso.

On April 5, 1989, one week after Gino Milano testified, a Common Pleas Court jury returned a guilty verdict against all eight defendants in the case. Scarfo, Philip and Frank Narducci, Faffy Iannarella, Joseph Ligambi, Salvatore and Lawrence Merlino, and Nick Milano were all convicted of first degree murder. The day after the jury verdict was announced, a Common Pleas Court judge imposed life terms on all eight defendants, sparing the jury the task of debating a capital punishment sentence in the case.

And so it was over.

Between May 1987 and April 1989, Scarfo had been convicted three separate times. The mob boss, who had celebrated his fifty-ninth and sixtieth birthdays behind bars, would now most certainly spend the rest of his life there. Most of his soldiers were looking at twenty to thirty years. Others, like Leonetti, could expect thirty-five to forty.

With Gino Milano as a witness, the District Attorney's Office didn't even bother using Caramandi in the D'Alfonso murder trial. He watched the proceedings from a safe distance, surrounded by FBI agents, while the world in which he had lived for most of his life was destroyed.

"It would have been a beautiful thing, this business. But the point is, Nicky really didn't give a fuck for us guys. We just were tools to him.

"When he put me and Charlie with him direct, we were on top of the fucking world. We were so happy. I mean, I would have died for this guy. I even told him, he came first. I said, 'You come before my mother, my father.' See, this is the way this thing works. It has to. We're told that. This thing comes before anybody. The button. The badge. The Mafia.

"And Scarfo knew this. He knew I was a loyal. I mean, Jesus Christ, you name it, I did it. I took my chances. Any kind of way to make money, I made it. And Scarfo knew this.

"I don't know what happened. This guy just turned on me. Still today, I believe this guy was gonna kill me. There's no doubt about it. Because he figured I fucked up with this Pastorella guy.

"I had a real serious problem. That fucking Long John scared the shit out of me in jail, brother."

Sentencing in the RICO case began the first week in May and stretched over eleven days. Judge Franklin S. Van Antwerpen sentenced two defendants each day, culminating on May 11 with Leonetti and Scarfo, the underboss and the boss of the now decimated crime family. Leonetti got forty-five years. Scarfo got fifty-five. The sentence was to run consecutive to the fourteen years Scarfo got in the Rouse case and the life sentence in the D'Alfonso murder trial.

Gino Milano's sentencing was postponed. He was now a cooperating witness. Ciancaglini, Iannarella, and Salvatore Merlino each got forty-five years. Charlie White, Nick Virgilio, Joe Grande, Tory Scafidi, Phil Narducci, and Joe Pungitore were sentenced to forty years each. Wayne Grande got thirty-eight years. Frank Narducci, Jr., got thirty-five, Ralph Staino, Jr., thirty-three, and Anthony Pungitore, thirty.

Like Gino Milano, Lawrence "Yogi" Merlino also skated away from the imposition of a jail term. Facing life for the D'Alfonso murder conviction and looking at thirty years in the RICO case, Merlino reached out to the FBI and agreed to cooperate. The decision sent shock waves through the underworld. Merlino became the fourth made soldier from the Scarfo family to flip. *Omertà* was clearly a thing of the past in Philadelphia. With Merlino the FBI saw the possibility of opening up a whole new area of investigation. The focus would shift from South Philadelphia to Atlantic City, where Merlino was in the construction business. Just how Scarfo and company were able to arrange those construction contracts with casino developers would now become a central question. Another, with much broader implications for New Jersey, was whether the casinos themselves were part of the process.

The news of Merlino's defection was another underworld humiliation for Scarfo. But it was quickly overshadowed by perhaps the most dramatic posttrial development in the Scarfo saga. On a Sunday afternoon late in June, word leaked that Philip Leonetti, Scarfo's thirty-six-year-old nephew and underboss, had cut a deal with the FBI. In exchange for the feds' promise to speak on his behalf at a sentence reduction hearing, Leonetti agreed to give federal authorities chapter and verse of his life in the mob. What Leonetti hoped for was a reduction of his forty-five year RICO sentence to ten years. That, he figured, would offer him the chance to start life over while a still relatively young man.

What the feds wanted in return was entree to the next level of mob business. Leonetti, because of his familial and underworld positions, could provide a broader picture of how the Scarfo family operated and also how it interacted with other crime families. Federal authorities in New Jersey and New York would now take over where their Philadelphia counterparts had left off. In New Jersey, the target was Atlantic City in general and the Bartenders Union in particular. In New York, it was John Gotti, the man federal authorities considered the most powerful Mafia boss in America.

Leonetti and Scarfo met frequently in Atlantic City and occasionally in New York with Gambino family leaders. And on at least one occasion, federal authorities now say, they traveled to New York and met directly with Gotti. At that meeting, Leonetti has told authorities, Gotti bragged about arranging the murder of his predecessor, Paul Castellano.

It is not hard to imagine Gotti and Scarfo at a mob sit-down where such a discussion would take place. Castellano's murder, federal authorities believe, was a blatant power grab, part of an internal Mafia struggle rooted in greed and a desire for complete control. It was, in short, the kind of move that Scarfo would both understand and admire.

Caramandi had heard rumors for several weeks that Leonetti had put out feelers to the FBI. At first, he said, he was surprised. But later, he said it made sense. It was the smart thing to do. And Leonetti was a smart kid.

"Not too many people knew this, but Philip had tried a couple of times to get away from his uncle. One time he just took off and was gone for a week or two. Nobody knew where he was.

"But I don't think anyone ever figured he would go this far, that he would cooperate. He's a young kid, though. He's used to living good and he's looking at forty-five years, plus he knows the feds were still looking at him for some other murders."

Adding to Scarfo's embarrassment was the fact that his sister Nancy, who was Philip Leonetti's mother, also went under. She, Leonetti's girlfriend, and Leonetti's teenage son all entered the Federal Witness Protection Program a few days before word leaked of Leonetti's defection. But first Nancy Leonetti stopped at Scarfo's apartment on Georgia Avenue, where, according to several sources, Scarfo had a substantial amount of cash hidden behind a fake wall. Rumors put the amount at anywhere from $1 million to $3 million, money that ironically may have been marked to pay for the numerous and lengthy appeals that Scarfo and Leonetti were expected to mount following their convictions.

"Nicky had a lot of places built into the apartment where he used to stash money," Caramandi said. "He had these secret hiding places, but his sister and Philip probably knew about at least some of them."

The sixth Scarfo crime family soldier to turn government witness was a Newark-based mobster named George Fresolone. Fresolone began cooperating with the New Jersey state police at about the same time that Leonetti struck his deal with the feds. For more than a year, he wore a body wire and allowed his phone to be tapped as he conducted business for one of the few active remnants of the Scarfo organization, the North Jersey wing of the family that traced its roots back to "Tony Bananas" Caponigro.

Fresolone, a thirty-six-year-old construction worker, gambler, and loan shark, was not identified by authorities as a mob informant until August 1990, a month after he was formally inducted into the organization at a secret ceremony attended by a half-dozen members of the Scarfo crime family.

The ceremony was strikingly similar to the one in which Caramandi swore to live and die for La Cosa Nostra. There was the gun and the knife on the table, the pricked trigger finger, the burning tissue in the cupped hands of the initiate, and the blood promise to "burn like the saints in hell" for betraying the organization.

The one difference was that as he was being initiated, George Fresolone was wearing a transmitter.

Less than a block away, in an unmarked van, New Jersey state police detectives got the entire ceremony on tape.

EPILOGUE

ngelo Bruno had ruled the Philadelphia mob for more than twenty years. He used an iron fist covered with a velvet glove. Nicodemo Scarfo saw no need for the glove. In the end, that made all the difference.

Had Caramandi been arrested for a case like the Rouse extortion during Bruno's era, things probably would have played out differently. Bruno would have let Caramandi take his shot in court, confident that the mobster would do the right thing. In turn, Bruno would have made sure that Caramandi's family was provided for. If Caramandi had been convicted, he would have spent his time in prison under the mob's protection and would have returned to the Bruno family once he had finished serving his sentence. The $1 million shakedown would have been lost, but that was only money. The process, the system, the organization, would have remained intact. That was the old, time-honored way the mob took care of its own and ensured its continuity. There was a time to push and there also was a time to back off.

"It was a very feudal society," said Klaus Rohr, the FBI supervising agent whose squad tracked the Philadelphia mob. "Power was not to be flaunted. You didn't need to show a big Cadillac. People knew who Don Angelo was."

Bruno was the consummate racketeer. Scarfo, on the other hand, was a gangster. "If he could have gotten a running board and attached it to the side of his car, he would have," said Rohr.

Nicodemo Scarfo was transferred from Philadelphia to a maximum security prison in Marion, Illinois, shortly after he was sentenced in May 1989. From there all he could do was watch and listen as his two families collapsed. Twenty-two members of his criminal organization were either in jail or under indictment. Seven, like himself, were serving life sentences. Five others, including his nephew, were then known to be cooperating with law enforcement. A sixth was still undercover.

His sister was living in federal protective custody. His youngest son, Mark, was in a coma. His oldest son, Chris, would have nothing to do with him and, in fact, filed a petition in Atlantic County Superior Court to have his name changed. Christopher Scarfo now legally uses the maiden name of his wife. So does his young son, Nicky Scarfo's only grandchild.

Only Nicky Jr., twenty-four, had remained loyal. At the time his father was sent to Marion, the younger Scarfo was living with Caramandi's stepdaughter and doing his best to take care of his father's business. Federal and local authorities said that the younger Scarfo continued to collect a street tax from some bookmakers and loan sharks. He also traveled occasionally to New York and North Jersey, although mob figures there did not appear pleased to see him. It was all, investigators said, a futile attempt by the elder Scarfo to hold on to power by proxy.

And it nearly cost his son his life.

On October 31, 1989, Nicky Scarfo, Jr., and his cousin John Parisi drove up from Scarfo's home in Margate, New Jersey, to South Philadelphia. They spent part of the day on Passyunk Avenue before Nicky Jr. met with Bobby Simone at the lawyer's office off Rittenhouse Square. Then, shortly after 7:00 P.M., Scarfo and Parisi headed for Dante and Luigi's Restaurant at Tenth and Catharine streets, where they were to meet another associate, Johnnie Palumbo, for dinner. Dante and Luigi's was a small, family-oriented restaurant that had been a favorite of Nicodemo Scarfo.

Scarfo Jr., Parisi, and Palumbo had just sat down to dinner when Chaz Iannece, Charlie White's young son, stopped by. Iannece, whose father had been sentenced to forty years in the RICO case, greeted Scarfo Jr. with a handshake and an Old World kiss on the cheek. They chatted for a few minutes, and then Iannece left.

It was Halloween night in South Philadelphia. Children dressed in costume and carrying brown bags stuffed with candy were going from door to door. No one thought anything of the man dressed in black and wearing a yellow mask when he walked into the restaurant. He carried a brown bag and had the hood from his black sweatshirt pulled up over his head. He walked directly to the table where Scarfo Jr. sat, pulled a 9mm machine pistol out of his bag, and started shooting. Bullets ripped through young Scarfo's chest, neck, and arm, knocking him out of his chair and onto the restaurant floor.

"Help me," he said as the blood flowed out of his body. "Somebody help me."

The gunman turned and bolted out the door. He tripped as he went down the steps, dropping his gun, and then sprinted into the night. Scarfo was rushed to Thomas Jefferson University Hospital, where he was listed in critical condition.

As with the Bruno ambush of almost ten years earlier, speculation began immediately about why and from what quarter the shots had been fired. Some federal investigators pointed toward New York. They said the shots were retribution for the way Scarfo's father had allowed the Philadelphia family to disintegrate. With five former members then serving as government witnesses and with the heat turned up in both Atlantic City, where the New York wiseguys had strong interests, and Manhattan, where Gambino boss John Gotti was the target of a sweeping federal investigation, there was certainly enough evidence to support that theory.

Local police, however, said the shooting had all the marks of an internal dispute. The sons, brothers, and fathers of Scarfo family members who were then in jail were all considered potential suspects. Many were holding Scarfo responsible for the trials and convictions of the past two and a half years, and any of them would have had enough of a motive to take a shot at Scarfo Jr., his father's proxy.

Miraculously, Nicky Jr. survived the assassination attempt. Within twenty-four hours his condition was upgraded from critical to stable. Then it was fair. Nine days after the shooting, Scarfo Jr. walked out of the hospital. He had the scars from nine entry or exit wounds, but most of the bullets had passed through his body without hitting an organ. A broken arm would prove to be the most severe of his injuries.

Scarfo Jr. would not talk to police about the shooting. Parisi and Palumbo said they saw nothing more than a masked man with a gun. Iannece, who some investigators figured was a "spotter" sent to pinpoint where in the crowded restaurant

Scarfo was sitting, insisted he knew nothing about any murder plot.

The motive for the shooting remained a mystery. So did the identities of those behind it. But throughout the Philadelphia underworld the message delivered on Halloween night was clear. Nicodemo Scarfo's iron-fisted reign was over. Investigators saw signs of this almost immediately. Scarfo Jr. avoided South Philadelphia after his release from the hospital and relocated to North Jersey, where he lived under the protection of the Newark branch of the crime family. From there he would travel to the federal prison in Marion to meet with his father and, authorities say, transport messages back and forth between the imprisoned mob boss and his crippled organization. He also continued to collect "tribute" from a few Scarfo loyalists still willing to share their racket income.

For nearly a year following the October 1989 shooting, the New Jersey state police tracked Scarfo Jr.'s every move. They knew where he was living, whom he was meeting with, and what business deals he was trying to put together. They knew because the mob figure assigned to protect and guard him was George Fresolone, who by that time was already wearing a wire and working for the state police.

Fresolone stayed undercover until August 1990, four weeks after he had recorded his own initiation ceremony. New Jersey authorities disclosed that he was an informant during a roundup of mob figures and associates from six different organized crime families. Forty-one people were arrested in Operation Broadsword, including Scarfo Jr. The charges ranged from conspiracy and racketeering to loan-sharking, extortion, and drug dealing. By year's end the cases were presented to a state grand jury. Indictments followed.

Federal and Pennsylvania state prosecutors, meanwhile, had found a new weapon in Philip Leonetti. During 1990, he testified at three different trials, all of which ended with convictions of mob figures or their associates. Leonetti, frequently described as a stone-cold killer, brought that same cool, detached demeanor to the witness stand. "He's like ice up there," said one federal agent impressed with his courtroom appearance.

But his real tests are yet to come.

In late December 1990, the feds dropped two underworld bombshells, one on Atlantic City Bartenders Union Local 54, the largest and most powerful labor organization in the casino industry, and the other on John Gotti. Leonetti figured prominently in each case.

In a civil RICO suit filed in New Jersey, the U.S. Attorney's Office charged that Scarfo had turned Local 54 into a cash cow for the mob and that the union's leadership, past and present, had willingly gone along with what amounted to a classic case of labor racketeering. Among other things, the feds charged that for years Scarfo had been receiving cash payments of about $20,000 a month as his end of an elaborate scheme to defraud the union's welfare fund. Filed along with the sixty-six-page civil complaint were several lengthy affidavits, including one in which Leonetti said that the mob took control of the union shortly after the November 1976 casino gambling referendum. From that point on, he said, the union was under Scarfo's thumb. "No appointments, jobs, union cards or other favors were to be made or given without [his] approval," he said.

Local 54 officials vowed to fight the civil litigation. Instead, on April 12, 1991, they folded. Every union officer resigned and a federal monitor took over the local.

At the same time authorities in New Jersey were closing in on Local 54, their counterparts in New York moved on Gotti and three of his top mob associates, Frank Locascio, Salvatore Gravano, and Thomas Gambino, son of the late Mafia "boss of bosses" Carlo Gambino. All four were arrested after being named in a RICO indictment that charged Gotti with heading the Gambino crime family and with ordering four mob murders, including the December 1985 shooting of Paul Castellano.

Among the witnesses who would be used to prove that Gotti was a crime boss and that he had ordered Castellano killed, the feds said, was Philip Leonetti.

"He can hurt Gotti, but he's got his work cut out for him," Caramandi said of Leonetti. "It's tough being up on that witness stand."

For his crimes, Nick Caramandi was sentenced to eight years in prison. But he spent only a little more than one year behind bars. He is now living under an assumed name in a small town far from Philadelphia.

At his sentencing in July 1989, Joel Friedman, head of the federal Organized Crime Strike Force for the Eastern District of Pennsylvania, called the Crow "one of the most important

witnesses I have had in twenty-one years of combating organized crime" and said that as a result of his testimony "deeply
entrenched criminal institutions have been weakened or destroyed. The Mafia, which has operated in Philadelphia since
around 1920, is in disarray with its hierarchy and much of
its active membership serving long prison terms.... A major
P-2-P importation ring was crushed. Likewise, a substantial
methamphetamine manufacturing ring was destroyed. A corrupt city councilman was removed from office and sent to
prison where he belongs. A large labor union local was purged
of longtime mob influence and goon control."

Letters from Edward S. G. Dennis, Jr., then acting Deputy
Attorney General of the United States and former U.S. Attorney
for the Eastern District, and from Wayne R. Gilbert, Special
Agent in Charge of the FBI's Philadelphia office, were also
made part of the sentencing record. Both pointed out the significance of Caramandi's testimony. Gilbert also noted that
Caramandi would live the rest of his life under a Mafia death
threat.

Caramandi, who was facing a maximum twenty-year sentence, was hoping to get five years, which was what another
federal judge gave Tommy DelGiorno one month earlier. Instead, Judge John P. Fullam imposed an eight-year sentence.
Like DelGiorno, however, Caramandi got credit for time served
beginning on November 14, 1986, the day he called the FBI.
As a result, Caramandi had almost three years of prison time
to his credit when federal agents turned him over to prison
authorities in August 1989. Caramandi was transported to a
secure minimum-security wing of a federal facility in Arizona,
where, under an assumed name, he was housed with several
other soon-to-be members of the Federal Witness Protection
Program. From there, in October 1990, he was paroled, given
a new identity, and relocated to another part of the country.

He keeps tabs on what is happening in Philadelphia, however, and on the chain of events that he set in motion and that
is still spinning through the underworld.

If he has any remorse, it is not for his life of crime, or even
for those he helped kill. He is saddened, he says, by the fact
that his testimony resulted in the sentencing to prison of
many of his former friends. And he is dismayed by the dete-
rioration of a way of life that he thought would go on forever.

"The Mafiosi today, they're not like the old-timers of yesterday. Like in the thirties, forties, and fifties. I mean, Nicky used kids, for Christ's sake. That's no good. Half of these kids shouldn't even be in jail. They don't even know what the fucking world's all about. How do you know anything? They don't know what day it is, yet. And there they are, behind bars. I feel sorry for a lot of them. None of them ever did anything to me. I just can't hate them. But here I had to get on a witness stand and testify against them. That kills me, when I think about them kids. They're probably saying to themselves, 'What the fuck did I ever do to him, that he's beefing on me like this?' Meaning me.

"I mean, my beef is with Nicky Scarfo. But this comes with the package. I hadda do this. It was something I hadda do. My agreement was to tell the truth and I hadda tell the truth.

"For years Angelo Bruno didn't make anybody in Philadelphia. When he got in after the Apalachin meeting, he made a few guys then, maybe ten guys, and that was it. Maybe another twenty years later he had made a few more. Ciancaglini, Sindone, and Coo-Coo Johnny, Johnny Grande. That's Wayne Grande and Joe Grande's father. So you could see how tough it was. This thing was a closed book. But when Scarfo got in, he wanted to use these fuckin' kids. He built a regime and he didn't know what kind of people he had with him. Because he wanted to be a fuckin' movie star. Honor and respect were the things of years ago.

"Today it's betrayal, deceit, envy, jealousy, viciousness. It's not like it was.

"The Mafia. What is it? It's a brotherhood of evil. It's the code of silence, *omertà*. But it slipped away, because Scarfo let it slip away. Scarfo ended up betraying himself. But then he knew all the rules. He was around in the days when honor and respect were there. He knew what it was to be put on the side. He was held down. But his jealousy and deceit came out of him when he got the power, when he became boss. Mickey Diamond. Frankie Flowers. Salvie Testa. He settled old debts. He showed his animosity and his bitterness. The bitterness that was so thick in him, so deep in him. Whatever happened to this regime, he did it to himself."

INDEX